THE USES OF ERROR

FRANK KERMODE

THE USES OF ERROR

Harvard University Press
Cambridge, Massachusetts 1991

This book is printed on acid-free paper, and its binding materials have been chosen
for strength and durability.

Articles from the *Atlantic* appear courtesy of the *Atlantic*. The article from the
New Republic is reprinted by permission of the *New Republic*, © 1989,
The New Republic, Inc. Articles from *The New York Review of Books* are reprinted
with permission from *The New York Review of Books*, copyright © 1974–1985 Nyrev, Inc.
The article from the *New York Times Book Review*, © 1983 by the New York Times Co.,
is reprinted by permission. The article from *Raritan* is reprinted by permission from
Raritan: A Quarterly Review, vol. II, no. 2 (Fall 1982); copyright © 1982 by *Raritan*,
165 College Ave., New Brunswick, NJ, 08903.

Library of Congress Cataloging-in-Publication Data

Kermode, Frank, 1919–
[Essays. Selections]
The uses of error / Frank Kermode.
p. cm.
ISBN 0-674-93152-1 (alk. paper)
1. Criticism. 2. Literature—History and criticism. I. Title.
PN81.K43 1991   90-47100
809—dc20   CIP

To John Updike
il miglior marinaio

Contents

Introduction

Most reviews are written and circulated under conditions which ensure that they have a very short active life. There are deadlines, there are restrictions, normally quite severe, on their length; and when published they claim houseroom only for as long as the paper they are printed on – a day or a week, at most a month. Moreover, the literary status of reviews tends to be settled by their ephemerality. It is usually supposed, not only by the public but, quite often, by the writers themselves, that reviewing is the work of the left hand, work that nobody would do if there weren't some reason – shortage of cash would be cited most often, though another good reason is that you can't work all day on a novel or a 'serious' book of any sort – that prevents their occupying their time with something more valuable.

Yet reviewing is a skilled and many-faceted job. It is one thing to be bright, brisk and summarily fair in the six or eight hundred words of an ordinary newspaper review, quite another to control, without looseness of argument, the six or eight thousand words sometimes allowed by such journals as The *New York Review of Books* and The *London Review of Books*. And the fifteen hundred words of a leading piece in the weeklies present some of the problems of both short and long.

Not that length is the only consideration. For one thing, the reviewer obviously needs to think about the probable audience, the Sunday skimmer at one end of the scale, the person already interested enough in the subject to tackle a serious review-article at the other. Finally, a reviewer needs to know quite a bit about quite a number of things; and must be able to write prose that intelligent people can understand and enjoy. It follows almost infallibly that the reviewer will be somebody who writes other things beside reviews.

In his younger days Edmund Wilson, a great reviewer, liked to use his notices as building materials for more substantial writings, but later on he simply collected them in such volumes as *Classics and Commercials*, and everybody still seemed quite pleased. The novelist John Updike, who rather looks down on criticism – 'hugging the shore' he calls it – nevertheless enjoys some coastal reviewing in the intervals of his transoceanic novel-writing. Understandably reluctant to allow even his less ambitious voyages to have no permanent record, he gathers together his every notice, however short, into volumes with such mildly self-deprecating titles as *Picked-up Pieces* and *Hugging the Shore*. It might be thought that lesser persons should accept ephemerality as the penalty appropriate to their coastal caution; but it is hard to see why, if they can get away with it, they shouldn't be allowed to enjoy the measure of permanence, and the measure of vanity, proper to their station, especially if they believe, as I admit I do, that some of their best writing has been 'buried' in reviews.

My own principal occupation has been academic, and most of my 'serious' books are recognizably academic products, the sort of thing professors like, and are expected, to do as part of their jobs. However, the English-speaking literary world (I think fortunately) acknowledges nothing comparable to the sharp distinction Germans make between *Tageskritik* and *Literaturwissenschaft*, reviewing and literary study – and so with us it is quite usual for the same people to do both. The days are gone when other academics reviled reviewer-professors for unseemly self-display, or waste of academic time, or betrayal of the dignity of their institutions; for example, nobody now thinks it odd that Oxford's Merton Professor should have a *deuxième carrière* as the demotic lead reviewer of *The Sunday Times*. And complaints from non-professors, to the effect that the professors are taking the bread out of their mouths, are also less common than they were, partly because there is so much more reviewing nowadays that practically everybody can have some, partly, no doubt, because the bread is often such a meagre ration.

My own view is that these arrangements are good for both

reader – since they can be fairly certain the reviewer has at least some idea what he is talking about – and the professors, if only because the work helps to keep them sane. It also reminds them that they have a duty, easily neglected, to make themselves intelligible to non-professors. Talking among themselves they may feel some need to be impressively arcane, but when addressing intelligent non-professors they need to remember one of the less offensive precepts of Lord Chesterfield: 'Speak the language of the company you are in; and speak it purely, and unlarded with any other.'

Finally, it is clear that for a variety of reasons, and despite all that can be said to dignify it, reviewing must normally be a secondary occupation. It is something you can only do well enough if you are also doing something else well enough. If that other occupation is being a don and writing good donnish books, so much, in my view, the better for everybody.

The essays included in this volume are a selection merely; to have followed the admirable Updike – or picked-up-pieces – principle and put everything in, even if (an untidier fellow than he) I could have found everything, would have made a book too heavy for my purpose and the reader's patience, though in moments of self-intoxication I did find myself wishing the book could be twice as long as it is. I don't know whether I have chosen well, and I do know that others would have chosen differently. A few of the chapters were not, strictly speaking, reviews; and one of these I hesitated to include, because I do not like what is called knocking copy, and because I don't, even defensively, enjoy quarrelling with someone who cannot reply. But in the end I put it in because I had certainly been abused and misrepresented by the person to whom I was responding; and because that person had had plenty of time to reply had she wished. I could have published this rejoinder, when it was new, in a more prominent place, where more English readers would have seen it; but, wanting only to have it on record, I sent it to the excellent American quarterly,

Raritan, where it was sure to find a professionally interested audience. Now I have been persuaded that it is appropriate to a record of the present kind. Whether or not that particular decision was right, I think that what I have included gives a fair idea of what I have been doing along these lines over the past couple of decades.

Publishers are often said not to like collections such as this, gratifying though they may be to the egotism of writers; and I am all the more grateful that the idea of making this selection came not from me but from a publisher. While in this grateful mood I should also thank Anita Kermode, who had an active or corrective hand in many of the pieces, and who, by sorting with determination through the chaos of my clippings made this collection possible. Needless to say, I am also indebted to the authors who provided my material, and to the editors for whom and with whom I have worked, among them Bill Webb of *The Guardian* and Bob Silvers of *The New York Review of Books*, but especially Karl Miller, who has been editing me in *The Spectator*, *The New Statesman*, *The Listener*, and *The London Review of Books*, for thirty-odd years. Except for a few minor corrections the pieces appear just as they were when new, even though I have occasionally had second thoughts, and even wanted quite badly to make changes. That would have frustrated my intention, for the pieces, so refurbished, would no longer have been true reviews. I have for the most part allowed the original titles to stand; they are almost always the creations of editors rather than authors, and I think they help to retain some of the flavour the products had, or should have had, for their first consumers.

In trying to provide such commodities the reviewer is all too likely to err; the correspondence columns will sometimes tell him so specifically, and his own history as a critic will leave him in no doubt about the probability considered more generally. For an idle moment, reflecting that after all reviewing was what I had done in the spare time left me by another job, I did consider calling the book *Ill Met by Moonlight*, but the title decided upon at the suggestion of Stuart Proffitt of Collins (though it is attached to the one and only sermon I have ever preached or ever will preach, and not to a review) is better. It hints that even mistakes may turn out to be of some use; and it cannot be an error to think that if error proved to have no uses the life of the literary critic, whether in his *Tageskritik* or his *Literaturwissenschaft*, would be very wretched.

I

Augustine

It is a fact, but not a fact to which all can attend equally, that St Augustine is one of the writers who require to be known by any who would understand the shape of our world. The great intellectual discoverers and synthesists of the future usually reflect some aspect of his vast achievement – this could be said, for instance, of Aquinas and Dante, of Erasmus and Calvin, of Marx and Freud. Yet he was provincial, vain, enslaved to a fierce mother, born into the petty gentry of fourth-century Roman Africa; after a bout of literary and philosophical high society in Milan he went home and became a terribly argumentative clergyman, pouring out sermons and books against heresies now forgotten by laymen; while all about him the splendours of the province – the baths and arenas, the agriculture and the literary culture – faded. The Catholic victory under Constantine lost reality, paganism did not die, and the Vandals of Genseric, less likely to sack civilly than Alaric at Rome, stood outside the gates of Hippo, while the old Bishop lay dying within, comforting himself with a maxim of Plotinus. He was a Platonist to the end, this scholar who stumbled over Greek; a scholar to the end, this pastor who marvelled that St Ambrose could read silently, without moving his lips; a pastor to the end, this politician who terrified his flock and purged his enemies – 'the first theorist of the Inquisition'.

Why should one care about this ancient, disagreeable man? Mr Brown's masterly book* will provide some answers. It cannot be an act of ordinary ambition to become the umpteenth biographer of the first great autobiographer, and Mr Brown's aim seems to

---

* Peter Brown, *Augustine of Hippo* (London: Faber & Faber)

have been to make available to the common reader, not merely facts and opinions and historical contexts, but a sense of their relation to the way we live now. He does so with elegance, and with vast but unobtrusive scholarship; his style is diversified by mannerisms on the whole acceptable, and imitated from an obvious eighteenth-century model – the commas are archaically placed, and there is an occasional touch of scholarly camp, as when Augustine is said to have known less of the Latin classics than a modern schoolboy. But Mr Brown communicates with unhurried power a sense of the quality of life at the end of the fourth century, and a sense of the powerful relevance of those faded controversies. Above all, one grows clearer about the genius of Augustine, who reached out from Hippo and shaped the religion of the Mediterranean world and the future of that empire to which, in a sense, we still belong; who established, from his cathedra, the topics and the modes of discourse characteristic of Christian thought in the West. Working as usual under the pressure of controversy (adapting Platonism to Catholicism), he once invented the enormously long-lived and influential idea of *rationes seminales*, seminal reasons created by God which allowed for mutability without themselves changing, and so explained the coexistence of transience and eternity. In a sense Augustine is himself a *ratio seminalis* of our history.

He was born in 354 at Thagaste (Souk Ahras, in Algeria), in a region which had experienced but outlived what Mr Brown calls an 'economic miracle'. Christianity was the philosophy of the well-to-do, the heir of Ciceronian philosophy and rhetoric, and of Greek and Punic demonism, as much as of the New Testament; though it held to the Bible as a book better than the classics it was, as Mr Brown says, not a religion of suffering: there were no crucifixes. Augustine was a renegade from his mother's religion; he wept over Dido, took profane mistresses and lapsed into Manichaeism, a religion whose dualism always had a strong appeal for him. Subsequently he experienced two conversions, not clean breaks because he was intensely aware of the continuities of the personality. The first made of a Manichaean lecturer in rhetoric a Christian lay philosopher; the second, the famous one in the garden, made him a theocrat and defender of the faith.

But he was always an orator. The chief business of bishops was the exposition of Holy Writ. Augustine sat in his cathedra, surrounded by a standing congregation, and brought to the task all the devices necessary to squeeze out meaning and carry conviction: they included rhymes, puns, vulgarisms, homely instances. And these devices carry over to his more abstract books. In the *Confessions*, as Mr Brown's schoolboy knows, he called Carthage 'a cauldron of unholy loves'; in the Latin this is *sartago*, a frying-pan or skillet, to rhyme with *Karthago*. A critic of witty seventeenth-century Anglo-Catholic sermons speaks of 'the joke for God's sake'. This is its origin, in an oral society which knew how to persuade; and in the *Confessions* Augustine is addressing God directly. Needing to move the populace against the Donatists, he wrote a street song. His great task – to prepare, from this unpromising base, an empire for the people of God – required the use of any available power, the rhetorician's and the commissar's.

This combative habit characterises even the great speculative works of his middle years, the *De Trinitate* and the *De Genesi ad litteram*; and in the greatest of his books, the *Confessions* and *The City of God*, there is the same quality of contest: he was always *agonistes*. Augustine won all his major arguments; some would say because he was right, others that he was, more than his enemies, a man who knew the mysteries of personality and especially of guilt, and wanted a church that included sinners, not merely initiates. His rejection of Manichaeism was grounded on its psychological inauthenticity: neatly dividing spirit and body, white and black, it ignored the complex movements of lapse and regeneration familiar in real life. Though he loved Plotinus and even the anti-Christian Porphyry, he needed to adapt Neo-Platonism to a Christian humanism (the same need was felt in Europe 1,100 years later) because he would not have it that the *logos* could not be made flesh; the Incarnation was his link between the Plotinian *here* and *there*. With a typical pun he remarked that had he remained a mere expert in Platonism he would have perished: *peritus . . . periturus*.

Of course he remained *peritus*; Platonism furnished him with many arguments against Manichee, Donatist and Pelagian, and above all gave him a means to express the psychological insights of the *Confessions*. But the Bible, which is the book recommended by the voice of the child in the garden, was for the humble and not for the *peritus*. The arrogant exponent of its text wanted the humble in the church, as he wanted it in the language of religion: his *sermo humilis*, contaminating the Latin of Cicero with the vulgarism of the Bible, laid down, as Auerbach argues, the basis of our vernacular culture, and reflects a strange spiritual democratism.

About Augustine there is always an air of Renaissance and of Reformation. The reconciliation of Platonism and Christianity; the devoted study, in a Christian academy, of Plato and St Paul – these make one think of the fifteenth century. He is both reformer and counter-reformer, puritan and inquisitor. His episcopal responsibilities – which included much that would later have fallen to a magistrate – involved also the discipline of seminary priests, proto-Jesuits; yet his puritan devotion to the Word led him to develop a system of allegorical interpretation which was still a model 1,300 years later.

It is perhaps because Augustine was refuting heresies of a peculiarly archetypal character that his temporary polemical expedients achieved such permanence. The Donatists, with their extremist apocalyptic right wing, the Circumcellions – a sort of Direct Action Committee – held that the purity of the church depended upon that of its members: in putting them down he was attacking in advance many future heresies (for heresies, like art movements, repeat themselves). When, under pressure, he himself adopts extreme positions, he again forecasts the future; becomes, for instance, a Calvinist *avant la lettre*, too mechanically rendering his prevailing sense of the human consciousness as dislocated by an aboriginal catastrophe. But he was no fundamentalist, and never sold out reason, his Graeco-Latin inheritance.

His greatest controversy, with Pelagius, was conducted against a backdrop of apocalyptic war, in the old age of the world. The Pelagians thought that although custom had corrupted men, the will was entirely free, so that perfection, being impossible, was also obligatory. The old man opposed this with enormous strength and cunning, allowing the fallen their strict measure of freedom, asserting their dependence on grace; but even so his victory almost drove him back to the limits of Manichaeism, and Julian, the brilliant young metropolitan Pelagian, fought a 'Punic war' against this barbarous African heresy. Augustine won; his was the future we got; his, not Julian's, our Europe. At the revival of paganism and Greek speculation, his battles were fought again, and less decisively; but he dominated them. He systematised Pelagianism in order to suppress it; at last contesting with intellectual equals, he won world fame. History made him right. His library somehow survived the sack, and events on the whole complied with his writings.

If this did not matter, what would one say of the books to be bought now, in paperback – the *Confessions*, *The City of God*? The latter makes the ancient world a figure of the modern and predicts the imperial and national mythologies that still exist in our world. The former tells us that the fate of human beings is not a general doom, but a matter of mysterious personalities. If he had written nothing else Augustine would still be read for the subtleties of his thought on guilt and on habit and on memory: Freud and Proust and Beckett are still in his line of descent. He observes a child at the breast with unenchanted eye; he is horrified by the distorted operations of sex; he places each man in the terrible context of time. His conclusions were founded on an appalled recognition of the extent of suffering, which he had to reconcile with the justice of God. His answers may shock us, but if he extended the guilt he felt himself to the entire human race he was nevertheless talking about the real world, and seeking his answers in what he saw to be the unfathomable depths of the personality: so that we feel he had his priorities right when, as he lay dying in a collapsing world, he remembered the cold saying of Plotinus, that 'he is no great man who thinks it a great thing that sticks and stones should fall, and that men who must die should die.'

The Listener, 31 August 1967

7

Joachim of Fiore

Joachim da Fiore died in 1202, but his posthumous career has been long and full of interest. A conservative figure, always submissive to Rome, he could hardly have foreseen that by the middle of the thirteenth century his doctrines, interpreted by more fanatical thinkers and swollen by spurious additions, would earn papal condemnation; much less that seven centuries later they would still have the power to excite such prophetic temperaments as those of Yeats and D. H. Lawrence. It was his fate to be cited by many who had little idea of what he wrote, and to be associated with others who, though they professed what appeared to be vaguely Joachimite beliefs, had very likely never heard of Joachim.

Marjorie Reeves has already meditated the fortunes of Joachim in her books *The Influence of Prophecy in the Later Middle Ages* (1969) and *Joachim of Fiore and the Prophetic Future* (1976). This new book*, written in collaboration with Warwick Gould, a distinguished Yeatsian with a special competence in the nineteenth-century antecedents of that poet's ideas, concerns itself mainly with the modern efflorescence of Joachimism, but it does deal, more briefly, with the six intervening centuries. Although the authors are always looking for the true Joachim they naturally have to write quite a bit about various false Joachims as well, and the result is a book of which it is true to say that it is a landmark in the history of ideas. It raises the whole subject to a new level and discovers which of the many enthusiasts and commentators

---

* Marjorie Reeves and Warwick Gould, *Joachim of Fiore and the Myth of the Eternal Evangel in the Nineteenth Century* (Oxford: Clarendon Press)

really knew what they were talking about. No doubt there is a good deal to add, and there is still room for argument, but whatever is to be said on this subject will henceforth be said with direct reference to this book.

'Most of the passing references to Joachim do not prove the influence of his ideas.' What, in a paragraph, were these ideas? He left three main works, the *Liber Concordie Novi ac Veteris Testamenti*, the *Expositio in Apocalypsim* and the *Psalterium decem chordarum*, all first published in Venice in the early sixteenth century. Joachim believed that there had been an epoch of the Father and an epoch of the Son; the third epoch or *status* would be that of the Holy Spirit. The typological concords between the first two epochs, as illustrated by the Old and New Testaments, would be repeated in the third, which would not abrogate but fulfil the others. He thought that the third epoch would be heralded by a time of troubled transition, but that when it arrived it would be an age of monkish contemplation. Fifty years after his death there began to appear pseudo-Joachimite works which gave these ideas the development they seemed to invite.

The first monastic order to appropriate Joachim – others were to follow – was the Franciscan; and in 1254 Gerard of Borgo, an enthusiastic adherent of the Spiritual party, announced that the Old and New Testaments were now obsolete, having been re-placed by a gospel appropriate to the third *status*. This was the Eternal Evangel, or Everlasting Gospel, as prophesied in Revelation 14:6. It is important to note that Joachim, henceforth firmly associated with this new Evangel, had never even thought of such a thing, let alone supposed that the new gospel consisted of his own writings. Nor had he formulated the notions of an Angelic Pope and a Last World Emperor, which, by the time of the Renaissance, were also firmly attached to his name.

Gerard went too far when he argued that the existing Church would soon be superseded by the *Ecclesia Spiritualis*, to be run by barefoot mendicants. The Eternal Evangel was condemned to be burnt, and Gerard was condemned to perpetual imprisonment. Joachim was obviously implicated in this disgrace, and was accord-ingly remembered as a heretic, though granted a place in the *Acta Sanctorum*. Later he was assailed also by Protestants, who thought

9

the Eternal Gospel a papist plot against the Bible, though they also supposed Joachim to have identified the Pope with Antichrist, an identification they warmly approved; and they liked his use of the Seven Seals as divisions of history, for they had independently made use of them for the same purpose.

Some maintain that the Calabrian abbot has had as profound an influence on political thought as Marx, who, despite the greater accessibility of his texts, has also been submitted to some pretty elaborate interpretations. It may be that the influence of very potent thinkers always does take distorted forms, which can coexist with the purer doctrines of the scholars and the champions of *sola Scriptura*. The history of ideas would probably furnish instances of the superior effectiveness of the grossly simplified, or even the nonsensically embellished, over the plain and true. However, the purpose of *Joachim of Fiore and the Myth of the Eternal Evangel in the Nineteenth Century* is primarily to separate genuine from corrupt or derivative knowledge of Joachim. It is not a straightforward assignment. For one thing, the abbot's evidence for his theories came from the Bible, and was available to everybody with a similar taste for apocalyptic history and prophecy. For another, 'thinking in threes', which was Joachim's habit, is a habit of curiously wide diffusion, and the critical investigator must be careful not to assume that it is found only where somebody has been reading a rather obscure medieval text.

The genuine works of Joachim were not re-published, and the authors note carefully that the idea of three historical epochs could easily be identified with the standard Tripartite division *ante legem, sub lege, sub gratia*; even when the triad is expressly linked with the Trinity one needs to be cautious. They are confident that the millenarianism of mid-seventeenth-century England bears no certain trace of the abbot's influence, even though some vulgar apocalypticists talked about the Age of the Spirit. They accordingly dispute the opinion of A. L. Morton that there was a Ranter cult of the Eternal Evangel which was transmitted to Blake; 'The Everlasting Gospel', they say, is unrelated to the Joachimite idea. Moreover they dismiss all those attractive arguments about the Joachimite affiliation of the Familists and the Brethren of the Free Spirit. Jakob Boehme must also depart this scene, as a thinker 'cosmological rather than historical'; and the Rosicrucians fare no better. The tests for authentic Joachimism here applied are certainly rigorous, and the authors are no respecters of persons. There is a good deal of polite scolding, and not all the victims may be as ready as the present reviewer to kiss the rod.

By the same token, those who got it right, or began to, are honoured. One such inquirer was an eighteenth-century German professor, J. L. Mosheim, who worked in the Wolfenbüttel collections and by that chance left work available to Lessing. Mosheim was translated into English in 1803 and apparently much read in succeeding years, thus laying claim to some celebrity as a forerunner of the great nineteenth-century revival of Joachim. The idea that an élite was charged with the conversion of the world at the dawn of a new age – an idea which had previously animated his Franciscan, Dominican and Jesuit adherents – was now to assume a secularized form appropriate to the quite different patterns of nineteenth-century thought.

The principal, though not the only, foyer of the new Joachimism was Paris. There had been premonitory rumblings in Lamennais and Saint-Simon, whose tripartition was as follows: Christianity up to the Reformation; Christianity from the Reformation till now; and henceforth the synthesis, the age of the Holy Spirit and brotherly love. Comte's Third Age was the Age of Humility. The religion of humanity was preached all over Europe, always with the proviso that élites were required to advance it, and occasionally with allusion to the Angelic Pope and the Last World Emperor. The credit for recovering or recirculating the idea of the Eternal Evangel goes to Lessing (*The Education of the Human Race*, 1780), and Schelling knew enough to associate the Third Age with John the Evangelist, as Joachim had done. But a more influential voice was that of Michelet. He believed in an Eternal Evangel that was to be 'un Évangile d'intelligence et d'esprit; jusque-là l'Église n'avait que la lettre'. He thought of Joachim as a founder of the Renaissance; and a prophet who foretold the transformation of the Church appealed strongly to his religious anticlericalism. Michelet and his followers seized upon the deutero-Joachim, rather than the original; but it was Michelet's colleague Edgar Quinet who first (and, as it turned out, correctly) associated both Columbus and Savonarola with Joachimite thought.

Renan gave Joachimite studies a sounder scholarly basis; he understood, for example, that there never was such a book as the Eternal Evangel. But, like his predecessors, he saw his material through a haze of contemporary aspirations – he too wanted a new, human Church, such as the world might have had if Rome and Paris had not extinguished the creative power of the thirteenth-century proto-Renaissance. However, the most potent agent of the nineteenth-century diffusion of Joachimism was – and one can well add 'as usual' – not a scholar but an unacademic enthusiast, the novelist George Sand.

Sand, who had previously declined an invitation to be the female Messiah of the Saint-Simonians, was associated with Pierre Leroux, who professed the new religion of St John and the Eternal Evangel. Her acquaintance with this enthusiastic but unscholarly sect was in part responsible for her undertaking the novel *Spiridion*, serialized in the *Revue des Deux Mondes* in 1838–9, and supplemented by two sequels. The success of this funless ancestor of *The Name of the Rose* is astonishing to contemplate: it made a powerful impression on Mazzini, George Eliot, Matthew Arnold, Dostoevsky and, closer to home, Renan. It tells of Spiridion, a converted Jew, who was first a Catholic, then a Protestant and finally a subscriber to a third religion. After his death his fellow monks discover his secret book, which (in the 1842 revision of the novel) consists of the Fourth Gospel in the hand of Joachim himself, together with an introduction to the Eternal Evangel by John of Parma, the Joachimite General of the Franciscan Order who lost his job when Gerard of Borgo was condemned in 1255. This inflammatory document announced the birth of a new religion, free of sacraments and ceremonies. A third section of the book described a vision in which Christ was comforted by Moses, who had also experienced the supersession of his regime.

If we needed proof that the *frisson* of one epoch can be the ennui of another we could find it by reading a few pages of *Spiridion* and comparing our reactions with those of Renan and Matthew Arnold. Arnold read Renan on Joachim, and even copied out a passage from the heresy trial about the way things were in the *secundus status*: free in respect of the past, not free in respect of the future, so that people lived *inter utrumque, hoc est, inter carnem et spiritum, usque ad praesens tempus*, as it were between two worlds. But from *Spiridion* he copied more than from any other book – thirty-two passages, including 'Mon âme est pleine d'espérance en l'avenir éternel.' However, the authors acknowledge that despite his admiration for both Sand and Renan, Arnold could not accept Joachim as the herald of a new age and new hope, or at least not with comparable fervour.

That Joachim had some influence on *Romola* is not news, but its nature is now put beyond doubt. George Eliot's Savonarola is a Joachimite, and the reference in the Proem to the Angelic Pope is not a mere passing allusion. Reeves and Gould know more about the Joachimite prophecies of the Florentine 1490s than George Eliot did, but she had a very good idea of what was in the air, and knew that some of Romola's contemporaries expected a *renovatio*, to be conducted by a *Papa angelico* and a Last World Emperor or Second Charlemagne. The authors conclude that *Romola* has a Joachimite, not a Comtean, structural basis.

Yet strict as they are, it strikes me that at this point Reeves and Gould allow themselves some of the freedom of speculation for which they reproach others. When they wish to show that Romola's 'Drifting Away' is sound doctrine according to Joachim, they quote 'a striking phrase': 'Her experience since the moment of her waking in the boat had come to her with as strong an effect as that of the fresh seal on the dissolving wax.' This metaphor they confidently derive from Revelation 7:14, where the faithful, after great tribulation, are 'sealed', and from the sealing of the faithful in Joachim's *Expositio in Apocalypsim*. Eliot's comparison is itself weak, and the connection with Revelation and Joachim seems at best tenuous. Moreover, the attempt to extend Joachimite patterns to *Middlemarch* seems to me a failure, though I do not say it could not or should not be better done. A similar uncharacteristically wanton flourish occurs when the fondness of Pater and others for the adjective 'flowery' is taken to be a covert allusion to 'Fiore'.

All the same it is probably true that Pater felt the abbot's influence; like others later he probably saw him as the prophet of historical crisis, and himself evolved a very private version of that crisis philosophy. Like many of Pater's other preoccupations, Joachimism became extremely fashionable towards the end of the century; but the advocacy of J. A. Symonds was probably more effective. Developing the ideas of the French historians, he found in the Eternal Evangel the first stirrings of the Renaissance, and in the supposed democratic religion of the Spiritual Franciscans an indication of the happiness to come. Symonds brought off a notable feat of *aggiornamento* by associating Joachim with Whitman, both prophets of a humanist future. And in one way or another many notables of the 1890s professed what was becoming a fashionable allegiance to Joachim. They included Havelock Ellis and Oscar Wilde. However, the greatest names in modern Joachimism are not these, but Huysmans, Yeats and Lawrence.

Durtal, in *Là-bas* (1891), remarks that the end of a century in which positivism had its peak was just the moment for a revival of mysticism and 'les folies de l'occulte'. Huysmans knew a lot about these matters, not least the weird neo- Joachimite cult of Pierre-Michel Vintras, which expected the coming of the Paraclete any day, and the institution of an epoch of freedom, goodness and love. Reeves and Gould give their usual careful attention to these *fin-de-siècle* extravagances, but the hero of their narrative of modern Joachimism is undoubtedly Yeats, to whom they devote seventy rich pages.

It has long been known that Yeats's story 'The Tables of the Law' contained clear references to Joachim, but the extent to which the poet absorbed the ancient system (in forms inevitably somewhat dilute and distorted) has not been fully understood. Yeats's Aherne appears to believe that under the third dispensation everyone will have his or her own Law, which reminds one of the cabbalistic conceit that in the end every one of the six hundred thousand will have his or her own Torah and develop individual perfection. 'The Tables of the Law,' says these authors, 'deploys a conception of the Eternal Evangel which may be bizarre, but which is anything but deracinated.' They see the poet's vagueness about history as in this case a positive advantage, enabling him to convert what he read in Renan and elsewhere to his own peculiar purposes. These were strictly *fin-de-siècle*, since Yeats predicted apocalypse in 1900 (though he later advanced the date to 1927). He blended Joachim with Blake and Nietzsche, listened to the Joachimite speculations of the erudite Lionel Johnson, and worked it all into a larger occult tradition. He even read Joachim in the Bodleian, and married a wife who possessed Joachimite texts. It is here plausibly argued that the concept of Unity of Being is originally Joachimite. The 'multitudinous influx' of which the poet spoke in 1934 is attributed to the abbot's Holy Spirit, and Phase 15 of the System is where the thought of Joachim, now quite assimilated, finds it ultimate place. Although his own speculations grew more and more cyclical, Yeats habitually thought in terms of crisis, and so Joachim was never far from his mind, 'a constant part', say the authors, 'of his ruling mental set, his "phantasmagoria"'.

The long chapter on Yeats ends with a note on Joyce's interest in Joachim, indicated by an allusion in *Ulysses* but more extensively displayed in *Stephen Hero*. The last of the modern Joachimites to be discussed is D. H. Lawrence, whose interest in the subject has been studied, though perhaps less circumspectly, by earlier commentators. Lawrence went out of his way to celebrate Joachim in his school history textbook *Movements in European History*, but a trinitarianism with a Joachimite component powerfully affects almost all his work from *Sons and Lovers*, or at any rate from its unpublished preface of 1913, to *The Plumed Serpent*, and even, in some measure, to the posthumous *Apocalypse*. The source of Lawrence's information on the subject remains something of a mystery, though he could have read George Sand and Yeats's story, and Huysmans as well. The young Lawrence was a great reader, and it would be interesting to know whether he had come across Symonds; his interest in Carpenter suggests the possibility of an acquaintance with a vast undergrowth of occultism and of irregular speculation, from which seeds of Joachimism might well have been blown into the imagination of youth.

The provenance of Joachim's ideas in Eastern Europe, to which the authors devote their final chapter, is equally intractable, since there were indigenous triads, such as the three-Romes theory, with which those ideas could be confounded; but it seems likely that George Sand contributed something to *The Brothers Karama-zov*, and that Soloviev, Kandinsky and others were in one way or another affected by Joachim. The Czechs, it seems, were especially interested, and there is a cantata by Janáček called *The Eternal Gospel*.

The authors, habitually cautious, have avoided saying much about Möller van den Bruck and any possible Joachimite influence on the Nazis – not, it seems, because they think there was none, but because of the improbability of its having any direct connection with genuine Joachimite ideas. This limitation of interest is, of course, consistent with the method they have chosen to use, and it might well have been impossible to finish a study more receptive to ignorant and perverted versions. Yet such versions can as well, or even better, lead to political or religious action. 'Joachimism,' write Reeves and Gould, 'represents only one current in the stream of nineteenth-century thought about history,' and this is true; it is also true that those for whom it formed such a current – who saw in it a method of resolving dualisms and a hope for a religion unhampered by the Church – were intellectuals, capable of understanding Joachimism as 'a particularly powerful form' of the well-known historiographical habit of thinking in threes, but too obsessed with the idea of an intellectual élite to have much influence on affairs.

Ideas need not have a wholly respectable pedigree to stir the imagination. Renan was enthusiastic about *Spiridion* before he began serious work on Joachim, and Sand's novel, together with other works that came out of the unholy mix of late nineteenth-century anti-establishment thought, seem to have appealed more directly to that vague millennialism and that hazy typological yearning which form part of the uncritical inheritance of the European imagination. However, Marjorie Reeves and Warwick Gould are nothing if not critical, and we may be glad of it, for we now have a map of neo-Joachimism which will prevent error about its major features without inhibiting research in its less reputable byways.

Times Literary Supplement, 25 September 1987

16

Deciphering the Big Book

There are vast libraries of Biblical scholarship, and they are in the present age expanding at least as fast as ever before; but it does not appear that they are much frequented by the general reader. If he is a non-believer he is likely to think it none of his business; if a believer he tends to leave all this to his pastors and to buy and read books which obscure the interesting issues with a smokescreen of institutional piety, or, at best, attenuate and vulgarize them.

This is unfortunate, for it means that secular intellectuals are only vaguely aware of the achievements of a scholarly tradition which has, over two arduous centuries of inquiry, established criteria of exact research and bold speculation not often matched in the humanities, whose practitioners are likely to assume in priests and ministers an intellectual docility deriving from the nature of their commitment to a religion. This is presumably different from one's own commitment to a professional discipline, which need not be the consequence of some prior doctrinal preference, and is less obviously associated with a pious social role. There is the additional difficulty that the learned clergy are learned in their own way, and speak their own language, so that it isn't always easy for the otherwise-learned laity to know exactly what they are talking about.

So it comes about that while a student of the nineteenth century may be quite willing to agree that German Biblical criticism was one of the greatest achievements of that age, and a matter of some importance for our own, he is unlikely to pay much attention to the continuation of the tradition. It may be true that the greatest days are over, for we can never again have the sense that this kind of scholarly inquiry is undermining the foundations of a culture as well as those of a traditional faith. It may also be true that subsequent criticism has been affected by a desire to save the faith; for much of it benefits by a more sophisticated hermeneutics designed to permit the prosecution of 'scientific' research without disturbing belief in the ultimate truth and even, in some extremely refined sense, the historicity of the Gospels. Yet the achievements of this later scholarship remain worthy of the consideration of all secular historians and critics.

Much of the finest work has been German and Protestant, and it is in Germany that the subtler philosophical accommodations have been made. Catholic scholars worked under severe inhibitions deriving from the interpretative authority of the institution and the impossibility of challenging dogma. A simple instance of the cramping effect on scholarship is the fact that until twenty or so years ago it was impermissible for a Catholic to argue from the position that Mark was prior to, and an importance source of, Matthew – a position available to others for a century. (It is now under attack; few theories in this field can be said to have won permanent and universal assent.) Vatican II was a great relief; and Raymond Brown, an American priest of immense learning and application, more than once registers his delight at being able to work with this new liberty.

Yet, like his magisterial and enormous commentary on John's Gospel,[1] his new book,* a commentary on the Infancy narratives in Matthew and Luke, has been submitted to ecclesiastical authority and bears the *nihil obstat* and *imprimatur* of his ecclesiastical superiors (still in Latin, whether or not Milton was right to say that English would not provide 'servile letters enow to spell such a dictatory presumption'). But if it would be wrong to ignore it, it would be equally wrong to exaggerate the degree of restriction implied by this deference. The Catholic scholar is doubtless more sharply aware of the nature of his freedom, since it is institutionally

[1] In *The Anchor Bible*, 1,208pp. in two volumes (New York: Doubleday, 1970).

* *Raymond E. Brown, The Birth of the Messiah: A Commentary on the Infancy Narratives in Matthew and Luke* (New York: Doubleday)

defined, than his ecumenical partners in the Anchor project. Yet, though he must face them more directly, his problems are substantially the same as theirs. What is most striking about this huge new book is its awareness of what is implied by its choices and decisions, and its determination to treat these implications exhaustively and lucidly.

I can't hope, in this review, to attend to much of the detailed argument – only to give an idea of the undertaking and discuss a few examples. The four Gospels contain two Infancy narratives, in Matthew and Luke. Mark begins with the Baptism of Jesus, and John leaps back over the childhood to the pre-existence of Christ as Logos. Though lazily consolidated in the popular mind, the narratives of Matthew and Luke differ widely and are often incompatible. Matthew has the Magi, Luke the shepherds; in Matthew the Annunciation is made to Joseph, in Luke to Mary. Luke alone has the journey from Nazareth to Bethlehem (for an improbable census) and the birth in the manger. It is he who works in all the material about the conception, birth, circumcision, and naming of John the Baptist, the purification of Mary, the characters Simeon and Anna, and the story of the twelve-year-old Jesus in the Temple. Each of the two has an elaborate genealogy, but their versions disagree widely in detail. Matthew's starts with Abraham, Luke's with God and Adam; they differ about the identity of Jesus' grandparents, and in other ways hardly worth mentioning. A more serious difficulty is that Mark apparently knows nothing at all of these matters, and even represents Mary as hostile to Jesus when he visits his home town in the course of his ministry. A related, and celebrated, problem is the virginal conception of Jesus, proclaimed by Matthew and accepted by Luke, but no concern of Mark's, or indeed of Paul's.

The obvious answer to these problems is that it would be absurd to think either Matthew or Luke is offering a factual report; these narratives are fictions, though of a rather unusual kind. But in this form it is not an answer generally acceptable to people who study the matter in detail. Brown is willing to say that the problem of the historicity of the accounts is 'somewhat relativized' by the perception that they are 'primarily vehicles of the evangelists' theology and christology' (this is a solution which, in essentials, is as old as Herder), but he repudiates the expression 'fictions' with some indignation.

Yet the explanations he offers are at bottom perfectly consistent with the bolder way of putting the point, and one can only lament that the word 'fiction' has associations with lying or fraud. Certainly there is no need to suspect anything of that kind. What can be agreed is that these narratives of the birth and infancy of Jesus were written after the central parts of the Gospel dealing with the ministry (which in turn were originally written after the Passion narratives) when later curiosity came to demand some information about the pre-Baptism years. They would be made consistent with the later material, and with contemporary theological and apologetic needs. Placing the birth in Bethlehem, not Nazareth, answers Jewish scepticism about a Galilean Messiah, and the virgin conception may (perhaps) answer Jewish allegations of the illegitimacy of Jesus. More important, the recognition that Jesus was the son of God, originally associated with the Resurrection, was quite naturally pushed back first to his baptism (as in Mark) and then to his conception and birth – and finally, in John, to his pre-existence.

Matthew and Luke usually depended on Mark, but he was no help to them as they composed these narratives. Whether they had other sources, oral or written, is a question minutely pondered in this book. Brown has little time for the more naïve answers (for example that Luke's information about the Annunciation derived directly from Mary) but he does not altogether give up history, and there are long discussions of Jewish marriage customs and other relevant, and sometimes saving, considerations. But he is also keen to define the literary structures of the narratives; both *are* very literary, and especially Luke's, for it is he who elaborates the parallels between Elizabeth and Mary, and he who inserts the canticles later known as the Magnificat, the Nunc Dimittis, etc., which are based on Jewish hymns.

And this is the real question: how did they come to make up these stories? It is obvious to all that they contain what Brown calls 'historicized theologoumena', which I, not he, would gloss as 'fictions inserted into a history-like record on a later consideration of what ought properly to have occurred'. The documents are not histories in the ordinary sense, for they are records of speculations entertained three-quarters of a century after the events they purport to describe.

Yet even this polysyllabic euphemism is, at some points, too dangerous. Consider the virginal conception. Brown admits that in quoting Isaiah from the Greek text ('Behold, a *parthenos* shall conceive') Matthew established Mary's virginity against the original Hebrew sense (*alma*, translated by *parthenos*, has no connotation of virginity). And he carefully surveys all the arguments on this famous point, silly as some of them are. He rightly adds that if, having done this, Matthew (and Luke) nevertheless regarded the virginal conception as somehow historical, we need to guess how they contrived to do so. The answer is, as I've suggested, that by hindsight one could see the need of pushing back the idea of the divinity of Jesus to his conception. Apart from that, nothing seems very clear. The Christian version does not closely resemble any other myth of virgin birth, nor was it especially likely to impress the Jews. And in any case one can't simply treat it as something Matthew made up; that would be inconsistent with the teaching of the Church. Giving up the virgin birth might be bad for people; and 'one must make a judgment about the extent to which the creedal affirmation is inextricably attached to the biological presupposition', and remember that a miracle is a miracle.

Here it is dogma that restricts the handling of the theological fictions; but the same kind of inhibition is detectable in Brown's handling of the whole matter of midrash, which is probably the most effective clue to what Matthew and Luke are doing. Briefly, midrash was the general description of methods used by Jewish commentators in the revision of ancient texts to accommodate them to changed understandings of the Law, or altered social presumptions and needs. In one form it consisted in rewriting existing narratives, or making narrative insertions, a sort of *aggiornamento* of the old text. It is now widely accepted that free narrative invention founded on an Old Testament text is the mode of a good deal of the writing in the Gospels. Brown looks with his usual care at this theory, which is more complicated than I have said, and points out, quite correctly, that the purpose of the Infancy narratives is not that of midrash in the strict sense; for it is not the narrative interpretation of old texts that is in question but the use of old texts in the construction of new ones. However he does allow that in developing motifs from Old Testament stories for their own purposes the evangelists may be said to exhibit the *style* of midrash.

This is very important. 'The same kind of mind that would compose a midrash to make Scripture understandable composed the birth stories to make [the] christological insight [that Jesus was the Son of God] understandable.' And Brown rests on a compromise, allowing something to history and something to midrash. For example, Luke's manger comes from the (Greek) Isaiah: 'The ox knows its owner, and the donkey knows the manger of its lord; but Israel has not known me . . .' The other elements in the story have similar explanations; the canticles are adapted versions of scriptural poems – for example Mary's (or as some think, Elizabeth's) Magnificat is developed from Hannah's in 1 Samuel. Matthew worked in the same way, though producing a different story.

If one thinks of these as only one or two out of a great number of examples, it becomes plain that these stories stand in a unique relation to other stories – scattered episodes in the Old Testament. Some are typological in character: that is, they constitute a direct fulfilment, and a very unexpected one, of Old Testament promises which may not even look like promises, being perfectly self-sufficient (save to the special interpretative eye) in their original contexts. It is all the more remarkable that a good deal of the Passion narrative is similarly constructed; for Matthew and, perhaps especially, Luke allow a note of fantasy in the Infancy narratives, but the Passion narratives are celebrated for their quite extraordinary realism, which, as Erich Auerbach claimed in *Mimesis*, is unparalleled in the literature of the ancient world.

Brown's admirable caution prevents him from saying anything as bold as that. For an audacious (though equally learned) application of the midrash theory to the narratives, and indeed to the whole of Matthew, one may look to the British scholar M. D. Goulder,[1] who takes up the now familiar position that Matthew

---

[1] *Midrash and Lection in Matthew* (New York: Alec R. Allenson, Inc., 1974).

was a scribe learned in midrash, but develops it in a new way, arguing that virtually the *whole* of Matthew is a midrash on Mark, and Luke a midrash on Mark and Matthew.

He thus disposes, at a stroke, of all the complex rival hypotheses concerning the material that is in Matthew and/or Luke but not in Mark. Goulder is willing, for example, to maintain that the virginal conception is pure midrash, an explanation of Isaiah's *parthenos*;[1] his only worry is whether so well educated a Jew as Matthew evidently was could have seriously entertained the notion. (He concludes that an earlier Judaism than that which recorded its hostility to Christianity might conceivably have done so; after Jesus no Jew was likely to claim that the Messiah's conception would be virginal.) And with a bow to the Brownian view that the Church is unlikely to have been wrong, for so long, on such an issue, he consigns the whole story to midrash.

So, too, with the Annunciation to Joseph, which came about in this way. Joseph, in Genesis, is a dreamer. Matthew's Joseph dreams. What the angel says to him comes from the story of Abraham and Isaac ('Sarah thy wife shall bear a son, and thou shalt call his name Isaac'). Matthew then moves on from the Torah to the Prophets, and so Isaiah's *parthenos* comes in, prompted by the echo: 'and thou shalt call his name Emmanuel'. These developments were very desirable theologically, for virginal conception emphasizes the divine paternity of Jesus. But they entailed more narrative. To make sense of what the angel had to say, Joseph must be betrothed but not married to Mary (Brown works out the Jewish law and custom relating to such premarital relations). The Slaughter of the Innocents is developed from the story of Pharaoh's order to kill the Hebrew boys, especially Moses, who fled to avoid destruction and returned when those who sought his life were dead, the new story matching the old almost to the letter, but lacking any contact with historical fact; and from the story of Esau. As for Luke, he worked up the material in his own more elaborate,

---

[1] We may see the midrashic process continuing in later years; the virginity of Mary became 'perpetual'; she herself was immaculately conceived; and so on.

23

more cultivated way, but at bottom he was carrying out the same kind of exercise.[1]

Brown has not this panache; he mills everything very fine. What he calls 'the backwards process of Gospel formation' is only the beginning of a longer tradition of interpretation, whereby the Church inserted its authentic theological insights into the original story. It will now permit these processes to become the subject of disinterested inquiry, and this book is just such an inquiry – into every fact and speculation that could conceivably be relevant. The result is tolerant but conservative. Readers not much concerned with historicity or church doctrine may think the whole process a little overelaborate. Yet the more we know about these narratives the better we shall understand narrative in general. I mentioned Auerbach's all too brief treatment of Gospel realism, in which he found that contemporary generic and rhetorical conventions were significantly suspended; here began that *sermo humilis* which, after many transformations, would be the language of the novel.[2]

Auerbach saw that the use of this new realist style was accompanied – at first sight rather curiously – by the nonrealist practice of *figura*, which presupposes that

> an occurrence on earth signifies not only itself but at the same time another, which it predicts or confirms, without prejudice to the power of its concrete reality here and now. The connection between occurrences is not regarded as primarily a chronological or causal development but as

[1] *See* John Drury, *Tradition and Design in Luke's Gospel* (London: Darton, Longman and Todd, 1976). Among other things, Drury reminds us that midrash survives, for instance, in Christmas cards. The apocryphal Protevangelium of James (ca. AD 150) had already conflated Matthew and Luke, and the popular tradition still has magi and shepherds, Herod and the chorus of angels, all mixed together.

[2] Auerbach's pages on Peter's denial (*Mimesis*, chapter 2) contrast Mark's serious treatment of 'common people' with passages in Petronius Arbiter and Tacitus in which such people can only be represented under the constraint of stylistic and rhetorical norms directly related to the class structure of the society. The passage, for all its brevity, is central to the whole of Auerbach's work, for he will argue that future realism depends on this Christian radicalization of the representation of reality. The later history of the Christian 'humble style' he traced in the remarkable essay on *sermo humilis* (in *Literary Language and its Public in Late Latin Antiquity and in the Middle Ages*, translated by Ralph Mannheim, 1965).

a oneness within the divine plan, of which all occurrences
are parts and reflections.

Such relations, which he calls 'figural', are more often spoken of
as 'typological'. Auerbach's main interest was in later typologies,
but he knew that the evangelists used a form of *figura* based on
Jewish scripture, and briefly characterized their method as one of
'revisional interpretation'. A consequence of the method is that
the Old Testament progressively loses its authority as history
and law, becoming instead a repertory of promises and anticipations.

It would have been interesting to have his views on the kind of
'revisional interpretation' Matthew was going in for when he
narrated the birth of Jesus Christ with ample reference to the
patriarchs and the Exodus, so as to represent the child as the New
Israel; having him 'called out of Egypt' (Hosea's 'When Israel
was a child I loved him, and out of Egypt called my son') involved
the writing of a bit of realistic narrative. *Figura* and *sermo humilis*
coexist from the beginning, as Auerbach knew; yet he seems to
have thought that modern realism had lost, or utterly transformed,
the habit of *figura*.[1] It may be, however, that every narrative is
related to another in a fashion best illustrated by midrash. As
one counter-realism follows another (the *nouveau roman*, the

[1] Auerbach himself seems to have doubted whether the twenty specimen passages,
chosen from almost three thousand years of writing, were columns stout enough to
support the weight of his argument in *Mimesis*. And there are signs of collapse, notably
in the final chapter, where his entire discussion of twentieth-century realism rests on
a few pages of *To the Lighthouse*. He finds that the book's record of 'random moments',
mediated by no single consciousness, implies an expansion in the practice of registering
reality; and this expansion imitates 'an economic and cultural levelling process'. We
are making progress toward 'a common life of mankind on earth'. But this is to ignore
much of Virginia Woolf's book, which insistently offers, as a key to its own reading,
the painting of Lily Briscoe, which is anything but 'random'. It requires a wholesale
reduction or transformation of the casually or randomly human (for example, where
a photograph would have shown a mother and son, the picture offers only a wedge of
colour). The order of the painting, consummated by the celebrated single brushstroke
on the last page of the novel, is the order of a modern *figura*, a 'oneness within the
divine plan' with another word substituted for 'divine'. It is curious that Auerbach
should have chosen, as an occasion to celebrate demotic randomness, a text which
continually affirms figural rigour as well as recording multiplicity and contingency;
and which represents the artist's vision as intensely privileged precisely in its access
to that 'oneness' which is the ground of *figura*.

ultra-modern 'text' with its inescapable intertextualities) we may see them all as attempts to break the midrashic habit, with its peculiar presumption of an occult historical plot which establishes a strict relevance between widely disparate moments of time and bits of story. Certainly the study of the composition of the Infancy and Passion narratives should interest all students of fiction.[1]

Reynolds Price has had thoughts of this kind.* His thirty translations of passages from Old and New Testaments are re-searches into the origin of narrative as well as brilliant exercises in translation. In an impressive introductory essay he solves the problem of historical reference in a novelist's way – 'they bear their validation in their narrative bones . . . they are plainly not deceitful, and I plainly call them true.' The translations are meant to convey the formidable simplicity and directness of Hebrew and Greek 'realisms'. Often they are very forceful, but however surprising (as when John's risen Jesus calls out to the disciples as they fish, 'Boys, anything to eat?') they are quite literal.

---

[1] They should also read Hans W. Frei's *The Eclipse of Biblical Narrative* (Yale University Press, 1974, reprinted 1977). Frei's earlier work, *The Identity of Jesus Christ* (Fortress Press, 1975, substantially published as articles in 1967), studies the Gospels as belonging to the class of 'history-like' narratives which cannot be distinguished from their subject matter: 'there is no gap between the representation and what is represented by it.' This is not equivalent to saying that such narratives are, or claim to be, accurate reports of historical facts, and to think so is to make a category mistake. The history of this mistake, which had vast consequences for Biblical criticism and hermeneutics, is the subject of Frei's longer book, *The Eclipse of Biblical Narrative*. The meaning of Biblical narratives is not the occurrences they report, neither is it the historical situation in which they were written; as for any other realistic narrative, it is what they *say as stories*. The theological book, *The Identity of Jesus Christ*, tries to use this position for exegesis; in the historical work Frei traces the breakup of the traditionally firm connection between the narratives and their historical reference which began in the seventeenth century and grew palpable and worrying in the eighteenth. In describing the history of the hermeneutic bridges built between history and the history-like, Frei takes an unusual course through the history of scholarship up to Hegel, Schleiermacher, and Strauss, with glimpses beyond. The attempt to restore narrative to a position of logical independence makes him a sort of modern Spinoza; for Spinoza, long before the post-Kantian hermeneutic refinements became available, could directly state that when we are at work on a passage of Scripture our concern is not with its truth but with its meaning (*Tractatus Theologico-Politicus*).

* Reynolds Price, *A Palpable God: Thirty Stories Translated from the Bible with an Essay on the Origins and Life of Narrative* (New York: Atheneum)

Deciphering the Big Book

The most ambitious exercise is a translation of Mark in its entirety. For most people this is the cardinal Gospel, and if one wants to see how curiously its power derives from its bald rough Greek, Price's translation is probably the best there is, and I would recommend it to anybody who is puzzled by the proposition that Mark, who cobbled sentences and episodes together with such apparent awkwardness, is a great writer – the superior, perhaps, of the rabbinical Matthew and the more graceful story-teller Luke. I doubt if Price can expect total assent to all his translator's solutions, but they are all reached in the right spirit of reverent audacity. I hope he will take on the whole New Testament.

If he does so he will have at some points to involve himself in textual questions. The problems are, of course, enormous, arising from manuscript transmission over vast periods of time, in traditions which were early diversified. A standard work on the subject is Bruce M. Metzger's *The Text of the New Testament*.[1] Erasmus, in the edition which was for centuries the received text of the New Testament, relied mostly on two inferior manuscripts, and here and there, lacking a Greek text, himself translated the Vulgate into Greek. This poor makeshift was the basis of the Authorized Version. Now some thousands of manuscripts are known, and practically all have been collated (the computer vastly increased the speed of the operation) and, as Metzger remarked in his conclusion, it is possible to know what can be known, and also what cannot be known, about the original texts.

He has now, in *The Early Versions of the New Testament*,* turned to the study of early versions other than Greek, systematically surveying manuscripts in Syriac, Coptic, Armenian, Georgian, Ethiopic, Arabic, Latin, Gothic, Slavonic. To each section an expert in the appropriate language adds a postscript explaining the limitations of these languages in representing the original Greek. The Syriac and Latin are the most important. All that

---

[1] Oxford University Press, 1964; second edition, 1968.

* Bruce M. Metzger, *The Early Versions of the New Testament* (Oxford University Press)

remains of the Old Latin is a few imperfect manuscripts, but the Vulgate, which has some textual and immense ecclesiastical authority, is represented by 10,000, so that Metzger has to withhold a checklist.

The subject is dauntingly vast, and there is a learned argument at practically every point along the way. Once again the outsider is struck with something close to awe at the meticulous industry of the Biblical scholars, and his reaction may well be to let them get on with it, since there seems to be no easy way in. But the material they are entrusted with is of importance even to the most secular mind; and however ill-equipped we may feel, we must get some sense of it, and not allow it to become an institutional preserve. These books, in their different ways, will help us to do so.

New York Review of Books, 29 June 1978

The Lattimore Version

The abundance, in our time, of single-handed, non-institutional translations of the Bible, and especially of the New Testament – Richmond Lattimore's is the most recent* – is a phenomenon worth a moment's thought. The earliest versions were made in defiance of the religious establishment, but the Church eventually took them over and established a fairly effective monopoly. Some sort of doctrinal position-taking was inevitable; King James's translators used the older Protestant versions, but did not endorse them. The Catholic (Douai) translation was primarily meant for priests who would need to be able to confute, in the vulgar tongue, the heresies of Protestants with the vernacular Bible at their fingertips.

James's version turned out to be good enough to satisfy most of the requirements of the English-speaking world for a very long time; when people spoke of the Bible it was mostly that version they meant, rather than a collection of documents in Hebrew and Greek. And it was the work of good scholars. When it was mooted, the prelates had their doubts: why another version? 'If every man's humour should be followed,' said Richard Bancroft, Archbishop of Canterbury, 'there would be no end of translating.' But the royal plan went ahead; during the reign of Elizabeth the Geneva Bible had established itself as the popular translation; its tone was too puritan, it must be supplanted. And so we got the familiar text, owing much to its predecessors, archaic in language even at the time of publication. It was more 'numinous' than any other,

* *The Four Gospels and the Revelation*, translated by Richmond Lattimore (New York: Farrar, Straus & Giroux)

but responsible for a misleading association between the language of the New Testament and a vague, old-fashioned grandeur.

The new version was a success, but soon caused a certain amount of learned discontent. On the one hand it was felt that the so-called Authorized Version (never technically authorized) did not match the original, especially the brisk, clumsy, colloquial, and in its time very modern, Greek of the New Testament; on the other, the gap between the language of the AV and good modern English also seemed troublesome. In 1653 the great scholar John Lightfoot urged the Commonwealth Parliament to commission 'an exact, vigorous and lively translation'; it would need to be officially sponsored because individual translators might otherwise take it on without learned and devout supervision – 'a precedent of dangerous consequence, emboldening others to do the like'. No such version appeared; and the individuals moved in.

The *Cambridge History of the Bible* gives samples of the 'pert and colloquial' Daniel Mace (1729) who clearly believed in the propriety of rendering the Greek into the language of his moment, e.g., 'When ye fast, don't put on a dismal air as hypocrites do' ('Be not, as the hypocrites, of a sad countenance,' AV; 'Do not scowl like the hypocrites,' Richmond Lattimore). But Edward Harwood, in 1768, objected not to a lack of modern colloquialism in the AV, but to the contrast between its 'bald and barbarous language' and 'the elegance of modern English'. His *Magnificat* begins thus: 'My soul with reverence adores my Creator, and all my faculties with transport join in celebrating the goodness of God my Saviour, who hath in so signal a manner condescended to regard my poor and humble station' ('My soul exalts the Lord, and my spirit rejoices in God my saviour, because he cast down his eyes to the low estate of his slave girl,' RL).

Equally elegant variations are to be found in the version of Rodolphus Dickinson (Boston, 1833: 'When Elizabeth heard the salutation of Mary, the embryo was joyfully agitated' ('the babe leapt in her womb' AV). Much depends on one's view of the appropriate modern English: is the right choice the English of easy middle-class conversation, as Mace must have thought; or a statelier dialect, appropriate to the gravity of the matter (Harwood and Dickinson), or even a rougher tongue, more appropriate to the Greek original, and to the working-class status of the main characters in the stories it told?

The establishment once more intervened in the 1870s with the Revised Version; working with better texts and a more highly developed scholarship, the translators tried to observe a strict rule of literal fidelity to the originals without using language that did not consort with the language of the King James Bible. The result was not always happy. The latest major institutional effort, the New English Bible, is not a revision but a new translation throughout, and aims to employ 'a contemporary idiom rather than reproduce traditional "biblical English"'. The work of the scholars was gone over by a panel of literary advisers. It is not easy to imagine what this panel actually did; the prose, however accurate, is distortingly flat and lifeless.

So it happens that none of the great institutional translations (including, I think, the American Standard Version) has over-whelming authority to many people nowadays, pious or not. And this may be one reason for the proliferation of single-handed versions: every man's humour is followed, there is no end of translating. Another reason is that institutional control of the text has slackened, and so has the extra-literary authority of the text itself. There can be a genuine interest in the Gospels as works of literature, and in the problems they set translators, considered for their own sake; and these are indeed of high interest.

Richmond Lattimore, a translator of great experience, now has his turn. A brief preface tells us only a little about his method; he says that some years ago he translated Revelation and discovered that the language 'turns itself into English' with 'natural ease'; and he declares, as did the editors of the RV, that 'fidelity to the original word order and syntax may yield an English prose that to some extent reflects the style of the original.' One must not take this claim to fidelity at face value. Sometimes it is indeed possible to stick to the original word order, as in the first sentence of Mark ('The beginning of the Gospel of Jesus Christ'), but soon trouble arrives: 'And was the John having been clothed in hairs of a camel and girdle a leather round the loin of him and eating honey and locusts wild' becomes, in Lattimore, 'John was clothed in camel's hair, and a belt of hide round his waist, and he ate locusts and wild honey.' How is this smoothing out to be avoided? Reynolds Price, whose translation I praised last year (*NYR*, June 29, 1978: *see* previous chapter), is terser: 'John wore camel's hair and a leather belt round his hips, ate grasshoppers and wild honey.' But the original isn't terse.

Anybody who looks at an interlinear translation of the New Testament will see in a moment how inconceivable, save for the simplest pedagogical use, a translation faithful 'to the original word order and syntax' must be. There is a very interesting discussion of the problem in George Steiner's *After Babel*. Walter Benjamin, in his extraordinary essay on translation (to be found in *Illuminations*), argued himself into the position that scriptural interlinear was the model of perfect translation. The object is to change one's own language by allowing interference from the language of the original. In theory this gives you access to a sort of archetypal language in which all others meet; but as Steiner sensibly observes, it would be dangerous 'to carry the process of intermediation to an extreme of theoretical violence in the hope of fusion'. At the lowest level the product will hardly be language at all; higher up it will be no more than a 'codified strangeness'. A true 'interlingual, inherently unstable "mid-speech"' hardly exists, unless it is approached in Pound or Zukovsky. Since Steiner's is a huge book, and not everybody reads it all, I recommend his observations on Browning's (and, incidentally, Lattimore's) version of the *Agamemnon*.

Reynolds Price's Mark has something of the right creative instability; it is, to put it at its lowest, often surprising. Surprise is not a part of Lattimore's programme. One small instance of the difference: Lattimore translates all the 'ands' of the Greek, as of course he should on the principles stated. But although to a grammarian these conjunctions may suggest the paratactic quality of the original, for most of us they recall the 'numinous' King James version; and so they work against any effect of modern 'ease'. The translation certainly has merits, but they lie neither in any startlingly modern view of the original, nor in literal fidelity.

Here I'll give a few particular instances. The first is chosen by the translator himself to illustrate his practice: 'I have translated Mark 10:27: "for men it is impossible, but not for God, since for God all things are possible." I could have written: "Men cannot do it, but God can do anything."' He isn't, he says, trying to render the saying in 'contemporary idiom'; rather he means to reflect 'the style of the original'. But the original order is something like this: 'with men [it is] impossible but not with God, all things for [are] possible with God.' So the correspondence isn't very exact; 'since' is intrusive, and something of the gnomic quality is lost if one twice inserts the verb 'to be' when it is absent from the original.

Price also misses this quality: 'With men it's impossible but not with God for everything is possible with God'; and E. V. Rieu in the Penguin version: 'For men it is impossible, but not for God. Anything is possible for God.' That heavy stop changes the tone. Ronald Knox, whose Catholic translation follows the Latin Vulgate text, departs further from the Greek: 'Such things are impossible to men's powers, but not to God's; to God, all things are possible.'

Lattimore's version is almost the same as those of RV and NEB, inevitably, perhaps. The point to notice is that the translation he says he rejected: 'Men cannot do it, but God can do anything' – is not at all acceptable; it forfeits the structure of the original, with its contrast between *adunation* and *dunata* ([it is] impossible/ [all things are] possible) and the triple repetition of *para*, 'with' or 'for', and leaves a mere paraphrase; since the rejected alternative preserves nothing but the basic sense there is no particular virtue in the rejection.

Lattimore cites another passage – John 11–in which his version simply duplicates RV: he has both the sisters of Lazarus, Martha and Mary, say, 'Lord, if you had been here, my brother would not have died.' In the Greek, there is a slight variation in Mary's version, and Price, noticing this, reproduces it by the slightest of variations in the English: Martha says 'wouldn't' and Mary says 'would not'. It isn't the same as the Greek, but it is as faithful as anybody could hope for. (NEB also observes the variation, in a different way.) Perhaps success depends on such minute particulars. Lattimore may be just a little too smooth; his version of Mark 7:1–5 is certainly less glib than the one he offers in his preface as the sort of translation he wants to avoid – with the syntax ironed out; but it is less successful than Price's in simulating the bumpy ride of the original, with its enormous clumsy parentheses.

The whole matter bristles with difficulty. We suppose that Mark in Greek sounded pretty rough, especially to people who knew a more literary Greek; but we, when we read the morning paper, aren't constantly hearing it against a background of the prose of Burke or Gibbon. To me the original sounds astonishingly rugged, and its uncouthness powerfully affects my sense of what Mark's gospel is; but scholars who know a lot of first-century Greek might well say I exaggerate. Anyway, Lattimore often strikes me as less uncouth than his principles require; but that doesn't mean he fails to provide some unusually interesting readings.

In Luke 23:16, for example, Pilate is saying he finds in Jesus nothing deserving of death. 'I will teach him a lesson and let him go,' translates Lattimore. The AV has 'I will therefore chastise him . . .'; Rieu: 'I propose, after due correction, to release him.' Knox says 'scourge him'. It might be thought that 'teach him a lesson' is a weak euphemism for 'flog'. But the Greek word is *paideuo*, which means, in the first place, 'teach, instruct'. The sense inevitably gets extended to include 'correct', 'beat'; and the Latin text uses the word *emendo*, of which the senses are also extended to mean 'castigate', 'beat'. The ideal translation will preserve something of the range of the original word; that is what Rieu is unsuccessfully attempting. Lattimore has found a colloquialism which more exactly reproduces that range of sense; for 'teach him a lesson' *could* mean what it literally says, but in modern English always has the sense of physical assault. For good value he gives the clear extended sense of 'whipped' in a note. I suppose it is by such small triumphs that a new translation should, in part, be judged.

At John 5:41 Lattimore, agreeing with RV, reads 'I do not receive glory from men.' (AV: 'I receive not honour from men'; Rieu, 'I take no praise from men'; NRB 'I do not look to men for honour'; Raymond Brown in his *Anchor* commentary: 'Not that I accept human praise'). 'Honour', 'glory', and 'praise' here translate the difficult word *doxa*. In Plato it is sometimes used in opposition to 'knowledge' – opinion is uncertain, likely to be false. (The sixteenth- and seventeenth-century English usage preserves this sense.) It also means 'reputation', or 'the opinion others hold of one' (often distinguished from a true, inherent honour); and, to add to the confusion, it can mean, without disparagement, 'honour' or 'glory'.

Obviously it is this latter end of the sense range that is primarily at work in the verse under discussion, though it implies also that the sort of honour men can confer (what Shakespeare calls 'mouth-honour') is irrelevant to God. Four lines later Jesus is saying, 'How can you believe, when you receive your glory from each other, and do not look for the glory that comes from God alone?' (Lattimore). Here NEB uses 'honour'. Rieu, not very valuably, paraphrases: 'content as you are with praise from one another, and not seeking the approval that comes from the Only God?' For the Greek has *doxa* in both these places, as well as in 1:41; Rieu's liberty is self-condemned, and so is Brown's, who has 'praise' in the first place and 'glory' in the second. It is easy to see why they chose to vary the word in translation; internal puns on *doxa* are working in the original, and they are missed if you translate by the same word in both places; yet they are missed just as much if you don't. The translators of King James, far more familiar than we are with the sort of contrast involved (it is very common in the poetry of the period) still stuck to 'honour' in both cases. To sort out *doxa*-opinion was a work of length; such a work is Shakespeare's *Troilus and Cressida*.

So we cannot blame the modern translator; and indeed Lattimore has an economical note on the difficulty, pointing out (what is easily missed) that in 1:42 of the same passage John uses the verb *dokeō*, closely related to *doxa*, in the sense of 'wrongly suppose' and in direct contrast to *know*. I very much doubt whether he is right in saying, in his note, that 1:41 ('I do not receive glory from men') could mean 'I do not accept the opinion of men.' But to open up the subject in a note, when it is incapable of treatment in the text itself, is certainly fair dealing.

So much may well be said of the whole thing. Lattimore follows his humour, and though I don't think it is very close to mine (I seem to want more clangour, more roughness) he has thought about and tried to solve a large number of problems as they arose. He is as far from Benjamin's magical, unattainable interlinearity as he is from the bureaucrat's English of NEB; but he is very honestly not quite the same as anybody else, and follows his humour with much circumspection.

New York Review of Books, 19 July 1979

Sacred Space

Christian Verse

The editor of an anthology of Christian verse has, at the outset, to decide what the book is for. Pious browsing? Testimony to the predominance of Christianity in our culture, whether religious or secular? Evidence that adherence to Christian doctrine is compatible with the production of poetry that still seems good? An anthology of *religious* poetry would, you might suppose, be quite a different matter. Yet Helen Gardner's *Faber Book of Religious Verse* contains nothing that is manifestly outside the Christian tradition, unless one defines that tradition very rigorously. She includes Shelley, Hardy, Housman, and Yeats, but no Jewish poetry, to stray no further from the middle of the road than that. Dame Helen professes to distinguish between Christian and religious, but only to let in a few errant masters like those named above.

The lazy confidence of the English assumption that religious, give or take a few marginal cases, means effectively the same thing as Christian, has its amusing side, especially in these days when it is harder than ever to draw the line. A few years ago the American scholar Charles Anderson prevailed on me to abet him in his campaign to install a monument to Henry James in Westminster Abbey. The main task before us, apart from collecting the cash and commissioning the stone, was to persuade the dean and chapter of Westminster that they should give the enterprise their blessing. We were called upon to make our case with proper ceremony, and in due time waited on the dean with the most impressive group of senior establishment figures we could muster; I remember the late C. P. Snow (a lord) and V. S. Pritchett (a knight) and Iris Murdoch; there were others, all in their best clothes. The dean required an assurance that Henry James could properly be called a religious man. We gave it without reservation; if the question had been whether he was a Christian we should have sipped our sherry with less composure. We succeeded; James was installed with all due observances, and Professor Leon Edel preached a notable sermon to a very grand congregation. More recently, the fans of George Eliot have got her in too, though she was quite positively not Christian; and the two novelists now hobnob with Hopkins, Eliot, and Auden, who satisfy much more rigorous standards.

It is a safe guess that if Donald Davie had anything to do with it neither James nor George Eliot would be commemorated in a Christian church. You will look in vain for Shelley, Hardy, Housman, and Yeats in his sacred space. Yet there are obvious reasons why his anthology* is enormously superior to its Faber rival. The first is that he is himself a fine poet and critic, admittedly with strong and idiosyncratic tastes, but never likely to call a bad poem a good one. The second is that he has been thinking hard about Christian poetry. In a way his anthology is a companion to his recent book of lectures, *A Gathered Church* (1978), which argues aggressively that the literature of dissenters has had very unfair treatment in traditional literary history and criticism; to him it seems anything but marginal to English and American culture.

Davie's choice of verse is illuminated by some forceful doctrinal assertions in *A Gathered Church*. Having remarked that few of us 'would like to live with the Calvinist tenets of election and reprobation in their primitive seventeenth-century ferocity' – to which tenets he attributes both 'masculine force' and the power to create 'private terror and despair' – he says of Jonathan Edwards that his doctrine ('Calvinism in all its uncompromising rigour') 'has never been controverted, and perhaps it is incontrovertible'. We have simply set it aside. Davie shows contempt for softened versions of Calvinism, and seems to be sorry that John Wesley,

* *The New Oxford Book of Christian Verse*, chosen and edited by Donald Davie (Oxford University Press)

whom he admires, wasn't a Calvinist. So we know where Davie stands, and also, incidentally, why he shows so much interest in American Christian poetry, including poems by Anne Bradstreet, Edward Taylor, Jones Very, John Greenleaf Whittier, and Emily Dickinson. (Gardner shows no sign of having allowed American poetry to come under her notice; some things, and the literary inferiority of Americans is among them, are apparently not negotiable.)

Davie returns to his doctrinal position in the preface to the anthology, but poetry is an even more important test for inclusion than Calvinism. This isn't a work of piety, but as a matter of personal preference (he is 'specially drawn to the plain style') the editor chooses a lot of eighteenth- and nineteenth-century hymns, and leaves out the un-English baroque of Crashaw's 'Hymn to Saint Teresa'. Most of these hymns are the product of evangelical dissent, and they 'preach doctrines more bleakly challenging than most modern Christians are accustomed to'; yet many of them are still familiar, though often in expurgated forms, to modern churchgoers who probably don't even know they are chanting the words of John Newton, Isaac Watts, Charles Wesley, and Cowper. Such hymns treat, as a rule, of 'one or more of the distinctive doctrines of the Christian church', but for the present enterprise they must also satisfy the requirement that they be good poems; and since Charles Wesley alone wrote more than six thousand hymns we can see that the editor set himself no simple task. What he did, he says, was to assume that George Herbert, Henry Vaughan, Christopher Smart, and William Cowper were 'the masters of the sacred poem in English', and then ask of each candidate for inclusion whether it deserved 'to appear between the same covers as Herbert's "The Collar" or his "Church-monuments"' – a criterion as admirable as it is surely almost impossibly severe.

This preface is a strong critical essay, and it includes a subtle study of Cowper's hymn 'Sometimes a light surprises' from the collection he published in 1779 with John Newton (coming upon it in an index of first lines you might want to attribute it to Emily Dickinson).

One may have read this poem, or more probably sung it, many and many a time before realizing that the crucial word in it is the first. 'Sometimes' – only sometimes, not always, not even very often! The 'holy contemplation' that is thereafter evoked, the sweet security, the unforced adoration – all this is distinctly *not* what any one, it seems, should expect to experience at all often, in church or out of it. It is *not* presented as the normal condition of the Believer. Above all therefore it is *not* the pay-off, the guaranteed reward for going to church and trying to behave well. On the contrary one earns such fitful and infrequent benefits (though 'earn' is the wrong word anyway, for a Calvinist such as Cowper) only by first suffering through afflictions and desolations – the 'season of clear shining' comes only 'after rain', only 'when comforts are declining'; and there is no guarantee that it will come, even then. Similarly, one sings anyway; the consoling words that one sings strike dully and inertly Sunday after Sunday (one is even, so some might say, 'insincere' in singing them); it is only *sometimes*, on one or two Sundays out of many, that 'a light surprises' and the words take on heartfelt meaning, 'while he sings'.

The emphasis in the preface, once again, is on the doctrinal 'bleakness' Davie finds so attractive. For my taste there is a little too much relish in his admiration for the 'appalling' certainties of Calvinism, but perhaps he is sure of election and would expect those who have no such confidence to feel some unease or resentment. However, it is undoubtedly in consequence of his beliefs that Davie regards 'direct and unswerving English' as the only decent way to talk to God; 'any prevarication or ambiguity is unseemly'. And he is beyond question a connoisseur of such English; so the bleakness of the theology contributes after all to the strength of the poetry.

This 'New' Oxford book, then, reflects the personality of the compiler much more positively than its predecessor, the superseded volume of Lord David Cecil, or its rival, the *Faber Book of Religious Verse*. Resemblances are closest, not surprisingly, in the medieval sections; it is after the Reformation that Davie strikes out on his own. He includes three sonnets by the plain but difficult Fulke Greville, five of Mary Herbert's psalm paraphrases from *The Sidney Psalter*; Francis Quarles's one masterpiece which begins

> Like to the arctic needle, that doth guide
> The wand'ring shade by his magnetic pow'r,
> And leaves his silken gnomon to decide
> The question of the controverted hour,
> First frantics up and down from side to side,
> And restless beats his crystal'd iv'ry case,
> With vain impatience jets from place to place,
> And seeks the bosom of his frozen bride;
> At length he slacks his motion, and doth rest
> His trembling point at his bright pole's beloved breast.
> E'en so my soul . . .

He has found two poems by one Thomas Washbourne that satisfy his criteria, nobly unearthed from Grosart's Victorian edition. The many evangelical hymns seem worth their place. Wordsworth squeezes in with 'Resolution and Independence', on the faintly ridiculous plea that the old leech-gatherer of the poem is a Scottish Presbyterian. (Wordsworth, who says a lot about the old man in his remarkable letter to Sara Hutchinson, June 14, 1802, fails to make this point, speaking instead of 'the fortitude, independence, persevering spirit, and the general moral dignity' exhibited by this impressive figure, in spite of 'the necessities which an unjust state of society has entailed upon him'.)

The nineteenth century provides more hymns, and more American Christian poetry. From the twentieth century Davie gives us a highly individual selection: the anonymous Ozark Holy Roller song, 'The Heavenly Aeroplane', and, less contentiously, several poems by C. H. Sisson, including the remarkably fine 'Letter to John Donne'.

Even if it were to turn out that there aren't many readers who want Christian poetry so rigorously Christian and so rigorously poetry, this anthology will survive as the work of a distinguished poet when more conventional compilations are forgotten. Given the terms Davie so firmly and lucidly sets down there is, in my view, only one serious complaint to be made. Cowper is one of the heroes of the book, but his best poem, 'The Castaway', is omitted. This can hardly be because the editor thought it inferior as poetry. The reason must be doctrinal.

Cowper had earlier shown some fascination with the idea of death by drowning in the ocean, but 'The Castaway', written at the end of his life, grew out of prolonged meditation on a passage in a book about Admiral Anson's voyage round the world. A sailor is lost overboard near Cape Horn: 'We perceived that he swam very strong, and it was of the utmost concern that we found ourselves incapable of assisting him; and we were the more grieved at his unhappy fate since we lost sight of him struggling with the waves, and conceived . . . that he might continue sensible for a considerable time longer of the horror attending his irretrievable situation.'

Cowper might have written about this event as he did of the sinking of the *Royal George*, which capsized at the quayside with the loss of 800 lives: a patriotic lament for the brave that are no more. But he saw the lost sailor as a type of himself, and calls him 'such a destin'd wretch as I'.

That is near the beginning of the poem; the bulk of it describes, with feeling but in a slightly stilted diction, the plight of the sailor: 'Not long beneath the whelming brine, / Expert to swim, he lay.' The ship sails on, carried away by 'the furious blast'; at length the man drowns: 'by toil subdu'd, he drank / The stifling wave, and then he sank.' Heroic Anson shed a tear, and since this will immortalize the dead man there is no need for the poet to do so. There is a melancholy delicacy about all this, but the refusal to take on the job of commemorating the sailor is really a device to reintroduce the real subject; for 'misery still delights to trace / Its semblance in another's case.' And so to the last, worked-for stanza, with its complex peripeties:

> No voice divine the storm allay'd
> No light propitious shone;
> When, snatch'd from all effectual aid,

We perish'd, each alone;
But I beneath a rougher sea,
And whelm'd in deeper gulfs than he.

First, the comment or complaint that God had omitted to intervene; then '*We* perish'd' – all the more surprising in that one half
expects 'We perish', a generalization of the human condition. But
no, it is Cowper and the sailor, only those two; and the subsequent
claim that the poet's is the worse case divides him not only from
his 'semblance', the drowning sailor, but from the whole of
mankind.

It seems clear that Davie accepts reprobation, the damnation
of the non-elect, as the logical accompaniment of election. So did
Cowper. Many years earlier, while a patient in a private asylum
at St Albans, just north of London, he had been converted to
Evangelical Calvinism; but he subsequently suffered, as the elect
should not, from a conviction that he was damned nevertheless.
(If Thomas Pynchon's Scurvhamite sect had existed, Cowper
would probably have joined it.) Calvinism suited this poet's de-
mentia *almost* exactly; but it was not only mad but theologically
incorrect of him to suppose himself singled out from the rest of
humanity for both election and reprobation, and one can only
guess that this is the reason why Davie excludes 'The Castaway'.
Yet it is surely as Christian as it is bleak, and since Davie is not
given to failures of nerve we shall have to attribute this unhappy
reprobation of a fine poem to heresy-hunting.

Cowper of course wrote a great deal of jollier stuff. It is pleasing
that the Oxford University Press should, in these hard times, be
proceeding with their edition of his poetry and prose almost in
the grand old manner. The prose already runs to about 1,300
pages,* and there is as much still to come; the first of the two
verse volumes† only takes us up to Cowper's first volume of
poetry, though he was over fifty when it was published in 1782.

* *The Letters and Prose Writings of William Cowper, Volume I: 1750–1782
& Volume II: 1782–1786*, edited by James King and Charles Ryskamp (Oxford
University Press)
† *The Poems of William Cowper, Volume I: 1748–1782*, edited by John D.
Baird and Charles Ryskamp (Oxford University Press)

A second volume will include most of his best-known works; unfortunately the translation of Homer, which occupied the poet for eleven years and was in his view his principal work, is to be left out 'on grounds of expediency' (neither the publisher nor the editors can afford the time and the expense).

Charles Ryskamp, of the Pierpont Morgan Library in New York, is the most distinguished of Cowper scholars. Twenty-three years ago he published his admirable *William Cowper of the Inner Temple, Esquire*, which took the poet's life up to 1768 (his thirty-eighth year) and added many uncollected letters and poems. Now, working with collaborators, he shows himself an exemplary editor, deeply learned in the poet's life and times, ready but not over-ready to annotate. He and his helpers must have another gift – the capacity never to be bored by Cowper, an admirable letter writer certainly, but with a tendency to rattle on.

I suppose the high point of the prose must be the twin essays called *Adelphi*, the poet's record of his own conversion and the deathbed conversion of his brother, who was a Cambridge don, thought by Cowper perhaps too clever to be religious. Depression ran in the family and after a bright start, at Westminster School and then as a student of law, William fell prey to it. At twenty-one he belonged to a rakish and talented group of young men; at thirty-two he made his third suicide attempt, the proximate cause being his terror at the prospect of a House of Lords inquiry into his tenure of an easy and remunerative post there. He describes vividly an attempt at hanging himself:

> My garter was made of a broad scarlet binding with a sliding buckle being sewn together at the ends; by the help of the buckle I formed a noose and fixing it about my neck, strained it so tight that I hardly left a passage for breath or the blood to circulate. The tongue of the buckle held it fast. At each corner of the bed was placed a wreath of carved work fastened by an iron pin which passed up through the midst of it. The other part of the garter therefore which made a loop I slipped over one of these and hung by it some seconds, drawing up my feet under me that they might not touch the floor. But the iron bent,

44

the carved work slipped off, and the garter with it. I then fastened the garter to the frame of the tester, winding it round and tying it in a strong knot. The frame broke short and let me down again ...

So to the third attempt, jumping from a chair with the rope over the angle of the door; a voice said ''Tis over, 'tis over, 'tis over,' but he found himself face down on the floor, half dead only. All such failures Cowper attributes to the direct intervention of God, who, as he remarked in a famous hymn, moves in a mysterious way his wonders to perform.

The genre of confessions was in vogue, but Cowper meant it when he said that 'there was never so abandoned a wretch' as he. (As 'The Castaway' suggests, he felt a special horror at the idea of abandonment; his mother died when he was six.) He thought despair the unpardonable sin and Satan's greatest weapon; but he was saved from it, or should have been, by his conversion. After his stay at St Albans, he never went back to London but moved a little to the north, living first at Huntingdon and then, for many years, at Olney, as the boarder of the Revd and Mrs Unwin, and later, when Unwin died, of Mrs Unwin alone. The curate of Olney was the reformed slave-trader and hymn writer John Newton, author of 'How sweet the Name of Jesus sounds', and it was he who extracted from Cowper his large contribution to the volume *Olney Hymns*.

He was now leading a placid village life, but in 1773 he was mad again, perhaps from the anxiety of supposing that he must marry Mrs Unwin to put a stop to gossip. Thereafter he clung to the belief that he was, of all the elect, the only damned soul. This conviction is recorded in a remarkable poem, all the more horrible because of its stately Horatian sapphics:

> Hatred and vengeance, my eternal portion,
> Scarce can endure delay of execution: –
> Wait, with impatient readiness, to seize my
> Soul in a moment.
> Damn'd below Judas; more abhorr'd than he was,
> Who, for a few pence, sold his holy master.

Twice betray'd, Jesus me, the last delinquent
Deems the profanest . . .

[Not, need I say, in Davie.]

From the time of this breakdown he never entered a church, and was convinced that, irrevocably damned, he had virtually ceased to exist. But he achieved some kind of equilibrium, began to write a great deal of verse and made new friends. Then there were more relapses, in 1787 and 1792; the final collapse of 1794 lasted until his death in 1800.

Although a large quantity of biographical information survives, it isn't easy to guess the cause of these illnesses. It was at one time not uncommon to speak of his 'hereditary taint'. It appears, moreover, that sexual anxiety of some kind attended each collapse; the last coincided with the final illness and death of Mrs Unwin. There were strong rumours that he was a hermaphrodite, and Charles Greville says so positively in his *Journal*; or that he had some genital defect. But perhaps the behaviour that gave rise to such speculations was a consequence rather than a cause; we remember another uniquely elect figure, Dr Schreber, who believed he must become a woman. However, Cowper's fantasies were not messianic; they were fed by a demonic version of Calvinism. His sufferings arose from a conviction that absolutely nothing, including those sufferings, can occur without the direct concurrence of God; as he was so often hellishly depressed the moral seemed obvious.

Yet the great bulk of his writing is genial enough. He wrote about his Horatian retirement, his garden, his pet hares, his chats with ladies. Most of his letters – an immense collection – are gently animated and seem happy enough. Reading them, one remembers that he had almost no income and unashamedly depended on friends for his support and his luxuries. The quantity of good things sent him by coach from London is extraordinary – he is forever thanking people for salmon, halibut, oysters, sole, cod, mackerel, herring, and port. Now and again some political event excited him – the Gordon Riots of 1780 or the bad behaviour of the American colonists; and he was clearly shaken out of his country calm by hot-air balloons, though the one he saw was a failure. 'The endeavour was I believe very philosophically made, but such a process depends for its success upon such niceties as make it very precarious.' He decided against them.

But more often his letters are chit-chat, as might be expected from a correspondent whose only winter diversion is 'to walk ten times a day from the fire-side to his Cucumber frame and back again'. He cracks some jokes ('Vive la bagatelle!' he cries, quoting that other melancholy man, Swift). He is sometimes priggish, especially when writing to Newton, after his removal to a London parish; he agreed that it was disgraceful to celebrate the centenary of Handel's birth with a concert in a church. Worse, he consoles himself in a hard winter that the sufferings of the poor who can 'wrap themselves up warm in the robe of Salvation' are less than his own, since he lacks this recourse. He had about him a touch of the contemporary Man of Feeling; but true men of feeling probably don't become Calvinists.

Cowper wrote to hold off melancholy. In 1779, admittedly before he became famous, he told a correspondent, 'I have no more Right to the Name of a Poet, than a maker of Mousetraps has to That of an Engineer.' Verse is to him what a fiddle might be to a gentleman. But he thought himself a good judge of poetry. He was harsh on Dr Johnson, or rather he admired him as lexicographer and biographer, but declared he had no ear for verse. Of Pope he said that 'never . . . were such talents and such drudgery united'. He came to see his own Homer as superseding Pope's, which he repeatedly condemns in his letters. But he mostly clung to the idea of himself as an amateur, amusing the ladies with *The Task* and the whole nation with his poem *The Diverting History of John Gilpin* – for some time not known to be his.

Curiously enough, the event that did more than any other to propel him into serious authorship was a book by Martin Madan, the cousin who rescued him after his suicide attempt years before and consigned him to the asylum at St Albans. Madan was now advocating polygamy, on the novel ground that monogamy was the chief cause of ruined women. He wanted every seducer to marry his victim, whether or not cohabitation continued, and so be responsible for keeping her off the streets. Cowper, greatly disturbed by all this, wrote diatribes against Madan. 'Fear siez'd the trembling Sex, in ev'ry Grove / They wept the Wrongs of Honorable Love,' etc. Or, 'What is there in the Vale of Life / Half so delightfull as a Wife ... ?' Well, how would *he* know? But these exercises got him going, and by the time he took on Homer he was turning out forty lines a day.

'I am become the wonder of the Post Office in this Town,' he once wrote. 'They never sent so many letters to London in their lives.' Writing verse and letters is a palliative for melancholy little used, one supposes, in our day. But it kept Cowper for long periods calm and civil. Yet it was when depression mapped itself on to those bleak and appalling doctrines, and his writing faced in Calvinism a demonic projection of his own psyche, that he became, for a few moments in his seventy years, a great poet.

New York Review of Books, 21 October 1982

Beethoven at Home

W. H. Auden once reviewed, in these pages, Otto Deutsch's large *Documentary Biography of Mozart*.[1] Without research I can't be positive that it was the shortest review ever published here, but I'd bet on it. Auden found the whole enterprise redundant, even indecent. Mozart's life was none of our business; and he would have said the same of Beethoven's. One admires the purity of this attitude, but Auden himself was not always capable of holding it, for he was interested in great men and liked to pay them homage. And it is easier to do that to a person than to a shelf of books or scores. In celebrating Freud he spoke of a loved master, even of 'an important Jew who died in exile'; he mourned a man. And the wonderful epiphonema of his poem might be applied with almost equal justice to Beethoven:

> sad is Eros, builder of cities,
> and weeping anarchic Aphrodite.

Once allow this more sublime style of biography and how shall we keep out the more ordinary kind, in which homage takes the form of a passion for postmarks, the journals of innkeepers, memorabilia scribbled on the back of a manuscript; in which reverence is expressed in endless explanations, which, if they fail, at least breed wonder at all there is to explain?

Since facts accumulate and explanations decay, biographies of Beethoven will presumably continue to be written. Readers who want everything will go on consulting Alexander Thayer's *Life of*

[1] *NYRB*, August 5, 1965.

Beethoven in the latest edition (at present this is Elliot Forbes's, revised 1964, re-revised 1967). Middle-aged laymen may still look back to J. W. N. Sullivan's *Beethoven: His Spiritual Development*, now fifty years old. It was very rich, and we may gag a little at the remembered taste. Mr Solomon's book* is more sober, but may prove standard for the present generation. Without being vast it has much detail; it is up to, and occasionally ahead of, the progress of research. It registers efficiently Beethoven's Times, and records, with modest conviction, the Life and its psychopathology.

The Audenesque objection would be that all this, however serious, is gossip, and tells us nothing about the music. Knowing that love made him weep his pints, and that his father beat him, will not help us to understand how he came to write the Piano Trios, op. 1, much less the *Hammerklavier* Sonata and the *Grosse Fuge*. And that is true. All we get is a great man's Life. And Beethoven's, though he was recognized as a great man and often, though with some unease, behaved like one, lacks the colour and variety that great men's lives should have been. Bonn, and Vienna with its environs, represent virtually the whole of his world. He threatened to go to Paris, but stayed at home; he might have gone to London, but didn't; he even spoke of emigrating to the New World, but died in Vienna. His love affairs were abortive, his friendships sentimental but shallow, his intervention in others' lives clumsy without offering the narrative satisfactions of ultimate disaster.

Much of the detail in a biography of such a man is likely to be of the sort that gets recorded only because the greatness of his demeanour was slightly crazy, he blew his nose into his hand; he tried to sell the *Missa Solemnis* to several different people, and he wrote a letter now called the Heiligenstadt Testament, which calls forth intense efforts of interpretation but might not seem of very great interest if the life in question were that of an ordinarily odd, sad man.

In short, the greatness that justifies minute inquiry has no very obvious connection with the biographical detail the inquiry

* Maynard Solomon, *Beethoven* (New York: Schirmer Books)

uncovers. For example, his treatment of his nephew Karl might, in a lesser man, seem no more than pathetic and a bit sordid. Himself the son of a failed and alcoholic father, Beethoven more than once felt he must act as head of the family; and when his brother Caspar Carl fell ill Ludwig extracted from him a legal declaration that after his death he wanted his brother to be his son's guardian. Caspar Carl died when Karl was nine years old, and Beethoven about forty-five. The widow, Johanna, very reasonably disputed Ludwig's claim that he was now the child's sole guardian. There was a long struggle, during which the composer behaved like a madman. He despised Johanna because she had been pregnant with Karl before marriage, and because her husband had had her convicted on a specious charge of stealing money from him. Since practically all their money was her dowry, this was only a technical offence, but Beethoven called it a 'horrible' crime. Perhaps he held it against her that the marriage had been unhappy; perhaps, as Solomon suggests, and as later events partly confirmed, he unconsciously desired her. Anyway, he fought her with ridiculous ferocity, traducing her in the courts, and recording various fantasies about her, such as that she had poisoned her husband, and, after his death, taken to whoring (he called her, interestingly enough, the Queen of the Night).

During this long paranoid episode Beethoven harmed everybody concerned, including himself: his lifelong tacit pretence to noble status was exposed in court. Johanna suffered, obviously; and Karl had the worst of it. Though he seems to have deluded himself into thinking he was the boy's natural father, Beethoven treated him coldly, even cruelly; one assault caused injury 'in the genital region', whereupon the composer pleaded that his 'having been human, and erred now and then' was no reason why the child should be taken from its father. As Karl grew up the harassment continued; Beethoven seemed anxious to deny him any sexual life. And at nineteen he made a serious suicide attempt, openly attributing his misery to his uncle's behaviour. A little while after Beethoven died, leaving Karl his sole legatee, though he was well aware of the possibility that Johanna might be Karl's, for he was unmarried and in the army.

Even this brief summary of the affair may suggest that while it was at its height Beethoven was so obsessed by it that he can hardly have given much attention to anything else. Nothing could be less true; in the middle of his crazy litigation he wrote the *Hammerklavier* Sonata and the Kyrie, Gloria, and Credo of the *Missa Solemnis*, as well as sketching the *Diabelli* Variations. This certainly lends colour to Solomon's thesis, that major transformations in the music are usually associated with major biographical crises. The excesses that distort behaviour have quite a different effect on the inner life, enabling the discovery of what would remain inaccessible to conventional good conduct.

As Solomon is ruefully aware, it is difficult to develop the theme of these correlations by writing biographically about the music. In fact he fences off the music in four sections, one for each period of the composer's life (Bonn, Vienna, Heroic Period, Final Phase). The 'rather wide variety of categories – aesthetic, historical, psychoanalytic, sociological' that he uses are applied, mostly, to the life not the music; the category most enterprisingly used is the third. But before interpretation begins the facts have to be established. Thayer has the great mass of them, but there are questions about the dependability of early witnesses, the authenticity of transcripts, and so forth. And there is new research, including his own. This is, in other words, a major biography. Yet I doubt if Solomon would claim to have radically changed the chronicle of fact, except by one great coup, the discovery of the identity of the Immortal Beloved; and not everybody will find that knowing her name makes much difference. The main interest of *Beethoven* lies less in the continuous thread of the life than in Solomon's examination of certain large knots in it.

Beethoven was the second and eldest surviving son of a very minor musician, who beat him to make him practice. A drunken, irresponsible father and a melancholy mother, perhaps obsessed with the memory of her first-born son, gave him a childhood he rarely spoke of, and then confusedly. He is said to have lacked, throughout his life, the ability to mourn. At grade school he was backward; and though he later shared, 'in a sloganized and simplified form', such Enlightenment enthusiasms as the philosophy of Kant, he never became in the ordinary sense, an intellectual. He was a child virtuoso on the piano, but was slow to learn composition, and is said to have been doing unsatisfactory counterpoint exercises for Haydn in his early twenties. At the same age, and characteristically in a time of trouble, he had his first success as a composer; and it would be reasonable to say that thenceforth he did all his thinking in music. Always ambivalent about authority, he venerated the dead Mozart but envied Haydn, whom he treated disrespectfully, at least until he was very old, denying that he had learned anything from him. There is discernible in the history of Beethoven's music a pattern of convention-defying forward leaps, and subsequent withdrawals to positions established by the authority of others, that may reflect this ambivalence.

It was his virtuosity that won him his uneasy place in Vienna. The social order was changing, but a musician still needed, as Mozart had needed, any proof he could come by that he belonged upstairs. Beethoven had some generous patrons; but he had to sell his art (a word he used in a sense that belonged less to their world than to the later nineteenth century) as a commodity. His manners reflect the ambiguity of his position: deference, as in dedications, but with a developing attitude of eccentric defiance. He made aristocrats beg him to perform. He despised audiences; improvising pathetically, he would make them weep, then burst into loud laughter and tell them they were fools. Near the end of his life he was contemptuous of the audience at the first performance of the string quartet op. 130 because they applauded the early movements but were confounded by the great fugue – 'Cattle! Asses!' His laughter, sudden, uncouth, and loud, was remarked upon. One has noticed something similar in very withdrawn men – the inexplicable gust, outside the normal sociology of laughter, coming from an inner world with different rules.

His hearing first gave him concern in 1801, though sixteen years passed before he was totally deaf. In the Heiligenstadt Testament, a letter to his brothers written the following year, he used his affliction to excuse his misanthropic ways. They had, in fact, established themselves much earlier; but deafness or the fear of it must have deepened his isolation. Solomon finds here another benefit conferred by apparent disaster: by ending his career as a virtuoso, deafness gave the composer greater freedom in an inner world of silent tones. And the Testament, for all its talk of suicide, heralded eight years of prolific composition, mostly in a new 'heroic' style.

Beethoven's attitude to Napoleon, a curious blend of messianism and indifference, calls for a whole chapter. Like many others he cooled off his admiration for the First Consul when he had himself crowned Emperor; but the famous tearing up of the title page of the Third Symphony was not his last word. In fact he restored it, and finally removed all reference to Napoleon only when he might have lost a fee by retaining it. But his motives were more complicated than that. As late as 1810 he thought of dedicating the C major Mass to Bonaparte; and before that he had caused some comment by entertaining Tremont, an associate of the emperor's, after the French bombardment and occupation of Vienna. This sounds like some private hero-worship fantasy leaking into everyday life. During these years Beethoven was much influenced by French music, and Solomon rejoices that he decided against going to Paris, where his career might have ended in emulation of the sterile heroics of fashionable French music. One should add that during the bombardment and occupation he wrote not only the rather military Fifth Piano Concerto but the piano sonatas op. 78, 79, 80a, and the beautiful quartet op. 74, which Solomon, like most experts, thinks of as pleasant but backward-looking, though a lay ear finds it full of original sounds.

For homing in on Beethoven's 'Immortal Beloved', and for a sensitive interpretation of the whole episode, Solomon deserves congratulation. She was Antonie Brentano, to whom Beethoven later dedicated the *Diabelli* variations. He seems to have courted her in his usual way, choosing to do so because she was married and presumably inaccessible; it was his habit either to flirt ponderously or choose women likely to turn him down, at the same time acting in a manner calculated to ensure rejection. But Antonie seems to have dumbfounded him by saying she would leave her husband. A famous and obscure letter shows Beethoven moving toward a decision to break with her, presumably with an indeterminate mixture of altruism and selfishness; he certainly believed that marriage would be disastrous to his music. He never again had a serious relationship with a woman, though soon afterward he began going with prostitutes, and seems to have accepted the loan of friends' wives.

Now began the Final Period. The Congress of Vienna brought from Beethoven his worst music, in his moment of greatest popularity, although *Fidelio*, in its last recension, was at last successful. But after 1815 he rather lost touch with patrons and public. Almost completely deaf, he turned away from his own time and looked back to Handel and Bach. He took to drink, developed cirrhosis of the liver when he was fifty, and perhaps had a venereal disease. At the same time he began a series of masterpieces – the *Missa Solemnis*, the *Diabelli* Variations, the two late sets of bagatelles, and the Ninth Symphony, finished in 1824.

The remainder of his life was given to the five last quartets; only a little earlier he had remarked he might yet make a success of his life. We might say he brought it off anyway. It is right for the experts to tell us that this music is less original than we think; but all we learn from them of its Baroque elements and its debt to Palestrina reinforces our sense of its being a unique world which we understand only according to its own natural laws; a world only very tenuously related with the one in which biography moves most easily, bearing its explanations.

The chief instrument Solomon uses to untie those knots is the Freudian-Rankian Family Romance. Beethoven persistently refused to admit his true birthdate, claiming that the documents referred to his dead brother, also named Ludwig. He wanted to be illegitimate, and was reluctant to deny the rumour that he was a natural son of the king of Prussia. In drafting the Heiligenstadt letter he apparently could not bring himself to write down the name of his brother Johann; that was also his father's name. Such fantasies relieve guilt at the father's death, license incestuous desires, and satisfy a wish for grander parentage. Beethoven, in his dealings with his own drunken father as well as with Karl, showed himself ready to usurp the paternal role; and even his relations with Haydn and Napoleon display a filial ambivalence. Solomon develops this theme with subtle persistence, most effectively in his study of the strangely negative fantasy family Beethoven constructed, with Johanna as absent wife, Karl as absent son, and himself as absent father. And even these painful delusions turn out to be blessings in disguise Solomon says; for Karl and Johanna brought the composer's deepest conflicts and desires to the surface, and made possible a new release of creativity.

Occasionally, as in the Third Symphony, Solomon finds a musical reflection of a non-musical conflict; but he does not attempt to relate the history of Beethoven's delusions to his music in any specific way. *Fidelio* is an apparent exception, but only because it has a libretto; and the passage on the opera is the wildest thing in Solomon's book. Leonore, helping Rocco to dig the grave, is seen as collaborating in her husband's murder. But Florestan's place is taken by the evil father, Pizarro; so Beethoven's fantasy of parricide and his fantasy of father-rescue are reconciled. Moreover Florestan, in his soundless cell, is not only the deaf Beethoven but also the dying vegetation god, as Pizarro is the winter god; and mankind celebrates the new year with marriage hymns. There would be no need to change this reading if the opera were without musical interest, or even not an opera at all. It sounds like the kind of thing students used to write about *The Winter's Tale*, as in Simon Gray's *Butley*.

One sympathizes, however, with the feeling that the power of *Fidelio* calls for profound explanations. Solomon seems to agree with Winton Dean that with all the revising Beethoven never got it quite right, and that Marcelline remains too prominent. But what prevented him from making such an obvious correction? Perhaps he came to see the apparent imbalance as a true balance. Without the quartet, transfiguring the commonplace, the arrival of Pizarro and Leonore's *Abscheuliche* would feel very different, and so would the ecstatic reunion of the finale.

There is an element of the *unheimlich* in all Beethoven's greatest achievements. Charles Rosen[1] says that with the *Hammerklavier* Sonata 'the emancipation of piano music from the demands of the amateur musician was made official, with a consequent loss of responsibility and a greater freedom for the imagination.' But that freedom was dialectically related to the observance of self-imposed restraints, which Rosen defines; and so there is, together with the sense of frontiers mysteriously breached, a

---

[1] *The Classical Style* (Norton, 1972), p. 404.

sense also of a returning home. Solomon speaks of a recurrent homecoming in Beethoven's work, and one is reminded of Heidegger's unique meditations on the same theme in Hölderlin – a memory which prompts the reflection that the best complement we could have to a serious biography of Beethoven would be just such a meditation, if only there were anyone in the world to write it.

New York Review of Books, 6 April, 1978

II

Fighting Freud

The winter number of *Partisan Review* contains an editorial comment entitled 'Freud in the Seventies', in which it is maintained that the 'apostasy' of Frederick Crews from Freud – Crews having 'been one of the staunchest as well as one of the most flexible interpreters of psychoanalytic theory, particularly in relation to literature' – must be seen as an indication that the 'intellectual community' has almost completely lost faith in psychoanalysis.

The editor, William Phillips, goes on to give reasons for thinking that something needs to be done about this, but I mention his piece because it rather strikingly illustrates the point that the book under review,* and some associated shorter writings by Crews, have wider implications than at first sight appear. Since I intend to suggest that Mr Crews has got things wrong, and that his 'apostasy' (which is in any case not yet complete) may be caused by a corrigible misunderstanding, I had better admit now that my knowledge of psychoanalysis is lay knowledge, and that I have never been a 'psychoanalytic critic'. It would be dangerous to claim disinterest, always an ambiguous proposition in these matters; but I can at least claim to be concerned to avoid not a personal impoverishment but an impoverishment of the techniques and theory of humane interpretation – an awkward phrase I will try to justify.

Mr Crews is a strong-minded critic, and a writer of considerable rhetorical resource, but in this book it is himself rather than us

* Frederick Crews, *Out of My System: Psychoanalysis, Ideology, and Critical Method* (Oxford University Press)

he is trying to persuade. He had planned, he says, to write a book expounding a consistent position on psychoanalytic criticism; but the war and the student troubles of the Sixties intervened. He lost some of his old confidence in Freud; and, caught up in political debate and ideological self-scrutiny, he wrote in the heat of various moments the essays here collected. Looking them over later, he discovered to his surprise that they somehow added up to the book he had wanted to write in the first place. The discontinuities and self-contradictions could either be ironed out by the insertion of brief disclaimers, or offered as testimony of an intellectual odyssey – of a deconversion experience not yet quite complete. We are to read it as a study of 'the difficulty of mediating between empirical responsibility and urges toward deep and revolutionary explanation'. One gloss on this phrase is: 'A growing conviction that Freud does not make scientific sense.'

Since that is the central issue, I shall say nothing about Mr Crews's politics – his discovery that he was not born to be a fanatic, his eventual decision against the anti-cultural postures of the Movement. The main point is that a sense of empirical responsibility has seriously weakened his adherence to the 'deep and revolutionary' explanations of psychoanalysis. First we have a ten-year-old essay called 'Can Literature Be Psychoanalysed?' and giving the answer yes, though Crews now thinks it 'too charitable toward the scientific claims of psychoanalysis'. It is a low-keyed performance, addressed to doubting laymen, and draws on the ego psychology of Ernst Kris, who

> insisted that the 'reality' from which a literary creation
> proceeds is not only the reality of the author's drives and
> fantasies, but also the structure of his artistic problem and
> the historical state of his genre.

Defending analysis against the charge that it is unscientific, Crews here argues that it has a measure of verifiability; but later he read Karl Popper, and this was seemingly a critical moment for him, for it was then revealed that verifiability was anyway of small account, falsifiability being the criterion to apply. And Popper's application of this criterion to psychoanalysis appears to have made a decisive impression on Crews. But in those far-off days no such doubt had occurred to him. In the same essay, he warns against certain dangers – one must not produce 'ludicrous diagnoses of writers' mental diseases', for example; and he rightly emphasizes the general importance to critical theory of the interpretative concept of overdetermination:

> I submit that we are entitled to consider *both* overt purpose and the perhaps contradictory purpose (or purposes) that may emerge from imagery or the shape of a plot.

Only a year later 'the anguish and frustration of Vietnam' fired, among other things, Mr Crews's attack on Norman O. Brown. Interesting as this essay is in itself, I want to draw attention to one feature of it that here seems more important than the general disagreement it expresses. Crews opposes Brown because Brown is opposed to the dominant American ego-psychology, and because he takes an interest in other post-Freudian teaching, such as that of Melanie Klein. So far as I can see, Crews's references to Klein are always hostile (he likes to think of her as the showman of a sort of Grand Guignol parody of analysis) or contemptuous (ninety-five per cent of American practitioners think little of her). He shows no sign whatever of having given Klein any serious thought; and when he speaks of D. W. Winnicott, though he does so more kindly, he offers only a vulgarized allusion to the work of a theorist held by many to be, at any rate in the aesthetic implications of his achievement, the most interesting and perspicuous of modern analysts.

Winnicott's concern, though one might not guess as much from Mr Crews's allusions, is not mainly with teddy bears and grubby blankets but with the implications for human creativity of what he calls 'transitional' experience; the baby survives its necessary passage into a world of independent objects by creating an object which already exists, so acquiring in its play a capacity to transform and use the given object. All subsequent cultural experience is 'located in the *potential space* between the individual and the environment (originally the object).' Thus the problem of creativity is removed from the familiar context in which we endlessly discuss the intentions or the needs of an author and the external requirements of his genre; for Winnicott explains the precursor of the aesthetic event as an event neither 'subjective' nor 'objective'. He holds that the capacity for symbolization is possible only when this paradox is *accepted* and not regarded as a means toward some resolution.

Even in so crabbed and distorted a summary Winnicott must seem to have some relevance to current critical issues – more, perhaps, than the Freudian revisionists still preferred by Crews. I take these lapses to be characteristic of a curious provincialism in Crews; although his work is thoroughly footnoted with references to many diverse works, he rarely looks outside the limits he has chosen. And this may be one reason why he has despaired too early.

Still in 1967, he turned his attention to Conrad and demonstrated the methods of psychoanalytic criticism in order to shame ideologically corrupt critics who never get beyond Conrad's manifest content. His opponents here seem to be men of straw, and in any case his analysis of *Heart of Darkness* commits the very faults the author more than once warns us against. After an incautious dose of Freud, Crews says, a man may 'become the purveyor of a peculiarly silly kind of allegory', hearing everywhere 'the squeaking bedsprings of the primal scene'. But he himself hears them in Conrad's Congo, and blames Conrad for their audibility: 'the text threatens to become no longer a story but a clinical document... [It] is in the most agitated sense an autobiographical work.' Indeed, one of the difficulties faced by the reviewer of this book is that the author often disowns his argument before we can say why we don't like it; a prefatory note accuses the Conrad essay of 'biographical reductionism'. 'Reductionism' becomes henceforth one of his major worries, an obsession which, attentive to Crews's cautions, we should not attempt to explain clinically.

A couple of years later Crews is saying why he rejects Northrop Frye's injunction not to 'stray outside literature'. This prompts him to look again, this time with less confidence, at the question of how you defend Freud's 'revolutionary explanation' against the claims of 'empirical responsibility'. 'The few experiments thus far undertaken,' he concedes, 'while generally supportive of the theory, hardly close off alternative interpretations . . . The sceptic is free to say . . . that the Freudian theory is unscientific because its assertions cannot be verified.' And that fact, together with another very awkward one, namely that a book cannot, like a patient, be invited to 'support or refute' the analyst's hunches, explains why most literary criticism of the analytic variety is inept.

The suspicion that psychoanalysis was after all unscientific could only be strengthened by Crews's discovery, in the early Seventies, of his 'longstanding but hitherto tacit commitments to reason and democratic process'. He no longer felt able to support extremist movements, and attacked the revival of Wilhelm Reich ('the world can be made safe for genitality only through cultic delusion'), emphasizing the dangers that ensue when Freud's 'horrific' but still ironically humanist conception of the superego falls into the wrong hands. The commitment to reason continues to grow, and in the last chapter we are given another, more rational look at Freudianism, under the title 'Reductionism and Its Discontents'. Described as an attempt to 'renew appreciation of the criteria that enable rational, nonsectarian discourse about literature to occur', this chapter gives only a qualified welcome to Freud, who is needed among other things to counter the 'affect-stifling' procedures of Frye; but mostly it worries about reductionism. Freudianism can be quite properly reductive, but is too often reduction*ist*, as in the early work of the psychoanalytic critic Norman Holland.

This argument about theoretical reductions that are good ('reductive') and bad ('reductionist') seems largely internal to Crews himself. More interesting is the search for a reliable psychoanalytical model. Ego-psychology, it appears, remains the best, though even it is unsafe. And here Sir Karl Popper, after waiting some years in the wings, makes his decisive appearance. He maintains that science occurs only when there exists a community which agrees on certain empirical criteria by which statements can be falsified. But Popper, though he may be a useful ally if one is looking for a theory of institutional competence (a theory which psychoanalysis could doubtless use), is no help at all to anybody who would like to believe that the 'revolutionary explanations' of psychoanalysis are scientific. For Popper does not regard it as a science at all.

In his recent piece on Erikson (*NYR*, 19 October 1975), Crews moves on a bit and claims, for instance, that one of the things that let Erikson down was 'the empirical weakness of the Freudian tradition'; and he rehearses a number of fatal objections to the scientific status of that tradition. 'Very little,' he now admits – and this is the note caught by Mr Phillips in his editorial – 'very little remains obvious in the legacy of Freud.'

When Dr Robert Mollinger took issue with this conclusion in a letter to this review (February 5), he restated a position once held by Crews himself ('much of psychoanalytic theory has been supported by independent [i.e., empirical] investigations') and commented on the author's disregard of other modern developments of the tradition. Crews's refutation was a simple declaration of his Popperian faith ('a body of theory cannot be called scientific unless its hypotheses can be exposed to tests for falsification') and the casual dismissal of Melanie Klein I have already mentioned. Mr Crews says that he 'persists in thinking that psychoanalysis, whether or not it is an efficient therapy, has things to teach us,' but what they are is likely to emerge, one gathers, only after there has been 'an unsparing reassessment of it'. As things now stand, Mr Phillips's word 'apostasy' is only the slightest of exaggerations.

It might be useful to reduce the narrative of Crews's deconversion to four stages. (1) Literature can be psychoanalysed, and psychoanalysis is satisfactory because, as near as makes very little difference, its findings are verifiable. (2) We must be reasonable, resisting the extremism of Brown but also the 'affect-stifling' taxonomies of Frye: (3) We must be even more reasonable, or we shall fall into reductionism. Meanwhile we should feel no great enthusiasm for the only psychoanalysis that will serve as a model, namely American ego-psychology. (4) The Popperian phase: psychoanalysis is not falsifiable, so not a science; moreover its therapeutic value is very doubtful. It may have some uses, but it is far from clear what they are.

It seems possible that the situation is less desperate than is here suggested. Freud himself was in large part responsible for the assumption that psychoanalysis must and can be tested by the criteria appropriate to the physical sciences; and if you were already feeling uneasy about its capacity to meet such tests, a reading of Popper is likely to have just the effect it seems to have had on Crews. Yet it should be remembered first that Popper, in emphatically denying psychoanalysis the right to be called a science, allows that it is, like other 'metaphysical systems', capable of verification though not, at any significantly high level, of falsification.[1] And he adds that 'if a theory is found to be non-scientific or "metaphysical" it is not thereby found to be unimportant.'

There are admittedly versions of this position which sound stronger; see, for example, Frank Cioffi's 'Freud and the Idea of a Pseudo-Science', which tries to convict Freud of 'the habitual and wilful employment of methodologically defective procedures', such, Cioffi argues, as all pseudo-sciences use.[2] Thus to unfalsifiability Cioffi adds a further charge of bad faith, the deliberate obstruction of disconfirmatory procedures.

The principal procedure attacked by Cioffi is *interpretation*; he concludes that it is as vicious in psychoanalysis as in pyramidology, and for the same reasons: the data and the hypotheses can always be modified to evade disconfirmation. But there are objections to this argument, the most important being that there is a difference in kind between theories which are 'context-free', like those of physics, and those which are 'context-dependent', like psychoanalysis, the context being the therapy.[3] And this objection can be broadened into a criticism of all who try 'to fit Freudian theory into

[1] For possible ways of testing *see* J. O. Wisdom, 'Testing an Interpretation Within a Session', in *Freud: A Collection of Critical Essays*, ed. Richard Wollheim (Doubleday, 1974), p. 332 ff.

[2] *Explanation in the Behavioral Sciences*, ed. Robert Borger and Frank Cioffi (Cambridge, 1970), p. 471 ff.

[3] Jürgen Habermas will help to explain this point. He distinguishes between the 'explanatory understanding' that proceeds from 'general interpretations' such as those of metapsychology, and the rigorously formulated explanations of the empirical sciences. In the latter case the content of theoretical propositions is 'unaffected by operational application to reality'; in the case of the former 'theoretical propositions are translated into the narrative presentation of an individual history *in such a way that a causal statement does not come into being without this context*' (my emphasis). Thus metapsychology is not context-free. See *Knowledge and Human Interests*, 1968, translated by Jeremy J. Shapiro (Beacon Press, 1971), pp. 272–273.

an appropriate model of science, and then label the divergencies as indices of its pseudo-scientific nature.'[1] As I understand the matter it is not the physical scientists who cling to the notion that physics is the queen of the sciences and that all others must carry their heads at the same angle. Indeed some are now willing to argue that Popper's falsificationism itself depends upon a metaphysical theory of truth. At any rate there seems no urgent reason, while this refined debate is in progress, to give up psycho-analysis because Popper, or post-Popperians, call it unscientific.

I mention these debates – without going into them, lacking both space and authority to do so; the point is that Mr Crews, who has after all a profound interest in the theoretical status of psychoanalysis, has so far not attended to them.[2] B. R. Cosin, C. F. Freeman, and N. H. Freeman, for example, give strong reasons for rejecting Cioffi's account of the subject, and indeed they have a claim to be heard on the subject of certain crude assumptions which the falsificationists may be making (the notion that facts are neutral with respect to theory, that there can be 'theory-free' observation). Above all they insist that the anti-Freudians have seriously misunderstood the concept of interpretation itself, which is part of an active and developing relationship, to be welcomed and resisted by the patient, just as Freud's theory states. Modern psychoanalytical theory emerges from this long paper looking a great deal more healthy than Crews supposes.

The heart of the matter, whether for analysis or for critical applications of it, must be this question of interpretation. Certainly it is so in the work of Roy Schafer, whom Crews does mention in passing; Schafer defines psychoanalysis as the interpretation and reinterpretation, in the perspective of life history, of the utterances of the analysand during the session – a process of giving meaning to what had lacked meaning, and one with more affinities for the humanities than for the natural sciences. It is, in short, a hermeneutic activity; and such problems as the causal relation between infantile trauma and adult disorder, much

---

[1] B. R. Cosin, C. F. Freeman, N. H. Freeman, 'Critical Empiricism Criticized: The Case of Freud', *Journal of the Theory of Social Behaviour*, I (1971).

[2] He does not mention the important symposium *Criticism and the Growth of Knowledge*, ed. Imre Latakos and S. Musgrove (Cambridge, 1970).

emphasized by the falsificationists, can yield to a process of interpretation that is self-critical and self-correcting,[1] dependent on the context it affects.

It seems likely that Crews's difficulties could be met without abandoning psychoanalysis, or reducing it to the status of an outmoded methodology that still offers a few testable low-level hypotheses. It is simply a different kind of science and belongs to what discriminating Germans call the *Geisteswissenschaften*. 'The birth of psychoanalysis opens up the possibility of arriving at a dimension that positivism closes off, and of doing so in a manner that arises out of the logic of enquiry,' said the Frankfurt philosopher Jürgen Habermas, lamenting the long delay, even among German theorists, in implementing this programme. Psychoanalysis is of course different from other branches of hermeneutic enquiry; but the general laws we follow in interpreting historical or literary texts apply. The defensive procedures of neurosis are linguistic; the analyst has to translate a deformed and 'privatized' language into a public one, a task which has obvious analogies with that of the literary critic.

Freud's own theory, according to Habermas, was wrong in definable ways. These ways are not to be discovered by indicating differences between his theory and theory of physics, though he himself might have supposed so. 'He did not comprehend metapsychology as the only thing it can be in the system of reference of self-reflection: a general interpretation of self-formative processes.' This general interpretation is 'a systematically generalized history', which provides a scheme for many histories with foreseeable alternative courses, much like a general theory of history or of the novel.[2]

The relevant difference between the physical and the hermeneutic sciences is that the former base their explanations on context-free laws and the latter are context-dependent; their explanations and interpretations are part of the process of the context. We need not at present suppose that a methodology

---

[1] Mr Schafer's *A New Language for Psychoanalysis* has just been published; my reference is to his inaugural lecture as Freud Memorial Professor at University College, London, last autumn.

[2] See *Knowledge and Human Interests*, chapters 10–12.

different from that of physics is an offence to reason, as perhaps Mr Crews is tempted to do. Nor need he suppose that the only future for literary psychoanalysis is in detecting more and more manifestations of the primal scene in the Congo or in Highbury or Walden; or in the free-floating chaos of opinion that Norman Holland has recently favoured. Our point of departure (the French Freudians have long ago moved on) will lie rather in a fuller understanding that reading a text and reading a patient are interpretative processes of a very similar sort. What the practitioners of these two kinds of reading can learn from each other is a large enough subject to renew Crews's zest for responsibly confronting deep revolutionary explanation.

New York Review of Books, 29 April 1976

Freud is Better in German

Now in his eightieth year, Bruno Bettelheim has spent more than half of his life in the United States. He arrived here in 1939 after a year in Dachau and Buchenwald, and this book* contains an expression of his gratitude to his second country. His work as director of the University of Chicago's Orthogenic School, where he devoted himself to autistic children, as well as his books on children and other matters, has earned him the deep respect of his contemporaries. Yet this is the book of an exile, and its most potent, though tacit, theme is nostalgia for the Vienna of his early life.

He was born there in 1903 into a middle-class, assimilated Jewish family, about half a century after Freud, whose origins were very similar; and Dr Bettelheim says that the culture in which he was reared had not changed very much. From 1920 on he read Freud's books as they appeared. He studied psychoanalysis and was analysed in Freud's Vienna. The Gymnasium he attended still had the traditional humanistic curriculum, emphasizing Greek and Latin. Most important of all, he shared Freud's language. Obviously Mr Bettelheim can claim a degree of intimacy with the thought and the culture of Freud that few living people can match.

It is clear that on arrival in the United States Dr Bettelheim suffered some culture shock. Americans, he discovered, had very little understanding of Freud. They had converted psychoanalysis into a medical specialty, making it, in Freud's own words, 'a mere housemaid of Psychiatry'. They were not educated in the classics

---

* Bruno Bettelheim, *Freud and Man's Soul* (New York: Knopf)

and had little contact with culture as Freud understood it. Not to know the story of Oedipus is to miss the point of Freud's central doctrine; not to know the legend of Cupid and Psyche is to misunderstand the very term 'psychoanalysis'. Worse still, Americans were unfamiliar with the German distinction between the natural sciences and the sciences of the spirit (*Naturwissenschaften* and *Geisteswissenschaften*) and so could not see that psychoanalysis belonged to the latter. Hence the un-Freudian emphasis on cure and on adjustment or adaptation to society; in these, the great objects of American psychoanalysis, neither Freud nor Dr Bettelheim has any interest.

Dr Bettelheim says little of the other national schools of analysis, though Jacques Lacan, for example, agreed with him about the unimportance of cure and the British school differs considerably from the vacuously optimistic American school (as he sees it). And, of course, it is America he has in mind when he says that a failure to understand the tragic aspect of Freud's thought has allowed the growth of an intolerably vulgar Freudianism that supports the notion that 'unrestrained letting-go' and 'letting it all hang out' is proper conduct on all occasions and not just on the couch. Like Freud himself, Dr Bettelheim thinks that psychoanalysis met much less resistance here than elsewhere and that the reasons for this were incomprehension or shallowness of response.

One important reason for this failure was the general inability of Americans to read Freud in German, a second that the translations meant to ease this problem were unsatisfactory. It may surprise readers of the 'Standard Edition of the Complete Psychological Works of Sigmund Freud' to find that its chief editor, James Strachey, and his collaborators (including his co-editor, Anna Freud) are here made responsible for the failure of American psychoanalysis. Yet Strachey knew Freud and was not prone to vulgar error. Dr Bettelheim's suggestion that he ought to have made it his responsibility to tell ignorant readers the story of Oedipus or of Psyche is very odd, for Strachey could no more have supposed his readers to be in need of such help than Freud himself did. As Dr Bettelheim's book progresses, his condemnations of Strachey grow even stronger. At first he says only this:

'I do not doubt that Freud's English translators wanted to present his writings to their audience as accurately as possible.' But sixty pages on they are accused of using various devices to make it 'difficult to gain an understanding of what [Freud] had in mind' and of finding 'subtle ways of putting a distance between him and the reader'. In short, they distorted Freud on purpose.

No one, I dare say, would want to maintain that the 'Standard Edition' doesn't need some revision. It would be astonishing if it didn't. But the implication – or charge – of deliberate distortion is surely absurd. It may be true that the translators 'cleave to an early stage of Freud's thought, in which he inclined to science and medicine' – just as it is true that Dr Bettelheim cleaves to 'the more mature Freud, whose orientation was humanistic'. Indeed, it might be thought that Dr Bettelheim, though he gives a persuasive account of Freud's progressive abandonment of his medical attitudes, somewhat exaggerates Freud's independence of them. But in any case Strachey & Company were translating the whole of Freud, early and late. Some of the passages of which Dr Bettelheim complains may be too medical in tone, but some can be defended. He scores some hits, as might be expected, but fewer than he thinks.

In any translation there is a drift away from the tone and even the sense of the original, and this drift is likely to be stronger when the text is treasured by an institution that is split by doctrinal and national disagreement; as in theology, key terms acquire incompatible definitions. Moreover, the German language has the trick of making up new terms out of its own substance; lacking this capability, English has usually resorted to neologisms made from Greek and Latin roots. To Dr Bettelheim such words look affectedly learned, and sometimes they are. Strachey should not have translated '*Mutterleib*' as 'uterus'; 'womb' is better. '*Unheil*' is not 'trouble' but 'disaster'. '*Masse*' doesn't mean 'group' – it simply means 'mass' – and so an important book, 'Group Psychology and the Analysis of the Ego', has a mistranslated title. Worse still, '*Trieb*' does not mean 'instinct'; Strachey hesitated over the word, disliking 'drive', but he should have seen that 'instinct' was worse. 'Triebe und Triebschicksale' simply doesn't mean 'Instincts and Their Vicissitudes', though Dr Bettelheim's

'Drives and Their Mutability' is only slightly better. Perhaps 'Drives and Their Vicissitudes' would be the best compromise.

He insists that Freud was always trying to avoid technical words, so that it is a distortion to make him sound technical in a translation. For example, '*Besetzung*', which means 'occupation' or 'investment' or 'filling' in ordinary German, is translated as 'cathexis'. But granted the English habit of making up words from Greek, 'cathexis' means 'occupation', in what is obviously a special sense. And it must surely have a special sense in Freud. He also uses '*Uberbesetzung*'; not, I am told, a common word. Is 'hypercathexis' really more bizarre than 'over-occupation' or 'upper-occupation'?

A similar point arises with Freud's word '*Fehlleistung*', a combination of two ordinary words that means something like 'faulty achievement'. Freud used it (*pace* Dr Bettelheim) as a technical term, covering acts or speech-acts in which the unconscious enters to prevent our doing what we set out to achieve. Strachey translated '*Fehlleistung*' as 'parapraxis', which is rather brilliant and conveys the sense of Freud's word better than the clumsy circumlocution that would have otherwise been necessary. Dr Bettelheim says he has never heard anybody say 'parapraxis', which is odd, since I hear the word often and use it myself. It might be thought of as Strachey's little contribution to the tradition of classical culture in which Dr Bettelheim wishes we were educated. But such praise is not to be expected here. Strachey is even blamed for translating '*Versprechen*' as 'slips of the tongue', though it is an expression far older than Freud and an exact equivalent of the Latin '*lapsus linguae*', which Freud himself could have used. Dr Bettelheim says fancifully that Strachey was making the tongue responsible for the error, which is simply to misread the idiom.

Too often his notion of the range of senses of an English word seems to have been determined by looking it up in a short dictionary. He supposes, for instance, that 'anatomy' (used to translate '*Zerlegung*') has no use outside the biological sciences and must reflect a predilection for medical terms. Ignoring the complex history of the word 'association' in English philosophy and poetry, he declares that it must refer to 'a conscious process, deliberately engaged in', so that 'free association' is a false translation of '*Einfall*'. And so on.

But the substance of Dr Bettelheim's complaint is suggested by his book's title. Freud used the word '*Seele*' very freely: 'A dream is the result of the activity of our own soul'; 'the structure of the soul'; 'the life of the soul'. Strachey avoided the word, always translating it as 'mind' and '*Seelische*' as 'mental'. He must have known that this was inaccurate; his problem, as usual, was the different semantic range of the words '*Seele*' and 'soul'. It would be disastrous to say in English 'psychoanalysis is a part of psychology which is dedicated to the science of the soul'; Strachey said 'part of the mental science of psychology', which is bad but lacks the religious, or religiose, overtones of the more literal version. Perhaps he should have used 'psyche' and 'psychic', but there are obvious dangers in those words too. Dr Bettelheim's observations are here more justifiable, but perhaps he should address his complaints to Babel rather than to Strachey; some of these problems are inherent in the diversity of languages and cultures.

The same may be said of his strictures on the words 'ego', 'id' and 'superego'. The true equivalents of Freud's '*Ich*', '*Es*' and '*Uber-Ich*' are 'I', 'it' and 'over-I' or 'upper-I'. Dr Bettelheim points out that in German the word for child is neuter ('*das Kind*'), so that children are used to being referred to as 'it' during their earliest years; consequently, Germans would be comfortable with a neuter word for aggressive and asocial impulses. But if Strachey had decided against his Latin technicalities and used 'it', he could not in any case have saved that important childhood association. When Georg Groddeck's translator translates '*Es*' as 'it', we find it no less odd, I think. And we should surely be glad not to have to talk about the 'upper-I'. Moreover, 'ego' has a long history of use in psychology and philosophy, a use quite independent of the pejorative senses Dr Bettelheim takes to be unavoidable.

None of this means that Dr Bettelheim is wrong in claiming that it would be better to read Freud in German, and better still to do so in Vienna, and best of all to do so 60 years ago. It is salutary to have instruction in what we have lost. But on the evidence here presented, he has treated rather harshly a huge labour of translation, carried out with devotion and skill, and has unfairly visited the failings of American psychoanalytic practice on that translation. When that is said, we can sympathize very sincerely with this remarkable man as he looks back after a lifetime of achievement in an alien culture and an alien language to the happiness and security of the Gymnasium, the city and the language of his youth.

The New York Times Book Review, 6 February 1983

Work and Play

Here is a book* on a subject of obvious importance; it is based on serious though unobtrusive research and meditation; and it is written in a lucid and unaffected style. Reading the early pages one has little doubt that one is in for a quite memorable course of instruction, and that one had better be thinking of the appropriate ways of celebrating an investigator of insight and originality. However, something goes wrong: the author's hand, elegantly opened, stays open, the fist is never made, and the material dribbles away.

Mr Clayre undertakes to examine the notion, which according to him is about two hundred years old, that work should be the central interest of every life. The antithetical faith, which he takes to be of more recent origin, holds that the right course is to drop out of the cycle of production and consumption into freedom and nature. In between there is a third term, the 'instrumentalist' belief that the object of working is to finance leisure and pleasure.

The first task of the book is to look at the tradition of the primacy of work. This tradition is middle-class-intellectual, to be sought among people who talk about physical labour rather than do it. Such people, says Clayre, are apt to dismiss any dissenting views held by the workers themselves, attributing them to alienation or self-estrangement or 'false consciousness', concepts which he thinks have not travelled well down the years that have gone by since the end of the sixteen-hour day. Believing that workers are entitled to their views, Clayre wants among other things to

* Alasdair Clayre, *Work and Play: Ideas and Experience of Work and Leisure* (New York: Harper & Row)

measure the gap that exists between those views and the doctrines of the intellectuals.

Many of the theories about work that are still current have eighteenth-century origins. Rousseau, who believed that membership of society entailed an obligation to work, wanted Emile to be a carpenter and avoid monotonous and repetitive labour, even though this was before the power-machines came in. Schiller argued that individual liberty would be possible only after a transformation of the state, and also introduced the notion of play – creative activity of a disinterested, Kantian kind – as the sole satisfaction of the legitimate demands of men living in society, and indeed an index of their humanity. Fourier thought work and play need not be divided and set great store by variety of tasks. The early Hegel saw machines as mechanizing workers, and sketched the concept of alienation.

Evidence of this kind suggests to Clayre that there may be 'a tendency in critical concepts to outlive the cosmology and methods of argument which gave them their original force'. This is in fact a commonplace of the history of ideas; it might even be said to have outlived its own epoch. The classical instance is the survival for centuries of antithetical primitivisms, labelled 'soft' and 'hard', and reflecting complementary attitudes to work. Both kinds are involved in the story of Adam, who lived in a paradise of pleasure but had to cultivate it: a situation Milton found a bit difficult, for having declared the work virtually unnecessary, a mere disinterested tidying up of superfluous growth with prelapsarian secateurs, he gave Eve victorious arguments for the division of labour. The interesting question about all such perennial survivors is not whether they are true today, but why thought and feeling tend, over extremely long stretches of time, to assume these forms of expression.

In fact it is not very surprising that, for example, the concept of alienation should be older than the machinery we now identify as its principal agent. There has always been repetitive labour and it has always been stupefying; this of course does not entail the view that powered machinery may not be more stupefying than nonpowered, or nonpowered machinery than repetitive manual labour. Mr Clayre's real point is that he is disinclined to believe that the stupefaction of workers is to great that they do not know what they are talking about, and this is why he is keen to prove that the intellectuals are too ready to apply to modern conditions 'methods of argument' designed to deal with conditions as they were over a hundred years ago, closing their ears meanwhile to the views of the workers themselves. For this reason they perpetuate the error of William Morris, and are quite unable to understand that some people actually like machines and are fascinated by their precision, just as they cannot understand that workers rarely entertain lofty ideals of work in the manner of their betters.

Since loss of work entails the ruin of leisure – the two, by long habit, are thought of as complementary – people who work rarely waste their time in fantasies of total idleness. They do of course discriminate between different kinds of work; it needs no academic investigation to convince them that clockbound workers are worse off than men who regulate their own time, or that noisy work, or work carried out under strict surveillance, or work with a very short cycle, is more exhausting than work which, though physically tougher, is more varied and spontaneous. Most obviously, they are aware that hours spent at work are stolen from leisure, which is why the major effort of unions has hitherto been toward shorter hours and higher wages, rather than toward sophisticated improvements in working conditions. What they go for is more leisure and more money to pay for it.

It is when he turns to the question of what workers think about work that Mr Clayre, it seems to me, begins to waver. He has little difficulty in demonstrating that nineteenth-century workers, unlike their bourgeois sympathizers, liked leisure and play more than work, and would not have understood Engels when he pitied them not because they had to work but because they had to work for money. This is strictly a gentleman's worry. And even in Engels's Manchester, work was inextricably involved with play – with the jokes, songs, and rituals of the workshop (in so far as masters permitted them) and the finery of the holiday processions, deplored by Marx for the waste of money involved. Then as now, says Clayre, workers set a higher value on play than writers do, which partly explains the gap between their views on work.

As my account no doubt suggests, Clayre is somewhat obsessed with this difference. And yet it cannot come as a surprise to anybody who is or has been a worker, or has known workers, to learn that they like playing better than working, and combine to improve the rewards of work rather than to make it more varied or productive or even safer. To develop an interest in Ruskin or Morris or Marx was a fairly sure sign of upward mobility and a changed style of life. The capacity of the working classes to spend all they earn, even in the best of times, though it invariably irritates the middle classes, arises naturally enough from their conviction that they spend the week doing what they do not freely choose to do in order to purchase the right to do as they please in their 'own time'. There are plenty of reasons, no doubt, for thinking this an unfortunate or even a false attitude; perhaps, as Clayre suggests, there was a primitive state in which work and leisure were undissociated, where the satisfactions now associated with leisure were intrinsic to hunting or agriculture; but it seems clear that this is over.

At this point Clayre worries about the possibility that the lowering effect of repetitive work in modern factories may have a damaging effect on the worker's leisure. The automobile worker often dislikes his job and does it only for the money; but it has tired him in a peculiarly destructive way and may have impaired his creativity in leisure tasks also. He cites some evidence that this is so, and it does not seem improbable. But on the whole his promised treatment of the workers' view of the effect of their jobs on their lives is disappointing and sketchy.

There is a great deal of evidence he does not use, for example on the element of play in nineteenth-century work: the rough fun, the songs that not only lamented the passing of a traditional way of life but sometimes celebrated the virtues of the new order, the vitality of town life, the pretty clothes that the new money could buy, even the achievements of ur-Stakhanovite workmates, and the traditional craft obscenities. Clubs and unions fostered a class-ideology, and with it a new concept of the dignity of the working man. The music-hall songs of the later years of the century, a commercialized development of working-class play-songs, can be used to show how complex were the interactions of work, play, and status; such are the subjects of Martha Vicinus's book *The Industrial Muse*, published last year. By comparison Mr Clayre often sounds very abstract.

Moreover, like the predecessors he condemns, he concentrates on the theory of work, relying largely on Huizinga for what he says of play. It may be, as D. W. Winnicott remarks, that 'the natural thing is playing', but it does not follow that the concept needs less exploration than that of work, especially in a book like this. If work is the social reality, leisure is the space between it and the soul of the individual, the space in which he makes the rules, runs the clock, and is necessarily creative. It is the modern version of what Morris called creative activity and Marx free work. And it is, of course, precisely the space that advertising seeks to invade and corrupt. Of the forces which act upon playtime, and which, in their more complicated fashion, attempt to fulfil the failed prophecy of the nineteenth-century economists and keep labour at something like subsistence level by taking its money in exchange for trash, Mr Clayre has nothing to say, though they must be at least as important as the carry-over of ill effects from tedious work into leisure; and they also have a bearing on the question of 'false consciousness'.

We should need, in short, more generous and subtle notions of play-creativity and its enemies before we could add to Clayre's book the final section it lacks. They would not be easy to develop, and we should have to be especially careful not to give play to our own false consciousness, for example by undervaluing leisure activities which are to us inexplicably tedious or insipid. On the other hand we should not simply ignore the intrusions of a stupefying propaganda into the space of play.

For want of such discriminations this elegant and in its way rather distinguished book seems in the end tentative and inconclusive. It is also, despite its initial claims, uninformative on the opinions of workers – further testimony, indeed, to that 'gap in consciousness' between them and their intellectual sympathizers of which Clayre so often complains.

New York Review of Books, 27 November 1975

Sic Transit Marshall McLuhan

The fame of Marshall McLuhan in the late Sixties, a period more favourable to guruism than the present, was beyond the dreams of even the most ambitious don. His slogans were quoted everywhere, he travelled the world – now, on his view, electronically reduced to a global village – addressing his fans, advising admen, businessmen, politicians and theologians, telling us all what reality would look like if we broke our habit of contemplating it only through the rear-view mirror, firing off his 'probes', his heavy puns and his strangely old-fashioned jokes. (He was very keen on these jokes, and freely offered them to anybody who might need them for after-dinner speeches – Prime Minister Trudeau, for instance.) He was a pioneer in the movement, now seemingly irresistible, which has carried English literature professors out of literature into larger and, one must suppose, more exciting studies – philosophy, law, psychoanalysis, history, 'culture', 'theory' and prophecy.

These emigrants don't, however, pay homage to the trailblazer. As a prophet of epochs, a connoisseur of epistemes, McLuhan was early superseded by Foucault. The supersession of gurus is by no means invariably the result of a discovery that they were wrong about everything, and it remains possible that there was a good deal more to McLuhan than it has this long while been fashionable to say. He was certainly wrong about quite a number of things, as various people pointed out at the time. But just as it is not clear that these critics were responsible for his occultation, so is it not certain that in some form his celebrity couldn't, given some appropriate resuscitation therapy, be re-established.

Sic Transit Marshall McLuhan

McLuhan was born in Alberta in 1911. This hefty selection* from what, in the second half of his life, must have been an enormous correspondence, begins in 1931. The early letters, mostly to his mother, are neither prodigious nor duller than most letters on comparable occasions. Writing home from the University of Manitoba, he professes admiration for Shakespeare and declares Goethe to be a barbarian. More important to him than either of them was Chesterton, to whom he adhered faithfully, with demonstrable consequences, throughout his life.

When he was 23, he went to Trinity Hall, Cambridge to take another first degree. 'Everybody writes books here,' he told his mother, 'not many of them worth reading either.' From this general and doubtless just censure he exempted Quiller-Couch; and *GK's Weekly*, together with Father D'Arcy's 'succinct and admirable little volume, *Catholicism*', made up for the deficiencies of his instructors. Non-Cambridge dons fared no better: Dover Wilson came to lecture, and managed to do so despite 'a pigeon chest which only criminal indifference to his body could have left so undeveloped' (McLuhan was a rowing man).

However, as time went by the 'exceptional advantages' of Cambridge grew more evident: 'The easy accessibility of Willey, Tillyard, Lucas and Leavis, makes for an intellectual variety that not even my wildest hopes had prefigured.' He was able to discover T. S. Eliot, who, though a genius and a poet, had arrived at the same position as McLuhan 'concerning the nature of religion and Christianity, the interpretation of history, and the value of industrialism'. I. A. Richards, on the other hand, was a humanist engaged in a quest for objective standards of criticism, which, rejecting religion, he could never find: hence his 'ghastly atheistic nonsense'. However, a few years later, applying for a job, McLuhan claimed to be 'the only man in the USA who had a thorough grounding in the techniques of Richards, Empson and Leavis at Cambridge'. Nobody tells all in job applications.

Though admittedly deficient in other languages, he regarded English literature as foreign; nor did he think his talent was really

---

* *Letters of Marshall McLuhan*, selected and edited by Matie Molinaro, Corinne McLuhan and William Toye (Oxford University Press)

literary. He obviously read widely, though with his own emphasis
– for instance, he came upon books by Maritain in the English
Faculty Library, and was thus enabled to see why Aristotle was
'the soundest basis for Christian doctrine'. At this time, about
1935, he was moving sedately towards the Church, and also
rehearsing his Canadian version of agrarianism. And although he
regarded his mind as nothing out of the ordinary, he began to
sense a vocation, and to feel 'a strong sense of superiority that is
utterly incommensurate with my abilities'.

In 1936 he went as a teaching assistant to Wisconsin, which
then had a remarkably powerful English department. While he
was there, he studied, among other things, Pound, Joyce and
Yeats, but more important to him than any of these was Wyndham
Lewis. At this time he was received into the Roman Catholic
Church, and soon afterwards moved to the Jesuit University of
St Louis. With an interval during which he went back to Cambridge as a graduate student he stayed at St Louis until 1944,
when he returned to Canada. One of his pupils was Father Walter
J. Ong, who was to apply great learning to an explicitly Catholic
development of McLuhanite ideas.

From this period there are some curious letters to his fiancée:
a lengthy exposition of Catholic theology, with some vitriolic
material on Reform, and some over-confident assertions ('Today
England is returning to the Faith'). He is equally confident that
there will be no war in Europe. 'The real villains of the piece,'
he writes, 'are not Hitler etc. but the Comintern, the free masons
and the international operators who have their headquarters in
Prague. Hitler is being backed by Chamberlain and Roosevelt.'
The trick of expressing minority opinions with unwavering assurance was to stand him in good stead later on.

At Cambridge his thesis on the poet Nashe got him the doctor-
ate necessary to his academic advancement. Subsequently he
repeatedly undertook to publish this work, without ever doing so.
And though he wrote many literary-critical articles, including a
rather celebrated piece on Tennyson and Hallam, none of his
full-length books was, like the Nashe, a literary study. 'I feel I
must first make my mark as a "scholar" in Eng Lit,' he explained,
'before seriously embarking on any other careers.' Nashe had

introduced him to all manner of interesting issues, such as the history of rhetoric, in those days a topic of very marginal interest to literary critics generally; his thoughts were already straying outside the purely literary canon. He began to make his students read Pudovkin and Eisenstein on film technique, for he admired, and was later to adapt for his own writing, Eisenstein's ideogrammatic mode of exposition. So the confluence of an interest in Scholastic Catholicism with an interest in modern technologies, so essential to his developed thinking, was already established. Sigfried Giedion's *Space, Time and Architecture* was the sort of book that excited him most.

He now formed, with the exiled and poverty-stricken Wyndham Lewis, a friendship which not even Lewis's eccentric temper could shake ('I am not "insulted" at your lack of trust in me. You have no reason to trust me or anybody else'). McLuhan spent a great deal of time, though without much success, trying to get the toffs of St Louis to commission portraits from Lewis.

By the end of 1947 McLuhan seems to have worked out the historical basis of his ideas, encapsulating it in a formula which, with variations and accretions, he would continually repeat in the rest of his writing. He was convinced not only that modern sensibility was formed by the Symbolists, but that Symbolism had its roots in Patristic and Medieval theology: 'the Fathers fathered French symbolical linguistic technique'. He says, without giving references, that there had been a Patristic revival in France around 1800; I don't know whether this is true; he may have been thinking of Migne, though he was a bit later.

He now projected many more books than he ever had time to write – for example, a book on Eliot and, simultaneously, two on popular culture. These last were boiled down by 1951 into one book, *The Mechanical Bride*. Since popular culture reflected the new epoch in technology and education ('popular icons as ideograms of complex implication') while Eliot, whose views on the dissociation of sensibility appealed so strongly to McLuhan, was a Catholic heir of the Symbolists, there was no real incompatibility in these interests. Soon McLuhan was corresponding with Pound, who also perceived that simultaneity of presentation was necessary to the understanding of modern experience.

As his programme developed, he began to wonder how he could fulfil it singlehanded, wishing he had power to hire his own colleagues. He badly needed to write a book about 'the men of 1914', the Modernists so critical to his version of history. He explained to Pound that the vortex he created with Gaudier-Brzeska and Lewis had been debased, had become 'a kiddie's slide', at least partly in consequence of the malignant influence of Freud and socialism. He was particularly severe on Orwell, whom he called a 'duffer' and 'a complete ass'. His letters now begin to go on about usury, and the dissociation of sensibility between Dante and the Impressionists.

With the appearance of *The Mechanical Bride* McLuhan, at forty, was set on a course he never changed. It treats of advertising, comic strips and so on, with the intention of showing us how we are shaped by these and other modern media – for instance, radio and the press; avoiding linear exposition, the book uses an ideogrammatic technique developed from Eisenstein and Pound, and perhaps also from the 'simultaneity' of newspaper lay-out. There had been some delay in finding a publisher, the reason being that 'publishers' offices now are crammed with homosexuals who have a horror of any writing with balls to it.' Homosexuals here join modern gnostics, Freemasons, puritans, people who favoured abortion, and others as the enemy. (It is surely to his credit that the list doesn't contain Jews.) These élites, he told Pound, have the arts and sciences in their pockets. A few years later he remarked that 'the real animus' against *The Gutenberg Galaxy* 'will be felt in gnostic and masonic quarters', as if criticism of his arguments could only come from such secretive and powerful heretics.

The later letters, some very long, offer many rather repetitive summaries of McLuhan's thought. Just as printing imposed on us a visual and linear mode of thought, and gave sight the prime place in the hierarchy of the senses, so the electronic age provides information from all directions at once. Thus the ratio of the senses is altered in favour of hearing with its superior kinaesthetic qualities, and we have to adjust to a new relation with space and time. The oral world was 'put under great strain' by the invention of writing; then print destroyed it altogether, and along with it the analogical Thomistic view of consciousness. Now that electricity has put our senses outside us, made them 'discarnate', we must seek the equivalent of Aquinas's *sensus communis* for them in their externalised state. The consequences must be that the individual will melt into the community, and the world become a global village. As in Symbolist poetry, process will in all things be more important than product. (One of McLuhan's oddest achievements was to make Poe's essay on 'The Philosophy of Composition' a blueprint for the electronic age; he also used the story 'A Descent into the Maelstrom' as a parable showing that the way to behave in the modern vortex was to stay cool, and by noticing – as he was doing – the smallest indications of what was going on, learn to survive like Poe's hero.)

Tirelessly seeking new implications, new sympathizers, he dictated torrential letters, explaining the relevance of his thought to business, education, the American South ('new electric technology favours the old southern cohesion of awareness'), the Russians (still oral), and practically anything else that came up. The old technology, he asserted, is always the content of the new, as movies become the content of television. And television, unlike radio, is a *cool* medium, because of its low definition and back-projected image. Not surprisingly, the people at the sharp end of the media were absolutely enchanted, and indifferent to any ideological subtext that might have seemed inconsistent with their own enterprises.

What emerges more clearly from the letters than from the books is, first, that subtext, the theological-historical basis of the whole project: 'I am a Thomist for whom the sensory order resonates the divine Logos.' Lost at the Renaissance, this scholastic insight was redeveloped by the Symbolists and their modern descendants, who accurately foresaw the (providential) crisis, now upon us, when the next galaxy moves in to supplant the old.

Secondly, the letters seem to show that McLuhan felt an increasing need to convince not just enthusiasts but everybody, and a natural failure in this respect gave him an increasing sense of isolation. He repeatedly insists that he is misunderstood because he is very deliberately not thinking in the old linear rationalistic way, but either simply making observations of a world of whose complexity he has, perhaps uniquely, been vouchsafed some sense, or sending out what he calls probes, speculative shots which may or may not be on target. 'All of my work has been experimental in the sense of studying effects rather than causes, and perceptions rather than concepts. That this is not the normal way of proceeding in the Western world, I know from the public response of distrust and disbelief concerning my motives. My motives, so far as I have been able to discover them, are simply the intellectual enjoyment of play and discovery.' Everybody who demurs at the method or the findings is a slave to the rear-view mirror. Even the Church, which failed to take account of the implications of Gutenberg at the Council of Trent, has now, at Vatican II, ignored the electric galaxy and declined to understand media. When General Electric came up with some electroencephalograms proving that the medium really was, in real life, the message ('the basic electrical response is clearly to the media and not to content differences within . . . TV commercials'), he was happy. But when his views were contested, he was, in spite of his protestations of indifference to rear-view mirror opinion, quite profoundly upset.

His irritation with criticism grew stronger in his last years, and is perhaps related to his increasing willingness to be outrageous, as when he defends capital punishment, preferably done in public, as 'an intensely creative outlet for the entire society'. Detecting a hardening of the tone of his opponents, he hardened his own, explaining (in 1975) that the young people of the Sixties, who turned to him as a way of zapping the establishment, were now 'squaring up again', running for cover and leaving him alone to withstand the rage of the academics.

On the evidence of this collection, the critic who upset him most was Jonathan Miller, whose little book on McLuhan, published in 1971, accompanied it, if it did not partly cause, the rapid decline in McLuhan's reputation. The two men were acquainted: indeed they had got on very well together, partly because McLuhan, large and genial, considerate and full of conversation, was very easy to like, and no doubt partly because of some temperamental and mental affinity between the two – for Miller was equally conversable and also enjoyed running ideas up the flagpole. However, as time went on the differences between them grew visibly deeper. They emerged menacingly as Miller worked on his book.

'I am perfectly prepared to scrap any statement I ever made about any subject,' said McLuhan, 'once I find it isn't getting me into the problem . . . I have no proprietary interest in my ideas and no pride of authorship as such.' But it turned out to be otherwise when Miller called this an attempt to profess a scientific disinterest to which McLuhan had, in his view, no genuine claim, and which in any case he misconceived. The offence was compounded when Miller accused him of having an undeclared interest – his Catholicism, with its strong scholastic base, together with his reactionary agrarianism. Miller added other criticisms: McLuhan made much of Ramus, but didn't understand him; he dealt in gross historical, philosophical and physiological simplifications and committed downright errors (for instance, there is no evidence to suggest that hearing is 'hotter' than the other senses or has a more privileged status with regard to synaesthesia, and none that reading something is less 'simultaneous' than hearing it).

Reading Miller's book seventeen years on, one might think it rather laboured; and of course people nowadays have sharply different ways of speaking about the relation between the oral and the scripted (which wouldn't, as it happens, have helped McLuhan's case). Miller was determined to give McLuhan the serious criticism his thought merited, and in his last pages he testified to the impact it had on him personally. McLuhan had changed the way he thought about print, the telephone, the photograph, radio and television, even though he did so by arguments Miller found quite unacceptable. And with a final glance back to the earliest of the sage's masters, Chesterton, Miller declared that McLuhan 'has accomplished the greatest paradox of all, creating the possibility of truth by shocking us all with a gigantic system of lies'.

Miller's book has the virtue of making his objections clear, but McLuhan's response was not so much to debate them as to express his sense of injured merit. He wrote rather crossly to me, as general editor of the series in which Miller's book appeared, reducing me in his salutation from first name to surname, and saying that Miller was 'debating at a juvenile level' by refusing to do so on the lines McLuhan had opened up. 'The last thing in the world anybody wants if proof of anything I am saying. The evidence is plentiful for those who are interested. The poetry of the Symbolists, from Baudelaire until now, is a massive and explicit testimony to sensory change.'

A review of Miller's book by Alan Ryan brought on a correspondence in the *Listener*, and Miller wrote an article for that journal, thus continuing, said the aggrieved subject, 'his anti-McLuhan crusade' and going on like some nineteenth-century rationalist attacking Catholicism. He even suspected his opponent of strong left-wing tendencies.

Some of his anger was probably due to his having thought of Miller as a friendly sympathizer (Miller had tried but failed to show a documentary about him on the television programme *Monitor*). Yet he might have seen which way the wind was blowing from Miller's contribution to a radio discussion in 1966 ('very poorly assimilated ideas . . . how inaccurate he is about it all'). Perhaps he did not notice it amid the contemporary torrent of discussion, though a letter to Miller in April 1970 professes to welcome the latter's dissent. (His letter to me says he has no idea of my attitude to his work, though he had certainly read my lengthy reviews of *The Gutenberg Galaxy* and *Understanding Media*, and discussed them with me on Miller's television programme.)

On looking back at the fracas, it seems fair to say that Miller's emphasis on the not very explicit Catholic basis of his thought was just, and that it was therefore misleading of McLuhan to claim, as he continually did, that he was totally disinterested. And since he objected to 'linear' and rational discussion, it is difficult to see how he could ever have engaged in a considered defence of his position, even had he admitted to having one. He objected, understandably perhaps, to Miller's conclusion – the 'system of lies', misquoted as 'a pack of lies' – and ignored the rest of the statement which said he had 'created the possibility of truth'.

The detail may now seem unimportant, but Miller's conclusion may not be, for it is in a way a palinode, a sudden admission that there might after all be something to be said for McLuhan's way of doing and saying things: that his concealments and self-deceptions and errors were almost necessary to getting the truth, or its possibility, across. And one can't help thinking he would have enjoyed the computer-generated stock-market collapse last October. Communications satellites were not yet commonplace, yet his system – he may not have wanted a system, but like Blake, had to have one, or be enslaved to another man's – accommodates them perfectly. His general assumption that new technologies change human ways of perceiving and feeling may have been expressed in an allegorical system as arbitrary and bizarre in its way as Spenser's House of Alma, or Blake's prophetic books, but experience seems to be showing that he was sometimes on the right track.

In innumerable ways the linear men could show how wrong he was about the manuscript-print transition, and the print-electric transition, how he built his nests of ideas from any and every scrap of information that caught his eye. Yet the idea of living at a great moment of transition is one we have long been unable to do without, and McLuhan provided it with what was, for the moment, a rather thrilling mythology. We are not as we were in the Sixties, and tend to use leaner and more arcane authorities: Foucault predominantly, but also Derrida. But the idea is still in place, still a cause of excitement and anxiety. McLuhan would have found himself quite as easy as Lyotard with the implications of the personal computer, or with modern political advertising, fundamentalism and civil war. He would have known exactly what was really going on in Sri Lanka, Nicaragua, Afghanistan and Palestine. He might even have retained a habit of mind that sometimes baffled his admirers: his optimism, his conviction that he had read the signs, that he knew how the maelstrom worked, and given some co-operation, could probably get us out of it.

Finally, a word about the editing of the letters. A lot of trouble has been taken, much information dug out, so it is a pity that the finish is not all it might be. There are lots of avoidable errors, simple typos and worse (*The Mechanical Bridge*, 'unitiated', 'mediam', 'seiminar', *Sunt lacrimae verum*, 'the King of Heaven doth suffereth violence'). The editors throw *sics* about beyond necessity, but miss many urgent occasions for them. A footnote may refer only to itself (p.425, n.1 says: 'See p.425, n.1'). Bartlett's *Remem-*

bering is misleadingly dated 1961. Hetta Empson is called Heather, without benefit of *sic*. And so on. Nobody's perfect, but the less perfect you are the more careful you need to be with *sics*. Still, the notes are generally helpful, and this collection offers us a good chance to take another longish look at McLuhan, in letters which make no bones about saying what, according to Miller, he deliberately concealed in his books.

London Review of Books, 17 March 1988

Philippe Ariès'
Bumper Book of Death

This book* is a history of the collective consciousness of the 'Latin West' (with Britain and New England included by association or out of courtesy) during the last thousand years; its focus is death, or changing attitudes towards death, but it is part of the argument that such attitudes must be related to our feelings about many other matters.

Ariès is a researcher of genius, and I shall be saying later that his gifts are sometimes the cause of certain faults or excesses. As in Burton's *Anatomy of Melancholy*, of which this work is a modern avatar, there is an armature of theory which is almost lost under the vast quantity of illustrative material. Much of this is unfamiliar, for Ariès has looked in unusual places – wills, journals, epitaphs and the like – in an attempt to avoid the more formal literary and iconographical kinds of evidence, though he uses that evidence whenever he needs to. What he wants to do is to get behind the standard theological, liturgical and rhetorical formulas, and touch some common imaginative deep structure from which we generate our changing attitudes to death.

The thesis maintains that there have been, in the millennium under consideration, five distinct historical phases. The first, and longest, was the phase of what he calls the Tame Death: at this time death was not feared but thought of merely as repose. The manner of suffering it, its effect on survivors, their ways of

* Philippe Ariès, *The Hour of our Death*, translated by Helen Weaver (London: Allen Lane)

representing it, of disposing of the corpse and remembering the departed, all reflected this calm acceptance. The Tame Death was as devoid of terror as it was of medical attendance; when possible, it was public and ceremonious. The worst fate that could befall one was sudden and unexpected death: it is a measure of the changes that have occurred between the early and the late years of the period that nowadays it is on the whole thought a benefit to die without knowing it – for example, in sleep.

The second phase is that of the Death of the Self. The individual begins to conceive of his death as personal, and as preceding an intimate accounting with God. Elaborate wills, giving among other things detailed instructions for the disposal of the body, for masses, tombs and epitaphs, accompanied a new anxiety about Judgment and the after-life generally. Anonymous burial, the normal lot of all but the rich and powerful, gave way to the desire of more ordinary persons to have some memorial. Death was well on the way to becoming 'untamed', and in the third phase the melancholy appropriate to the death of the self gave way to the more fantastic responses of the Baroque; death even grew erotic. There followed, in the Romantic period, the age of the Beautiful Death. The loved one might now be identified with nature, and a cult of the dead, indeed of death itself, might co-exist, as in *Wuthering Heights*, with exotic Gothic terrors. Last comes our own Invisible Death.

Such, in brief, is the historical scheme. Ariès admits that it can't really accommodate all the facts he has collected, or all the ideas they have given him, and he urges us to look out for the *obiter dicta*, the less schematic speculations, that he comes up with in the course of the work. These are undoubtedly interesting, and make the work even more like Burton's: but most readers, I think, will come away, not with a handful of ideas, but with a mass of strange, often gruesome information.

For instance, there is the changing history of graveyards. At the beginning of Ariès's thousand years it was the custom to bury bodies inside, or just outside, the church, so that they might have the protection of the saints. There were ecclesiastical and practical objections to this practice, but they were overborne. Later it was probably the fashion for personal monuments that led to intolerable overcrowding in urban graveyards, which had formerly

94

been rather temporary places of deposit, the bones being removed later to an ossuary. In the nineteenth century people began to complain that the urban cemeteries were unhygienic. The great Paris graveyard, Les Innocents, was closed, and corpses were dispatched to the environs by the trainload. Ariès asks why the city sites, fundamentally unchanged for centuries and presumably always rather grisly, came so suddenly to seem intolerable. Had there been a change in the sense of what a city ought to be? Or was this a new form of an old fear, a new mechanism of rejection? We can never answer such questions satisfactorily, because the evidence provided is so extensive and complicated. It won't support a simple thesis. At times it has appeared that the living are anxious to keep themselves well apart from the dead, and the revulsion against vast urban burial grounds might well be an instance of this: yet at much the same time the desire to commune with one's dead seems to have grown stronger, and Ariès cites some instances to show that in roughly the same period there was a revival of interest in mummification. One late eighteenth-century gentleman had his wife made into a mummy, and kept her in the house after he remarried – a state of affairs imaginable, in our time, only by Thurber. Somebody else wanted to patent a method of vitrifying corpses and making of them glass beads to be worn by the bereaved.

We read here of medieval emperors who, at death, were instantly boiled to remove the flesh, which occupied one tomb; bowels, heart and, noblest of all, bones were each consigned to separate tombs. We see a photograph of the great ossuary at Palermo, stuffed with the bones and skulls of monks. We read of a hundred different ways of thinking about dead bodies and getting rid of them. Customs that must have seemed natural and universal turn out to be merely cultural and local. All that is certain is that the body has to be disposed of somehow; whether it is to be tended or even remembered, let alone prayed for, whether it is to be loved or feared, depicted as beautiful or disgusting, seems to be optional. We continue to make such choices. Here in Britain we prefer to burn the dead, in the United States the preferred procedures are at once more profitable and less briskly like garbage disposal.

Among thousands of almost equally startling bits of information, Ariès offers us the news that in Britain today widowers are ostracised, and that in the first year after the death of the wife their mortality rate is ten times that of men of the same age not so bereaved. I mention this fact because I do not quite know what to do with it, and there are a great many more of the same kind. One sees why Ariès needed his big scheme to accommodate them. He also needs, and has, strong views as to what are good and bad ways of thinking about death. Both the scheme and the *parti pris* tend to distort the evidence.

The argument is for deep historical change. Of course such change does occur, but Ariès wants its course to be chartable in terms of abrupt turning-points, violent contrasts. He is always anxious to dispute received opinion. A notable instance of this anxiety is his pronouncement that human beings never knew the fear of death until the seventeenth century. 'Of course they were afraid to die; they felt sad about it and said so quite calmly.' This formula distinguishes the fear of dying from the fear of death, which is probably fair; but it also switches from being afraid to feeling sad, which probably isn't. But Ariès badly wants to establish that there was a major change in feeling at a particular historical moment.

Behind this need there is a very strong feeling that in the centuries since we gave up the tame death we have gone terribly wrong on the subject. Death is regarded as a scandal. 'It should have disappeared along with disease, but it persists; it is not even any longer in retreat.' Ariès believes that we need to humanise, or rehumanise, death, to change its image. At present that image strikes him as more cruel than ever before: a man or woman in a hospital bed, stuck all over with tubes, lacking the nobility of even the most grotesque St Sebastian.

Yet it is hard to believe that death has only recently become a scandal. Even in the centuries when it was tame, when it was accepted without fuss, when the passing was orderly and the mourning quick and simple – there must have been something scandalous about it. Rachel mourned her children and would not be consoled: it seems improbable that she had no successors before the present century. Where there is an imagination of happiness, death is a scandal. That is one implication of the Genesis myth, and it was of particular interest to Milton, admittedly a post-tame-death poet. His poem is always astonished by the brutality and finality of death's intrusions into bliss; even before it has ever happened to anybody it is thought of as a dreadful penalty:

> the pain
> Of death denounced, whatever thing death be.

The most appalling indication of the enormity of the loss suffered by Adam and Eve is Eve's proposal to meet death half-way by suicide:

> Why stand we longer shivering under fears
> That show no end but death, and have the power
> Of many ways to die the shortest choosing,
> Destruction with destruction to destroy?

Since their deaths would presumably have prevented all the deaths that have happened since, Eve's seems a reasonable argument, but of course it is also wicked, and Adam knows better than to annoy his Judge, the inventor of death, with such 'acts of contumacy'.

A scandal is, literally, a stumbling block or trap; when there is no way round it, the only thing to do is to accommodate and explain it. That is why the human imagination has a plasticity in regard to death no less admirable than what it displays in its dealings with sex. The arts of dying, like the arts of disposing of the dead, remembering them, assisting them, are therefore extraordinarily various, and fashions change in time: but whether they change with the decisiveness postulated in this book is very doubtful. When you listen to the arguments in *Measure for Measure*, you may be impressed by the Duke's grand formulation of the *Contemptus mundi*: there are ways of dealing with the fear of death, and the Duke specifies some of them, but Claudio is closer to the real thing and speaks like a man with a dread of it in his guts. *Measure for Measure* admittedly scrapes into the seventeenth century, but it is hard to believe that nobody ever felt like Claudio before that date.

Ariès, however, might value the play as a document of transition. He alludes to *Hamlet* only in passing, though it is also full of interest for his argument. The reader of this book will abandon any notion that the graveyard scene is merely an instance of the literary macabre: the burial grounds of the period would have been littered with bones and skulls, and the gravedigger would have known who had lain where, and even the corpse's prospects of slow or rapid decomposition. Hamlet's reaction to the skull of Yorick is especially apposite. Ariès notes a change from the *memento mori*, the generalised injunction to remember that you must die, to the *memento illius*, the reminder of a particular person. Hamlet treats the jester's skull as both of these. You could also say that rapid remarriage – using the funeral baked meats cold at the wedding reception – was good medieval thanatology, acceptable to Gertrude, but not to Hamlet – another mark of transition. Anyway, that is the sort of thing Ariès is always looking for.

He wants to discover 'a hidden language' – a deep structure which has sharply different period manifestations. 'The desires and fantasies that had risen from the depths of the human psyche were expressed in a system of symbols provided by the Christian lexicons. But each age spontaneously chose certain symbols in preference to others, because they better expressed the underlying tendencies of collective behaviour.' In favour of this view it can be said that whole tracts of the language of death might remain unused for centuries. For example, St Matthew's pronouncements on judgment, Heaven and Hell, though perfectly familiar to the literate, seem to have had little influence on attitudes to death until the late Middle Ages. The Last Judgment was not until then a matter of much concern; even at Chartres it is not represented as terrible. Its depiction on baptismal fonts suggests merely that to have been baptised ensures one a place among the sheep rather than the goats: the matter was already settled. But soon it grew in importance, and flourished in the popular imagination and in painting. Another instance is Purgatory, familiar to the theologians and Dante, but having no popular imaginative acceptance until the sixteenth century; prayers for the souls in Purgatory, like the Mass for the Dead, are a relatively late innovation. The notion that one needs the help of intercessors at the time of judgment also appears quite late, and the Ave Maria, which requests such intercession at the hour of our death, came in in the sixteenth century.

This is all persuasive. Yet even at the time when the moment of death assumed such critical importance, there were voices strongly insisting that the final account would take notice of a whole life, and not just its end. The simultaneous existence of conflicting opinions is something of a nuisance to Ariès. It might suggest that although there are recognizable differences in prevailing attitudes to death at various periods, most of the possible responses can co-exist, so that the irruption of apparently new or neglected forms of expression need not be read as marking an epoch in the subject. But that is too simple, too dull, for Ariès: anything that seems obvious, or is widely believed, must be challenged. Is there a relationship between the high mortality rate of the plagues and the development of the macabre in funerary art? No, for that might imply the too early onset of the fear of death. So macabre 'images of death and decomposition do not signify fear of death . . . They are the sign of a passionate love for this world and a painful awareness of the failure to which each human life is condemned.' Max Weber remarked that only capitalist man wants to go rich to his grave. 'In fact the truth is exactly the opposite': it is pre-capitalist man who wants to 'go to his grave loaded with gold and riches and to hold on to his fortune *in aeternum*'. He accepted the idea of dying but could not bring himself to 'leave houses and orchards and gardens'. Yet another common error is the belief that the family is now on the wane: in fact, it dominates our society as never before.

There is probably something in all these paradoxical contentions, but they are too unqualified to convince. Researchers of genius love to find intricate and occult patterns in their material, and they love to show that everybody else has been not slightly but entirely wrong.

Characteristically, he has little praise for his rival inquirers into the depths, the psychoanalysts. Freud and Abraham were, he thinks, right to deplore the modern refusal to mourn, but wrong in their analysis of it. They assumed that complex dealings with the love and hate felt by the survivor for the deceased were universal, that the death of the other always induces the same sort of psychic situation. But Ariès has been labouring to show the great diversity of the human response to death, and to prove that it is subject to periodization: so he concludes that the analysts were unwittingly dependent upon a local and cultural model of mourning, which they mistook for a universal condition: their ideal mourner is a nineteenth-century invention based on the eighteenth-century invention of the Beautiful Death. Before that there was grief, but not guilt, no persistent prostration.

I suppose the analysts would dismiss these arguments as mere symptoms of denial, saying, for example, that mourning recapitulates inescapable infantile losses and conflicts common to all mankind; death is always construed as an act of violence, however the culture works to conceal and deny the fact. For them, Ariès's denial of denial is simply another form of the same denial. He himself shows how various are the forms denial can take – for example, in his study of the practice of concealing or revealing the face of the dead, of changing fashions in tomb sculpture. But these are cultural, not psychic changes. The analysts have a deeper deep structure. Ariès rejoices in diversity; analysts, despite all the variations of doctrine, are what used to be called uniformitarian.

His love of change can be seen in the emphasis he places upon the fear of premature burial, as the starting-point, virtually, of modern attitudes to death. For centuries, nobody seemed to bother about it, but then an epidemic fear developed. Finally it disappeared again, so that although it instituted a major change it was in itself no more than a period fashion. This seems very doubtful. I myself have known a man with a pathological terror of being buried alive: he extracted all manner of undertakings from his friends, who were to carry out a series of tests and install alarms in the coffin. I dare say the consulting rooms are still haunted by such unfortunates, and Ariès himself cites instances from earlier periods. The fear of premature burial – and the fear of the prematurely buried – may be closer to universal than he allows. Epidemic manifestations may have temporary and local explanations, but that the dead and living states should be clearly distinguished, that any intermediate state is felt to be intolerable to all concerned, may be matter for the analyst rather than the historian.

Ariès's attitude to psychoanalysts is nothing like so hostile as his attitude to doctors. He looks back with admiration at times when death occurred without medical attendance, at home; the dying knew they were dying, and how to behave, and the neighbours dropped in to say goodbye. Nowadays the doctor is in charge, prolonging our lives into the worst terminal indignities, then dismissing our bodies as of no further relevance, or of medical failure. A strong dislike of modern modes of dying may be one of the forces that animate this very excited and eloquent book.

Indeed, I have given a rather poor impression of its scope, variety and interest. It is likely to be read less as an example of a fashionable way of doing history than as a sort of bumper book of death. It is very large, but then so is its subject, and part of the pleasure for everybody will be that, large as it is, it doesn't include everything. The main pleasure, of course, is that it protects us from its subject by making it a subject, a mere matter of cultural history.

London Review of Books, 1 October 1981

Paul de Man's Abyss

Paul de Man was born in 1919 to a high-bourgeois Antwerp family, Flemish but sympathetic to French language and culture. He studied at the Free University of Brussels, where he wrote some pieces for student magazines. When the Germans occupied Belgium in 1940 he and his wife fled, but were turned back at the Spanish frontier and resumed life in Brussels. The Germans closed the Free University in 1941, so frustrating one possible career; but de Man's uncle, the socialist politician Hendrik de Man, helped him to a job on *Le Soir*, the biggest newspaper in Belgium, which was then under German control. Hendrik de Man had supported the King's decision to surrender, and for a time persuaded himself that the German takeover, though not quite the revolution he had looked forward to, was a revolution none the less, and might bring about what men of good will had wanted so desperately in the pre-war years – an end to decadent pseudo-democratic capitalism and a new era of socialism, even if it had to be national socialism.

Until November 1942, when his contributions abruptly ceased, Paul de Man wrote copiously for *Le Soir*. He later claimed that he left the paper as a protest against German control, though the paper was already under German control when he joined it – it was known as *Le Soir volé*, and its present management say it was 'stolen and controlled by the occupier'. The signs are that at least in the early days de Man did not regard German control as a deterrent; of course the German bosses are quite likely to have turned much nastier in 1942, as they did about many matters. In addition to the hundreds of pages he wrote for *Le Soir* de Man wrote some reviews in Flemish for another German-controlled journal. He also did a lot of translating – including a Flemish version of *Moby Dick* – which had no connection with war or politics.

After the war he was briefly associated – his opponents suggest feloniously – with an unsuccessful art publishing venture. In 1948 he went to America, where he worked in a New York bookshop and made useful contacts – for example, with Dwight Macdonald and Mary McCarthy. Soon he was teaching at Bard College. Remarried – his opponents say bigamously – he went to Boston and taught at the Berlitz School. He registered for the Ph.D. at Harvard, became a teaching assistant in Reuben Brower's famous course, Humanities VI, and was recognized as a remarkable teacher, the kind that makes and keeps disciples. In spite of Brower's advocacy he failed to get tenure; in 1960 he moved to Cornell, and thence to Zurich and Johns Hopkins. He ended his career at Yale, where, throughout the Seventies and early Eighties, he was the most celebrated member of the world's most celebrated literature school. He died in 1984.

As academic curricula vitae go, de Man's was certainly unusual, and an account of his publications might seem to make it more so, for his first book, *Blindness and Insight*, appeared only in 1971, when he was 51, and even then, it is said, he published only because Yale drew the line at bookless professors. There were to be only two more essay-collections before his death, but now we have two posthumous volumes, and there may be more to come. Considering the ever-increasing density and strangeness of his work, and its ever-increasing fame, it would take a very tough dean to say de Man had under-produced.

The corpus is now augmented by a volume he would not himself have wanted to see. This collection of his wartime writings* looks like what it is, a heap of ephemera, ill-printed and hard to read in the photocopies. They testify to the exceptional industry and ability of the young literary journalist – he wrote a long succession of literary chronicles and reviewed large numbers of books in various languages – but it is unlikely that any degree of later

* Paul de Man, *Wartime Journalism, 1939–1943*, edited by Werner Hamacher, Neil Hertz and Thomas Keenan (University of Nebraska Press, 1988)

eminence would have induced anybody to re-publish them had not their discovery caused such a tremendous bother. The editors, friends of de Man, decided, probably rightly, that in view of all that had been said and written about them on hearsay it would be as well to make them wholly accessible. The editors have not obtruded themselves; they neither justify nor condemn.[1] And they seem to have been thorough. Here are 170 pieces from *Le Soir*, ten in Flemish from *Het Vlaamsche Land* – these with English translations – plus 100 brief notices written for a book-distributing agency in 1942–3, and a few earlier pieces from student magazines, one of which is here palpably misdated (4 January 1939 for 4 January 1940).

Keen to extenuate nothing, the editors also include a facsimile of page 10 of *Le Soir* for 4 March 1941, which is headed *Les Juifs et Nous*, and consists of one violently anti-semitic piece on Jews in general, and another claiming that French painting between 1912 and 1932 was *enjuivé* as a result of a plot by Jewish dealers, so that an influx of foreign blood had deflected French art from its natural course, making it morbid and corrupting both to painters and their public. A third essay condemns Freudianism as a further instance of Jewish decadence, and the fourth and last is de Man's now notorious article on the Jews in modern literature. Dissociating himself from vulgar anti-Semitism, for which he nevertheless holds the victims themselves partly responsible, he accepts the view that Jews had a lot to do with the disorders of Europe between the wars: but since national literatures evolve according to their own strict laws, they remained largely unaffected by the Semite invasion of other aspects of European life. There were no first-rate Jewish writers anyway; de Man lists some second-rate ones (he doesn't include Proust) and concludes that if the Jewish problem were solved by the creation of a colony isolated from Europe the consequences for 'us' would not be deplorable. It must be added that the page on which this article was printed is decorated with boxes containing comments about Jews from such authors as Ludwig Lewisohn, Hilaire Belloc and

---

[1] The same editorial team has compiled a volume in which thirty-eight contributors respond to the wartime writings (*Responses*, University of Nebraska Press).

Benjamin Franklin, who is said to have wanted Jews, described as 'Asiatics', excluded from the United States by the Constitution. This last citation is spurious.

Some commentators, including Geoffrey Hartman, say that by the standards of the time this was pretty lukewarm anti-Semitism. Jacques Derrida – a Jew and a close friend of de Man's – finds it inexcusable, but demands that it be dealt with justly. He repeats that the article deeply wounded him, but discovers in it some redeeming qualities: for example, 'to condemn "vulgar anti-Semitism", *especially if one makes no mention of the other kind* [i.e. "distinguished anti-Semitism"], is to condemn anti-Semitism itself *inasmuch as* it is vulgar, always and essentially vulgar'. Certainly these interrogations should be carried on justly, but this is all too manifestly a desperate plea. Others have suggested that this article is virtually a unique aberration in de Man's contributions to *Le Soir*; yet others have conjectured that at this stage he was unlikely to have known much about what was already going on in 'colonies' within Europe – the Final Solution wasn't ordained until January 1942. But as even the charitable Geoffrey Hartman feels obliged to remark, and as a reading of this collection makes obvious, neither of these excuses is plausible.

By now these wartime writings have been passionately scanned, especially by Jacques Derrida in the long article quoted above, which was published in *Critical Inquiry* last year.[1] Here there is room for only a few observations. First, there is certainly more than one anti-semitic piece. An article in Flemish (20 August 1942) about contemporary German fiction deplores the way some Expressionist writers came into conflict with 'the proper traditions of German art which had always before anything else clung to a deep spiritual sincerity. Small wonder, then, that it was mainly non-Germans, and specifically jews, who went in this direction.' Again, it is surely odd to find in a piece on Péguy (6 May 1941) a short, but not all that short, account of the Dreyfus affair which omits to mention that Dreyfus was a Jew; de Man is seemingly at a loss to understand why the straightforward case of an officer

---

[1] 'Like the Sound of the Sea deep within a Shell: Paul de Man's War', *Critical Inquiry*, Spring 1988. Derrida at the time of writing had seen only twenty-five of the essays from *Le Soir*.

wrongly accused and reinstated by due course of law should have caused such a furore. He admires Péguy, a Dreyfusard, for quarrelling, at the cost of his job, with other liberal-socialist Dreyfusards. Christopher Norris, in a page devoted to this curious essay, remarks that 'any mention of the Dreyfus affair must of course raise the question of anti-Semitism', but fails to add that de Man's mention of it rather pointedly did not; Derrida likewise omits to notice the omission in his *Critical Inquiry* piece, also preferring to emphasize that de Man was here writing admiringly of a Dreyfusard. In fact, the drift of de Man's piece is best expressed in the words *au fond, il ne s'agit pas de grand'chose.*

Even if we recall that the affair lasted over a decade, that the opponents of Dreyfus forged and suppressed evidence, and that the victim spent a long time in prison, it might still be maintained that the level of anti-Semitism over all these articles is fairly low. But to confine attention to specific references is misleading, for a survey of the whole collection makes it apparent that anti-Semitism was at least not entirely inconsistent with de Man's ideas about the national spirit and the need for cultural development to take place on national (and at any rate in some measure xeno-phobic) lines. Like his uncle, he was, it appears, ready to believe that the 'revolution' brought on by the *événements* of May 1940 had introduced a new and promising epoch of German hegemony in Europe. Flemish is a Germanic language, and it may have seemed opportune and possibly just, even for a writer of de Man's French formation, to score off France, the dominance of whose language and culture was inveterately resented in Flemish Belgium. Yet there is an obvious difference between the French and the Jews. Given a spell of German discipline, the French might yet pull themselves together: but what hope was there for the Jews with their non-European, 'foreign blood'? At the rather abstract level of discourse preferred by the young de Man, there was not much need to be as specific and insistent as some of his fellow contributors, either about Jews or about the flowering of the German spirit demonstrated in the conquests of 1940. Just as he refrains from further overt reflections on the Semite invasion, he silently declines to comment on the continuing progress of German arms, on the Italian alliance (though one article praises the successes of Italian nationalism), on the Russian campaign, the fighting in the Balkans and Africa, the entry of Japan and America into the war. Perhaps he regarded these matters as outside his cultural brief, though the fall of France had not quite been. Yet the military and political developments of 1941 and 1942 must have been of keen and at times disquieting interest to one who had taken the German victories of 1940 as final. For de Man had at first written, understandably, as if in 1940 the war was over, saying more than once that the difference between the two world wars was that the first was long and the second very brief, so that only in the first did people settle down to observable wartime behaviour. Since the Germans had won so completely, any future was going to be a German future, whether one liked the idea or not. But by the time he stopped writing for *Le Soir* the case was somewhat altered, with the Wehrmacht surrounded at Stalingrad, beaten in Egypt, and facing future battles in the west against forces enormously augmented since the American entry into the war. Meanwhile the Final Solution was well under way.

All these events, perhaps along with an increase of supervisory rigour in the office, may have been his inducement to leave *Le Soir*, but there seems to be no evidence for this except de Man's own remark quoted above. And he is said to have offered on occasion rather unreliable versions of his wartime career – for instance, that he worked in England.

In student articles, written during the phoney war or *drôle de guerre* period, de Man argued that the war had been inevitable, and that after the annexation of Czechoslovakia it could no longer be maintained that Hitler merely wished to correct the injustices of Versailles. As an anti-imperialist, he said, one must choose the less objectionable of two imperialisms – namely, the British. But when the war was won we would have to deal with all the problems left over from the Thirties – unemployment, for example; and that would require a vast reform of European (and imperial) politics generally. May 1940 changed his mind, and a year or so later we find him claiming that the invaders, far from being the barbarians of propaganda and of leaders in the pre-Occupation student paper, are highly civilized. He rejoices at reports that the

French are working alongside their victors in a *solidarité purifiante*. Soon he is recommending some German hand-outs explaining National Socialism, and observing that the Germans have made much more generous armistice terms than the French had allowed at the end of the first war.

He sometimes speaks of the irresistible force of a nation's desire for unity, recommending Belgians to study the Italian example and commenting with severity on the record of the French. Ever since Richelieu they had striven to divide Germany. And they had made a bad mistake by refusing to collaborate when they might have done so on equal terms: for they must now choose between doing so on terms much less favourable, and passively submitting to England. He admires the traditional qualities of the French (expressed in the customary terms as clarity of intellect and expression), but rarely loses a chance to compare them unfavourably with the Germans. Under Hitler, he contends, there flourished a pure literature, very different from recent French writing. The Germans would give the French, at this decisive moment in the history of their civilization, what they now most needed: order and discipline, and presumably purity also. However, in April 1942 he complains that the French do not appear to be responding satisfactorily to 'the reforms at present in progress'.

Opinions of this sort surface from time to time in pieces of which the ostensible purpose is simply literary criticism, and the contention that in the mass these articles are just neutral accounts of books and concerts, leaving only one or two collaborationist obiter dicta to explain away, is simply absurd. Taken as literary criticism, they seem to offer few hints of the writer's future interests, though in saying so I find myself slightly, and unwillingly, at odds with both Lindsay Waters and Jacques Derrida. Some of de Man's judgments are routine – he thought very highly of Charles Morgan, for instance, as the French did in those days. He speaks well of Valéry, and that does remind us of the links between his later thought and his early interest in Symbolism. But his views on history, if he remembered them later, must have seemed embarrassingly undeManian. So with romanticism: an essay from the hand of the scholar of whom it is commonplace to maintain that he changed everybody's attitude to that subject says that romanticism was pretty feeble in France, but strong in Germany because deep in the German national spirit, indeed *la consécration définitive de la nature nationale* (21–22 November 1942) – a version of literary history which he was later to condemn.

Unlike some commentators, both friendly and hostile, I see nothing very reprehensible about his failure to talk about this body of work (as distinct from parts of the work itself). Generally speaking, few writers, of whatever kind, and even if conceited enough to think anybody else would be interested, would volunteer to bring their juvenilia to judgement, even if they didn't contain opinions later seen to be embarrassing or perverted. However, this writer's subsequent fame – and the continuing row between deconstructive admirers and more conservative academics – ensured that people *were* interested, some hoping to use the wartime pieces to discredit de Man and the movement associated with him, the rest needing to defend themselves and their hero. So the significance of these juvenilia is strenuously debated.

Few would deny that at least some of the wartime writing is odious, that of a clever young man corrupted by ideas, and corrupted by war (for in wartime the intellect grows as sordid as the conflict), or merely opportunist, or a mixture of all these. To work for *Le Soir* and *Het Vlaamsche Land* was manifestly to forego any right of dissent. To appear on that anti-semitic page was, as almost everybody would agree, an act amounting to full collaboration. The repeated triumphing over the defeated French, having a possible origin in Belgian domestic conflicts, was presumably not done under direct external compulsion. And it is hard to find indications of concealed dissent in this collection, though some have tried to do so. The simplest explanations may be the least damaging in the end; the young man, on his return from attempted flight, found reasons for thinking it intellectually honest as well as expedient to collaborate with the victors. Others, especially in France, did likewise, until, their reasoning invalidated by events, they saw they must cease to do so; and it could be that de Man gave up his job for similar reasons. One wonders whether, had the Germans occupied Britain at the end of 1940, there would have been no clever young people willing to say in collaborationist newspapers (and wouldn't there have been collaborationist news-papers?) that this was at least not altogether a bad thing.

Lindsay Waters's long and interesting introduction to *Critical Writings 1953–78** amounts to an apologetic intellectual biogra-phy of de Man. He dwells on the forces – the failures of democracy, the desire for national redemption, the longing for action – which induced intelligent people in the pre-war period to succumb to 'the fascist temptation'. The comparison with Heidegger is here as elsewhere – and doubtless justly – used in de Man's favour. But the main argument is that in his earliest work de Man embraced an 'aesthetic ideology' – its political manifestation is a rather mystical nationalism – of just the kind he was later to attack with such contemptuous subtlety. This implies that the youthful errors were intellectual rather than ethical, though Waters is in no doubt that anti-Semitism, a rather more than merely cerebral blunder, was an essential constituent of German nationalism, and he has no way of excusing de Man's endorsement of it. However, he finds in these 'marginal texts' the seeds of much later work: they display de Man's abiding interest in 'inwardness, interiority', so 'there is a fair degree of continuity'.

This connection seems rather tenuous, but Waters goes on to give a convincing account of the later career, from the early Sartrean phase through the decisive encounter at Harvard with American New Criticism, and the revisionary studies of romantic thought, to the decisive 'turn' to rhetoric and the concord with Derrida, which were the features of de Man's last and most influential phase. His rather exotic academic career in America was a genuine European intellectual adventure, typical of what the writer himself, in a letter of 1955, called 'the long and painful soul-searching of those who, like myself, come from the left and from the happy days of the Front Populaire' – which, though it takes us back to a date before there is any substantial record, is plausible enough, as is the highly metaphysical mode of the soul-search.

In support of his argument for continuity, Waters also supplies

* Paul de Man, *Critical Writings 1953–1978*, edited by Lindsay Waters (University of Minnesota Press, 1989)

what many disciples have been demanding: a selection of uncollected essays from the years before the publication of *Blindness and Insight*, with one uncollected late piece at the end. Many of these items are reviews, some long celebrated, like that of Michael Hamburger's Hölderlin translations. Some – on Montaigne, Goethe and Mallarmé – were originally in French. All have that air of quiet, even tolerant authority which, despite occasional severities and bursts of ill temper, was of the essence of de Man's personality. In an essay called 'The Inward Generation' he remarks of certain 'near-great' writers of the pre-war period – Malraux, Jünger, Pound and Hemingway – that they had all been 'forcefully committed politically, but their convictions proved so frail that they ended up by writing off this part of their lives altogether, as a momentary aberration, a step towards finding themselves.' The whole passage has concealed autobiographical interest. It attributes the course of such careers to the collapse of an aesthetic inherited from Symbolism, and used as a protection from real problems; but the war brought these into menacing actuality, and the political was now a matter of life and death. The political and aesthetic beliefs of such writers make them 'vulnerable targets for today's conservatism – more vulnerable, in fact, than they deserve to be, because their predicament was not an easy one'. Although he distances all this by talking about 'the political and aesthetic beliefs of the Twenties', it seems obvious enough that de Man here had himself in view: and in essence this is the best defence that could be offered. Reviewing books by Erich Heller and Ronald Gray, he remarks that both authors 'too readily call "German" a general feature of the romantic and post-romantic intellect', just as he had done himself.

The most intense of these speculations concern Mallarmé and Hölderlin, whose question *wozu Dichter in Dürftiger Zeit?* seems to have haunted de Man: he quarrelled over it with the august interpretations of Heidegger. There is a measure of self-absorption about even the least of these pieces. They look forward as well as back, and one of their merits is that they often demonstrate how much can be said in a review or a relatively brief essay: which explains why de Man was so slow to publish a book, and why all his books are collections of essays.

The Uses of Error

It seems that Christopher Norris had almost finished his book on de Man* when the young Belgian scholar Ortwin de Graef uncovered the articles in *Le Soir*, so he comments on them in a postscript. He finds that they contain 'many passages that can be read as endorsing what amounts to a collaborationist line'. It would have been enough to say 'many passages that endorse a collaborationist line', but in general Norris is under no illusions. Before he knew about *Le Soir* he had already noticed National Socialist sympathies in the articles for *Het Vlaamsche Land*, and even in a pre-Occupation piece for the student newspaper. These pieces 'uncritically endorse such mystified ideas as the organic relation between language, culture, and national destiny' – ideas de Man would later 'deconstruct with . . . extreme sceptical rigour'. You can tell how shocked Norris is, for 'mystified', a favourite term of de Man himself, is his usual epithet for ideas he dislikes, and 'rigour' is what deconstructors ought always to use in the necessary business of 'demystifying' them.[1] So he won't excuse the wartime writings as 'youthful aberrations': but de Man is nevertheless a hero and somehow to be excused, if only by a 'totalising' account of his interior life, 'totalising' being a very mystified practice and tolerable only in these very unusual circumstances. Norris outlines the problems of Belgian national politics and the life and opinions of Hendrik de Man, by means of which the young man could, with fatal ease, have got hold of mystified ideas; and argues that the course of his subsequent intellectual travail can be in part explained by the disenchantment that followed their demystifying.

[1] Norris has recently published yet another set of rigorously demystificatory exercises in *Deconstruction and the Interests of Theory* (London: Frances Pinter, 1988). They show, among other things, that he is not unwilling to be rigorously demystificatory about the very Theory which ought itself to be so, especially when it is put to right-wing or 'irrationalist' purposes, or does its own demystifying with insufficient philosophical rigour. The chapters exhibit a considerable range of interests – from Bloch and Adorno on music, de Man on Kierkegaard, and Rudolf Gasché on de Man, to Pope and Shakespeare post-structurally considered. Norris himself emerges as a demystified left-wing rationalist.

* Christopher Norris, *Paul de Man: Deconstruction and the Critique of Aesthetic Ideology* (London: Routledge, 1988)

Others, less charitable, have declared that deconstruction is a means of destroying the value of any historical record, or at least blurring a past, as if de Man's work were 'nothing but a series of oblique strategies for pretending it never happened, or at least that there existed no present responsibility for past thoughts and actions'. This is Norris's account of a view that he of course rejects. It has been expressed with much indignation by Stanley Corngold and others – the holocaust, and de Man's own past, they say, conveniently vanish – but it is dismissed, in my view correctly, as founded on a false idea of the relation between deconstruction and history, admittedly a very dark topic. The alternative reading, vigorously expounded by Norris and more or less the same as that proposed by Waters, is that de Man's later life was dedicated to the purging of the false ideology that had once possessed him – in short, an aesthetic ideology, related to an organicism equally responsible for romantic error and for German nationalism with its attendant evils. Looking with 'principled scepticism' at these youthful beliefs, de Man perceived that they must all fall together, as romantic fallacies he had now seen through.

Some may think it strange to regard Nazism and anti-Semitism largely as intellectual errors, corrigible by the mere taking of further thought. And although defences of de Man are decently animated by affection for a dead and admired friend, these attempts at biographical exculpation, these rakings through his evolving, exacting, rather melancholy writings, often seem to lack any serious understanding of how even people of high intelligence are sometimes induced to behave, especially when they may be under stress of a kind the exculpators have the good fortune to know nothing about. De Man himself has some tortuous but interesting observations on excuses in an essay on Rousseau's *Confessions* (in *Allegories of Reading*, 1979). For example, he distinguishes between confession and excuse. The former is 'governed by a principle of referential verification', whereas the latter lacks the possibility of verification – 'its purpose is not to state but to convince': thus it is performative whereas confession is constative. He is interested in the curious interaction, in Rousseau, of the two rhetorical modes, but at the same time he is willing to say that Rousseau was clearly dissatisfied with his performance as judge of himself, and unable to get rid by excuses of a recurrent sense of shame. For the childish theft of a ribbon is only a beginning: it is followed by other faults that likewise call for excuses, such as the abandoning of one's children. (De Man, we are told by some of his accusers, abandoned his own wife and child, but I do not know whether the known facts really permit this inference.) The critic's interest is expressly not in any simple way biographical or ethical: it is firmly expressed as devoted to an entirely rhetorical problem. It nevertheless passes belief that anybody could write an essay such as this without reflecting on his or her own life, and it may surely be assumed that de Man did so.

It is true that such considerations are not strictly germane to rhetorical theory. Norris quotes an admiring judgment of Minae Mizimura: 'The shift from a concern with human errors to a concern with the problem inherent in language epitomises [de Man's] ultimate choice of language over man,' adding on his own account that it is here – 'at the point of renouncing every tie between language and the will to make sense of language in acceptably human terms – that de Man leaves behind the existential pathos that persists in his early essays'. This apathetic purity is what his disciples admire and emulate, though the need to defend the master must sometimes hinder them from quite so scrupulous an avoidance of pathos: the enemy, after all, was representing him as a devious, opportunist, dishonest human being. Furthermore, even if one breathes the air of pure theory, it must sometimes seem strained to argue that it is always impossible to say what one means, even if the statement you wish to make is that it is always impossible to make such a statement; or to combine this belief with the belief that one can and should intend to say, and say, what will make sense of de Man's life as a whole.

Norris is sometimes critical of his subject – for example, of the way in which his views on undecidability are given what sounds like inappropriately decisive and even authoritarian expression. This is his explanation: de Man's style has 'a rhythm that alternates between claims of an assertive, self-assured, even apodictic character, and moments of ironic reflection when those claims are called into doubt'. This is true: de Man almost always achieves this kind of internal tension, the undecidability of his own writing reflecting the unavoidable undecidability of language itself. He was always looking for the point where necessity encountered impossibility, or intention its fated undoing. He is the great impresario of the rhetorical impasse. The title of his first book, *Blindness and Insight*, reflects its thesis, that in critics the two must exist in inseparable tension. In the late essay 'Resistance to Theory', to be found in the book of the same title, he argues that 'rhetorical readings' are theory and not theory at the same time, the universal theory of the impossibility of theory. It would be easy to extend the list of such paradoxes: de Man's quarrel with the aesthetic is the quarrel of an aesthete, his refusal to accept customary distinctions between literature and philosophy is philosophically-oriented, the denial of any differences between literature and non-literature is highly literary. Some such aporia – another favourite word – is the goal of de Manian meditation, a kind of substitute for the obsolete satisfactions of closure, now known to be impossible because of the very nature of texts.

Norris, it must be said, is very clear about de Man's positions. He hasn't enough patience to give a fair hearing to anything that he can dismiss as mystified, but one hardly reads him with any hope of that. Within his own ballpark he is lucidly competent. He makes bold use of digressions. The point of a long one about Hillis Miller is to demonstrate that two colleagues, both deconstructionists, may have, within their sympathy, very different attitudes and styles. There is another on Adorno, registering with approval his view of the negativity of knowledge, in order to confer on de Man the increment of this particular virtue of Adorno. The object is to confute those who accuse de Man of nihilism; they are just as wrong as those who accuse him of quietism. The real problem is to discover in him anything, outside rhetoric, that can be stated unequivocally as a belief; and Norris's book does help one to grasp the nature of that problem.

For a while, given the extraordinary veneration in which he was held, it must have been difficult for admirers to write about de Man without referring first to the man and his death, and then, for it emerged almost before the period of mourning was over, to the wartime writing. One impressive thing about *Reading de Man Reading** is that apart from the fine leading essay by Geoffrey Hartman, mentioned above, the contributors go about their rhetorical deManian business without such allusions. Hartman writes as a Jew, and as one who knows more than most about wartime anti-Semitism. He admires the intellectual power of de Man's late work: 'the only peculiar thing is that a philosophical mind of this calibre should turn against the pretensions of philosophy and toward literature.' And now he wonders about the *purity* of these deconstructive essays. 'Hegel or Heidegger or Kant or Proust are not sources but materials only; there is neither piety in this critic for their achievement nor any interest in strengthening their hold on us, consecrating their place in the canon.' He clearly thinks of de Man, the philosophical critic, as having made an extraordinary effort of self-dehumanization, as if the kind of interest Hartman speaks of were somehow base or inauthentic. Nevertheless he speculates that there may be hidden, in the later essays, 'the fragments of a great confession', and that one might 'link the intellectual strength of the later work to what is excluded by it, and which, in surging back, threatens to diminish its authority'. And when de Man asserts that 'what stands under indictment is language itself and not somebody's philosophical error,' we are to understand that this is a reflection 'by de Man on de Man', for 'the later self acknowledges an error, but does not attribute it to an earlier self – because that would perpetuate its blindness to the linguistic nature of the predicament.' In short, the conscience of the rhetorician is such that it forbids the exercise of conscience in the person.

This gives one a fair notion of the complexity of the problem. Some of de Man's admirers have properly assumed that their business is finally with his mature writings, with the power of his rhetorical procedures; and their ability to continue them is well illustrated in the remainder of this book. Among the most impressive are Neil Hertz's essay on de Man's essay on 'Wordsworth and

* *Reading de Man Reading*, edited by Lindsay Waters and Wlad Godzich (University of Minnesota Press, April 1989)

the Victorians' (in *The Rhetoric of Romanticism*) – a deManian interrogation of de Man, like Carol Jacobs's 'Allegories of Reading Paul de Man' ('*Allegories of Reading* is an elaborate allegory of the impossibility of the fundamental condition of allegory' which 'necessarily relapses into the condition it deconstructs'). Like the master, these critics have become connoisseurs of the symmetry between the impossible and the necessary: as he himself pointed out, 'the impossibility of reading should not be taken too lightly.' Hillis Miller speaks of the 'austere rigour that makes de Man's essays sometimes sound as if they were written by some impersonal intelligence or by language itself, not by somebody to whom the laws of blindness and impossibility also apply, as they do to the rest of us'. On such matters it may, he feels, be best to keep silent, as he says de Man does.

But blindness and impossibilism, a love of the aporetic, seem, among initiates, to promote not silence but an endless linguistic fluency. This is in a way strange, for the prevalent deManian tone might be called depressed; every critical victory, to be recognized as a victory, must be a defeat. You may win the local skirmishes of deconstructive reading, but you have to lose the war. There must, it seems, be a peculiar pleasure in encountering language allegorized as something resembling the great Boyg, with no defence that can be used in that formidable encounter except language itself, now allegorized as a weapon treacherous and very easily broken. In a rare jocular moment de Man himself compared undecidability and aporia to getting stuck in a revolving door, which is perhaps a better figure. Anyway, a definition of reading which claims that hitherto it has never been attempted, and now that it has turns out to be impossible, might well have seemed dispiriting, but it turns out to be positively exhilarating. One might compare these writers to the early Christians, who thought they were the first people ever to read the Jewish Bible properly, were caught in the aporia of an end-time that could not end, and managed to feel pretty exalted about it.

Norris speaks of the essential inhumanity of de Man's views on language, summarized in a neo-Nietzschean manner as 'a wholly impersonal network of tropological drives, substitutions and displacements'. 'To call de Man's position counter-intuitive,' he says, 'is a massive understatement.' Yet it is just this bleakness, this disclaimer of human authority over language, that attracts de Man's luxuriously ascetic followers. They mourn the man but rejoice in his 'inhuman' teachings.

The theory that theory is self-defeating, that it cannot possibly control or comprehend the workings of figural language, is part of the master's charm, but it is also a strange foundation for the ambitious institutional and political programmes now being quite stridently proposed by some – for instance, Jonathan Culler in his recent book *Framing the Sign*.[1] Norris, no less committed but rather more critical, is less confident of the imperialist possibilities of theory, though he would like some sort of concordat with Marxism. De Man himself, with his 'extreme and principled scepticism', would possibly have thought this out of the question, as it must be if the inevitable terminus is that revolving door, where language moves in, impossibly, on an understanding of language, and is at once thrown out. The noble course is not to submit to the bewitchments of language, and to recoil from the Acrasian temptations of the aesthetic 'ideology'. But people outside the cult are probably less principled and more prone to mystification. Trilling's students, when he introduced them to the abyss of the Modern, gazed into it politely, said 'how interesting!' and passed by. Others may do the same to de Man's abyss, and carry on thematizing and totalizing because it is their pleasure to do so, even if it is shamefully human to do so; and they have a long history of resistance to puritanical imperatives. As a rule they will do so without reference to the youthful errors of Paul de Man, and the insiders should now be happy to stop worrying about them and get on with their necessary and impossible projects.

London Review of Books, 16 March 1989

---

[1] *Framing the Sign: Criticism and its Institutions* (Oxford: Blackwell, 1988)

Talking About Doing

The Deconstructionists and the New Historicists

Anyone presuming to review works of modern literary theory must expect to be depressed by an encounter with large quantities of deformed prose. The great ones began it, and aspiring theorists usually carry their heads grotesquely to one side in emulation of these models. What begins as servile mimicry soon becomes a pathological condition. It is a relief that two of the present five books may be pronounced orthopaedically sound.

Opinions differ as to whether Deconstruction will take over the academy, or be 'co-opted' by it, so dwindling into a slicker version of the old New Criticism. Some think or hope that it will simply fade away. The intemperateness of its propagandists seems to be increasing; large claims are made for its beneficially cathartic effect on the institutions which house it, and this could be construed as a sign of desperation. On the other hand, some assaults on Deconstruction, by eminent but not very well-informed elders, have provided the defenders with a good deal of scornful merriment as well as some useful ammunition. On the side of the elders it can be said that it isn't altogether easy to find out what Deconstruction really is: its practitioners automatically object to any and all descriptions of it, and invariably claim that all adverse criticism depends on the very presuppositions that have already been terminally deconstructed.

The virtue of John Ellis's book* is that he insists on putting his questions in pre-deconstructive terms, refusing to believe that

* John Ellis, *Against Deconstruction* (Princeton University Press)

they can be dismissed as inapposite. For, as he remarks more than once, the importance of a new way of thinking can only be estimated by what intelligent people regard as intelligent discussion of it, not by brusque refusals of such discussion on the ground that it does not accept in advance the rules the inventors of the important new way of thinking have laid down. One can only ask legitimate questions by becoming an insider, and then the questions become irrelevant. Sceptics have to understand that they can say nothing to the point without ceasing to be sceptical.

Ellis thinks there is something very odd about accompanying announcements of a major intellectual development with a ban on attempts to state what it is, or to evaluate it. All he asks for is a serious dialogue between the parties, such as we have not yet had. In the end, the obstinate refusal of such a dialogue makes him angry, but for a while he keeps cool and contents himself with 'examining the logic of the central issues and arguments' in a mannerly prose which clearly marks him as an outsider. His book is worthy of the serious response it asks for, but all he really expects is the rejoinder that logical analysis is inappropriate; Deconstruction is not a theory but a 'project', and has a different 'logic'. Ellis wants to know what this alternative logic is. But to answer him the defenders would have to use his old logic, which allows for alternatives such as either/or and true or false, as the new one does not. He points out that among themselves the deconstructors are ready enough to say that X's position is wrong, or that Y has absurdly misunderstood something: so that there are circumstances in which rational argument creeps back – Derrida notoriously accused John Searle of misunderstanding him even when what he was saying was perfectly clear. Ellis therefore assumes the right to judge some of Derrida's main arguments, and accordingly takes on the *Grammatology*.

Before long he is vigorously denouncing the treatment of Saussure in that book (very central to Derrida's 'project') as based on the palpable error of representing Saussure as ethnocentric, and holding him responsible for perpetuating a general failure to notice the priority of writing over language, a failure related to the dominance of the 'metaphysics of presence'. Ellis is willing to question this cardinal doctrine and ask in what sense writing *is* prior to speech – even though that question is now assumed to be so naive and ignorant that people have long been ashamed to ask it, and Derrida's expositors have usually passed over the topic in silence. Ellis thinks the whole argument depends on a piece of legerdemain, intended to conceal the fact that what is really being talked about is the much more familiar problem of the relation of words to things, of signs to referents. The wrong view of this is what Derrida calls 'logocentrist', but his refutation of it looks less sensational if you reflect, as Ellis does, that it is now rarely held, having been exposed in other terms by other philosophers, notably Wittgenstein. But 'the resistance to any awareness of other critiques of logocentrism means that all criticism of the deconstructive critique must be regarded as a return to logo-centrism.'

Why is nobody willing to say exactly what this word means? Because, says its users, 'a demand for clarity begs the question at issue.' Ellis disagrees, and offers this old-style definition: it is 'the illusion that the meaning of a word has its *origin* in the structure of reality itself and hence makes the *truth* about that structure seem directly *present* to the mind'. But this position was familiar long before Deconstruction came in with its mystifying demands for demystification. What is now obscurely attacked is a view generally agreed to be naive and uninformed, especially by readers of Wittgenstein, Sapir, Whorf and others. And according to Ellis, Derrida has done little more than add to the existing consensus a kind of gratuitously revolutionary fervour – a 'rhetorical absolutism'.

None of this will be accepted or perhaps even discussed. Ellis complains that what he takes to be the deconstructive habit of simply putting something 'in question' and then moving on ought not be preferred to the old-fashioned way of thinking, which tries to move the argument along, not simply to find something else to put into question. When he himself moves on from linguistics and philosophy to deconstructive literary criticism, he makes similar points, arguing that since it is admittedly at its best when expounding hidden complexities in texts, it is much more like other sorts of criticism than it tries to look: here again what is striking is not the new achievement but the new self-admiring rhetoric. Is it the case, he asks, that there is a general belief in the obvious (traditional, authoritarian) single meaning of a text, a belief which must therefore be demystified and deconstructed? No, few hold such an opinion; what is being demystified anew is merely the old Lansonism, long since discredited everywhere except in France, where it required the Sixties revolution to supplant it. Moreover it is 'vacuous in theory, and counterproductive in practice' to insist on 'ironic' readings in *all* cases.

It cannot be said that Ellis has dealt with every aspect of Derrida and Deconstruction, but on the ones he tackles – such issues as the famous reversals of centre and margin, the doctrine that all interpretation is necessarily misinterpretation (reduced by calmer exponents such as Jonathan Culler to the uncontentious assertion that no interpretation can ever be final), and the dashing new formulation of the old problem of intention – Ellis argues with force and clarity. Moreover he happens to believe that some writings are more complex and more valuable than others, and has little difficulty in showing that this is covertly assumed by deconstructors, who ought not, according to their own light, to assume anything of the kind.

Ellis concludes that what Deconstruction provides is largely an emotional bonus – if gives its adherents 'a routine way to a feeling of being excitedly shocking'. They get the feeling that might attend a genuine piece of original thinking, but here it can be achieved without comparable effort. Along the way, 'shared enquiry' which characterizes genuine intellectual research is sacrificed. It might be a good idea for people who want to adjudicate between Deconstruction and Ellis to read or reread the *Grammatology*, and perhaps the Searle-Derrida debates, plus Rudolf Gasché's *The Tain of the Mirror*, which gives a more sympathetic philosophical account, indeed treating Derrida more or less simply as a philosopher (it is almost as hard as Ellis is on the literary criticism). They would, I think, conclude that there is here a case to answer, and that the answer that Ellis is using the wrong logic, or is simply ignorant of what Deconstruction really does, won't wash.

The most powerful rival to Deconstruction in the literary field

is at present the New Historicism, and H. Aram Veeser's large
and uneven collection of essays* sets out to explain what it is,
why there are so many different kinds of it, so many differences
of view within its ranks, and so much opposition from outside
them. The prefatory explanations of Veeser himself are enthusiastic but in some respects inaccurate. He believes the New
Historicism has given us what we sadly lacked, a chance to
cross disciplinary boundaries, to use the findings of anthropology
(mostly Clifford Geertz's 'thick description'), politics, economics,
and so forth. The assumption seems to be that hitherto all modern
literary criticism has been 'empty formalism', blind to history and
to these other subjects. Once more a revolutionary banner is
raised, and the old guard is accused of misrepresenting this
splendid new thing as a mere cover for a revived academic
Marxism.

There is an able and fastidious piece by Stephen Greenblatt, a
pioneer of the style, but the shrewdest essay is Hayden White's
survey of the whole collection. White considers this new style of
doing history from the point of view of a professional philosopher
of history, or metahistorian. He points out that in its simplest
form – a combination of formalist practice with an increased
attention to the historical contexts in which literary texts originate
– New Historicism contains little that might ruffle most conventional critics or historians. It is in thinking overmuch about the
theoretical implications of an initially reasonable ambition that
the New Historicists get themselves into internal arguments
and attract external opposition – for example, by destroying
distinctions between text and context, so that the records intended
to illustrate or provide the context become texts of equivalent
status to the 'literary' works which were the ostensible motive of
the enquiry. Literature thus becomes just one function of a
cultural system, one discourse among others.

This attitude is reflected even in the work of Greenblatt, whose
rhetorical strategy is to begin with some text apparently very
remote from the central interest and move in from that periphery
on to *King Lear*, or whatever the 'literary' work in question

* H. Aram Veeser, ed., *The New Historicism* (London: Routledge)

happens to be. That there can be a genuinely fresh look at texts for the most part already well-known to historians, including literary historians, may be seen from Steven Mullaney's book about the London theatres of Shakespeare's time, which studies the civic or political margins, the 'liberties' and the Southwark bank, in relation to the cultural and social patterns of the City which excluded them, and considers their effect on the plays. But even this kind of interesting quasi-archival work isn't theory-free: White makes the point that you can't have history without a theory of history, so that to view it as 'a sequence of integral "cultural systems" of which both literature and social institutions and practices are to be regarded as manifestations' is to speak for an ideology as surely as a Marxist might.

Veeser himself lists five assumptions as common to all practitioners: 1. 'that every expressive act is embedded in a network of material practices'; 2. 'that every act of unmasking, critique and opposition uses the tools it condemns and risks falling prey to the practice it exposes'; 3. 'that literary and non-literary "texts" circulate inseparably'; 4. 'that no discourse, imaginative or archival, gives access to unchanging truths or expresses unalterable human nature'; 5. 'finally . . . that a critical method and language adequate to describe culture under capitalism participate in the economy they describe.'

I suppose No 3 is the most worrying of these, for it raises the question of text and context, and also the whole unexamined question of literary value. The others are familiar under many different guises, and in any case seem not to impinge very strongly on the practice of all the New Historicists. I myself find that their yoking together of disparate texts – I don't say 'heterogeneous', for that would beg the question – can make a serious point yet have the effect of a pleasing historiographical conceit. Veeser correctly remarks that rather similar and indeed much more complex feats have been achieved in the past – for example, at the Warburg Institute – and without the support of Geertz or Foucault.

For Greenblatt the work of art 'is the product of a negotiation between a creator or class of creators, equipped with a complex, communally shared repertoire of conventions, and the institutions and practices of society ... the process involves not simply appropriation but exchange.' These 'negotiations' are the material of what I have called his 'conceits', and it is hard to find much to dislike in them, though some Post-Structuralists will object to the 'negotiations' as diverting attention from language. Greenblatt's 'cultural poetics' can, in fact, be thought of rather simply as a blend of the formalist and the historical, very interestingly applied but essentially less 'new' than others tend to make it sound. As with Deconstruction, there is a certain amount of hype. You'd think, reading some of these pieces, that professional exponents of Renaissance literature had until yesterday still been swearing by Tillyard's *Elizabethan World Picture*.

It is interesting that in an academy now engrossed in Theory even this new development, which could be represented as an adjustment of normal practices rather than a shocking paradigm-shift, has quickly become a locus of theoretical dispute about what it is and how it stands in relation to other disciplines: so that there already seems to be more theory than practice, which is, after all, the trend. As Stanley Fish remarks in a magisterial afterword to Veeser's collection, most of these people are not *doing* New Historicism but only talking about doing it, often in prose that has taken on that self-important semi-illiteracy of which I have already complained.

There is also a tendency among the contributors to avoid the ostensible subject of the collection; a few of the essays have little perceptible connection with the question at issue, let alone with literature. Stronger contributions are Gerald Graff's calm, exploratory essay on 'co-optation' – the power of the institution to absorb and neutralize new fashions – and Elizabeth Fox-Genovese's convincing demonstration that the New Historicists haven't really given enough thought to history, or even to the sense in which the word 'historicism' has formerly been used. This chimes with Fish's observation that in the modern academy people often do very well by talking about what they are not actually doing, thus ascending to a new and comfortable level of contentious idleness. The best practitioners escape this charge, not because they espouse superior versions of the New Historicism, but because, even willy-nilly, they say something interesting about what, as one contributor puts it, used to be known as literature.

Rethinking Historicism * is a shorter collection and deals with a rival brand of New Historicism, with a main interest not in Renaissance but in Romantic literature. An Introduction by Marjorie Levinson is followed by a long essay from the same hand, with the consequence that nearly half the book is written in unacceptable prose and offers some opinions that will always remain pretty mysterious. One typical claim is that Marilyn Butler's contribution to the collection is distinguished by a calculated absence of Theory, and that this lack is a subtle snub to Mrs Thatcher: for it 'undermines the deeply abstract objectivity used to legitimate the deeply concrete interests of the groups in power'. The even more deeply abstract point seems to be that good historical writing is always presentist. This branch of historicism is distinguished sharply from Greenblatt's, which has an unhappily pastist bias, so missing the point that 'the real power of art-works' is 'to flare up at a certain moment, thereby introducing their distinct order of production into the alien formations of another age . . . We do *to* the past what it could not do *for* itself.'

There follows Marilyn Butler's Inaugural Lecture at Cambridge, a plea for a new canonical openness and for the relevance of Southey to the Romantic scene. Paul Hamilton's 'Keats and Critique' argues that 'the interchangeability in Keats's poetry of its ideal status and its political reticence gradually begins to expose the contemporary politicizing of the ideal and the idealizing of the political.' Jerome McGann, the remaining contributor, starts from Frantz Fanon and argues that the works of the past must be freed from the 'imperial imagination' or, if you prefer, 'the burden of the past'; a re-imagining of the past, illustrated here by re-imaginings of Aeschylus and Blake, Byron and Pound, gives us poems containing more history than they themselves were aware of, and affords us a chance to break with the Kantian aesthetic of disinterest, to see poetry as concerned with knowledge and with

* Marjorie Levinson, Marilyn Butler, Jerome McGann & Paul Hamilton *Rethinking Historicism: Critical Essays in Romantic History* (Oxford: Blackwell)

present and also future history, and to call into question 'all that is privileged, understood and given'.

McGann's Clark Lectures,* the title referring to de Quincey's distinction between the literature of power and the literature of knowledge, state these views more extensively. They are described by their author as part of a larger project to make a severe theoretical adjustment to literary history. The topics are mostly Romantic, though the *Cantos* come in as a clinching case.

McGann knows the fine print of scholarship in the relevant areas but has also read the indispensable books of the theoretical moment. The manner is not, as in so much of the writing I've been discussing, vulgar, but it is ponderously modish, its intention seemingly rather more to impress than to please. However, McGann does apply himself intently to particular texts, and finds new things to say about them, so it cannot be said of him that he talks about doing and doesn't do.

He thinks we continue to be seduced by that originally Kantian idea of disinterest, as mediated by Wordsworth and Coleridge and endorsed by many later poets and critics – an idea fatal, he thinks, to the recognition that literature has to do with knowledge. The Romantics who did not fall into this error were Blake and Byron (of whom McGann is the Clarendon Press editor). He then puts D. G. Rossetti and Pound – one marginal and one clear case – on the good side of the Romantic tradition. If this strikes us as an odd group, that is because we are still using old and false categories. Blake is there because he understood that knowledge in poetry is an activity, not a content, and that poetry assumes ideological positions with regard to its own activity. Byron in turn, though in a very different way, understood that 'the truth-experience of poetry is always transactional', or, as Habermas expresses it in an admittedly different context, it is 'communicative action'. The largely biographical chapter on Rossetti explains how his intimate associations with the trade practices of the period irked him in his mistaken attempt to show that art 'occupies a transcendental order'. This attempt was also fatal to Elizabeth

* Jerome McGann, *Towards a Literature of Knowledge* (Oxford University Press)

Siddall, whose suicide is described in a rather typically murky way as 'no more than ·he exponent and capstone of his disastrous quests for the Beatrice which his experiment required'.

McGann knows a lot of interesting things about all his poets but the fit still seems dubious, especially that of the Rossetti chapter, which is only made possible by the contention that literary historians have hitherto been wrong about Rossetti, which anyway follows from their being wrong about everything else. By the way, it isn't likely (page 75) that Rossetti wrote a grown-up letter to Ford Madox Ford, who was only nine when Rossetti died. F. M. Brown must be meant. Pound, to put it mildly, provides ample material for the study of the relation between poetry and ideology; the *Cantos* (fascist, but 'one of the great achievements of Modern poetry in any language') is a work that 'embodies a disturbing mode of truth: equivocal authority, uncertain knowledge – a fascist, not a Daniel, come to judgment'. The *Cantos* thus illustrate Benjamin's dictum, that the documents of civilization are also documents of barbarism.

I happened to hear the Blake lecture and found it difficult or even impossible to follow, mostly, I thought, because we were asked to study plate three of *Jerusalem* on a slide so dim that the detail to which the lecturer constantly and confidently referred was invisible. But the text as we now have it, with a clear photo-graph of the plate in question, shows that it would have been hard to follow anyway. The general point is that Blake is, in the 'modern revaluation of imagination', an 'originary' figure (this word is wrongly described in the latest *OED* as 'now rare' – the question is how we managed without it until Derrida's translators came to the rescue). And it does become clear that the virtue of this lecture lies in the detailed study of the Blake plate, with its rather mysterious excisions, here gnomically referred to as the 'representation of an absence'. It's by no means the case that this author has nothing to say, but it is unfortunate that he has developed such modishly obscure ways of saying it.

In this, as in other respects, there is a world of difference between A. D. Nuttall and most of the writers I've discussed. His criticism is strongly based in philosophy and the Classics, a product of Oxford Classical Moderations: but this provenance doesn't entail a lack of audacity. He calls himself solitary but sociable, and it is a pleasure to follow him on 'the fiery track of a certain idea'. He's indeed something of a wild man, who once sought (in a book on Herbert) to demonstrate that Jesus was insane, and now offers speculations equally original (whether they will turn out to be originary only time can tell) on Shakespeare, Pope, Swift, Ovid, Virgil and C. S. Lewis.* One essay is a piece of straight philological research into Latin 'causal *dum*'. Another is a philosophical enquiry into the good old problem, or should one say the good new 'problematic', of Intention. It is called 'The Intentional Fallacy Fallacy'. The long opening piece argues for a strong affinity between Shakespeare and Homer and Euripides, supposedly via Virgil. The title essay is a discourse on ancient Stoicism in its relation to two later types of the philosophy, one that eschews emotion altogether and another that seeks it out in order to repress it. This 'dynamic' variety attracted, among others, Augustine and Virgil, whose Aeneas weeps and loves. There is an elegant and learned essay on the *adunata* topos, the catalogue of impossibilities. Nuttall has a special talent for extracting large significances from a single text; his characteristic move is to say, 'But of course there is more to it than that,' before making some original and sensitive comments on, say, Pope's Homer. He remarks that 'the phrase "as a matter of fact" is commonly used to introduce a lie.' If this is so, the rather similar but more mannered expression 'in a manner' is also under suspicion, and he uses it far too much. But the fault looks venial to anybody who has just read through tracts of mortal prose by some of his contemporaries.

London Review of Books, 26 October 1989

---

* A. D. Nuttall, *The Stoic in Love: Selected Essays on Literature and Ideas* (Hemel Hempstead: Harvester Press)

III

Frances Yates and Imperial Secrets

It is not customary to say so, but there is something in common between the lifework of a scholar and that of a creative artist. We should not ordinarily devote to the scholar the peculiar attentions reserved by cultural convention for the oeuvre of a major artist – the passion for occult continuities discoverable under the surface, evidence for abrupt transitions and discrete 'periods' – but from time to time we are confronted with a body of work in which we intuit precisely this kind of variety and homogeneity. We become aware that we are dealing not with a writer who is to be admired for his labours of correction and accumulation, and not even for his brilliant insights and explanations, but with one who, in the course of time, remained ingeniously and beautifully faithful to some hint of illumination that was worth a life.

Wallace Stevens once remarked, I think memorably, that 'a vocation recognizes its material by foresight', and added in illustration some words spoken by Focillon of the *Prisons* of Piranesi. In their first state they were 'skeletal', but

> twenty years later Piranesi returned to these etchings, and on taking them up again he poured into them shadow after shadow, until one might say he excavated this astonishing darkness not from brazen plates, but from the living rock of some subterranean world.

Frances Yates might find the comparison immodest, and yet in her way she has done something of this kind. In her new book*

---

* Frances Yates, *Astraea: The Imperial Theme in the Sixteenth Century* (London: Routledge, 1975)

we see her at work on some of the early plates into which she has subsequently cut so deep: she has added a touch and reformed a line here and there, but the extraordinary fact is that this collection is of immediate significance to everything she has done since she started work over forty years ago.

That was before the arrival in London of the Warburg Institute, with which she was early associated, and which has fostered her work ever since. Yet even her earliest books, on John Florio and *Love's Labour's Lost*, can be read as sketches of, or tentative probes into, that deep layer of meaning which, she thought, must exist and must give coherence and sense to the art, literature and politics of the sixteenth century. In the years that followed she came more and more to understand its depth and the amazing variety of its detailed manifestations, but she never abandoned a faith in its essential simplicity. She would call her subject the Imperial Theme, and might have used that as the title of her new book had it not been pre-empted, long ago and for quite other purposes, by Wilson Knight.

Among the explorations of the theme which were written later than the first versions of the essays in this book were the study of the French academies of the sixteenth century, so solidly researched, and the delicate and laborious enquiry into the contexts and meanings of the Valois tapestries. This book crowns the work of others, but in its final form – arrived at by minute scholarship and brilliant guessing, by the establishment of connections where none had seemed possible – it could have come from no hand but hers; and who now can walk past these tapestries in the Uffizi without reflecting that they are not merely delectable extravagances but documents subtly woven into the fabric of cultural and political history? She gave another book to Bruno, as the philosopher of the new eirenic imperialism, the magus who wanted to tie together French and English, politics and cosmology, the divided religion of Europe. Her recent work, *The Rosicrucian Enlightenment*, carried the story of these phantom imperialisms into the court of the Elector Frederick and the English Elizabeth. *The Art of Memory* and the book on Shakespeare's Globe, sometimes dizzyingly speculative (for on the Yates method it is necessary to make bold leaps) are equally part of the vast unitary enterprise. Few scholars have the intellectual equipment for such a task, and of them even fewer have the necessary daring. The clue might be in the *editio princeps* of a forgotten Greek poet, or a set of accounts in the Bibliothèque Nationale. You must know what kind of thing to look for, and where; much of the work will be tedious, yet, when the detail begins to jump and proliferate, you must have the strength to control it. The learned may help, but they cannot provide the power to detect occult resemblances, or the stamina to seek them out.

The long essay 'Queen Elizabeth as Astraea' is one of Miss Yates's seminal pieces. It first appeared in the *Warburg Journal* for 1947, but was in the making some years before that. It is here preceded by an essay on Charles V and the idea of empire, available in French since 1960; and there will henceforth be no excuse for writing about Elizabethan literature and politics without reference to both these articles. (The few who have used them over and over again can now abandon their battered offprints.) The importance of the Emperor Charles is that he was responsible for a phantom renewal in the early part of the century of the medieval doctrine of Empire. This unlikely success was due not only to his personality and vast domains, but the skill of his artists. We see him in Titian's Prado portrait – based on the antique statue of Marcus Aurelius – the stoic *dominus mundi*. And Charles was to set a new style, that of the Reforming Emperor, a hope for a divided world. Though he never exercised the controverted right of the Emperor to summon a Council of the Church, he came very near to realizing 'the age-old Ghibelline dream of the Just Emperor', the answer to the urgent question as to how, in a new world of nationalism and religious division, Europe might be held together.

Charles did not achieve this, and what happened was that the national monarchs, especially of England and France, appropriated his propaganda methods. The great contribution of Miss Yates to our understanding of Elizabethan literature is that she refused to consider the many manifestations of devotion to the imperial Elizabeth – the poems, the tilts, the portraits, the Accession Day ceremonies – as disparate and charming manifestations of a lost culture. The imperial theme unites them. Astraea, the Virgin of Justice returned to earth, as in Virgil, was not a merely decorative allusion but a claim, subtly enforced, to imperial dignity, and in the end a matter of hard political manoeuvre. It is extraordinary how much of Spenser that seemed merely pretty becomes charged with urgent sense to readers of this essay, and how vivid and immediate the text of Foxe, down to the famous initial C with its woodcut of Queen triumphing over Pope – an imperial revenge given another dimension by the use of the same figure in the frontispiece of John Dee's *Memorials*, where imperial politics and astronomy grow together. A poem, an entertainment, a courtly ceremony, can yield to the right scrutiny its imperial secret; so we are instructed in the mythological, emblematic, and balletic auspices under which an imperial union between Elizabeth and Henri III against Spain might have prospered. Imperial diplomacy might be an elaborate dance, with the King leading it. And, as the essay on the Accession Day Tilts shows, the cult of the imperial Virgin with its elaborate chivalric rituals – mostly designed by Sir Henry Lee – was part of that 'imaginative re-feudalization of the culture' which was a means, and not only in England, of attaching old religious fervours to the worship of a national monarch.

Half the book deals with the French monarchy. Here the plot is much more elaborate, the imperialist scenario more professional, and the politics very complicated. Again Charles V provided the imagery, but the imperial idea was harnessed to the doctrine of the quasi-imperial descendant of Charlemagne, the French king, *rex Christianissimus*. As in 'The Valois Tapestries', Miss Yates studies the records of particular ceremonies in depth: the entry of Charles IX into Paris, 1571, after his marriage with the imperial Elizabeth of Austria, when Paris was decorated according to a programme devised by Ronsard and Dorat, executed by Dell'Abbate, and accompanied by the wonder-working music of Baif's Academy. Here, as in the Magnificences devised for the dynastic marriage of the Duc de Joyeuse ten years later, the themes were imperial – not only the greatness of France but the peace of the world and religious toleration. Within these beautiful and devastatingly expensive ceremonies were hidden the hopes, soon to be defeated, of a solution to the desperate political situation caused by the enmity of the Catholic League. Miss Yates turns from the gloomy allegorical religious processions of Henri III – half auto-da-fé, half masque – to the revival of the imperial idea under Henri IV, the French Astraea. But Henri was murdered and Bruno was burned, and the survival of the liberal imperial politics was entrusted, hopelessly, to the unfortunate Elector Frederick and his wife. So, it appears, ended the last century of the life of the imperial idea.

There are, perhaps, moments when some of the cards, formed into patterns of ever-increasing complexity, slip out of Miss Yates's hands, when one is giddy because too much seems to have meaning, because of the variety of the detail that must be accommodated to the theme. But this is what gives her work its peculiar force: whether she is looking at a portrait of Elizabeth, explaining the globe in it, and the scenes from the *Aeneid*; or speaking of magic, memory or music; or recreating the political tensions of Elizabeth's Garter Embassy to the French King in 1585; or speaking of Dee or Bruno or Shakespeare or Spenser, she is always acting in obedience to the foresight which enabled her to recognize her vocation. *Astraea* is a very important book in its own right, but it also serves as a witness to that vocation.

New Statesman, 17 January 1975

Roy Strong

Policy and Pageantry

When the emperor entered an Italian city he passed through triumphal arches proclaiming him the descendant of Augustus and lord of the world. A diplomatic encounter between monarchs, like the Field of Cloth of Gold, must be celebrated with palpable magnificence; the enormous cost of such occasions was as important as the political messages elaborated into visual imagery by architect and artist, and these imperial and royal practices persisted beyond the point where rational statecraft could justify them, in the superb extravaganzas of baroque court entertainment.

Dr Strong's subject* has increasingly engaged the attention of historians over the past twenty years, and his plan, which was to bring together a great deal of scattered and relatively inaccessible material in a form that would make manifest its importance and interest to non-specialists, is fully realized; his book is as splendid, and as ingeniously designed, as the great celebrations it records. He is an efficient compiler rather than a writer, but something over 200 excellent illustrations compensate for any defects in the expository prose; and the publishers have somehow contrived to dissociate splendour from expense.

The myth of universal empire has proved very resistant to the chill scepticism of actual history; its most recent English manifestation was in the political thought of Eliot. Historians are always ready to say of Eliot's hero Dante that his imperialist

* Roy Strong, *Splendour at Court: Renaissance Spectacle and Illusion* (London: Weidenfeld & Nicolson)

propaganda came fifty years too late, that the death of Frederick II ended all hope. Nationalism would supplant universalism when Western Christianity broke up, and the kingdoms came into their vernacular heritage. Yet the Dantean aspirations persisted; and the sixteenth-century career of the Emperor Charles V constitutes one of the strangest episodes in the strange history of the imperial idea.

Imperialists were well accustomed to the unpredictable mutations and translations of empire, but the advent in 1519 of an emperor who for forty years retained his authority over most of Europe and much of the New World must still have been surprising. Charles travelled indefatigably over his enormous territories and came as close as any of the successors of Augustus to the Dantean ideal of a ruler who, having all, could envy nothing. Dynastic marriages and conquest extended his sway, and wherever he went his artists and poets proclaimed the mystique of empire: the emperor supreme over all, leading the people of God to their terrestrial paradise, which had been announced in 40 BC by Virgil in the Fourth Eclogue. Antiquarians revived the ancient imperial imageries which, often blended with the chivalric tradition associated with Charlemagne, adorned progresses and entries, tournaments and ballets and masquerades; all proclaimed, in stories elaborate with moral and political allegories, the virtues of the emperor, his partnership with the Pope (so long the enemy of the emperor) in the historical process which would reunite Christendom.

But lesser rulers were not slow to adapt the splendours of this imperial propaganda to nationalist uses. The English had long held their monarch to be emperor in his own kingdom, and Elizabeth had about her ingenious and devoted men able to demonstrate her right to be both empress and head of a Catholic church which had at last thrown off the yoke of the Bishop of Rome. The French, who had a special claim to the imperial dignity, developed its revived liturgy and its emblems on an even more extravagant scale, culminating in the vast and subtle cult of Louis XIV, but evident already in the propaganda of the Valois.

Dr Strong describes many varieties of politico-mystical spectacle from the Italian *intermezzi* and French *ballets de cour* to the court masques of Charles I of England. Throughout his book one senses the presence of his teacher Frances Yates. Miss Yates now has some of the celebrity she deserves, but her studies in the imagery, philosophy and politics of these spectacles and of related Renaissance manifestations are not well known. It has always astonished me that her article on the political use of Astraean imagery in the cult of Elizabeth – which transforms the entire study of Spenser – should lie, so little known, in the files of the *Journal of the Warburg and Courtauld Institutes*, together with other important work, for example on the Accession Day Tilts. Her studies of Charles V are even less known, buried as they are in French periodicals and reports of conferences. The combination of intellectual boldness and inspired research which characterizes Miss Yates at her best virtually created this subject: and her books on the sixteenth-century French academies and the Valois tapestries are as essential to the French as her Elizabethan studies are to the English scene.

Other scholars to whom Dr Strong is deeply indebted are D. P. Walker and D. J. Gordon, pioneer of modern studies in the court masque; I should add that he himself has made original contributions, notably in his essays on the celebration of Elizabeth's Accession Day, his book on the portraits of the queen, and the recent work, in collaboration with Stephen Orgel, on Inigo Jones, who gave Stuart imperialism its visible language.

Throughout this book one notices that political ideals and political opportunism may co-exist, and that art and scholarship could be made the instruments of policy. From Titian and Ariosto to Inigo Jones and Ben Jonson the greatest artists of the time could be hired to foster a political ideology of which the expression grew ever more explicitly absolutist. A simple instance of the ingenuity called forth is the imperialist play on the ancient idea of the emperor as he who brings the virgin Astraea, Justice, to earth; she was the last goddess to desert it at the end of the Golden Age. The propagandists of Elizabeth were quick to exploit one of her few advantages over male monarchs; *iam redit et Virgo* could be treated more literally in England, and the cult, which developed in very extravagant ways, was a true imperial cult.

Later everything grew much more elaborate. The view that

truth could be expressed in enigmatic visual images was accompanied by a delighted acceptance of the new and spectacular use of theatrical machinery, and the development of perspective scenes. These, says Dr Strong, developed along with absolutism; for in a theatre with such scenes only one person, the monarch, could see the sets without distortion; such sets are 'the ultimate apotheosis of the monarch'.

So to the extravagant absolutist spectacles of Charles I, who really believed that their enormous cost was justified, even, somehow, good in itself. The masque showed disorder giving way to order under the gaze, and with the participation as dancer, of the divine representative himself. We cannot have a very accurate notion of these strange sumptuary rituals. We can read the texts preserved by Jonson and others, but the words are often unimpressive without the painting and the carpentry, the gorgeous costumes and the music. We can read Jonson's learned notes, and marvel that the simplicities of the old maskers should have been capable of such sophistication. But even in the Banqueting House itself, with the Rubens ceiling to help us, and even with the drawings of Jones, and all the comments of the learned on the machinery and the political point of the entertainment before us, we cannot know how it felt to participate in these once-for-all events. There is often in accounts of them a note of melancholy, that they should be so fugitive – the note of Prospero ending the revels.

Yet even if they could be reconstituted we should, I think, find it hard to like them, to enjoy a magnificence so calculated, or the prospect of such exquisite skills devoted to the service of dangerous political ambitions. Unlike true ritual and liturgy, the Renaissance and Baroque spectacles were not capable of repetition; but their archaeological remains are often extraordinarily beautiful, which is why Dr Strong has been able to make this dazzling book.

New Statesman, 30 November 1973

Protestant Poetry

As times change, some of the unquestioned assumptions of the quite recent past may come to look extremely odd. How, for example, was the poetry of Spenser depoliticized? This remarkable achievement cannot be credited to any single authority; it was the work of many independent critics and reached its most intransigent form in the 1960s, when at last it became feasible to devote an entire book to Book V of *The Faerie Queene* without paying much attention to historical allegory; a neat trick if you consider the presence of such characters as Belga and her seventeen daughters. Of course not everybody followed this trend. Some were finding out in detail about the intimate relations between the Book of Revelation and Tudor Protestant propaganda, with implications for Book I; others tried to crack the political allegory of the obscure Church of Isis; but on the whole they were not thought of as doing the poet much service. If he was to be saved for the canon it must be by other means.

Great poetry in the post-Symbolist era was not allegorical, and, whatever the opinions of the poets, rarely political. If religious, it mustn't be radical or hectoring, prophetic or apocalyptic. David Norbrook believes that the *Scrutiny* group, which wanted Milton dislodged and cared nothing for Spenser, must bear much of the blame for the neglect of the Protestant prophetic tradition; they preferred a poetry of the middle Anglican way, Donne, Herbert, Jonson. In fact that group was less wantonly negligent of the political implications of poetry than the New Critics, and the attack on Milton developed spontaneously from many sides. To rescue Milton, or Spenser, it seemed necessary to soft-pedal their Protestant prophetic strains.

The novelty of Dr Norbrook's thesis* is that he looks at these and other poets of the same tradition and finds them valuable not in spite of but because of their politics. He aims to correct the distortions of history we have all inherited, and in bringing off that ambition he has written a book of exceptional interest. Nothing he discusses will be quite the same again.

Of course he has predecessors; Frances Yates long ago documented the apocalyptic imperialism of courtly Elizabethan and Jacobean propagandist history, and changed the look of Spenser for anybody who cared to read her. But Norbrook's concern is less with the court than with radical Protestants the court mistrusted, and he owes less to Yates than to dozens of lesser scholars. He has sucked the honey of a hundred articles. It seems evident that he himself holds quite strong views, but they haven't got in the way of his historical scholarship; in the nature of the case he has to neglect some aspect of the poetry he discusses, but on the whole his treatment of the subject is just, as well as novel.

The book begins with More and ends with Milton, with Spenser, Sidney, Greville, Jonson and the Stuart Spenserians in between. There is very little on the dramatic writings of the period, and Shakespeare is hardly mentioned, but the undertaking is quite large enough as it is to disqualify complaint on that score. Norbrook uses Walter Benjamin's formula (uses it, indeed, rather monotonously) to divide writers into those who politicize aesthetics and those who aestheticize politics. The second of these types is represented principally by Jonson, with the court masque as its characteristic genre. The first is the radical, prophetic Protestant, using many kinds but retaining an interest in the eclogue as a vehicle for political and ecclesiastical comment. It is not to be thought that such adverse comment is often very bold, nor that it is uniform. Spenser, for example, had very illiberal views on Ireland, and was the proponent of a quasi-imperialist militancy much in excess of anything the Queen approved. But he can still be quite properly seen as opposed to the sort of cultural conservatism represented by Jonson; and it is certainly wrong to

* David Norbrook, *Poetry and Politics in the English Renaissance* (London: Routledge and Kegan Paul)

think of him as a 'mouthpiece of official policies'. Norbrook remarks with some justice that critics have behaved as if Ficino and Hooker were better guides to Spenser's thought than his own writings.

Our interest in the celebration of royal authority has tempted us to forget the traditional opposition to its excesses. Humanism was by no means invariably at the service of monarchical pretensions; like La Boétie in France, though perhaps more cautiously, More was willing to venture across the boundaries of conventional politics. And when, as Norbrook puts it, the humanist dialogue yielded place to Protestant prophecy as the dominant literary mode of the reign of Edward VI, political comment became for a time more stringent and more open.

We needed a new look at this 'drab' literature, and at its influence on the Elizabethans. We could have read the pseudonymous 'Luke Shepherd' in W. C. Hazlitt's nineteenth-century collection; but we probably didn't, and he is mentioned neither in C. S. Lewis's Oxford History nor in the *Cambridge Bibliography*. So his lively satire on Corpus Christi may be a surprise. It appeared in 1548, the year in which Cranmer abolished the feast – another blow to Catholic sacramentalism, along with Bible translations and the campaign against images. Edwardian Protestantism also revived Langland; *Piers Plowman* was edited by Robert Crowley, and supposed by John Bale to be the work of Wyclif. Crowley, briefly mentioned by Lewis as a 'poetaster', is for Norbrook an apocalyptic poet. The Ghibelline views of Dante were imported; *The Pardoner's Tale* was 'radicalized'. Altogether, poetry and politics came close during the years of triumphant Protestantism.

This rather populist apocalypticism faded in the new reign, though it did not die. The new poetry was more complex and ambiguous, as *The Shepherd's Calendar* testifies. Norbrook is less interested in this strange work as a set of paradigms for poetry than as a set of rather obscure political-ecclesiastical observations. He changes our view of it without claiming to have solved all its problems, or even suggesting that they are all soluble. The older conventions of anti-Catholic polemic are now used against the Anglican hierarchy, but Spenser is not so clearly 'Edwardian' as Marprelate; he is, of course, not even anti-episcopal, since he admires Grindal. He is simply Low Church. He opposes the Alençon marriage, though cautiously, and wants active support for fellow-Protestants in the Netherlands. Spenser is less militant than Leicester, but although he veils some of his opinions the poem is very topical and unmistakably reformist; it is meant to be useful, as Harvey, against Nashe, maintained poetry ought to be.

The Faerie Queene is, perhaps understandably, less fully examined. It is certainly elusive, and, as Norbrook remarks, it has 'a deeper suspicion of false resolutions, or deceptive claims to transcendence'. He is less persuasive on its supposed 'alienation effects', giving as an example Arthur's erotic vision of Gloriana in I.ix. It is right, though, to set the poem in a context of courtly love, here seen in its political bearing, as actualizing a metaphor of subjection. There is no attempt to provide the large-scale analysis of Book I which, as the author says, we badly need; and on particular allegories such as those of Mercilla and Isis Church the book has little to add. This is a disappointment, but Norbrook's aim is rather to clear the ground than to work it. He makes much sense of Spenser's politics in general, and that is a notable service. It may be too much to say that 'the allegorical core of Book V portrays a predominantly Puritan Parliament approving the execution of a reigning monarch', but that it is a strong defence of the Leicester–Essex foreign policies, in a generally apocalyptic context, is clear enough. And it is in accord with his usual moderation that Norbrook finds little politics in Book VII, refusing even to mention the old and improbable conjecture that the Titaness represents Arabella Stuart with her unacceptable claims to the succession. Part of the skill necessary to making sense of Spenser is to know when this sort of proposition is plausible and when it is not.

On the *Arcadia*, treated as a politicized Italian courtly romance, and on Sidney in general, Norbrook is excellent; and the study of Greville may be the most impressive part of the book. This dark poet, this poet of 'hurt imaginations', comments on the 'voluntary servitude' of peoples without departing from the position that there was no remedy but resignation. He knew that 'the Neoplatonic conception of the political world held together by love' was one more of the 'shows' by which we are beguiled, 'a deceitful disguise behind which the true relationships are those of domination and exploitation'. And indeed shows and shadows are as important to Greville as to Shakespeare, and much more clearly in the service of a dissenting politics. Not surprisingly, Greville fell foul of the rampant censorship of the 1630s. And although in him 'the voice of radical humanism has lapsed into a self-protective stutter', he of all these political poets seems to have something to say to our own times. Norbrook suggests that his adoption of the Tacitean manner reflects the melancholy view of his Latin original that there was no hope of restoring the virtues of the republic, the politicians being so corrupted by imperial rule. The people, who in principle make kings and tyrants, can in principle also depose them; but they are kept at an impossible and ignorant distance by the use of the doctrine of 'mysteries of state', or, if you like, the Official Secrets Act; and their attention is fixed elsewhere by the provision of 'shows', while the state moves towards what Greville in the *Life of Sidney* called a 'precipitate absoluteness'.

Yet a hundred read Jonson for every one that reads Greville; and Jonson is in some ways the villain of this book, the great purveyor of deceptive shows, the laureate anti-prophet and collaborator with Stuart absolutism. He would willingly have celebrated the marriage of Charles to a Spanish Habsburg; he dignified the most extreme hierarchical assumptions; he professed to celebrate the old 'organic order' but hobnobbed with the crooked usurer Sir William Cockayne. It will do us no harm to have available this harsher portrait of a poet who, for all his boldness and for all the vicissitudes he brought on himself, did comply with ultimate authority. It enables Norbrook to bring out the shadows the poets of the rival tradition. They were not given much rein under the Stuarts. James was a great disappointment to them; their hopes in Prince Henry were dashed by his early death; their ambitions for Protestant empire were irrevocably broken by the defeat of Elizabeth Stuart and her husband the Elector Palatine at the White Mountain in 1620. But that these were lost causes should not entail the total oblivion of their poetic supporters. Norbrook shares Milton's admiration for William Browne, with his Protestant shepherds, *Calendar*-like complaints, and pointed topical allusions, suggesting that this apparently incongruous association of faerie mythology with political radicalism remained a feature of the English poetic tradition down to *Queen Mab*. He also has good words for another poet not very accustomed to hear them, namely George Wither, whose work sometimes harks back to the militancy of 'Edwardian' Protestantism, with its European and indeed world-wide ambitions.

The great scandals involving Frances Howard, Countess first of Essex and then of Somerset, provide an occasion for sorting the poets into rival camps. In order to marry the royal favourite Robert Carr, this young woman needed a divorce from the Earl of Essex. The stately celebration of this second marriage would be undertaken only by those who wanted to get on at court: Donne, for example. Ben Jonson showed his colours by writing masques for both the marriages: the first was the great *Hymenaei*. Two years after the second, Sir Thomas Overbury died of poison, and Frances and her husband were convicted of murder, though the sentence was not carried out. The opposition made this an occasion for further attacks on the court, but Jonson's courtly panegyrics simply grew more bland and fulsome. 'It was becoming a little difficult', says Norbrook judiciously, for Jonson 'to maintain credibility as a moral authority'. The poets of the Protestant apocalyptic strain, on the other hand, remained moral and consistent, attacking the pro-Spanish policies of Charles, criticizing Buckingham, detesting Laud.

Milton, who knew these poets, also knew Jonson. This book ends with a long and original study of the early Milton as inheritor of the prophetic tradition. The Nativity Ode reflects the apocalyptic revival of the 1630s, and so, in its way, does *Comus*. But *Comus* sets us some notorious problems. It is a 'show', produced in collaboration with a royalist composer and in some measure indebted to Jonson's masque *Pleasure Reconciled to Virtue*. The argument here is that *Comus* is a 'reformed' masque, having perhaps a relation to Jonson's of the sort that Grindal's position has to Laud's. That doesn't dispose of all the difficulties. Much has of late been made of a possible connection between the Castlehaven scandal and Milton's poem. Lady Alice Egerton, the fifteen-year-old who played the Lady, had a wicked kinsman, the Earl of Castlehaven, who three years earlier had been executed for virtually unspeakable Sadist perversions. Has the emphasis on the Lady's chastity anything to do with the *cause célèbre*? Not really: the enchanted cup of Comus is the traditional apocalyptic image of idolatry, and the chastity of the Lady, like that of Una, is an image of the true faith. She is given a correct political philosophy to match, one that is critical of courtly excess, including excessive authority. And what she has to say on this subject is markedly different from anything the Cavalier poets would expect from a woman.

Here the feminism that smoulders throughout the book is allowed a brief flare-up. One is glad of this, if only because it gives the author a chance to quote, as a slight indication of change in the air, from the anonymous Coleorton masque of 1618, securely hidden from modern eyes in R. Brotanek's *Die Englischen Maskenspiele*, Vienna, 1902. The masque is 'playful' but its arguments may not be without 'a certain seriousness' and might now be thought wholly serious:

> know your Strength & your own Vertues see
> which in everie Several grace
> of the mind, or of the face
> Gives women right to have Prioritie.
> Brave Amazonian Dames
> Made no count of Mankind but
> for a fitt to be at the Rutt.
> free fier gives the brightest flames;
> Menns overawing tames
> And Pedantlike our active Spirits smother.
> Learne, Virgins, to live free:
> Alas, would it might bee.
> weomen could live and lie with one another!

Like Spenser's Acrasia and the Blatant Beast, Comus is still 'on the loose' at the end of the masque; it would hardly be sage and serious to suggest otherwise. Moreover the Lady's heroism is passive, as always in Milton. She argues aggressively, but needs divine aid. At the end of *Pleasure Reconciled to Virtue* we learn that Virtue is 'By her own light, to every eye / More seen, more known when Vice is by'; but *Comus* ends with a variation of some significance: 'if Virtue feeble were. / Heaven itself would stoop to her'. This may not quite mean what Norbrook says, that Virtue 'may be "feeble" without divine aid', but it is satisfactorily different from Jonson's conclusion. And it surely is significant that these rational and principled lectures should be given by a woman. Norbrook tells us about the formidable Lady Eleanor Davies, sister to the appalling Castlehaven; an apocalyptic prophetess banned from publication in England, she went to Holland and wrote a poem about Belshazzar, foretelling the doom of those who feasted in Banqueting Houses. She was unkind enough to reprint this work after the King's execution outside the Banqueting House Inigo Jones had built for his father's absolutist celebrations. Milton, in these early days at any rate, is milder than Lady Eleanor, but his reconciliation of virtue and pleasure is not in the Jonsonian manner of the Banqueting House but in the manner of the Protestant shepherds.

Lycidas, despite the obvious assault on the clerical establishment, is also apocalyptic and prophetic in obscurer ways, and Norbrook does justice to the originality with which it handles a long-established genre, giving it a high political charge: he makes useful comparisons with the contemporary elegies on the death of Jonson. *Lycidas* joins the other poems here treated as a response to the increasingly reactionary mood of the time, and as an attempt to politicize aesthetics just when Charles, trying to impose his views on rationalistic Scottish Protestants, was unavailingly seeking to do the opposite.

This bold, finely researched and well-written book should have a decisive effect on our thinking about the poetry of the English Renaissance. It therefore seems essential to enter a protest against its mean, cheeseparing presentation. It is set from camera-ready copy without a justified right margin and with too many thinly printed words crowded on to the page. Corrections have been made carelessly, the type even thinner and the inserts slanting down from the line. It is, I'm persuaded, not only my dimming eyes that were tested; for there are things that ought to have been corrected and weren't, perhaps because nobody could bear to read through the book. The notes are ample and valuable, but if you miss the first reference to a book or article and have only the author's name to go by, you are at the mercy of the index, which does not always record that name: e.g. p.307, reference to 'Hough', who isn't indexed. Everybody interested in the period should soldier on through these 150,000 words, but a work of such importance shouldn't be so grimly reader-repellent. I suppose it will be said that nowadays you can't expect anything better for a mere £15.95.

Times Literary Supplement, 18 January 1985

How Do You Spell Shakespeare?

When Oxford decided to do Shakespeare they clearly made up their minds that the scale of the operation must be very grand, and a team of scholars has been working hard for eight years to get it done quickly, done right, and done with the greatest possible display of novelty. One has to admire not only the industry of Professor Wells and his associates, but their flair for publicity, as evidenced by the enormous solemn fuss about the poem 'Shall I die?', now accorded an honoured place in their canon, and also by the proclaimed scope and originality of their enterprise, which, though not essentially different from other such enterprises, is different in many eye-catching ways, and must have set the Press some unique problems.

The work is not yet fully finished. What we have at present is two vast volumes, the Complete Works in modernized* and again in original† spelling, and a fair number of the single-play volumes edited by a lot of able people who are presumably in agreement about the general editorial line and who can provide the detailed introductions and notes missing from the big collections. Of these more portable and more useful books I can't say much; they will be judged by comparison with the New Arden editions, some of which are now showing signs of age (some of them always did), and possibly with the New Penguin. There is a Cambridge set now well under way: the Oxford *Hamlet* is the third considerable edition of that play in five years, following hard upon Harold

---

* William Shakespeare: *The Complete Works*, edited by Stanley Wells and Gary Taylor (Oxford University Press)

† William Shakespeare, *The Complete Works: Original-Spelling Edition*, edited by Stanley Wells and Gary Taylor (Oxford University Press)

Jenkins's magisterial Arden and Philip Edwards's serious Cambridge version.

It may well be asked by non-Shakespearians and non-publishers whether all this editorial activity is needed, and by whom, and the Oxford team anticipates the question by asserting the boldness as well as the unparalleled scope of its enterprise. It is worth asking how much there is in this claim.

The Original-Spelling volume greatly increases the size of the undertaking and is probably the greatest novelty. In some respects it is a very odd compilation. Back in 1960 John Russell Brown wrote an article, celebrated in the trade, in which he argued against the value of old-spelling Shakespeare, saying among other things that the amount of 'silent alteration' an editor would have to introduce would make such a text almost useless for close study; that it would be naive to suppose the spelling reproduced was that of the author; and that to believe the old spelling imparted 'an Elizabethan flavour' to the words was a pseudo-historical nonsense, for the strangeness of the spelling isn't something the Elizabethan reader could have been expected to notice. Brown's article caused a stir because, as he remarked, it ran counter to assumptions rarely questioned. W. W. Greg had been firm about it in the Prolegomena to his authoritative book, *The Editorial Problem in Shakespeare* (2nd ed., 1951), where he argued that modernization seriously misrepresents Elizabethan English when it changes 'murther' to 'murder', 'mushrump' to 'mushroom', 'vild' to 'vile', 'wrack' to 'wreck', and so forth. Less controversially, he indicated that modernization can in some cases destroy rhymes, and hinder the business of emendation (but surely nobody would be ass enough to try that without recourse to the original). Greg's case really depends upon a conviction that the needs of critics and of ordinary readers are different, which is true, and another conviction, that there is always a chance that the original spelling has some trace of the author's hand and should therefore be preserved. Of course he knew better than anybody how slim this chance was.

Brown saw that Greg's general case, though somewhat dogmatically stated, was less strong than it appeared. Why not work from photographs instead of type facsimiles or old-spelling editions?

His opponents minimized the treachery of type facsimiles and stressed the fallibility of photographs: but that was before Hinman's Norton Facsimile of the First Folio (1968) – a remarkable achievement. By using only the best leaves of a great many copies of the Folio, Hinman produced photographs of an 'ideal' version, so that his facsimile is in practice a better copy than any genuine exemplar, and anybody who wants to see what Jaggard's compositors actually printed, without modern editorial interferences except for line numbers, should look there.

In 1965 Fredson Bowers, who more or less inherited Greg's authority, took a look at the problem in the light of the enormous recent expansion of bibliographical techniques, in part at least brought on by himself. Though he did not deny that an original-spelling text was desirable, he maintained sadly but strongly that it couldn't yet be achieved: there was still so much to be done in the way of studying printing-house practices, compositors' vagaries and so forth, along the lines of Hinman's extraordinary investigation of the printing of the First Folio, published in 1963. A great deal of recondite research has gone on since then, but work of this kind, as the present Oxford editors admit, usually opens up rather than closes the prospect of more work, and one would have expected Bowers's prediction, that an old-spelling edition of Shakespeare was a matter for the twenty-first century, to have held at least into the Eighties.

It is also a reasonable inference that such an edition would take a lot of people a long time: yet this has apparently not proved to be the case. An old-spelling Oxford edition was mooted long ago by R. B. McKerrow, but he produced only the *Prolegomena* (1939) before he died, and Alice Walker, who took over the project, did not issue a single play. With this discouraging history behind him, Professor Wells seems not to have been thinking of old spelling when he mounted the present assault on the Shakespearian summit. 'The newly proposed Oxford editions,' he wrote in 1979,

> will be in modern spelling. This procedure, traditional in editions of Shakespeare, removes unnecessary barriers to understanding, making it possible for the reader to concentrate on the text itself, undistracted by obsolete and archaic

accidentals of presentation. Thus, his reading experience is closer to that of Shakespeare's contemporaries, who also read the plays in what was, for them, a modern form. We plan both a new single-volume edition of Shakespeare's works for the Oxford Standard Authors (OSA) series, and a detailed scholarly edition, devoting a volume to each play, for the Oxford English Texts (OET).

Wells went on to give by far the best account of the problems of modernizing (*Modernising Shakespeare's Spelling*, 1979), but said nothing whatever about an old-spelling edition, and it is reasonable to infer that eight years ago the very idea of one must have seemed terrifying to the Press is not to the general editor, who was in any case ready with all manner of good reasons for doing without such a thing. So it is at least a little surprising that the decision was reversed, and that the work, once undertaken, occupied not the decades of editorial drudgery envisaged by McKerrow and Bowers, but five or six years at most of doubtless frenzied activity, years during which work continued on the modernized version, on the single-play volumes, and on the *Textual Companion*, still missing but promised for later this year.

Apparently the editors decided that the objections to old spelling were less cogent than they had thought. Does the present volume show their second thoughts to have been right? To answer with confidence one would need to have worked with the edition for a long time, and I have only sampled it. The most obvious difficulty is 'silent alteration', and so I thought I might look at a few passages celebrated for their difficulty, and see how the 'original spelling' of this Oxford edition compared with the original spelling.

1. There is a well-known crux in *Antony and Cleopatra*, I. iv. 47, where the original (Folio) text speaks of an 'Arme-gaunt Steede'. In Oxford OS we read 'Arme-iaunct'. The modernized text has 'arm-jaunced'. Presumably these readings will be defended and explained in the volume that we have not yet got, but the point is clear: an emendation of 'Arme-gaunt' has been read back into Elizabethan spelling, and the word 'Arme-iaunct' is a pretty modern guess at what the author, or a compositor, or a proof-reader, wrote or rewrote. It is, in fact, a fake antique.

2. There is another crux in the same play, solved by the eighteenth-century scholar Hanmer in one of the most brilliant and certain of all Shakespearian emendations. Antony is complaining that all is lost by Cleopatra's treachery. His followers have deserted him:

> All come to this? The hearts
> That pannelled me at heeles, to whom I gaue
> Their wishes, do dis-Candie, melt their sweets
> On blossoming *Caesar*: And this Pine is barkt,
> That ouer-top'd them all.

Hanmer read 'spanieled' in the second line. Antony has picked up the idea of 'discandying' (melting) from Cleopatra a little earlier.

> Ah (Deere) if I be so,
> From my cold heart let Heaven engender haile,
> And poyson it in the sourse, and the first stone
> Drop in my necke: as it determines so
> Dissolue my life, the next Caesarian smile [smite]
> till by degrees the memory of my wombe,
> Together with my brave Egyptians all,
> By the discandering of this pelleted storme,
> Lie grauelesse . . .

The idea is of the hailstones melting ('discandering' = 'discandying') and so killing her, her son and her other children, and then all the Egyptians. But the word for melting stays with Antony and he remembers its other association with candy, a sweet resembling ice: so he launches into a strange conceit, supposing the 'hearts' of those who followed him, dog-like, to have let his gifts (their 'wishes') melt in their mouths (the candy discandies), and then go and drop the sticky remnant fawningly before Caesar, represented as a tree in blossom, while Antony is a tall barked pine. In this extraordinary sequence the verb 'pannelled' must refer to the fawning action of a dog, which is why Hanmer, conscious no doubt that Shakespeare had elsewhere linked fawning and slavering dogs with candy, emended to 'spanieled'. In the Oxford modern-spelling edition this emendation is accepted. In the original-spelling version we get 'spannell'd', 'spanel' or 'spannel' being an old form of 'spaniel' presumed, no doubt, to have been familiar to the compositor, though not current in Shakespeare's time so far as the *OED* is aware.

The point is that the Oxford editors, having accepted the emendation and printed 'spaniel'd' in the modern version, have to invent a likely-looking older form as what the compositor misread as 'pannelled'. This is a guess, and a 'silent alteration' – and it is not easy to see that a modern reader is better-off with it than he would be with Hinman's photographs and a modern edition to tell him or her how the original 'pannelled' has been altered to 'spaniel'd'.

3. The most famous crux of all is in *Henry V*, when it is said of the dying Falstaff that 'his Nose was as sharpe as a Pen, and a Table of greene fields.' Theobald's emendation is widely though by no means universally accepted, and occurs in the Oxford modern version as 'a babbled', in the 'original' as 'a babeld' – again an attempt to reproduce the manuscript reading a compositor might have misread as 'a Table'. I don't know that every expert would think this a probable misreading, but it is in any case pure conjecture, and argues back from Theobald's bright guess – which took little account of the peculiarities of secretary hand – to a version which looks more plausible and scientific. No doubt the whole matter will be argued out in the missing *Textual Companion*, which, as we see from the bits and pieces of it sent out in advance, devotes so much grave argument to the text of 'Shall I die' that it is sure to be very expansive on rather larger issues.

4. At the beginning of the third act of *The Tempest* Ferdinand remarks that 'these sweet thoughts, do euen refresh my labours,/ Most busie lest, when I doe it.' Much ink has been expended on this difficulty, which Oxford-modern resolves by printing 'busil'est' – an emendation duly defended in Stephen Orgel's excellent single-play Oxford version ('my thoughts of Miranda are most active when I am busiest at my work'). The Oxford-original gives 'busielest' as what the compositor or possibly the scribe misread or wrongly divided in an attempt to make sense

where there seemed to be none. There is of course no guarantee, and some would say 'lest' means 'least', while others might give up and say there is here, as elsewhere, an indeterminable corruption: that, as anybody who has ever read proof knows perfectly well, minds wander, and it is sometimes impossible to explain how things came to be as they are. But the original-spelling editor is obliged to produce a rational fake.

5. The Oxford editors have decided that the differences between the Quarto and Folio versions of *King Lear* are so considerable that they must treat them as two separate plays: they therefore print them as two separate versions, *The History of King Lear* (Quarto) and *The Tragedy of King Lear* (Folio). This is one of their bolder innovations, but at present I am interested in what happens when the two versions differ only slightly and not, on the face of it, as the result of revision. Here is what Kent says about Oswald in the Quarto:

> . . . such smiling roges
> As these, like Rats oft bite those cords in twaine,
> Which are to intrencht, to vnloose . . .

In the Folio this is:

> such smiling rogues as these,
> Like Rats oft bite the holly cords a twaine,
> Which are to intrince, t'vnloose . . .

Since they give both versions, the editors naturally have both 'intrencht' and 'intrince' in the original-spelling text; in the modernized version they have 'entrenched' (Quarto) and 'intrinse' (Folio). But it is quite difficult to believe that these are independent versions, or that one is an improvement made in revision. The holy cords must always have been 'too intrinse' and never 'too entrenched', since the rats are biting at knots that have dug themselves into something. The Quarto must be wrong, perhaps because the compositor or proof-reader changed an unfamiliar to a familiar word; and the editors, pursuing their idea of two independent texts, have given canonical status to a sophistication.

'Silent alteration' would here have made a small point against the independence theory, or at any rate complicated it. Once again we shall have to see how the *Textual Companion* argues the matter, or consult the single-volume edition, not yet published. It will also, no doubt, offer explanations for pastiche stage directions. It certainly shouldn't be supposed that this old-spelling edition remains very close to the original, and in the absence of annotation in the volume itself the reader who hasn't got the *Companion* will always be uncertain, even when the spelling of everything looks reassuringly Elizabethan, as to what is editorial and what is not.

These complete editions are alike in their sparing provision of ancillary material, and the passages I've been discussing are of course random samples, for hundreds of such cases exist. The modern-spelling version, like many of its rivals in the market, is content to provide bare texts, rather handsomely printed though in double columns, plus a general introduction, a list of contemporary allusions to Shakespeare, and 17 illustrations, many though not all of them perfectly familiar. The general introduction includes a short Life of Shakespeare, a section on the drama and theatre of his time, a brief survey of the early printing of the plays, and a final section called 'The Modern Editor's Task', which usefully indicates the remarkable variety of problems set by the different sorts of copy used when the plays were printed, but also raises the question as to when variation between two Jacobean versions becomes so great that it is best to think of them as distinct and independent.

This is the point at which the Oxford editors have been boldest. In *Hamlet* there is a Quarto of authority, probably set for the most part from Shakespeare's own papers, which contains 230 lines not in the Folio version of 1623, and does not contain 80 more that are in the Folio. Since the latter was set mostly from a theatrical manuscript, the editors regard it as a revision of the Quarto which Shakespeare presumably authorized. Not feeling that they could print the longer early version as well as the slightly abbreviated Folio one, they have used the latter. Formerly editors following F have included the Q parts, but here they are printed as an appendix to the play, on the ground that if you put them in you have a composite that was never performed. The editors seem proud of this decision, though it means that their text no longer includes some famous verse from the opening scene and the Closet scene, a lot of Osric, and the whole of the final soliloquy, 'How all occasions do inform against me . . .'

We may well applaud this move as brave and logical, and it is true that modern editors tend to err on the side of timidity: yet there is something to be said against it. The habit of editors is understandably to climb back as far as possible towards the version they think had the final approval of the poet; they know very well that the best they can hope for is a rough approximation, but, given a choice between an early version and a version used in Shakespeare's lifetime and possibly under his direction, they will, if forced to choose, choose the latter, even if the reason for the cuts is uncertain (since the Folio version is extremely long without additions from Q, the reason is unlikely to have been simply performance time; a net cut of 150 lines would save only ten or twelve minutes, and by the same arithmetic the remaining 3900 lines would occupy around four and a half hours; to get it done on a winter afternoon at the Globe you would need to cut another two hours of it, roughly half the play).

However, the real objection to leaving out the bits of the first scene and the Fortinbras soliloquy is simply that they belong to *our Hamlet*. The problem is one that comes up in Biblical studies: it is recognized for instance that two independent and mutually contradictory versions have been combined in the opening passages of Genesis, but the canonical Genesis is the one we have, not the disentangled fragments. They are, we may say, too intrinse to unloose; they are entrenched in tradition and have for millennia been one book and not more. The Oxford editors profess amazement at the timidity of their predecessors, all save one, who was brave enough to put the intrusive Q material into square brackets. G. R. Hibbard, editor of the Oxford single-volume *Hamlet*, argues strongly that the Folio was printed from a fair copy made by the author himself; naturally he would make changes, some slight, as he worked his way through, and 'the cuts and additions seem to be parts of a definite policy designed to make the play more accessible to theatregoers in general by giving it a more direct and unimpeded action, pruning away some of its verbal elaborations, and smoothing out its more abrupt transitions.' But he admits that many of the changes seem not to further this cause, and it is obvious that the most striking of F's additions, the comments about the boy actors, didn't exactly promote direct and unimpeded action. Hibbard also relegates the Q parts of the opening scene, and the great soliloquy, to an appendix. We are being told to get used to a new *Hamlet*.

The whole question of the text of *Hamlet* is horribly complex, and the editors must have been tempted to print Q as well as F, but they decided that it would be 'extravagant' to do so, and forced to choose, chose the more 'theatrical' version. However, they made an exception for *King Lear*, because in that case the differences between the two versions affect the story-line, especially in the last two acts. A tendency to think of this play as extant in two versions has been growing of late. The arguments are extremely technical, as several books have recently shown, but the immediate question is whether readers of such plain texts as these will benefit much from the editors' decision. They may not be very interested in the conduct of the military operations which lead up to the deaths of Cordelia and the King – as Albany says of the death of Edmund, 'That's but a trifle here' (both texts). It is a perpetual irritation to scholars that so many people still think of these plays as they first came on them in such editions as the old Globe, and it is their pardonable professional deformity to exaggerate the differences superior information can impose. This doesn't mean that editors should simply mark up the texts of other editors, only that the scope for sensible change is less than it pleases them to believe. Bowers was right to warn his colleagues that the incredible refinement of bibliographical technique in our time might not succeed in making many substantial emendations to Shakespeare's text, and it is worth remembering that Hinman's work on the printing of the Folio, which made available vast quantities of new information about the way it was put together, the habits of various compositors, etc. didn't, so far as I know, establish or make certain a single new reading.

The principal effort of the main Oxford editors has gone into the text. Each play, in both original and modern spelling, is given a page of bland appreciative comment ('In *Titus Andronicus*, as in his early history plays, Shakespeare is at his most successful in the expression of grief and the portrayal of vigorously energetic evil'; in *Romeo and Juliet* 'Shakespeare's mastery over a wide range of verbal styles combines with his psychological perceptiveness to create a richer gallery of memorable characters than in any of his earlier plays,' etc.). It is claimed that the chronological order of composition has been freshly established, but the evidence isn't available here, and will, when it appears, chiefly concern the order of the earlier plays. Some may think it a nuisance to have the second and third parts of *Henry VI* before the first part, with *Titus* in between: it was sensible of Heminge and Condell to give them in the usual order. *Pericles*, a special case because it survives only in a quarto which is dependent on memorial reconstruction, and does not appear in the First Folio, is the kind of challenge the editors most enjoy. They offer a 'reconstructed' text in the modern-spelling volume and a diplomatic reprint in the original-spelling, which excuses them from the job of inventing Elizabethan-compositor's spellings.

The ancillary material in the original-spelling version is ident-ical with that in the modern version, except for an impressive essay on 'The Spelling and Punctuation of Shakespeare's Time' by Vivian Salmon. It is mostly what it says it is, but it is also a defence of the original-spelling version, suggesting that the funny appearance of the old spelling is less off-putting than Professor Wells supposed in 1979. As far as can be told, Shakespeare was himself a fanciful speller ('scilens' for 'silence') and despite some efforts to control them the compositors made almost as free; certainly they added letters to fill lines, substituted letters they had for letters they had temporarily run out of, and so on. Sometimes they can be identified by their orthographical habits. Nor were they the only re-spellers; occasionally they worked from copy prepared by a scribe, notably the well-known Ralph Crane, who also had his own way with a text; and there were proof correctors, who perhaps added their pennyworth. But Ms Salmon is still alert to the evidence for genuine Shakespearian spellings, and hopes that when fully armed with the *Textual Companion* as well as 'a critical old-spelling edition' we shall join in the game of identifying 'patterns of Shakespearian orthography'. Well, perhaps. At least if we make ourselves aware of spelling conventions we can judge for ourselves 'the meanings and the forms which Shakespeare and his fellow actors found appropriate to a printed text, unaffected by the cumulative modernizations of generations of editors'. 'The general reader' is included in this invitation, though it is not explained why he would be worse-off with Hinman's photographs.

My overall impression is that despite the undoubted learning and skill of the editors the edition suffers in two main ways. First, it is altogether too anxious to surprise us. There may be an argument for calling Falstaff 'Oldcastle' in *1 Henry IV*, and there is certainly an argument against doing so, but it is characteristic of this edition that the former argument prevails.[1] There is a case for calling *2* and *3 Henry VI* *The First Part of the Contention* and *Richard Duke of York*: it isn't a very good case, since by the time *1 Henry VI* was written and so entitled it is evident that the second and third parts had acquired the titles by which they have been known ever since, but these editors have committed themselves to the odder choice of title and of order.

There will doubtless be a vast amount of detailed comment and criticism when the whole operation is completed. At the moment it seems that the single-play volumes and the modern-spelling collection, despite the absence of apparatus and the continual self-advertisement, can hold their own against most opposition. The *raison d'être* of the old-spelling collection is doubtful: for defences of its silent alterations and for readings at present lacking any explanatory support we shall have to wait for the *Textual Companion*. At £50 it is going to be an expensive supplement, but if you want to know exactly what is going on in the Collected Editions you will have to have it. One can't help thinking there were some flaws in the strategic thinking of those who planned this large publishing enterprise.

---

[1] David Bevington, the editor of the single-volume *1 Henry IV* (Oxford), stubbornly calls the character 'Falstaff'.

This *Textual Companion** is described by the publisher as 'an indispensable companion to *The Complete Oxford Shakespeare*', which indeed it is, and it was reasonable to complain, when *The Complete Works* and *The Complete Works: Original Spelling Edition* appeared in 1986 and 1987, that they were badly in need of this third to walk beside them. The *Companion* is a very fine thing, and the publisher is again within his rights to call it 'probably the most comprehensive reference work on Shakespeare textual problems ever assembled in a single volume'.

Its practical disadvantages are too obvious to dwell upon for more than a moment. Weighing about half a stone, it brings the total of pages in this Collected Edition to something over 3500, and the total cost to £170. Not many readers will have desks large enough to do as the editors pleasantly imagine they might, and have all the volumes open at once. Moreover, the annotation is purely textual, and explanatory only when the editors need to justify a reading; so anybody who craves the sort of help to be had from, say, the Arden Shakespeare, or the single-play editions of the Oxford, or even from some rival collected editions such as the Riverside, will need an even larger desk. And we learn from the Preface, with mixed feelings, that the editors have compiled 'a glossarial commentary (at present unpublished)' which will no doubt in due course create further demands on pocket and space.

A rather tetchy review of the *Companion*-less volumes of the *Complete Works* (see above) complained at some length about the Original Spelling edition, partly because it represented what I took to be an unexplained change of editorial policy (there are arguments against such an edition, some of which the senior editor had quite recently endorsed); and partly because justification for some of its readings – 'fake antiques', as they were unkindly dubbed – was to be withheld until the appearance of this ancillary volume, only a few scraps of which had been sent to reviewers.

As one would expect, the *Companion* learnedly defends its choices in these and the hundreds of other places where choice is

* *William Shakespeare: A Textual Companion*, by Stanley Wells and Gary Taylor, with John Jowett and William Montgomery (Oxford University Press)

an editorial necessity; and emendations for an 'original spelling' edition require some imaginative exercises in Jacobean spelling. Still, it is a fair guess that the principal reason for having an original-spelling edition after all was that it made the business of explaining and defending editorial choices and emendations rather less clumsy for the editor, though at the cost of making the edition as a whole much harder to use by the reader.

However, it seems right to stop carping, for a while at any rate. The editors have thought hard about their policies and, conscious of their many arrogant and intemperate predecessors, explicitly disclaim infallibility. They point out that successful as well as erroneous work in this field almost invariably calls for correction, and, though quite firm in their treatment of other scholars, they avoid what Johnson called 'the acrimony of a scholiast' and generally preserve a civil tone. 'No edition of Shakespeare can or should be definitive ... Our own edition ... is inevitably not only fallible but arbitrary.' Gary Taylor's General Introduction carefully explains why this is so.

It does a great deal more than that, tracing with learning and amenity the history of editorial interferences from the moment when Shakespeare's 'plot' and his 'foul papers' were transcribed for the prompt book, licensed by the Master of the Revels as the Lord Chamberlain's deputy, annotated by the prompter, and divided into actors' parts. Publication, whether in authorized or unauthorized editions, or in the Folio collection of 1623, involved further interference, sometimes by scribes and always by composi- tors. Modern editors have to consider not only the work of all their learned predecessors but, much more importantly, the probable character of the lost manuscript material, a ghostly presence behind the early printed versions. To this end, they study with extraordinary minuteness the habits of particular scribes and compositors – journeymen now known and even loved for their idiosyncrasies, though for the most part named only by letters of the alphabet. To edit Shakespeare you need to know a great deal about contemporary conditions in the theatre and in the printing-house. And then you must make and defend firm de- cisions.

The Oxford editors do so. For example, they have decided that when they think they have detected an original of theatrical provenance (for instance, a text printed from a prompt book), they should choose it as their control-text. So they choose the Folio rather than the Second Quarto text of *Hamlet*: which is why, in their text, they omit the last of Hamlet's soliloquies, 'How all occasions do inform against me,' and some other well-loved lines. 'We do not wish to pretend,' they demurely admit, 'that this is the only rational choice; but we do insist that a choice has to be made, and that editors and readers must live with the consequences.'

Readers may very occasionally find it hard to do so – for instance, when Falstaff disappears, or rather turns into Sir John Oldcastle, since it is known that in early performances (though not in any printed form of the plays) that is what he was called. Oldcastle's descendants protested, and the consequence was the presumably unique disclaimer in the Epilogue to *2 Henry IV*. The decision to do away with Falstaff is characteristic of a certain archaeological rigour in the editors' procedures. Of course they are right to say that if we use their work we must live with their decisions, but it may simply be too late for most of us to start thinking of Falstaff as Oldcastle, and we may even find reasons for refusing to do so. There is a possible view of the plays, never considered here, and perhaps thought merely sentimental, that gives some weight to what they have become (especially when the change happened so early) as well as to what they originally were.

Another editorial decision, defended at length in the General Introduction, goes against the weight of tradition in supposing that Shakespeare, like other authors, sometimes revised his own plays, though not for publication. Of the six plays which exist in forms such that authorial revision may be suspected, one – *King Lear* – is included in this edition in both variant forms. *Hamlet* might have been treated likewise but for considerations of space. The editors are here again acting on examined convictions, though admitting they may be wrong. And it is true that the plays in question are, as usually printed, cobbled together in forms that lack historical justification. In the Folio version of *Lear* no servant brings Gloucester flax and whites of eggs to apply to his bleeding face, and if we are as severe as these editors, and if we want to keep that moment (Peter Brook, for example, didn't), we have really to accept a version of the play that lacks over a hundred lines found only in the Folio.

The General Introduction ably defends these editorial principles, and along the way gives a very lucid and engaging account of Shakespearian textual problems. It is followed by a minute examination of the canon and its chronology, an impressive blend of history and statistical analysis, right up to the minute in these and other respects, which weighs all the evidence and most of the methods by which it has been and might be analysed. The learned have laboured at these problems for over two centuries, and here receive proper tribute. We probably now have a clearer notion of the order of the plays, and the nature of Shakespeare's collaborations, than ever before. There is still room for disagreement about various assumptions, and even for dissent on matters of principle, but the material for argument, against as well as for, is set out here.

These prefatory considerations take up a quarter of the space, the remainder being devoted to textual annotation of the plays themselves. There is bound to be something in the treatment of almost any Shakespeare play that will upset somebody, whether the cause is the general position on the nature of the text, or just irritating individual readings. Such quarrels will often be about plays which are more interesting to scholars than to the world at large – for example, the second and third parts of *Henry VI*, which we are now invited to refer to as *The First Part of the Contention* and *Richard Duke of York* – *1 Henry VI* comes later, after *Titus Andronicus*. The two parts of *Henry IV* are similarly split by *The Merry Wives*, which shows how fiercely attentive to chronology we are required to be.

For simplicity's sake, the following remarks on individual textual decisions will be confined to some of those about which queries were raised in the review of 21 May 1987. The 'Armegaunt Steede' of *Antony and Cleopatra* I,v,47 (wrongly given as I, iv, 47 in that review) became, in the old-spelling edition, 'Arme-iaunct' and in the modern version 'arm-jaunced'. We are now told why one mysterious word is replaced by another: disliking all existing attempts to explain 'arm-gaunt', the Oxford editors point out that Shakespeare used the word 'jaunce' several times. *OED* says it means '?To make (a horse) prance up and down'. 'The sense is good,' say the editors confidently, 'implying that the horse that Antony "soberly" mounted was exhausted by being ridden by one in armour or by its own armour.' This seems no better than the rejected explanations of 'arm-gaunt' – such as 'lean with much war service'. Antony is only just getting on to the animal; he is leaving Egypt to join in a war, but his army hasn't recently been in action, and in fact the horse has no obvious reason to be tired, and doesn't seem to be, neighing so prodigiously that what Alexas is saying to Antony is drowned.

The original epithet is surely more likely to have meant 'power-ful' or 'ready for battle' or even just 'wearing armour' than 'worn out by fighting'. However, having chosen 'jaunced', the editors can without much difficulty find scholarly reasons for printing the brand new Jacobean word 'iaunct' in their text. In the nature of the case this kind of thing must often recur in such an edition. Theobald's celebrated 'babbled of green fields' in *Henry V*, which licenses the editors to print 'babeld', is not even discussed.

Another and possibly more serious problem arises from the two texts of Lear, and specifically from the two versions of Kent's speech about Oswald in II,ii, where the Quarto has him speaking of rats biting cords that are 'to intrencht, to vnloose' and the Folio gives us 'holy cords' that are 'to intrince, t'vnloose'. The review last May argued that the cords can never have been called too 'entrenched' – they must always have been too 'intrinse', since the idea is of biting through something that cannot be untied, not of digging something out by gnawing at it. The clear implication is that the Quarto reading is corrupt. But following their decision to treat Q and F as independent texts, the editors do not feel obliged to consider the two versions together, and the *Companion*, quite logically, has no note at all on 'intrencht'. This silence gives canonical status to what must be a sophistication, perhaps introduced by a compositor who couldn't read, or didn't under-stand, the unusual word 'intrinse'. A director favouring the Q text might therefore count on their editorial blessing if he stuck to 'entrenched', wrong as it almost undoubtedly is.

We might also ask whether it is likely that Shakespeare ever referred in this passage only to 'those cords', as the Quarto has it, making the cords 'holly' (holy) only later: the metaphor surely needs 'holy' to do its work, and one might think it had been there from the beginning. But the only editorial comment on 'holly' is by way of defending it as a spelling of 'holy'.

These may seem small matters, but, properly considered, they show how much can be at stake in the handling of detail, and how more is required of editors than bibliographical and palaeographical know-how. And, as I've remarked, these editors insist that decisions once taken – such as the decision to have two versions of *Lear* – must be carried out unwaveringly. They will have their cost.

To an extent one can't really suggest in a review of this kind the Oxford editors, tearing like a hurricane across the terrain of the Complete Works, have altered many familiar features. If they still sometimes seem over-bold, the laborious and civilized arguments of the *Companion* volume should exempt them from the charge of having been simply *épatants*, though the suspicion lingers that they have been capable, all else being equal, of choosing the more spectacular alternative. And the question remains as to the practicality of the whole vast edition. We can only suppose, since everybody concerned with it is highly professional, that its bulk and its price have been preferred to alternatives after due consideration; once a decision was made they stuck to it, except when, somewhere along the way, they changed their minds about Original Spelling.

London Review of Books, 21 May 1987 & 21 April 1988

Shakespeare for the Eighties

From time to time one hears somebody asking how it can be that the output of Shakespeare studies actually increases every year; why don't they exhaust the subject? Nothing could more clearly reveal the questioner as a layperson. Within the clerical institution that concerns itself with these matters, Shakespeare remains a privileged text. A few weeks back the British playwright Trevor Griffiths said to me on a television talk show that there were at least thirty (or was it three hundred?) British dramatists alive today who were better than Shakespeare. It was his way of establishing his status as an extreme heretic. We all respect Mr Griffiths, of course, but if he wants to change anything he will have to do better than that. He might as well walk down Piccadilly with a placard announcing The End.

Because very large numbers of people are compelled to study Shakespeare, or to go through the motions of doing so, many thousands of pastors are gainfully occupied in helping them to do so, or seeming to be doing so. A proportion of these workers must get tenure and improve their position in the hierarchy; they can do so only by writing books. These books must at least appear to say something new, and there is an endless sequence of new fashions, each generating the next, which develops or challenges its predecessor. The mode of the Seventies was predominantly feminist; the first two books under review offer a corrective response to extremist versions of that fashion; I can now comment on the revisionist position, and anybody who wants to can comment on mine. This is known in the profession as a Shakespearian Research Opportunity, and it helps to explain why people who wonder why we never exhaust the subject are simply working with the wrong model.

Linda Bamber's book *Comic Women, Tragic Men** begins with a brief history of feminist criticism since Kate Millett's break-through in 1970, and runs through the list of feminist Shakespearians since that date. Lisa Jardine does the same thing,† for each wishes in her own way to qualify and correct the work of the pioneers. Both take issue with Juliet Dusinberre, whose *Shakespeare and the Nature of Women* (1975) discovered that the myriad-minded one was deep into 'Renaissance feminism', and Coppelia Kahn, who found that Shakespeare's maleness inescapably affected his drama, which is nevertheless worth attention as a representation of his masculine anxieties about identity (*Man's Estate: Masculine Identity in Shakespeare*, 1981). Between the extremes of a feminist Shakespeare and a male chauvinist Shakespeare there is obviously much room for manoeuvre; and the existence of this new critical tradition also means that one need not dig very deep into the bottomless deposits of pre-feminist criticism. Bamber's allusions to the androcentric era before 1970 tend to be selective and cursory; it seems symptomatic that she attributes John Holloway's excellent book *The Story of the Night* (1963) to John Hollander, an entirely different poet-scholar. It is as if, over millennia, the frailty of paper or of scribes had merged into one the identities of two remote scholiasts.

Bamber's revisionism takes the following form. She sees Shakespeare as 'a man who takes the woman's part' in comedy but not in tragedy, an apparent incoherence she is ready to explain away. Of course all the plays have a masculine perspective; but that doesn't mean they must be sexist. Although 'men must write as men and women as women', they can do so without assuming superiority over the opposite sex. This seems sensible, and will not bring demonstrators on to the streets; it becomes critically useful only when expressed as a requirement that authors of either sex must grant to their opposites 'the privileges of the Other'.

* Linda Bamber, *Comic Women, Tragic Men: A Study of Gender and Genre in Shakespeare* (Stanford University Press)

† Lisa Jardine, *Still Harping on Daughters: Women and Drama in the Age of Shakespeare* (New York: Barnes and Noble)

Shakespeare granted women the privileges of the Other in comedy, but not in tragedy. He wasn't a feminist, for to him the Self was male, but feminists ought to like him because he respects gender Otherness. When the opposition of Self and Other can be called a 'dialectic' you get a new critical approach. On this subject Bamber is candid. She is very much against 'projection', the idea that the Other is a mere 'projection of that which has been repudiated by the Self', because if that were so she would have very little to say: 'It offers me too short a ride. The idea of dialectic simply takes me further.'

This is a bold and lively book whenever it is dealing with something that will take the author further. Thus it is true of some of the tragedies that there is a 'firm connection' between self-hatred and misogyny. When this connection is harder to spot, or harder to develop, as in *Macbeth* and *Coriolanus*, there must be something wrong with the play. Thus Hamlet resents the loss of the old world he was comfortable in, and his misogyny is his anger against the Other for taking it away. 'The sexual atmosphere of *Hamlet* improves' when Hamlet, on his return to Denmark, ceases to doubt his own 'manliness'. Coriolanus, however, 'loses our interest' precisely because he has no such moment. (That 'our', I must suppose, issues from my Other.) Incidentally, Hamlet purges his sexuality of aggression at the moment when he steals into the cabin of Rosencrantz and Guildenstern and makes off with their royal commission: 'in the dark / Groped I to find them, had my desire, / Fingered their packet . . .'

Here are a few more revelations offered by the dialectic of Self and Other. 'The flip side of [Antony's] romanticism is his Roman instinct to limit relations with the Other.' In marrying Octavia he is choosing 'a *limited* relation with the Other', whereas Cleopatra, though of course she also represents the Other, represents more of it. Bamber is most energetic when confronting difficulties which had not been thought to exist until she arrived with her dialectic. For instance, in the 'Romances' you can say that 'the feminine Other is lost and found or dies and is reborn.' Yes, but *The Tempest* is usually thought of as one of the Romances, and it contains no Return of the Feminine. There is no suggestion that Prospero's wife, only glancingly alluded to in the play as a

171

necessary condition for the existence of Miranda, is going to show up. The answer to this brand new problem is that the mother's absence is 'a central fact in the world of the play'. It makes for a very unhappy sexual atmosphere, and puts Prospero in some danger of committing incest with Miranda, but his desires are displaced onto Caliban. For him, the Other is irredeemably lost.

The play in which all this is going on is said by Bamber to have a geographical location 'near Bermuda' and a perpetually mild climate. Since in Shakespeare's play the island is obviously in the Mediterranean, and the weather over the three hours of its duration includes the terrible storm from which it derives its title and much collecting of firewood, Bamber is talking about something as absent as Prospero's wife; but between absence and presence there are well-known dialectical possibilities.

Lisa Jardine is a historian of longer reach, and what bothers her about recent feminist criticism of Shakespeare is that it is insufficiently careful about the ample historical record of the position of women in Shakespeare's time. So she provides a vigorous report on this matter; in due time it is bound to qualify any feminist hypothesis that is at all susceptible of historical control. She lends no support to either of the extreme positions – that Shakespeare's 'vision of women transcends the limits of his time and sex', or that he was entirely chauvinistic. She doesn't think Shakespeare was holding up a mirror to the condition of women, or that he had strong views about the need to change it. Very generally she supposes that the drama of the period shows a persistent interest in female character because of 'the patriarchy's unexpressed worry' about social change in general.

Still Harping on Daughters starts, however, with an amusing and important essay on the use of boy actors in female roles, a custom attacked by the Puritans as conducing to perverse lust of various kinds, and also as forbidden by Scripture. These divines were probably right on both counts; the playwrights exploited the possibilities of the double meanings implicit in 'the woman's part', wrote up 'the wanton female boy', 'the lovely garnish of a boy', and so on. Shakespeare gave his boys dressed as girls dressed as boys gay names like Ganymede and Sebastian (the nom de guerre of Julia in *Two Gentlemen of Verona*). Observe also that the best stage image of the master-mistress is the confrontation of the twins Viola and Sebastian in *Twelfth Night*, boy-girl and ephebe.

These charming ambiguities were honoured in the metropolitan culture of Jacobean London, which is more than can be said for ordinary women. Since the only free choice they had was in sex, all stepping out of line was likely to be represented as evidence of sexual rapacity, which is why there are so many insatiate women in the drama of the time. Jardine makes the interesting and possibly controversial point that social change had the effect of constricting women, not, as the books more usually say, of liberating them. The suppression of Roman Catholicism cut them off from the cult of the Virgin and the female saints. The vaunted humanist education offered to women of high rank was only an adornment, and prevented them from taking up forms of study that might have equipped them to seize the opportunities that were opening up for social and political emancipation. They tended to learn Greek, rather than the still useful Latin; it kept them out of mischief. They must not display eloquence: 'The woman of fluent speech is never chaste.'

The need to keep women down engendered the myth of their dangerous sexuality. Thus, says Jardine, a Jacobean audience would certainly start by thinking Desdemona's desire for Othello was an indication of 'driving sensuality', and their suspicions would not be allayed by the scene in which, waiting for the return of her angry husband, she remarks with apparent irrelevance that 'This Lodovico is a proper man'; we might think it a characteristic naiveté, but they would see at once the marks of 'sensual strain', so that Iago's reading of her propensities was after all not far from the right one.

The almost superstitious Jacobean fear of female sexuality has of course been noticed before, but Jardine is, so far as I know, the first writer to relate it firmly to a substantial reduction in the liberty of women. She demonstrates with much legal detail that they became more and more the mere instruments of patriarchy. The priority of financial interests tended to diminish what we should think of as normal family affection, and the implications for widows and children were sometimes cruel. She thinks Hamlet's disgust at his mother's remarriage derives from the consideration

173

that it virtually disinherited him – if Gertrude had another son, as in the absence of contraceptives she very well might, he would lose everything. And indeed Hamlet was so offended by his mother's going to bed with Claudius that it might not seem unreasonable to argue that a little brother would upset him even more.

Perhaps his reason for not saying so was that the notion of Gertrude 'honeying and making love over the nasty sty' was so disgusting that he shirked following out all of its consequences. However, he does not say so, and he does have the king's assurance, for what it is worth, that he would get the nomination for the elective kingship next time. The first task of historical scholarship is to attend to what the text invites us to attend to, and it doesn't invite our attention to Claudius, Junior.

There are a few similarly dubious points. Can *All's Well* be used as evidence of a general belief that one night of love was enough to secure conception? Shakespeare's source story prudently allows for quite a few. But the odd quibble with Jardine doesn't alter the fact that in all manner of ways – in discussions of contraception, pregnancy, perinatal mortality, clothes symbolism, etc., hers is a more than useful book. The large question why increased oppression of women took place under a female monarch is left to the end. We are told that Elizabeth, like Mary Queen of Scots and Lady Jane Grey, was 'a pawn in the English royal inheritance struggle', and that the elaborate symbolism that surrounded her made her sex insignificant, reducing her to a mere 'token woman'. Much might be said against this view and others here expressed, but this is a book that ought to have beneficial effects.

Lydia Pasternak Slater clearly believes that a woman can write about Shakespeare without being a feminist.* She ingeniously follows up on an idea itself not new, namely that to know what was actually done on the Elizabethan stage one should not only look at existing stage directions but infer directions from the dialogue; and, her strongest point, look closely at Bad Quartos.

* Ann Pasternak Slater, *Shakespeare the Director* (New York: Barnes and Noble)

These were unauthorized editions of the plays, usually put together from actors' memories. They tended to put in remembered moves as well as remembered lines ('Enter Juliet somewhat fast, and embraceth Romeo', or 'wounded, with an arrow in his neck') and one can often suppose that these details were in the original.

Working with these editions, and scanning Shakespeare's sources as well as the canonical texts, Ms Slater makes some shrewd inferences about performance, as when she deduces from the dialogue the necessary facial expressions of Angelo at the dénouement of *Measure for Measure*: relief, a smirk, rising confidence, anger. She sometimes seems to use too many documents, sometimes dwells on the obvious, and occasionally is too speculative (it seems unlikely that the reason for making silence a female virtue was the uncertain voices of boy players, who had large parts as well as small ones). But *Shakespeare the Director* is, in its intellectual style, quite a dashing book, though its passion for facts may make it seem old-fashioned – more akin to the work of the veteran scholar Muriel Bradbrook, whose papers are about to appear in several volumes, of which the first is *The Artist and Society in Shakespeare's England*.*

Bradbrook's essays here fill the interstices of her major books in the field. They have range of reference rather than depth of interpretation. Her essay on *The Taming of the Shrew* contrasts rather poignantly with the sort of reading given it by younger women, for her concern is not to argue that the piece is chauvinist or ironical, but to relate it to the tradition of Shrew literature, to see it in what is offered as an illuminating literary context. Thus there are sixteenth-century plays in which women dominate feeble husbands: 'I carry the whip,' says one of them. Shakespeare's play is indeed a novelty in that it makes the husband the tamer. A further measure of her disregard for fashion is her treatment of Jacques Derrida, rather mysteriously described as 'not a literary critic but an anthropologist', and of Paul Ricoeur, whose theory of metaphor is with equal obscurity made responsible for John

* M. C. Bradbrook, *The Artist and Society in Shakespeare's England: The Collected Papers of Muriel Bradbrook*, Volume I (New York: Barnes and Noble)

Barton's *The Greeks*. Those who reject the fashionable *in toto* rarely think it worth their time to find out what it is they are rejecting.

Nothing could be more traditional than a layman's book on the sonnets. Robert Giroux, a well-informed layman, offers an autobiographical interpretation and a facsimile edition of the Quarto of 1609.* He writes as a publisher with much experience of poets, some of it painful. People who are cautious about treating the sonnets as referring to the poet's life in just the same way as the poems in, say, Robert Lowell's *Notebook* refer to his, are described as 'absurd'.

Giroux has a go at most of the cruxes in which these poems abound. For him, all save the 'mortal moon' sonnet (107) were written about 1594–1595, and they are more or less in the right order. Southampton is the young man. Of the opening sequence of 'marriage' sonnets it is maintained that they began as a commission, but that around no. 10, where the poet first refers to himself as 'I', there is a great change of tone, the young man now being his 'love'. Giroux does not ask why the 'thou' of the opening sonnets changes to 'you' at no. 13, and in nos. 15–17, yet it is an oddity, for Shakespeare was normally careful about tutoyer; and it is even odder that 'you' should coincide with calling the addressee 'my dear love'. It is one more tiny obscurity in a sequence that remains a good deal more obscure than Giroux admits.

These early sonnets, in Giroux's view, were meant to persuade Southampton to marry Lady Elizabeth de Vere. They failed, but got Shakespeare a generous patron. Giroux rather likes the story, as old as Nicholas Rowe's edition of 1709, that the nobleman gave the poet £1,000 to make a purchase, assessing the modern equivalent as £20,000; actually it must be about eight times as much as that, and the story is no more probable than many other eighteenth-century tales of Shakespeare.

As to the identity of the Dark Lady, he rejects A. L. Rowse's Emilia and G. B. Harrison's Lucy Negro, saying that somebody called Rosaline is at least as likely (because of *Love's Labour's Lost*).

* Robert Giroux, *The Book Known as Q: A Consideration of Shakespeare's Sonnets* (New York: Atheneum)

Since Chapman was a bad poet, he can't be the Rival; it must be Marlowe. (But Chapman, one might be allowed to believe, was *not* a bad poet.) Some of Giroux's lesser inferences are idle or simply wrong. 'Speak of my lameness and I straight will halt' would lose its force if Shakespeare was actually lame. The argument that 'a widow's eye' in Sonnet 9 refers to Southampton's mother is absurd, since the point is to ask whether the young man is determined to remain unmarried in order never to leave a widow, not in order not to have a mother.

Some of the finest sonnets escape all mention ('They that have power to hurt' has given autobiography hunters a particularly bad time). The magnificent No. 138 is avoided, except for a reference to its early publication in 1599. In that year Shakespeare was thirty-five, and could plausibly admit that his 'years were past the best', a claim that might seem a little more affected in a thirty-year-old, as Giroux conceives him to have been when writing all save the 'mortal Moon' sonnet to celebrate South-ampton's release from prison on the accession of James I. I suppose books of this kind are meant for a specialized kind of addict, who will not mind the omissions, the forced readings, and the lack of genuine interest in the poems themselves. Readers who have such an interest are referred to Stephen Booth's *Essay on Shakespeare's Sonnets* and his edition of the sonnets, works of which Giroux unfortunately has little good to say.[1]

Another branch of Shakespeare publishing seems to flourish even in the hardest times: editions of the plays. Kenneth Palmer's *Troilus and Cressida*** has been on the way for many years, once destroyed by fire, once imperilled by flood, but now it is published as almost the last of the new Ardens, the first having appeared more than thirty years ago. Some early volumes show signs of wear, and in any case all are not equally good, but this is obviously the best multi-volume edition in existence, and Harold Jenkins's

---

[1] *Essay on Shakespeare's Sonnets* (Yale University Press, 1969); *Shakespeare's Sonnets* (Yale University Press, 1977).

* William Shakespeare, *Troilus and Cressida*, edited by Kenneth Palmer (The Arden Shakespeare; London: Methuen)

monumental *Hamlet*, published last year, should, along with some others, maintain its preeminence for another generation. The style has changed a bit since 1950, when it wasn't even known, for instance, that Jacobean compositors cast off their copy. Textually the Ardens grew more and more refined. Palmer has a vexatious text, and deals with it urbanely, without disputing the conventional wisdom but looking at everything with due care.

By a coincidence this belated Arden is met head-on by the first three volumes of the new Oxford Shakespeare. *Troilus and Cressida* is in the practised hands of Kenneth Muir.* He does not differ from Palmer on textual principles, dates, or indeed anything of importance, though there are, as there must be, different preferences when an editor has to choose between variants and the copy text is suspect. Muir's introduction is terser, and his annotation scantier, but a keen student might conceivably wish to use both of these editions. *The Taming of the Shrew* also issues from an old hand, H. J. Oliver,† and is properly gone into, though with no surprises.

These come with Gary Taylor's *Henry V*,‡ a lively and adventurous volume which, because it takes a part of its text from a quarto generally deemed to be without authority, offers a text different from any other. Taylor is a skilful bibliographer, and his reasons for novelty seem good; no doubt they will be ruthlessly examined in the specialist journals. Meanwhile the ordinary reader will hardly notice any difference. It is reasonable to ask who needs another edition of this kind and on this scale, especially as Cambridge University Press has yet another in preparation. Every edition, I suppose, will add something; and a few may even make more substantial contributions. But for the most part, the novelties will be few and small, especially in editions of relatively uncontroversial plays. The case for *complete* editions is not primarily a scholarly one; it is the need or desire to share the market. But

* William Shakespeare, *Troilus and Cressida*, edited by Kenneth Muir (The Oxford Shakespeare; Oxford University Press)

† William Shakespeare, *The Taming of the Shrew*, edited by H. J. Oliver (The Oxford Shakespeare; Oxford University Press)

‡ William Shakespeare, *Henry V*, edited by Gary Taylor (The Oxford Shakespeare; Oxford University Press)

there is this secondary consideration: it is important that experts should be given opportunities to disagree; how else can we provide subjects for yet more experts? They will adjudicate between old views and think up new ones, all in the privacy of their college studies. Occasionally they will descend into the classroom to instruct the draftees who make all this possible, but who will probably pass out into the world in total ignorance of the difference between Q and F, if not of that between Self and Other.

New York Review of Books, 28 April 1983

IV

Grandeur and Filth

The Victorian Cities

Millions of us still live in Victorian cities; 'the structures outlast the people who put them there', as Messrs Dyos and Wolff observe in the epilogue to their absorbing book,* 'and impose constraints on those who have to adapt them later to their own use'. Their contributors offer some striking images of these constraints. Take, for example, Sybil Baker's cool, minute, and frightful account of Victorian Belfast:

> Belfast's a famous northern town,
> Ships and linen its occupation.
> And the workers have a riot on
> The slightest provocation –

the provocation being, usually, an attempt to repress their sectarian and ethnic 'walks'. Just the situation of Bloody Sunday in Londonderry not too long ago; and on Miss Baker's map there, embattled as now, are Shankhill and the Falls Road.

Other cities, if they have shorter memories and less religion, are still in large part nineteenth-century structures. London, though already in the previous century what Morris called 'the horrible muckheap in which we dwell', took on its modern randomness and enormity. Bagehot, in a famous passage twice quoted in this book, compared it to a newspaper: 'everything is there,

* *The Victorian City: Images and Realities*, edited by H. J. Dyos and Michael Wolff (London: Routledge & Kegan Paul, 2 vols.)

and everything is disconnected'. All possible worlds co-exist in contiguous but discontinuous columns; life and death, wealth and poverty, instantaneously and pointlessly associated. The new city partook of no familiar order, had no apprehensible structure.

Mr Craig quotes a song called 'I can't find Brummagem' – the trouble was not that Birmingham was small or elusive, but that it was everywhere and nowhere. Engels had to work to get some idea of where Manchester was; even now 'the shortest way out of Manchester' is a euphemism for strong drink. And in London he memorably registered the brutal indifference of a city crowd, people not looking at one another, mankind dissolved into monads. That sense of ricocheting off thousands of meaningless urban objects, identified by Walter Benjamin in the experience of Baudelaire, is part of the consciousness of all modern city-dwellers.

L'immonde cité: nothing is better documented than the filth of Victorian cities, unless it is their grandeur. That filth and grandeur should coexist seemed to many the inevitable consequence of Political Economy, of laws as invariant as Newton's. The grand municipal centres celebrated and exploited a system which necessarily packed the poor into slums; the roads and railways required for the conveyance of the middle classes away from such areas occasionally ripped right through them, tearing up the homes and graveyards of the poor, and for a moment offending the newly refined senses of the rich. Meanwhile the sewage of a vast population fell untreated into the rivers. In the summer of 1858 the House of Commons had to suspend its sittings because of the stench from the Thames.

The Victorians took much interest in all these developments; they loved statistics, and compiled them tirelessly; and, as *The Victorian City* sumptuously shows, they also recorded the scene, in all its black majesty, with pencil and camera.[1] They were

[1] The magnificent editing of the volumes is reflected as much in the 434 illustrations – brilliantly chosen and often beautiful in themselves – as in the organization of the thirty-eight essays. G. H. Martin and David Francis contribute an authoritative

* *The Victorians by the Sea*, edited by Howard Grey and Graham Stuart (New York: St Martin's Press)

further aware that cities don't all develop in the same way; Birmingham, as Jane Jacobs says, was inefficient, felicitously so, having achieved industrialization by trial and error, and retained something of its old character – many small workshops, the old sporting traditions of cockfighting and bear-baiting. Manchester was infelicitously efficient – cotton, the first industry to develop mass-production techniques, simply took it over and monstrously specialized it; which is, in Jane Jacobs's view, why Birmingham now thrives and Manchester does not.

Manchester achieved its city status only in 1853, though by then it was the second largest city in England. It was never to be one of the really vast aggregations – in 1890 it was seventeenth in the world, when New York was second and Chicago seventh. But its growth from a town of 24,000 in 1773 to a conurbation of 250,000 in 1850 was startling even in a period of rapid population growth; and the growth was all to one purpose. Now cotton has dwindled away, but urban structures outlast the people who put them there, and to live in modern Manchester is to suffer under the constraints of which Dyos and Wolff speak. There it lies, spilled shapelessly over its almost featureless plain; and around it are its satellites, the smaller mill towns, some of them on the edges of containing hills and moors. Of one of these, Oldham, the reporter sent by the *Morning Chronicle* in 1850 wrote:

> The visitor to Oldham will find it essentially a mean-looking straggling town, built upon both sides and crowning the ridge of one of the outlying spurs which branch

chapter on the Victorian camera. The daguerreotype of the Forties, with an exposure so long that sitters had to wear iron clamps, was a superior replacement for the portrait (in the US it was greeted, by both Morse and Hawthorne, as superannuating the fallible artist, and that included Rembrandt) but it could not be replicated, and Fox Talbot's photographic negative replaced it.

It was, as the authors say, the image of the mass-production techniques of the society it would serve. The wet-plate arrived in the Fifties, cutting exposure time to ten seconds. Photography as art could still hold its own against photography as a means of record, but the Seventies saw celluloid roll film and lightproof cameras. The last step was the development of the two-tone block for newspaper printing. *The Victorians by the Sea** documents the democratization of the beaches, and in so doing uses some exquisite photographs by F. M. Sutcliffe, perhaps the greatest of the photographers, and some interesting 'candid' shots taken on the seashore by Paul Martin, with a camera hidden in a bag.

from the neighbouring 'backbone of England'. The whole place has a shabby underdone look. The general appearance of the operatives' houses is filthy and smouldering [mouldering?] . . . Pieces of dismal waste ground all covered with wreaths of mud and piles of blackened brick and rubbish – separate the mills . . .

Ninety-five years later I was discharged from the service, heaven knows why, in Oldham. I remember a warehouse, in which I was given the regular off-the-peg blue chalkstripe suit of the time, and turned out into what English soldiers call 'civvy street'. For me this was a dismal downhill slope, the Victorian back-to-back houses in a perspective obscured by fog and smoke; on that bald street no blank December day had broken, it could not pierce the dirt. It seemed an allegory; I walked down into a future.

Years later, when I went to work in Manchester, I learned to hate most not the fog and the damp (good for cotton, and thus essential to the city's style) but rather the days of sun, of raw light on a city built for the dark. Like my betters a century earlier I retreated to the Cheshire Fringe and drove to work down those streets which, as Engels noted, enable the rich to pass through, without seeing, the houses of the poor. They had moved steadily southward. At first I thought of living in Victoria Park, now virtually downtown, swamped by 1890; a private suburb of large houses with its own gate and porter, like Rolling Hills in Los Angeles; but now crazy, choked with smoke, with enormous holes in the roads. And so to the south. The prevailing wind blows the smoke northward, and Manchester has the highest rate of chronic bronchitis in the world; so you take your children to the Cheshire suburbs. These places have amazingly high per capita incomes and no pleasures except the television, the car, and the pubs it takes you to.

In its magnificent years Manchester built a great orchestra, a great library, a great university (though it nearly foundered in the first decade from underendowment), and a great newspaper, which has now moved to London and omits the name of the city from its title. Corporate civic wealth is no longer much in evidence; things have changed. But among the features of the city which don't change much one must count the poor. The Irish have lost their place at the bottom of the heap since the West Indians arrived, but the poor still have their quarters, sometimes the old ones.

A few months ago the *Observer* (February 3, 1974) ran a piece by Polly Toynbee headed 'If Engels could see it now', about the district Lower Broughton, which Engels once described after he came from north Germany to live in Manchester in 1842. The houses he wrote about in his book on the *Condition of the Working Class in England in 1844* are still inhabited. The city, having in 1965 declared them unfit, purchased them in 1968, intending to destroy them, but meanwhile it exacted rent. They had no lavatories until three years ago, when a TV programme got some action; before that the buckets were emptied into street drains. No hot water, of course, and no bathroom. The sewers still back up into the kitchens.

Meditating the text of Engels, Mr Marcus reflects that in 1844 the Manchester workers were living in shit. It seems that some of them, in Lower Broughton, still are. When a TV programme or a newspaper momentarily lifts the veil (though never as persistently as the *Morning Chronicle* did in the late 1840s) our suburban calm is ruffled exactly as, again and again, such revelations disturbed the Victorian middle class. We, no more than they, reflect that this wretchedness is directly related to our contentment. We prefer to say that in spite of everything things are much better. We see evidence for, and approve, slow but sure social change. But perhaps, in the early and more explosive years of the city, it was right and reasonable to expect change of quite another kind?

Manchester, it was always agreed, was the most dramatic instance, but to live in a city of some sort was now to be almost everybody's fate or choice. By the end of the century three quarters of the population had moved in, and even at that date housing and sanitation lagged far behind. We read today of what happens when the strip miners move in on a small Wyoming community; the most obvious and disagreeable consequences are always sanitary. This was so to a quite unbelievable degree in the first industrial expansion; for, as George Rosen notes in his sombre essay on 'Disease, Debility and Death' in *The Victorian City*, civic water technology and bacteriology were late nineteenth-century inventions. The consequences of not having them were already well understood in the Forties, when death rates were rising fast; and the desire to do something about the situation was not altogether altruistic. If the poor lived in shit the rich caught their diseases; fevers bred in Tom All Alone's in Southwark struck down the rich across the festering river.

The Victorians were quite early able to prove a direct correlation between bad housing and death rate (infant mortality in Manchester was over 50 per cent, with the usual class spread). But doctors had trouble distinguishing between different sorts of fever and 'malaria', and it took time to sort them out: typhus and typhoid were not properly distinguished till 1870, and the role of the body louse in the former was a discovery of the present century, though sanitation improvements had more or less eliminated the disease before then. Many other communicable diseases were epidemic, including some that killed mostly children and some that were psychiatric in character and so never tabulated by the statisticians. *The Victorian City* adds to Rosen's meticulous account of these matters Anthony S. Wohl's study of the role of the Medical Officer of Health, employed by the middle classes to control a dangerous situation yet constantly hampered by their unwillingness to spend much money in the process. These men continued to assert what was already known: overcrowding means a high death rate. They added that families living and sleeping in one room are likely to fall short of the highest moral standards, and many are the euphemisms for incest, which was still perfectly commonplace when Beatrice Webb was doing her fieldwork. If this news did not stimulate the burghers to action, it may at least have given them a thrill; their covert envy of the unconfined sexuality of the poor is often noted. In one of the oddest and most entertaining chapters Richard L. Schoenwald studies psychoanalytically the motives of the great sanitary reformer Chadwick, and the resistance of the populace to such instruments of civilized discontent as the water closet, which, three centuries after Harington invented it, was still by no means in general use.

The danger here may be that one can make very sophisticated the old naïve assumption that the poor are somehow responsible for their own ills – sexual abandon and a friendly attitude to shit are their 'natural habits' – an expression used by the *Morning*

Chronicle of the Irish. Of course the slums, as Dyos and Reeder explain in a penetrating essay, were essential to capitalist enterprise as reservoirs of casual labour, and as economic counterweight to the suburbs. However feckless, the poor did not actively desire hunger, hard labour, and early death.

It is not, of course, in doubt that they were systematically and minutely exploited. Reading the novelists, or the reports of Mayhew and his fellow investigators, one has some difficulty in resisting the conviction that the class responsible for these exploitations was guilty of monstrous and deliberate cruelty. Bullied and cheated by the masters (the pettier the more brutal), the poor had to contend not only with the rape of their labour but with short weight, adulterated food; one reads of a trade in used tea leaves. Even their pleasures were reduced or adulterated: urban parks replaced the old open spaces, severe fines eliminated talking and singing from the factories.

The documentation of poverty and its indignities reached a new level of public exposure in the famous series of articles run by the *Morning Chronicle* in 1849–50, and collected in *The Victorian Working Class.** Coming at the end of a decade of investigations, the series followed a fashion set by Dickens in the *Daily News.* 'We have allowed them,' said an editorial on the poor, 'to quench their thirst and cook their food with water poisoned with their own excrement.' Readers were shocked; they showed a capacity for reacting to such news as if hearing it for the first time. Similar revelations proved shocking in the reign of Edward VII and even in 1938, when the first evacuation of children from the cities revealed, as forcibly as a railway or motor road, the conditions of life among the poor. The horror soon wears off.

Mayhew was the *Chronicle*'s ace reporter. Parts of his work he incorporated in *London Labour and the London Poor*, others were published three years ago with long and authoritative introductions by E. P. Thompson and Eileen Yeo.[1] Selections from the

---

[1] *The Unknown Mayhew*, edited by E. Yeo and E. P. Thompson (Random House, 1971).

* *The Victorian Working Class: Selections from the Morning Chronicle*, edited and introduced by P. E. Razzell and R. W. Wainwright (London: Frank Cass)

other reporters are now available in *The Victorian Working Class*. They deal with rural labour and with the industrial workers, the 'hands', in the new cities. The reporters lacked Mayhew's gifts and also his opportunities – the weird trades and the fantastic topography of London, 'the attraction of repulsion', as Dickens called it. The provincial scene lacks colour and variety; and the reporters are more committed than Mayhew to the 'system' as an aspect of natural law.

The *Chronicle* led, as might be expected, with Manchester. Work there begins at six, the 'hands' summoned by bells or, later, sirens – still used (and accepted: half- and full-time are called by sirens in the northern game of Rugby League, familiar from David Storey's novel *This Sporting Life*). The engine starts, and the workers are in their places by six; to be late is to be exorbitantly fined. (The fines were among the workers' deepest resentments.) At 8:30 master and man broke for breakfast; at one o'clock for dinner. Work (after the Ten Hour Act) then continued from two to five.

The *Chronicle* represents everybody as reasonably happy with this arrangement, and as well fed and clothed. There were snags, of course: 'Unhappily the bulk of Manchester arose during a period in which . . . master and man more commonly regarded each other as mutual enemies rather than as mutual dependants . . .' A vast new population had to be housed, and they fell into the hands of jerry-building speculators, heedless of amenity or sanitation. The 'constant flux and reflux of poor renders the city hardly a fair test of the social condition created by the factory system.'

Perhaps it did take an Engels to see through such cant, as it took a Dickens to demonstrate that the schools admired by the *Chronicle*'s reporter were merely extensions or agents of the factory system. The reporter does notice that the children of the workers are habitually drugged; day-nurses kept them quiet with opium, which often killed them. For opium, not religion, was the opium of the people. It could be regarded as further evidence of their fecklessness.

It must have been a fear of fecklessness, of 'natural habits', that prompted the almost senseless severity of the masters; for it goes much beyond what they could have thought necessary to the maintenance of profit. David Craig, in a fine essay on 'Songs of the Bleak Age',* argues that the suppression of the old practice of singing at the loom contributed to the formation of a new working-class culture, organized, adversary, and eventually powerful; by 1919 the songs had disappeared and labour was formidably organized.[1]

But in the early days there was a powerful sense, recorded by Mrs Gaskell and the dialect poets described in *The Victorian City* by Martha Vicinus, of a lost happiness, of better times. The new city was toughest on those who remembered something else, who has experienced *Gemeinschaft* and had now to accustom themselves to *Gesellschaft* – a distinction borrowed by J. A. Banks, in another excellent essay in the Dyos-Wolff book, from Ferdinand Tönnies. People had to be kept down; at work the repetitive work-cycle accomplished this, and the pattern was extended as far outside the factory as possible. Which may explain what was often remarked: the peacefulness and reasonableness of the workers, their extraordinary deference. Of course, when they did protest they were violently repressed.

An instance of extra-curricular control is the temperance movement. Pubs, it is true, were often wicked places; there was, especially in dockside pubs, an evil custom of allowing the publican to pay out wages, and since he had a hand in rehiring he saw that most of the money was handed back to him at once. But the pub was also, for all practical purposes, the only community centre of the poor. Brian Harrison, in *The Victorian City*, gives a detailed account of its development, especially in London. There were forty-six pubs in three-quarters of a mile of the Strand; and although landlords like the Duke of Bedford in Bloomsbury improved their estates by cutting down on pubs, they elsewhere grew ever more brilliant with gas and glass, and more diversified:

---

[1] Craig has also a particularly good essay on *Hard Times*, and others on topics remote from the theme of this review. I'm often in deep disagreement, but his book is one of the most serious collections of literary criticism to appear in recent years.

* David Craig, *The Real Foundations: Literature and Social Change* (Oxford University Press)

there were pubs for medical students, prostitutes, actors, lawyers, foreigners, and so on.

These developments occurred in the teeth of the temperance movement, which got going just at the moment of major industrial change, around 1830. Its methods were pretty ruthless: the Band of Hope persuaded children to take the Pledge (I, in my laggard province, was perhaps one of the last children to swear this oath, which I break every day of my life). Temperance was powerfully associated with respectability, always in some measure desired by the upper working class. It mimicked its enemy, the pub, for the temperance society was valuable as a source of companionship, and of advice to newcomers; there were entertainments and soft drinks.

Yet in the Manchester of 1896 there was a pub for every 168 persons (though judging by some of the survivors they were as gloomy as temperance societies, and the ban on singing persists). Temperance prevailed no more absolutely than did the hysterical evangelical crusades launched even by the Catholics ('Get him under the drip of the Precious Blood'). 'Enthusiastic' tendencies were always present among workers, and especially those connected with the weaving trade, but they held out pretty well against middle-class evangelism. Nor, for that matter, did proletarian enthusiasm play much part in the early efforts to organize labour. Chartism was peaceful and reasonable, which, as Engels observed, was why it must fail. There was not even anger, or at any rate useful anger.

What, then, did happen to induce militancy, to encourage the construction of a new culture for the world of *Gesellschaft*? Was it the Hungry Forties? It is now commonly argued that the Forties weren't particularly hungry, and that writers such as Mayhew distorted the truth. Gertrude Himmelfarb's formidable essay in *The Victorian City* claims that the section of the population Mayhew studied was much smaller than he pretended, that he treated 'a relatively small, highly distinctive group of moral and social aliens as representative of all the poor, so imposing on them the image of the pauper. The Forties, it is argued, were anxious rather than hungry; and Mayhew was feeding this anxiety.

Here is an impressive modern version of the contemporary

complaint against Mayhew in such papers as *The Economist*, which called his book 'an encouragement to communism'. The opposite view is Eileen Yeo's that Mayhew made the 'first empirical enquiry into poverty as such'; that he defined a poverty line; that he grasped the connection between the plight of the poor and 'the perils of the nation', the slumps caused by overproduction and underconsumption – 'too many shirts and too many shirtless' –; and that he saw the iniquity of an arrangement by which 'the proportion of the wealth which is to come to the labourer is to be regulated by no other principle than what the capitalist can induce or force him (by starvation or chicanery) to accept'.

In this debate some scholars remain agnostic. It may be that when standards are in general rising poverty becomes more conspicuous; so that not poverty but the observer's consciousness of it grows more acute. What, then, of Engels? Was his shocked reaction to the Manchester poor merely another reflex of this middle-class consciousness or conscience? The answer may be that he had a deeper view of poverty, understanding it as a condition of not only material but also of psychic privation. This he could have partly learned from Carlyle, though not from the statisticians. But it was from his own philosophical education that he acquired the means to think of the condition of the working class in Manchester as of world-historical moment, dialectically an inevitable prelude to revolution.

Engels's Manchester book doesn't always enjoy a good press. His translators and editors, W. O. Henderson and W. H. Chaloner, call him 'no historian' – he peddled an unexamined myth of pre-industrial happiness, and by asserting that conditions had worsened in the Forties helped to establish another myth. As a prophet he was no better, jauntily asserting that the next slump must bring the revolution, whereas England got through that slump in 1847, and through the year of revolutions that followed. And 'the British working-class movement has developed on quite different lines from those Engels confidently predicted.' He was wrong about the widening gap between rich and poor; wrong about the inability of the system to continue when child-labour was banned; wrong about so much that the wonder is why people bother about a work so low on scholarship, so prone to unacknowledged use of secondary material, so garbled. The reason may be that *The Condition* is a brilliant political tract ('I charge the English middle-classes with mass-murder') and that this alone enabled it to be more than ephemeral; which is the view of Henderson and Chaloner.

Lenin took a different view: 'many descriptions of the dreadful conditions under which the workers lived had appeared before Engels came on the scene . . . But Engels was the first to show that the workers were something more than a social class in distress. He explained that the degraded economic condition of the proletariat was in itself the stimulus which would enable this class to make progress in the future.' If you hold this view you must believe that the condition of the working class had worsened, or that a new consciousness of that condition – enriched by the concept of *Verdinglichung*, or reification – had the same effect. Statistics might feed but could not found such a consciousness, which in one form might stem from the imagination of Dickens, in another from the Hegelian conceptual array of Engels.

Mr Marcus is interested in the Hegelian version.* He does not trouble to confute those who suggest that Engels exaggerated the whole thing, though he seems to have a grudge against Henderson and Chaloner rather deeper than a distrust of their translation will explain. This is perhaps unfortunate, since it might tempt some readers to reject his study before it is fairly under way. But he is avowedly a literary critic rather than a historian; and if he declines one contest he energetically accepts another, the struggle to rescue his discipline from what he sees as mere fashionableness and academicism – to upgrade the critic from man of letters to 'critical intellectual'. The heart of his book is in its close readings of Engels's and other relevant texts.[1]

---

[1] As Marcus notices, that Engels's text is in German doesn't make his task any easier; but he gets around this difficulty rather well. There is evidently need for an accurate translation; a pity Marcus didn't do one. (Sound translation and authoritative editing are much harder to come by, nowadays, than competent literary criticism, and it is unfortunate that they excite less interest.) Mrs Wischnewetzky's version of 1877 had the advantage of Engels's editing, but he cut down on his old 'semi-Hegelian

* Steven Marcus, *Engels, Manchester, and the Working Class* (New York: Random House)

Marcus provides a historical sketch of Manchester, then a brief account of the life of Engels as a young man, as preludes to a report on the confrontation of the two. The city he claims as the paradigm, the archetype, the site of the 'world-historical experience', neatly recounting the peculiar history which prepared it for this fate. For Marcus, unlike some Victorian and some modern optimists, there is no possibility that the condition of the populace was a merely transitory or accidental misery. 'Something new had happened. In part that newness consisted in the actual conditions that were being created and disclosed; in part it had to do with human consciousness struggling to make, and often to resist, the radical alterations and accommodations within itself that these conditions required . . . What had entered the world was the distinctive modern conscious experience of the extreme.' And he proceeds to examine, in his capacity as critic, the language of some who consciously responded to this 'grand historical crisis'.

Here he is of necessity very selective, preferring to say little of Mrs Gaskell, who for all her faults knew Manchester from within – you get a scanty and false notion of *North and South* from his one quotation, and of *Mary Barton* none at all; and curiously enough Mrs Gaskell is omitted from the index. Kathleen Tillotson's essential *Novels of the Forties* escapes mention anywhere.

On his own showing, the value of Marcus's book depends on the success of its deep scrutiny of texts. He scores some hits and some misses. He makes a good deal of Dickens saying of his first visit to cotton mills that the worst differed little from the best: '*Ex uno disce omnes.*' Dickens's use of Latin at this point is supposed to be his way of emphasizing the strangeness of his experience,

language' and could not cure the lady's graceless English. 'Mrs Wischnewetzky, he pertinently snorted, "translates like a factory"' – so Marcus, reporting Engels. He does a fair amount of pertinent snorting himself; a tendency to awkwardness in his own style seems to assert itself most frequently when he is rather obscurely blowing on other writers – as when he assaults Erving Goffman, in a gratuitous footnote, for falling into 'the fallacy of misplaced abstractness', having just himself committed this sentence: 'What in Engels and Mill is a rich blending of historically concrete instance that tend to reveal an emerging universal, has here been leached out into ahistorical generalities and empty inclusiveness.'

and the psychic space he needed to put between it and himself. But although it may be true that Dickens was not much given to Latin, this tag is simply part of the period lexicon, to be used when you wanted to say, like a former vice president, 'When you've seen one you've seen them all'; and even a writer not much given to classical tags would reach for it. This is making too much of a casual epistolary expression.

A more serious distortion occurs, I think, in the treatment of Carlyle's first reaction to Manchester:

> At five in the morning all was still as sleep and darkness. At half-past five all went off like an enormous mill-race or ocean-tide. The Boom-m-m, far and wide. It was the mills that were all starting then, and creishy [greasy] drudges by the million taking post there.

Marcus rightly observes that the water imagery suggests a 'radical transformation' of nature, but by misinterpreting the expression, 'taking post' he diminishes his own point. It does not mean 'taking up their posts' – this puts the workers inside the mills, and locates the metamorphosis there. What they are doing is rushing through the streets *to* the mills, themselves tide and mill-race, so the city becomes an extension of the factory. The whole environment exhibits life and power subordinated to the clock and the machine. You can still see it happen, in a modified way, in towns dominated by large factories.

However, Marcus makes keener observations than these. Disraeli thought Manchester 'the type of a great idea', just as surely as Athens. But when his Coningsby went there he noted the machines that had replaced men, and described them as 'mysterious forms full of existence without life' – a phrase 'packed with intelligence', as Marcus rightly remarks. However, Disraeli then undermines it, and falls into silliness: he lacked the intellectual resources of Engels.

Marcus isn't infatuated with Engels; he remarks a certain overconfidence, even a proneness to misunderstanding, as when Engels supposed the Plug Plot riots of 1842 had political significance. He was not altogether free of class feeling, witness his constrained reaction to the death of his working-class mistress. But he had the right training, and he had the intelligence and the energy. From the Wuppertal of his youth he knew the connection between puritanical money-making and civic gloom. Finding in Manchester a high rate of unemployment and inadequate responses to it – Chartism, like Owenism, left him unimpressed, the one legal, the other mystical – he set out, with Mary Burns as guide, to get to know the workers and to 'read' the unknowable city.

He already understood that want could not be satisfied out of mere charitable vanity, an eighteenth-century notion inappropriate to this terrible modernity. It can be said that he brought a philistine energy to the task of understanding what he saw as a revolutionary situation. But he could also see and feel. London horribly dissolved mankind into monads; but Manchester was still more important, the centre of class exploitation, where a gentleman might live without ever seeing a working-class quarter; where the streets were façades to cover the evil; where, if you looked, you could see people living in shit:

> ... generations of human beings, out of whose lives the wealth of England was produced, were compelled to live in wealth's symbolic, negative counterpart. And that substance which suffused their lives was also a virtual objectification of their social condition, their place in society: that was what they were. We must recall that this was no Freudian obsessive neurosis or anxiety dream; but it is as if the contents of such a neurosis had been produced on a wholesale scale in the real world. We can, then, understand rather better how those main street palisades were functioning – they were defensive-adaptive measures of confinement and control. And we can understand what they were concealing: plenty.

This passage shows Marcus at his best – perceptive and indignant – yet with a failure at the end, for *plenty* is an unhappily ambiguous colloquialism. (What was concealed was precisely its opposite.) But it conveys the depth of Engels's feeling about that proletarian indignity and misery which he thought to be the essential pre-requisite of the workers' resurrection from the spiritual death of agrarian paternalism, the precondition of their move toward authenticity. Once understood as 'the universally negated', they could be seen in dialectical terms. The loss of their *Lebenstellung*, their place in life; of their pleasures; even of their children, half of whom died before they reached the age of five, while the survivors faced the same life of psychological and economic privation – these would stir up the necessary anger against the righteous masters. Even crime became, for Engels, romantic rebellion. And out of conscious anger would come the revolution that would end the demoralization not only of the workers but of the masters too, of the class that oppressed as well as of their victims; revolution would prove, as cholera did before it, that all men were members of one body.

This conducted tour of *The Conditions of the Working Class in England* certainly leaves one with the feeling that Engels understood an alien scene differently and more deeply than most native observers; and that the way was here prepared for the first volume of *Capital*, a generation later. Meanwhile the English critique continued in its less systematic way, and produced the master-pieces of Dickens as well as the slow process of reform and the growth of an indigenous labour movement Engels had little time for.

No doubt Engels's insight was more precise than Carlyle's, more practical than Dickens's. But *The Victorian City* demonstrates that the situation was more complicated than he supposed; and also, perhaps, that the life of the 'negated' class was richer than he allowed. Human diversity, and even gaiety, were harder to crush than he thought. One thinks of the mining communities, whose culture is so private that politicians can never understand it – even D. H. Lawrence, who came out of one, grew ambiguous about it as he moved up the ladder, for his miners are sometimes dancers, sometimes demons; there is a taint of the middle-class envy and fear. So, too, with life in the mill towns. Oldham is not a prospect of misery to its inhabitants; it is, and has been, the ground of a life they would not change. The Victorian culture was one of very great diversity defying monolithic explanation; and the one thing everybody is right about is that we must find in it the origins of our own complexities.

New York Review of Books, 30 May 1974

Tennyson's Nerves

Robert Martin's book* is not one of those literary biographies that reshuffle a familiar narrative and perhaps add a few bits of new information or conjecture. It is a full-scale life, founded on primary sources, many of them previously unpublished. As the first major biography since Hallam Tennyson's pious memoir of 1897, it has obvious importance. Moreover, it is for the most part very well-written, affectionate without idolatry, well-proportioned and full of entertaining detail. Mr Martin, in short, has scored a considerable success.

His narrative will help us to a better understanding of the process by which Tennyson became the type, for his contemporaries, of what a poet ought to be. Only a few of them believed that apotheosis was bad for his poetry, or at any rate that it tended to obscure his genuine gifts, which were not of the kind that can expect the admiration of a large public. And of course it was the official Great Poet rather than the subtle inquisitor of language who provoked, a generation later, a reaction so violent that it has probably had more influence on the subsequent history of English poetry than anything Tennyson actually wrote.

It is true that there are more traces of him in the work of later poets – Eliot, for instance – than this account of the matter might suggest; it is difficult to forget altogether a once-loved voice. But the co-existence of such muted tributes with a general distaste for the Victorian cult of the poet merely confirms the rightness of the minority view – there was little correlation between the nature

* Robert Bernard Martin, *Tennyson: The Unquiet Heart* (London: Oxford University Press)

of Tennyson's finest achievements and his character as the ideal type of poet. He was in truth so far from being true to that type that to read him after a long interval is to be astonished by his strangeness, almost his foreignness (the word, applied to one who prided himself on his mere Englishness or chauvinism, is paradoxical or even insulting). The effect of that entranced research into the possible sounds of English, that phonological potholing in the recesses of language, far below the level of official sense, is very private, very idiosyncratic. Try reading aloud, with exaggerated attention to what is going on phonetically, so well-known a poem as 'Come down, O maid, from yonder mountain height.' The topic may seem reasonably familiar, but the sound of the poem is extraordinarily remote from the commonplace, and it is clearly part of the peculiar strength of Tennyson's verse that it can propose such a topic in such a way as to subvert its plainness.

Consider these stanzas as a further instance of such subversion:

> Unwatched, the garden bough shall sway,
> The tender blossom flutter down,
> Unloved, that beech will gather brown,
> This maple burn itself away;
>
> Unloved, the sun-flower, shining fair,
> Ray round with flames her disk of seed,
> And many a rose-carnation feed
> With summer spice the humming air . . .
>
> As year by year the labourer tills
> His wonted glebe, or lops the glades;
> And year by year our memory fades
> From all the circle of the hills.

What is unwatched and unloved seems, and very properly, commonplace enough, but from the simplicities of 'sway' and 'flutter down' we move to the maple consuming itself in its own fire; the fire is repeated in the sunflower petals (though they magically protect the seeds, a future), and the waste is repeated in the scent of the carnations (which continues by attracting insects to perform its natural, inhuman function). The introduction of the labourer, human exploiter of natural growth, reducer of natural disorder, is a necessary link between the plants and the higher beings at present neither watching nor loving them. He is touched in with an eighteenth-century formality, part of the scene and not capable of grieving over it or over the sensitive who no longer see it. They have memories but *become* mere memories, distanced first by the brook which occupies the two stanzas I have not quoted and comes between them and the garden, then by the vague view of the circle of the hills, fading into permanent loss (unlike the plants or the labourer).

Verlaine's criticism of *In Memoriam* ('when he should have been broken-hearted he had many reminiscences') is odd, coming from a poet who might, more than most, be expected to see how much thicker the plot of such lines is than the apparent simplicity of the topic (roughly, reminiscence) might seem to require. The disparity may provide a rough measure of the distance Tennyson habitually established between what, on the face of it, required to be said, and the far less public utterance that actually occurs. His strong sense of that distance is presumably what made him so docile about accepting other people's proposals of themes to write about. On one occasion, often recalled, he remarked that in his opinion there had not been since Shakespeare 'a master of the English language such as I', though he added: 'To be sure, I've got nothing to say.' And on another occasion he told Edmund Gosse it was only the dunces who 'fancy it is the thought that makes poetry live; it isn't, it's the form, but we mustn't tell them so, they wouldn't know what we meant.' Among the dunces must be counted his adoring friends in Cambridge, the Apostles, who were always urging him to deal with important subjects. But Gosse, usually thought less bright, took the hint, and Mr Martin rightly commends his summing-up of Tennyson on the occasion of the poet's eightieth birthday:

He is wise and full of intelligence; but in mere intellectual capacity or attainment it is probable that there are many who excel him . . . He has not headed a single moral reform nor inaugurated a single revolution of opinion; he has never pointed the way to undiscovered regions of thought . . . Where then has his greatness lain? It has lain in the various perfections of his writing. He has written, on the whole, with more constant, unwearied, and unwearying excellence than any of his contemporaries . . . He has expended the treasures of his native talent on broadening and deepening his own hold upon the English language, until that has become an instrument upon which he is able to play a greater variety of melodies to perfection than any other man.

Mr Martin can tell us, sometimes, how the feel of a scene got into Tennyson's head, where, for whatever length of time necessary, it would lap around, changing slowly into the shape his mind must give it. A visit to a sea cave at Ballybunion produced these lines from (or worked into) *Idylls of the King*:

> So dark a forethought roll'd about his brain
> As on a dull day in an Ocean cave
> The blind wave feeling round his long sea-hall
> In silence . . .

These are lines to which Keats, and perhaps nobody else, might have aspired: accurate, melancholic, menaced; inaugurating no revolution of opinion, of course, but emblematic of the poet himself, and not of the sage publicly venerated. And any biography of Tennyson as full and communicative as this one is bound to raise the question how it came about that so private a gift, an endless mouthing into shape of sounds, a fumbling at dark phonetic limits, could be transformed so completely into the statuesque representative of poetry as a popular force.

Most of his contemporaries, great and small, saw him thus; as I have said, a few abstained, including his friend Edward FitzGerald, but at the same time had to acknowledge the majority view; and Tennyson himself came to share the general opinion of the nature of his greatness. Confident of an exclusive vocation, he was able to devote his entire life to poetry (he simply assumed that it would be wrong for him to do anything else) and to make himself rich in the process. His title, the friendship of the Queen, the affection and admiration of such peers as Dickens, Carlyle, Browning and George Eliot, and the veneration of almost everybody else, somehow came to seem the natural outcome of his use of his talent; and much in his later life may be attributed to his having grown into his role. Yet through it all he retained his right as poet to be a bit odd, unconforming, eccentric in manner, demanding and even selfish, victim and exploiter at once of poetic 'nerves'.

Reading this volume, one may wonder at the social and genetic cost of making a major poet. Tennyson's father was the eldest son of a tough Lincolnshire businessman who accumulated a great fortune, but he was early disinherited and made into a clergyman, though wildly unsuited to such a career. Noisy and ungovernable from earliest youth, he was, as father of a family, morose, drunken and idle; one of the nicest things about him was that he rose in the late afternoon and then played the harp, but he was also violent and spendthrift. His wife was odd in more agreeable ways, and their twelve children exhibited a great variety of eccentricities, ranging from downright insanity to opium addiction, alcoholism and every kind of psychic instability. Edward entered a home for the insane at 19 and died there 60 years later, Charles went in for opium, Arthur for alcohol. Septimus would introduce himself to a stranger by rising from the hearthrug where he had been lying, extending a languid hand, and saying: 'I am Septimus, the most morbid of the Tennysons.' The daughters were noted for their strange manners; Mary, very beautiful till savaged by a mastiff, took to Swedenborg, Spiritualism and Mesmerism; Matilda was never quite right after a fall into a coal-scuttle as a child, and would embarrass Emily (who had been engaged to Arthur Hallam) by raising her umbrella in church to keep off the draught.

Since the crowded rectory had plenty of books as well as many peculiar persons, it provided an atmosphere conducive to poetry. But no less helpful were the fears that Tennyson experienced in perhaps even greater measure than his kin. A general anxiety about inheriting 'the black blood of the Tennysons' was more sharply focused in the fear of epilepsy, a disease to which the family was probably prone; it was, at the time, thought to be a

shameful affliction, related to excessive sexuality and masturbation. Tennyson experienced 'trances', and his verse is much
indebted to them, but they must have been terrifying in the
early days, when he could think of them as manifestations of
the disease. He feared to become like his father, and there
must have seemed a fair chance that any member of the family
would be mad, suicidal or addicted. The poet also feared
blindness, and spent a lot of his youthful time reading the
medical literature on the subject.

Martin is very good on all this, unsensational and asking the
right questions – for example, about the relation of these fears to
the poet's long delay in marrying. As to addiction, Tennyson
hated opium but was always a heavy smoker, and he drank rather
a lot. In time, he lost his fears (lost also his trances) and tended
to attribute his troubles to gout, a much more elastic diagnosis
then than now; as it happens, he did, in later life, become gouty
in the narrower and still current sense.

Before he was seven, Tennyson knew the Odes of Horace by
heart, and at eight was capable of writing verses of remarkable
felicity. It may be said, then, that a talented family justified its
extravagances and unmannerly ways by producing a prodigy, for
Tennyson was such as surely as his contemporary Mendelssohn,
though prodigious musicians are much more spectacular. Since,
conscious of such endowments, he never intended to do anything
except write poetry, the question arose as to how his career was
to be financed. Like the rest of the family, he always assumed that
he was owed a living. When the rich grandfather died, all his
descendants seemed to expect that his estate would keep them in
comfort for ever; the bulk of it went to the uncle who had replaced
Tennyson's father as heir, but the rector and his family, though
they complained stridently, still did quite well out of the trans-
action. Tennyson lost much of his inheritance, and that of his
family, by a rash investment; but he was never desperately hard
up, though he often represented himself as being so.

Relations between the rector and his father were always bad,
and some of the trouble arose from the son's combination of
financial extravagance and outrageously-phrased demands. The
poet inherited a tendency to require lots of money on demand,

and he was also remarkably stingy. At the time when he accepted a Civil List pension it was already possible to ask whether his case was truly deserving: what is remarkable is that he went on accepting it for the rest of his life, in times when he was making £10,000 a year (£150,000 in our money?) from poetry, while others sought relief in vain. In his bad years, FitzGerald gave him £300 a year out of an income of £800; later, though he never actually dropped him, Tennyson treated FitzGerald very off-handedly, and with little sense of gratitude for such a favour. This meanness extended to very small matters, such as his borrowing Samuel Rogers' court dress when received as Laureate, though Rogers was a short and Tennyson a tall man; later he borrowed robes to enter the House of Lords, and often schemed to avoid paying his full dues to clubs. Perhaps his habit of hanging onto his money (except when spending it on his own houses and *bella figura*) was necessary to his survival as a poet. Carlyle and FitzGerald both told him that he should take some employment, not only to ease his financial position but to strengthen his work. He refused to listen – very properly, says Martin, and one is inclined to agree.

If part of his right as a poet was to be kept in some style, another part was to lead a life of what must, to more obviously industrious friends, have seemed like indolence. He rose late, like his father, but instead of playing the harp, wrote poems. He kept other people up half the night, belching tobacco or reading *Maud* (Jane Welsh Carlyle claims that he once read it to her three times in an evening, over six hours of it altogether, though there may be some hyperbole there). Invited to stay, he would lay down conditions: he need not come down to breakfast, must be allowed his pipe, must be provided with port. Or he would descend, often inconveniently, on old friends, and stay as long as he chose. From his earliest days he had needed adulation; the Apostles had provided it at Cambridge, later friends served, and then his wife; when old friendships fell away, he replaced them with relationships of a different sort, and adulators like Allingham and Palgrave. At the same time, he required to be protected from hostile reviews (he never got over his early savaging by Wilson and Croker). Sensitive as well as demanding, he was clearly difficult: yet he was evidently much loved, and not merely as a great man. He gaucherie was itself charming.

He was to reach an eminence almost beyond criticism, and beyond self-criticism too. With great fame, he grew somewhat snobbish and reactionary. Martin, who gives admirable accounts of Tennyson's houses at Farringford and Aldworth, deftly points up the parallel between the aging poet and his extraordinary cousin Charles, an endearing snob who had inherited the grand-father's estate and spent it on a strange and extravagant house encapsulating the history of English building under the Planta-genets and Tudors. Callers would likely be told that the master was walking on the barbican. He changed his name to Tennyson d'Eyncourt (though his claim to noble ancestry was more than dubious) and waited to be granted a peerage. The cousins despised each other, and the poet was particularly hard on the pretentious name and the house – the newly-rich and their mansions always had the power to annoy him. Yet, says Martin, Aldworth is 'a distant and diminished cousin' of Tennyson d'Eyncourt's Bayons; the *Idylls of the King*, whatever else may be said of them, faintly reflect the Victorian medievalism of Charles; and, most remark-ably, the poet, when ennobled, seriously considered taking as his title Tennyson d'Eyncourt.

Such foolishness is a reflex of his extraordinary fame, an indi-cation that he thought it no more than his due, though some aspects of celebrity he found disagreeable. He thought himself hounded by the press, by 'cockneys' – the lower classes who took trips into the country in the hope of seeing him – and Americans, for whom he had an unreasoning contempt. One anecdote suggests that his fears were not altogether groundless. Sophia and Nathaniel Hawthorne stalked the Tennysons round an exhibition, without presuming to accost them: but before they left, Sophia seized the younger Tennyson boy and kissed him. 'I was well pleased to have had in my arms Tennyson's child,' she boasted. The poet could not sign hotel registers until his departure, for fear of being mobbed; and at public readings there was a real risk of hysterical outbursts on lines now familiar from the recitals of rock stars. All this makes him sound intolerable, yet he was, as I say, though vain and selfish, capable of winning genuine affection:

Browning, for instance, was perfect in his generosity to a more successful rival, though Tennyson treated him with some suspicion, reluctant to praise his poetry and thinking him forward because he dandled one of the Tennyson children at its christening.

Despite his fear of publication and reviewers, his success was almost unbroken. *Enoch Arden* sold 40,000 copies on publication in 1864, and made him £8,000 within the year – in terms of financial success, at any rate, no falling-off from *In Memoriam*, 'the pinnacle of success', fourteen years earlier. Without ever thinking himself a secure man, he was always able to do his work at his own pace – *In Memoriam* was 17, *Idylls of the King* 40 years in the making. He gave the public poetry, but also a commodity it perhaps wanted more – the image of the Poet who, inspired as he was, fitted the general preconception of what a great man must be, aloof and grandly moral. He feared that the story of Vivien might be called immoral, but by that time nobody would have thought of saying so. The man himself hardened in the mould of his greatness, growing reactionary in politics (his relations with Gladstone, Hallam's other great friend, were uneasy on political as well as personal grounds) and very puritanical in matters of sex.

J. M. Gray, in a thoughtful new book* on the *Idylls of the King*, argues that Tennyson took a strong line on masculine morality because he knew there was no possibility of relaxing the rules for women, and so the only way to get equality was to tighten them for men. Mr Gray thinks so highly of the *Idylls*, and makes out so elaborate a case for their refined structural complexity, that he is undoubtedly keen not to fall out with Tennyson about sex: but his line of defence remains curious, rather as if the inhabitants of Margate should be forbidden sea-bathing on the ground that it is not available to the inhabitants of Wolverhampton. Of course the poet believed, and told the Queen, that England was going to blazes, and that sexual wickedness was an important cause of this state of affairs, as it is nearly always held to be. But his own

---

* J. M. Gray, *Thro' the Vision of the Night: A Study of Source, Evolution and Structure in Tennyson's 'Idylls of the King'* (Edinburgh University Press)

undoubted chastity didn't stop him from cuddling young girls. He took the 21-year-old Margot Tennant on his knee and told her an improper story, afterwards condemning her because she did not blush.

Martin is, of course, required to speculate on the poet's sexual interests, especially in regard to Arthur Hallam. He does so very judiciously. Hallam died at 22, and was perhaps never quite the phoenix he was made out to be, but that says nothing about the quality and endurance of Tennyson's attachment to him, which was the occasion of much great poetry. An ardent lover of neither men nor women, Tennyson is unlikely to have thought of Hallam as other or more than his best friend, though the maps of love have been so redrawn that such observations are likely now to seem naive. Martin thinks it possible that the poet was particularly upset by Croker's sneering at 'O darling Room' because he suspected that the reviewer had 'caught him saying more than he intended, or even knew, about his affection for Hallam'. But this seems uncharacteristically far-fetched, a concession to modern knowingness. On the matter of Tennyson's marriage, Martin seems convincing. He delayed it for years, and rather inconsiderately; fear of poverty and anxiety about epilepsy may have had something to do with this procrastination, but to marry, a virgin, at 41 does not argue hot blood. It is fair to add that a man so interested in, and so fearful of, madness, and so taken with the idea of 'nerves' as a necessary element in the poetic temperament, might well choose less risky comforts. 'I doubt poets are an ill-starred race,' said FitzGerald, thinking of his friend – 'that is poets who deal in their own susceptibilities.' Tennyson was a voluntary patient in an asylum, and when the law was changed to prevent that practice, he frequented hydropathic establishments in which simple water, in large quantities, purged one of everything from gout to nerves. Presumably all this was instead of sex. Tennyson's half-hearted courtships – quite lacking the fervency of his love for the true alter ego, Hallam – also suggest that he was simply incapable of being as interested in another person as in himself, and his indifference to others' feelings, and carelessness in friendships, support the view, proposed by Martin, that he was constitutionally insensitive to the personalities of others. Martin indeed kindly suggests that a man so myopic could never see the reactions on other people's faces, and so had no idea of how he was affecting them, but this is not easy to believe of someone who claimed to have seen the reflection of the moon in the eye of a nightingale, and the truth must be that there was a profound narcissism in the poet – some arrestation of the power to invest emotionally in others.

Time and again Martin's narrative produces evidence of this. The poet had a powerful and personal epistolary style, but hated writing letters. Even among the Apostles at Cambridge he found it difficult to speak; and later he was silent if he could not dominate the company. He had a taste for sycophantic admirers; at first, Cambridge, ungratefully described as 'that college-studded marsh', provided them, later they offered themselves plentifully as the tribute due to fame. With his strong Lincolnshire accent and occasionally uncouth manners he passed for a very natural man (an important element in public greatness). But it was hardly probable that as he grew in age and celebrity he would separate his life from the myth of supreme greatness. Martin's account of the deathbed finely celebrates the immersion of the man in the myth.

Almost to the end there was a stream of visitors, keen to be among the last to see the poet alive. Then, the visitors forbidden, the family prepared for the end, notebooks in hand. 'It is perhaps churlish,' says Martin, to feel that Hallam 'occasionally lost sight of a worn-out old man dying in a draughty bedroom on a Sussex hillside and saw instead the apotheosis of Victorian poetry'. Tennyson asked for *Cymbeline*, but could not read it; the next day he was forbidden it. He spoke of the Queen, the Press and Gladstone, then called again for his Shakespeare; 'he fumbled with it, then put it face down with his hand laid heavily upon it, cracking the spine, so that today it still falls open to the speech of Posthumus to Imogen: "Hang there like fruit, my soul,/Till the tree die," a passage that had always moved him to tears.' According to Hallam his last words were 'Hallam, Hallam', and, to his wife, 'God bless you my joy,' though Hallam's wife, the practical Audrey, recorded that 'it was almost impossible to make out more than a word here and there of what he said owing greatly I think to his having no teeth in.' The presiding physician, in his account, paid more deference to the myth: 'On the bed a figure of breathing marble, flooded and bathed in the light of the full moon streaming through the oriel window; his hand clasping the Shakespeare which he had asked for but recently, and which he kept by him to the end; the moonlight, the majestic figure as he lay there, "drawing thicker breath", irresistibly brought to our minds his own "Passing of Arthur".' Almost everybody, but not Gladstone, went to the Abbey funeral.

London Review of Books, 6 November 1980

Victorian Vocations

Frederic Harrison and Leslie Stephen

Frederic Harrison once climbed Mont Blanc and found Leslie Stephen on the top. Not an improbable location for the encounter of two eminent Victorians: and they might equally have met in George Eliot's drawing-room. Whereas Stephen was much the more distinguished mountaineer, Harrison probably knew George Eliot better: he helped her work out the legal plot of *Felix Holt*, a service for which she may have owed him more gratitude than we need to feel. Perhaps she was showing it when she warned Harrison against employing her cook's daughter, a girl whose underwear she described as 'arrogantly good' and whose manners with men she thought 'too refined'. Obviously unsuitable, and Harrison did not take her on, though in the way of eminent Victorians he had a lively conscience, and once, after dismissing a housemaid who knelt before him and wept, mused a while on the 'arbitrary power' wielded by persons in his position.

His position, as these remarks are intended to suggest, was very like that of Leslie Stephen only more so, since he was rather better-off. They were upper-middle-class intellectuals, though they might not have called themselves so, and in their day that status ensured an unusual degree of both comfort and influence. From Ann Thwaite's biography of Gosse one remembers the remarkable moment when Gosse passed a note to Haldane as he sat on the Woolsack presiding, on 5 August 1914, over a debate, and so helped to ensure Kitchener's appointment to the War Office. That may have been the high point of literary influence on great matters of state, but it may also have been a freak;

certainly neither Harrison nor Stephen was ever in a position to exert such influence, and Stephen would probably not have wanted to. But they were listened to, and in various ways honoured, as their modern descendants cannot hope to be. And although they were probably more industrious than their successors, they also had more privilege. Work was a duty, but it could not be done without means.

Harrison was of yeoman ancestry, but his father was a rich and generous stockbroker. As a young man, Frederic had the means to lead a very agreeable life, his hard reading interrupted at will by cricket at Lord's, boating and climbing. When he married, his father increased his allowance, and did so again as each child was born, for he assumed that his son could not do his proper work in the world if he had to earn his own living. He gave Frederic the best available education; King's College School in the Strand produced, during the 35 years of Major's headship, almost a hundred boys who got into Leslie Stephen's *Dictionary of National Biography*; and if Oxford seemed a bit disappointing after that, Harrison could still claim that he read enough there to ensure his conversion from orthodoxy and Toryism to republicanism and free-thinking.

Oxford and Cambridge, virtually the sole nurseries of upper-class English intellect at the time, figure prominently in these biographies. Of Cambridge in particular we have in Noel Annan's book* an account that is not only detailed but exceptionally animated. And I suppose we need help to imagine a Cambridge with little time for science and a suspicious attitude even to the newly-established Moral Science Tripos; a celibate institution which applied religious tests that sometimes drove men to hypocrisy and sometimes to agonies of conscience, as, though somewhat belatedly, they did Leslie Stephen. (He eventually resigned his fellowship at Trinity Hall, and we now learn that he may have been brought near to suicide.) Not that life was always so thrilling; Stephen, in fact, found Cambridge dull. 'The only persons I thoroughly liked were Jebb the Public orator and Mrs Jebb,' he

* Noel Annan, *Leslie Stephen: The Godless Victorian* (London: Weidenfeld & Nicolson, revised edition)

wrote later: 'but Mrs Jebb is an American lady and so is naturally unlike Cambridge and indeed thoroughly charming.' In the first version of his book, published in 1951, Lord Annan obviously thought it sensible of Stephen to get out: 'most young dons who tear themselves away from the numbing embrace of that insatiable being, who is at once their mother and their bride, never regret the step they take.' When he wrote that sentence Annan was a don himself, but twenty years or so after leaving Cambridge he has found no reason to change it. Like Stephen, he saw all the administrative absurdities; like Stephen, he proposed reforms. But Cambridge takes very little notice if it chooses not to, and in time the young émigrés may be reconciled, as Stephen was. In time, as Annan reminds us, he won the rather improbable sponsorship of Mrs Leavis as a progenitor of *Scrutiny*; and the Leslie Stephen Lecture is still a considerable occasion. For his part, Harrison became an honorary fellow of Wadham, and had his ashes, mingled with his wife's (though of course she wasn't at Oxford) laid to rest in the ante-chapel of the college.

Such were the bonds placed upon men of this sort by their *almae matres*, though they couldn't help noticing the extraordinary ignorance of the undergraduates, the studious indifference of the dons, and the ridiculous examination system, attacked by both Harrison and Stephen. And it is clear from Annan's book that the higher education provided by the university was not much of a preparation for the intellectual struggles to come. If Stephen had stayed in Cambridge, he might have done very little of the work he is known for; we see him being not wholly serious in his teaching of New Testament Greek, coaching the boat, being a don. His real work lay elsewhere.

So, indeed, did Harrison's. Ms Vogeler's biography* is the first, and it is hard to imagine a reason for its not being the last. It is full of detail and documentation and it is very well written. Whereas Annan's *Stephen* is at once censorious and intimate, very much at ease with a figure who feels rather like a venerated but not wholly adequate ancestor, Vogeler's tone is both compassion-

---

* Martha Vogeler, *Frederic Harrison: The Vocations of a Positivist* (Oxford University Press)

ate and rather tart; her man had a kind of success in the world, but really did very little that now seems right. He was unusually intelligent, unusually active, and unusually silly; he was immensely public-spirited yet prejudiced to the point of absurdity. Although he had some immutable convictions, it is quite hard, even with the help of Vogeler's explanations, to decide why, on this or that occasion, Harrison acted as he did. When an answer is to be had, it usually has to do with his Positivism, which explains, for example, his altruistic attitude to public service, and also his indefatigable opposition to female suffrage, a cause in which he enlisted many intelligent women, including his wife and Mrs Leslie Stephen.

Positivism is a philosophy or religion that presents grave problems to the modern understanding. Comte was the Foucault and the Althusser of his day rolled into one and multiplied by ten, a prophet then quite unignorable but now almost entirely devoid of interest. Though Harrison had the usual religious struggle – he read Strauss and decided against Pusey and Newman – the main event of his whole thinking life was his encounter with Comte, and Vogeler is concerned to explain why this was so.

Comte divided history into three: there had been a Theological epoch, followed by a Metaphysical one, from which the world was now emerging into Positivism; Science would now come into its own, along with Sociology and Ethics. To all this prophetic history Comte added a quasi-religious ritual, for he was instituting the religion of Humanity. The tripartite scheme is essentially very old, but here it had a modern tone: the need for something to take over from religion was everywhere felt, and Evangelicalism had prepared the conscientious for altruism, a word Comte invented. There was an evolutionary element, too. Harrison was never altogether happy with the ritual, and was later to split the English movement on that issue: but everything else he apparently accepted. Something had to replace hell as the preservative of law and order; Fitzjames Stephen, Leslie's brother, thought the answer was to beef up legal punishments, but neither Harrison nor Leslie Stephen agreed. After his fashion, Harrison remained faithful to Comte throughout his long life. When he died at 92 there were few Positivists left, though their influence survived in various transformations – for example, the work of Patrick Geddes.

Positivists were supposed to be active in public affairs, and Harrison had strong opinions on practically everything. Though a keen patriot, he thought India should be returned to the Indians, and Gibraltar to Spain. Still under thirty, he wrote for the *Westminster* a bold notice of *Essays and Reviews*, a collection of essays which in 1860 outraged fundamentalist laypersons much as the hair-raisingly novel *obiter dicta* of the Bishop of Durham have been doing more recently. Harrison called the book an instance of 'Neo-Christianity', meaning that it was an attempt to show you could still be a Christian without believing anything in the old way. Clearly Positivism was superior to this ignominy.

The review attracted much attention, as did Harrison's forth-right views on other matters. Like Mill, he wanted to bring Governor Eyre to trial for murdering five hundred blacks and flogging hundreds of others in Jamaica: it may seem surprising that such men as Dickens, Tennyson, Kingsley and Ruskin took the opposite view – Carlyle indeed called Harrison's party 'nigger-philanthropists'. He wanted Home Rule for Ireland, and later stood as a Parliamentary candidate on Gladstone's side. He saw that the suspension of habeas corpus was not the way to handle the Fenians, and accurately forecast future troubles, though he rather spoilt this liberal record by suggesting in 1870 that five thousand Irish should be dispatched to help the French against Bismarck. He favoured the extension of the suffrage in 1867 – in part, because he believed that it would leave political supremacy where it belonged, with the 'richer classes'.

In an age which saw Ruskin calling John Stuart Mill a 'loath-some cretin' we needn't be surprised that Harrison was also capable of strong language. When Joseph Chamberlain was said to have hurt his ankle in 1906, Harrison prayed 'for the sake of our poor dear country' that the trouble was really paralysis. The poetry of Whitman, which was enjoying a vogue in England, he dismissed as 'spermatozoa and stink'. Fitzjames Stephen he described as a 'pushing ass . . . thrusting his carcase up the ladder of preferment, and turning round with pants to say: "I am for God, damn your eyes."' Harrison thought Fitzjames should be 'squelched'. He did not like climbers. Another thing he disliked was the mention of sex. As a good Positivist, ready at all times to rally to the support of freedom and progress, he might have been expected to do something about the imprisonment of the publisher Vizetelly for issuing translations of Zola. He did nothing. His inaction is possibly less surprising when one discovers that he deplored George Sand on account of her 'unwomanly proneness to lust'. Comte had ruled that women were to be accorded great respect but not allowed to do much in the world; his own relation with Clotilde de Vaux was entirely a matter of mutual uplift. Comte also ordained that the widowed must not remarry, and Harrison condemned George Eliot's marriage to Cross after the death of Lewes, deciding that the Lewes–Evans 'union' had to count as a marriage.

On the other hand, Harrison did a great many positive services to the community which happened also to be Positivist. He busied himself with the setting-up of the LCC and the London Library, and put forward a scheme for life peerages as a way of reforming the Lords. In his later years he had a mania for celebrating the anniversaries of great men, another Comtean trait, for there was a calendar of Positivist saints – all men, of course. However, Harrison's greatest hero was King Alfred, whose millennial celebrations he organized in 1902. Another great passion was warning the nation against the German threat. When the war came he argued that no constitutional principle could be found to justify conscientious objection to conscription: anybody who thought otherwise was a 'humbug and a sneak – in plain words, an ass and a traitor'. He devised brave punishments for the Kaiser, and thought very well of Lloyd George. He lost a son in the fighting.

In his old age Harrison wrote more than ever, including biographies of Chatham, William the Silent and Cromwell, whose bones and mummified head he wanted to re-bury in Westminster Abbey – a proposal that met with understandable resistance from Irish MPs. He wrote hundreds of letters to the *Times*, many of which were printed. He had by this time lost his early sympathy with the Trade Union movement (indeed he had always been suspicious of the TUC) and had come to regard Socialism as a curse; the miners' strike of 1921 was a Communist-inspired folly, and the General Election of the following year, which made Labour the official Opposition, a disaster. Vogeler remarks that on many issues he was at this time 'confused and desperate'; perhaps in a way he always had been confused. Some of the old optimism lingered on: he thought Einstein's relativity theories confirmed the basic tenets of Positivism. He seems to have quite enjoyed being very old. Although he disapproved of honours in the gift of prime minister and Crown, he liked being made a freeman of Bath and an honorary fellow of Wadham. His last book, *De Senectute*, is set in Oxford, and so, as we have seen, are his ashes.

What, on this very full account, are we to make of Harrison? Vogeler rightly observes that for him as for others Positivism was not only a substitute for religion but a defence against revolution, for which it substituted orderly progress. He wanted no unseemly social upheaval, for that there should be a class of the kind to which he belonged was essential to his conception of his role as man of letters and public affairs. He approved of Beatrice Potter's marriage to Webb despite his not having a 'socially attractive family': but clearly you needed to be as clever as Webb to extract such a concession. He was himself past fifty before he needed to accept payment for his multitudinous journalism, and he tried to use his privilege for the general good: but, as Vogeler remarks, he came to be seen as the prophet of 'an irrelevant philosophy and a failed religion'. He outlived his reputation, except as an improbable survivor and an authority on great men who had, almost incredibly, been his friends. Almost alone of that distinguished company, he lived to read and admire Lytton Strachey, which was very resilient of him. He died correcting the proofs of his thirtieth book.

Martha Vogeler, with her usual moderation, concludes: 'his story inspires pathos but does not deserve neglect.' In following his tracks for almost a century, from his birth in Euston Square to his Oxford rest, she has done all that could be done to justify that conclusion.

From where we now stand, Harrison will surely seem a lesser presence than Leslie Stephen. This is in part because Stephen's works are still in use: the *DNB* lives on though Harrison's biographical dictionary is forgotten, and many of us got our first introduction to the history of ideas in the eighteenth century from Stephen, whereas Harrison's historical work is likewise forgotten. But Stephen was also the father of Virginia Woolf and Vanessa Bell, the original of Mr Ramsay in *To the Lighthouse*, and a figure in many memoirs that happen to interest us because Bloomsbury interests us. We have a strong preconception of Stephen's rich melancholic character, and it has been reinforced not only by Virginia Woolf but by his own *Mausoleum Book*, an autobiographical work written for his children. A further preservative was the first version of Lord Annan's study, published in 1951. He has taken it up in the spirit of an engraver excavating his own plates, adding information that has come to hand in the interim, and, without disturbing the general design of the original, has incorporated his own later experience of Cambridge and London.

Annan's admiration of Stephen, even his sense of fellowship, is obvious, but he won't overrate him: he is only 'a peak set in the mountain range of a particular tradition of thought'. He had many shortcomings, including an indifference to art and music. As a philosopher, he was a failure. For all his reading and his industry he was trapped in the cage of mid-nineteenth century assumptions as to what was important and how it should be dealt with. Thus his main concern was to show that as 'belief in the dogmas of Christianity waned, there was still a morality as peremptory which men and women should accept if society was to improve'. 'Peremptory' in this context is George Eliot's word. She had a little more time for Comte than Stephen had, though, as Annan shows, he drew some important un-Comtean conclusions from his study of the great systematiser.

No more than Harrison did Stephen want the general arrangement of society to be unduly disturbed. He had the conscience and the industry, but also required the privileges, proper to a high bourgeoisie that had assumed responsibility for the national intellect. The characterization of this social class, made long ago by Annan, is now a familiar part of everybody's idea of the 'intellectual aristocracy' beginning with the 'Clapham Sect' and issuing in Bloomsbury and the ethics of Moore. It is a complicated tale – involving not only genealogy but the transformation of

Evangelicalism as well as of Cambridge – on which Annan loves to descant. It is his sympathetic grasp of such matters that gives both versions of his book their authority.

He is capable of Victorian candour – he calls Marcuse a 'miserable coward', which is almost what Stephen called Jowett – and he can be pretty hard on Leslie's shortcomings. Yet there is also a tenderness, and a willingness to defend his man from unjust strictures. One sees this in his remarks about Stephen's meanness, which is perhaps too notorious. Stephen, for example, once let it be thought that he was close to financial ruin, so that Gosse began lobbying to get him a Civil List pension: but it turned out that Stephen was talking only about his current account and not reckoning his securities or his income. His extraordinary tantrums over Vanessa's household accounts are well-known. A rational explanation of such conduct might begin by stating that money was a prerequisite of the kind of life a bourgeois intellectual must lead, so that in looking after it, even rather frantically, one was doing one's duty by oneself and everybody else. We hear Frederic Harrison at 80 lamenting that the £2000 a year which was all he then had was barely enough, and that although he approved in principle of the new national insurance and the employer's contribution, he feared that in order to pay it he would have to cut down on his staff of eight servants. 'The day of the middle-class and professional man of £1000 a year' was, he lamented, gone for ever; such a man could no longer manage on only about ten times as much as an artisan.

It might be thought that there is something pathological about such fears of poverty. Arnold, of whom Stephen did not approve, made famous a certain Mr Smith, secretary to an insurance company, who 'laboured under the apprehension that he would come to poverty, and that he was eternally lost'. Smith, according to Arnold, was typical of the middle class, which had two main concerns, making money and saving one's soul; and neither of these preoccupations seemed to Arnold conducive to culture. But Stephen, as we know, had other more admirable concerns, and was capable of generosity. Annan wisely remarks that the attitude of people to money is often at variance with their general character: but he goes further and discovers 'something fine' in Stephen's financial caution. He didn't want money for the usual upper-middle-class reason, to ape aristocracy, but merely to have enough to get on with his work. That, of course, is a difficult quantum. But Annan thinks he got it right, and praises both Stephen and his daughter Virginia for expecting to live as rentiers sheltered lives in which they could write as they pleased without turning out 'shallow things' to increase incomes 'which by the standards of their times were modest'. Stephen indeed said he was prepared if necessary to support his establishment on £1000 or £1200 a year – 'for millions of people do it'. But the last part of this statement is surely a delusion, and the first, one supposes, a desperate hypothesis; it sounds rather typical of Stephen's melancholic hyperbole, like his melodramas over the kitchen accounts.

This little excursion about money is characteristic of Annan's book: much of its charm comes from his having opinions and a willingness to give them ebullient expression. There is, for instance, a brief meditation on changing styles of mourning, and there are plenty of saws and instances: 'Most people's domestic life is an odd hotch-potch . . . Men and women are to be pitied: as we ourselves, too.' That third category, additional to men and women, is rather curious, but the effect is still agreeable.

Only about a third of the book deals directly with Stephen's life. The remainder is an attempt to situate him in the context of nineteenth-century ideas, and to trace the later course of those ideas: hence the unexpected presence in these pages of such as Habermas, Foucault and Heidegger. The early version of the book did of course deal with the disturbing influx of Continental and especially German thought into England, but the new one is more expansive, and expresses a general admiration for 'the German renaissance', that 'explosion of genius' which is characterized in a few pages on German music, philosophy and economic development which must have required real nerve to write. Stephen himself is represented as caught in the cross tides of Millian logic, secularized Evangelicalism, Darwinism and German critical thought. Occasionally his head disappears in the surf, for he is never allowed to look like a giant, and is usually called an industrious amateur.

All the same, he emerges as a figure of some weight and much dignity. If his book on ethics is a mess, it remains true that he was wisely sceptical about historical periodization – the Age of Reason or indeed the Age of Anything. He loved the eighteenth century best, and thought that Romanticism came when Methodist enthusiasm triumphed over bourgeois rationalism: hence he was keen that the conflict between science and theology in his own time should not have the same outcome as that between reason and dogma in the previous century. Admiring though he is of these and many other achievements, Annan is always judicial. Stephen, he points out, ignored all religions save Western Christianity; he succeeded no better than his brother or Harrison in solving the problem of providing secular to replace religious sanctions on conduct; he tried to work evolution into his solution, but alas, 'there is no logical connection at all between moral standards and the evolutionary process.' Such attempts only show how powerful was the effect of a remembered religion on the thought of these agnostics. Stephen could hardly have foreseen that in his daughters' generation ethics would be associated not with science but with art.

We are told about Stephen's more sporting achievements, especially on mountains and towpaths, and Lord Annan reveals an unexpectedly intimate acquaintance with these activities and the philosophy that lies behind them. But of course Stephen spent a lot more time at his desk than on mountains. After he left Cambridge, he wrote three or four articles a week, and sometimes six thousand words at a sitting. Much of what he wrote is naturally of small interest now; he had failings as a literary critic which Annan doesn't fail to indicate; he was not a professional biographer in the way Ms Vogeler, for example, is; indeed he was as unmodern as you might expect.

Yet his problems were real, and they were seriously engaged, and the fact that argument has moved away from them doesn't change that. Much that probably seemed advantageous at the time now strikes us as getting in his way. He was 'too ecumenical', too judicious, insufficiently *déraciné*; 'an amateur scholar, a Victorian gentleman' rather like Darwin or Acton (Annan's comparison), using outdated critical apparatus and techniques. Perhaps Cambridge had something to do with this: when Stephen visited Heidelberg he found that the only other person sculling on the Neckar was another Englishman. But in spite of all the defects, the emotional self-indulgence, the melancholy (after all, he lost two wives whom he liked), the meanness to his daughters (Virginia reckoned he spent about £300 on her education), he still emerges as 'an adorable man, and somehow tremendous'. It is Virginia Woolf's phrase, but Annan, having that intimacy of which I spoke, endorses it and makes it credible. It is not surprising that he retains the original ending of his book, a quotation from Lowes Dickinson's eulogy of Stephen:

> It does not become a Cambridge man to claim too much for his university, nor am I much tempted to do so. But there is, I think, a certain type, rare, like all good things, which seems to be associated in some peculiar way with my alma mater. I am thinking of men like Leslie Stephen . . . The world could never be driven by such men, for the springs of action lie deep in ignorance and madness. But it is they who are the beacon in the tempest . . . May their succession never fail!

This is the language of Forster's, and Annan's, King's, of an 'aristocracy' for which Annan long since supplied a history. And it explains why these books, good as they both are, concerned as they are with apparently similar subjects, are so different. Ms Vogeler, we may be sure, was not, any more than Mrs Harrison, educated at Wadham.

London Review of Books, 6 December, 1984

Squalor

On George Gissing

The books listed below have been my leisure reading for many weeks, and I have a glimmering as to what it is that prompts the converted to claim so much for Gissing. But my own view, which is very commonplace, remains the same: *New Grub Street* is a novel of extraordinary power, and without it the oeuvre would be no more than the interesting record of a pained but minor artist.

John Halperin, of course, takes a different view,* claiming that a dozen of the novels are 'first-rate'. In order to reach that total he has to include *The Paying Guest* – indeed, he thinks it a 'masterpiece'. As it is a short book, about thirty thousand words, which Gissing wrote in a couple of weeks in 1895, it might tempt readers to use it as a test case when considering such claims. Here it is, in a nice but expensive facsimile reprint, an easy and skilful little study of what happened to a suburban household when it took in a lodger, a girl from a vulgar family much richer than her hosts. Ian Fletcher's introduction does wonders for it; he has a fine sense of Victorian class nuances, for the consciences of the not-so-rich, for the servant problem, so agonising when only the poor didn't have them; but he also finds the scene in which the paying guest and her suitor set fire to the drawing-room 'hilarious', and here, I think, is the note of excess common to many of Gissing's supporters. It's a relief, certainly, to find Gissing in so relaxed a mood, still writing about the class and woman

* John Halperin, *Gissing: A Life in Books* (Oxford University Press)

questions, as he almost always did, whatever the ostensible theme, but for once finding them a matter of amusement. But if *The Paying Guest* is a masterpiece the world must be crammed with them.

Still, as Halperin remarks, admirers of Gissing tend to be decent folk, as generous in their praise as in their sympathetic interest in his appalling life, which was dominated, like his books, by problems of sex, money and class, gloomily interrelated. The degree of interrelation is indeed a perpetual theme of the commentators, and M. Michaux's collection* contains some good essays touching on it, and notably on its presence in *New Grub Street,* where all Gissing's woes and terrors come successfully together, so that we have a book notable for its critical power as well as for its account of several ways in which it was possible for a writer of this period to be *maudit* without being a poet.

George Orwell, who had been able to read very few of the books, nevertheless contrived to write one of the best pieces on Gissing, and his explanation of the novelist's wretchedness was that he felt acutely the horrors of life in Late Victorian England, horrors that were 'largely unnecessary'. Orwell's understanding of Gissing's response to these conditions was at least as full, and a good deal more tersely expressed, than that of his later admirers:

> The grime, the stupidity, the ugliness, the sex-starvation, the furtive debauchery, the vulgarity, the bad manners, the censoriousness – these things were unnecessary, since the puritanism of which they were a relic no longer upheld the structure of society. People who might, without becoming less efficient, have been reasonably happy chose instead to be miserable, inventing senseless taboos with which to terrify themselves. Money was a nuisance not merely because without it you starved; what was more important was that unless you had quite a lot of it – £300 a year, say[1] – society would not allow you to live gracefully

[1] Gissing's own estimate was £1,000, or about £40,000 today.

* *George Gissing: Critical Essays,* edited by Jean-Pierre Michaux (New York: Vision and Barnes and Noble)

or even peacefully. Women were a nuisance because even more than men they were the believers in taboos, still enslaved to respectability even when they had offended against it. Money and women were therefore the two instruments through which society avenged itself on the courageous and the intelligent.

Orwell then relates a rather typical Gissing episode from *A Life's Morning* (not a favourite with Halperin) in which a man loses his hat, has to steal money to buy another, since it is impossible to be seen without one, and so runs into a whole series of disasters. A taboo merely; hatlessness later became quite respectable, possibly because of the dashing manners of the Prince of Wales; though among the aspiring poor, as I know from my own childhood, men who earned three pounds a week still, in the Thirties, spent an absurd proportion of their income on hats, and a lot of time brushing them. Of course Orwell means by this example to illustrate prohibitions much more dangerously inhibiting, and equally absurd.

What Orwell doesn't quite see is the extent to which Gissing's own behaviour was affected by the taboos. To be a gentleman one needed to observe them, and Gissing had a hectic contempt for people who merely aspired to the class which could afford to do so with a measure of grace. 'Minor clerks' who dropped their aitches and lived on £2 a week were not entitled to be absurd even in the manner of the middle classes, and Gissing, better-educated and on the whole better-off than they, antagonized this large potential audience – the 'quarter-educated', as he called them, readers of *Titbits* – by his refusal to take them seriously or even to exploit them, as Bennett did: consequently, he ran the risk of falling between the two stools described by Reardon in *New Grub Street*, producing 'what is too empty to please the better kind of readers, yet not vulgar enough to please the worst'. His Reardon-like refusal to contribute to 'the multiplication of ephemerides' is a further sign of his gentlemanly contempt for the new reading public.

The worst of the middle-class inhibitions was the taboo on easy sex. Middle-class girls could not easily be got into bed without marriage, and they would not marry poor men. This theme is very powerful in *New Grub Street*, but it is heard throughout Gissing, in his life as well as his work. Sometimes it appears that nothing stands between the novelist and sexual bliss but a few pounds a week, though it is true that he often laments not only the impossibility of marrying an educated woman but the institution of marriage more generally; and his own third union, with Gabrielle Fleury, who had all the advantages of being middle-class, French and educated, proved almost as disappointing, though in a more genteel way, as his marriages with a prostitute and a working-class girl. In any case it seems possible that he could always have earned more if he'd really wanted to. Of course there was much competition; and some publishers were extraordinarily rapacious. But Gissing was a well-known writer, and although he was occasionally compelled to sell cheap because he was broke it is hard to believe, even allowing for his frightful domestic circumstances, that he could not have earned more than the £3 a week which seems to have been his usual reward for a relatively enormous output. As a matter of fact, he made over £500 in 1895, not a fortune but probably around £20,000 in our money. This was three years before he met his ideal, 'a woman of the intellectual bourgeoisie ... her voice carefully musical ... well read ... consciously refined and intelligent'. It should have worked, but it didn't: marriage itself, not money, was the problem.

Gissing's obstinate preference for domestic misery calls for some other explanation. He married wives whom he could not take with him when he went to see the sort of people he was entitled to know; he wrote stories about marital disasters, and then re-enacted them in his own life. Frederic Harrison, who knew him well, said that Gissing was 'the most hardened egotist and the most refined sybarite I know'; and there are sybarites who prefer nails to rose-leaves. He had a particular hatred for the middle ground between rich and poor – the mortgaged suburban house with its poky over-furnished parlour. It is a sentiment common among those who are bred in the more refined but still insecure stretch of territory that lies closer to the border of affluence than to that of poverty. Gissing said he wanted sexual union without marriage, and spouses with separate houses: but in spite of all this, he married into the certainty of squalor.

It is hard to avoid the conclusion that sex was the real problem, the others being mere sequelae. The resemblance between Gissing and Hardy, whom he much admired, is only superficial. Hardy also thought marriage hopeless: 'there is no satisfactory scheme for the conjunction of the sexes'. But Hardy felt this thought as a poet might. 'The emotions have no place in a world of defect, and it is a cruel injustice that they should have developed in it': Gissing could conceivably have said that, but Hardy's sense that sex is beautiful but necessarily blighted is absent from Gissing, who criticized the ending of *Tess* but could no more have matched the sexual poetry of that novel than he could have written the great poems.

Indeed, Gissing's world is more like that implied by Freud's essay of 1912, called 'The Most Prevalent Form of Degradation in Erotic Life'. A very common condition among modern men, said Freud, was a 'psychical impotence' which divorced desire and love; the sufferers 'lower their sexual object', and enjoy with women they could not love or respect pleasures unavailable from their well-brought-up wives. Respectable women, for their part, suffer not only from the lowered potency of their partners, but from the lengthy abstinence they must endure before achieving even that much satisfaction: so they become frigid, at any rate with their husbands. The remedy for this state of affairs is for men to overcome their deference for women and accustom themselves to the idea of incest with mothers and sisters; but if this seems utopian, Freud is willing to put up with things as they are, since he thinks that if everybody was able to use his or her sexual energy to the full, there would be no reserves for use in other ways, such, presumably, as writing novels.

Nowadays we may have got rid of deference, though expert friends assure me that degradation in erotic life has merely assumed different forms. What seems reasonably certain is that Gissing had it in something like the form outlined by Freud. When he was a student at Manchester he stole from the cloakroom to help the prostitute he later married: that is, the acquisition of money was not the motive of the theft – the real motive was sex with a degraded partner. Thus the 'guilty secret', which, as all commentators note, turns up again and again in Gissing's novels and is always traced back to the cloakroom episode and the subsequent prison sentence, is indissolubly related to degraded sex and fears of incest. His resentment of middle-class women is extraordinary, but he regards all women as ignorant and childish, more interested, if respectable, in moral attachments than in passion. He even scents an evolutionary purpose in female stupidity, and argues that 'the average woman closely resembles, in all intellectual considerations, the average male *idiot* – I speak medically.' It is true that one of his alter egos, Godwin Peak in *Born in Exile*, says that 'the daughter of a county family is a finer being than any girl who can spring from the nomad orders,' but the girl who fits that bill is called Sidwell Warricombe, which hints at a nominal promotion to masculinity.

Gissing seems to have disliked his mother, a cold untouching woman; according to his sister, whose memoir is reprinted in the Michaux collection, his father meant a lot to him, but he died when Gissing was 13. Discounting his remarks about the tortures of chaste celibacy, she denies that her brother had 'strong amorous propensities', attributing his misfortunes to the charitable disposition which led him to steal the money, and to the bitterness of his subsequent life. But it seems clear that he wanted women as much as he despised them. There is a revealing scene in *The Year of Jubilee*, published in 1895, when he had two bad marriages behind him. In that book we find young women of the fairly prosperous lower middle class, and they embody all that he coldly detests. A young man called Horace calls on the despicable Fanny; she is angry, and he stands before her, 'limp and tremulous'. To impress her with his seriousness and daring he speaks ill of his worthy father. 'And he knew his business; he was not ignorant of the girl's ignoble nature. Only the fury of a virgin passion enabled him to talk, and sometimes think, as though he were in love with ideal purity.' Fanny grants him a mild caress, 'passive, unconcerned; no second-year graduate of the pavement could have reserved a completer equanimity; it did not appear that her pulse quickened ever so slightly, nor had her eyelid the suspicion of a droop.' In the context of this novel Gissing's loathing for such women extends to practically everything that constitutes their world – the squalid Jubilee celebrations, the disgusting advertisements, the lodgings and houses of London itself, where live desolate men, 'imprisoned with wife and children amid these leagues of dreary, inhospitable brickwork'. In this *immonde cité* even the social services provide an obbligato of despair – 'the wailing shout of a dustman . . . was like the voice of a soul condemned to purge itself in filth.' In *The Whirlpool*, Harvey Rolfe exclaims that 'there is not a good word to be said for the ordinary life of an English household. Flee from it! . . . Domestic life is played out . . . All ordinary housekeepers' – i.e. not dukes, who 'breed' workers on their estates – 'are at the mercy of the filth and insolence of a draggle-tailed, novelette-reading, feminine democracy.' And when women, those agents of oppression, try to lead unusual lives, or educate themselves out of idiocy, they always seem to go wrong; like Alma in *The Whirlpool*, they may take up the violin and neglect their children, or become New Women, feminists (in whom Gissing took a suspicious and fascinated interest) – with similar consequences.

Not many years later Ford Madox Ford made the desirable Valentine Wannop (why, though, did he give her that despairing name?) a feminist *and* a Classical scholar. Gissing could never have done that. He was proud of his Classics, and in rare moods of exaltation would recite a chorus from Sophocles; when he had money he went straight to Athens, which he celebrated in several set-pieces, though he actually preferred Naples. His love of the Classics he derived from his father: it was a male passion. In the touching novelette *Sleeping Fires*, a father is united with his unknown son in Athens; the agent of reunion is a Classics don who is 'bear-leading' the young man. In this Classical setting, a natural sympathy declares itself between father and son: it would have been impossible for Gissing to imagine anything of the kind between father and daughter, or between two women. But for what he called Hap, Hardy might have been a parson and never bothered to write novels: but for Hap, Gissing might have been a don and escaped Grub Street (not that dons always do). A passion for the Classics was in his time a sure way of distinguishing the man of letters from the Grub

Street hack: but it also indicated membership of a male club. Their exclusion from it merely confirmed the idiocy of women, and provided some revenge for the indignities they imposed on all men with less than £1000 a year. Of course it was a woman who frustrated any hope he might have had of going to Oxford and becoming a true Classic.

Gillian Tindall, in her excellent general study of the novelist, shrewdly noted that the 'guilty secret' was a working-class crime. Its most absurd transformation in the fiction occurs in *Born in Exile*, when Godwin Peak suddenly flees from his college because he cannot bear the shame that must befall him when his uncle opens a cheap restaurant near the campus. It hardly matters how the Fall occurs: what counts is the horror of exile from happiness, from a paradise without the possibility of shame or want.

Gissing knew the particulars of want. *Born in Exile* specifies one of them that is still part of our social life: a 'poverty trap' set by the Inland Revenue, whereby a man with £100 a year escaped tax, but a man with £101 had to pay £4.16.9. (He is talking about the previous generation, but there is no suggestion that matters had improved in the meantime.) From a world rendered mean by such circumstances Peak decides to escape, even though he must lead 'a life of deliberate baseness to do so'. But his secret guilt emerges, and fortune, which had 'decreed his birth in a social sphere where he was ever to be alien', saw to it that he died, as he was born, 'in exile'.

Gissing's own fate was not quite so cruel, but his years in the lower depths marked him indelibly. He came to loathe the masses, and his best book about them is not one of the more sympathetic early ones like *Workers in the Dawn* or *The Unclassed*, but *Demos*, his seventh novel, written at the age of 28. It appeared at a time of socialist demonstrations against unemployment; its topicality was an unusual bit of luck cancelled out later when *The Crown of Life*, an anti-imperialist novel, coincided with the Boer War. Published anonymously, *Demos* was by some gossips attributed to Gladstone. Gissing went in for Victorian plots, and here the plot is based on an absurd will, but it is a strong book, reeking of hatred for the working class. By a testamentary confusion a working man becomes rich and undertakes a quasi-socialist exploitation of the mineral resources of a beautiful countryside. Meanwhile he abandons his working-class girl to marry upward. When the true will is found he loses everything, and is hounded to death by Demos. The aristocratic young man, his patrimony restored, rather improbably reverses the process of industrial disfigurement, and marries the dead man's widow: 'the untruth of years fell from her like a veil, and she had achieved her womanhood.' The old girlfriend, who had almost saved her unfaithful lover from the fury of the mob, did no such thing.

'In *Demos* it is particularly easy to observe Gissing's fantasies at work. Soon he gave up writing about the poor; and without altogether abandoning what Jacob Korg calls 'the iconography of degradation', he had occasional fits of relative jollity, as in the successful and lively novel of 1889, *The Town Traveller*. Less Dickensian than Wellsian, this novel is brightened by that rare person in Gissing, a high-spirited, noisy girl, whose relations with 'minor clerks' is part of the subject. 'Belonging to a class which, especially in its women, has little intelligence to boast of, she yet redeemed herself from the charge of commonness by a vivacity of feature,' comments Gissing on another woman in another novel, *Eve's Ransom*; it is set in Birmingham, and though it was written in a hurry we get some of the old iconography in a description of the statue of Peel, beside which stands 'a hansom, the forlorn horse crossing his knees and hanging his hopeless head'. Mr Halperin has little time for either of these interesting novels, and he also dislikes a lively novel called *Our Friend the Charlatan*, which has another guilty secret (this time plagiarism) but also a rich and comically ogrish woman called Lady Ogram. It sometimes seems he dislikes the idea of Gissing have a bit of fun.

Indeed, as I said at the outset, Mr Halperin's judgments are often mysterious to me. *Will Warburton*, Gissing's last novel, is about a young man who loses his money and becomes a grocer, which affects his relations with middle-class women. It's well done, but Halperin calls it 'one of his very greatest novels', which is to me as inexplicable as the judgment on *Sleeping Fires*, described as Gissing's *Antony and Cleopatra*, 'brilliant, highly dramatic, and wonderfully passionate . . . one of the greatest short novels ever written'. We have to remind ourselves of other books written at the same time – say, *The Red Badge of Courage* and *The Spoils of Poynton. The Whirlpool*, another of Halperin's 'great' novels, appeared in the same year as *What Maisie Knew*.

James, indeed, is more judicious than this later eulogist of Gissing. He had, he said, a 'persistent taste' for this author, a taste established by *New Grub Street* and triumphing 'even over the fact that he almost as persistently disappoints me . . . The whole business of distribution and composition he strikes me as having cast to the winds.' James had *The Whirlpool* in mind: it is an interesting novel and it testifies in some degree to Gissing's assertion that the effort of the novelist must be to embody his own 'shaping spirit'; it owes something to Dickens, something to Hardy, yet it is very much a Gissing novel. But James's criticism is fair.

All the same, Wells's judgment that Gissing was 'no novelist' is absurd. He had skill and fluency. His method seems to have been to work fast at an idea, write up to a third of a book, and then either abandon it or hurry to the end. Sometimes he might dash off a short novel in three weeks or so. Nowadays he might be doing quite other things, radio or television plays or film scripts, buying himself time to be the novelist he felt he really was, without ceasing to be a man of letters. 'It is ill to have been born in these times,' he said, 'but one can make a world within the world.' And that he did.

Mr Halperin gives us a thorough, if pedestrian account of both those worlds. Perhaps he exaggerates the remoteness of the world Gissing had to live in, calling it 'as remote from the aeroplane and automobile, the telephone and telegraph, movies and television, as that of *Adam Bede*'. Actually it would be a reasonable bet that more telegrams are sent by Gissing's characters than by those of any other author; his inner city was clogged by traffic, dirty, full of contrasts between rich and poor, just like modern London, and no one understood better than he that literature had become a commodity, and writers mere 'hands'. If he is worth reading it is not as an act of what Samuel Hynes calls 'Victoriolatry' but because he did make a world, and because, as he sometimes remarked, he could see the future. He wrote thirty-odd books, including a good one about Greece, a good one about Dickens, and the fantasized autobiography, *The Private Papers of Henry Ryecroft*. He was a more important writer than his doubles in *New Grub Street* but a lesser one than his champions are now trying to make out.

New Grub Street is published by Penguin (556 pp., 1980).

In the Year of Jubilee and *Eve's Ransom* are published by Dover/Constable (404 pp., 1982, and 129 pp., 1982).

The Odd Women is published by Virago (336 pp., 1980).

The Private Papers of Henry Ryecroft is published by Oxford University Press (298 pp., 1983).

The following novels by Gissing are available from Harvester Press:

Born in Exile, 470 pp., 1978.

Sleeping Fires, 230 pp., 1977.

Demos: A Story of English Socialism, 524 pp., 1975.

The Crown of Life, 320 pp., 1979.

The Emancipated, 484 pp., 1977.

Workers in the Dawn, 1983.

The following novels are currently out of print:

The Paying Guest, 200 pp., 1982.

The Whirlpool, 461 pp., 1977.

The Town Traveller, 336 pp., 1982.

Our Friend the Charlatan, 480 pp., 1976.

Will Warburton, 384 pp., 1982.

Isabel Clarendon, 720 pp., 1982.

Denzil Quarrier, 270 pp., 1979.

Thyrza, 490 pp., 1974.

The Nether World, 392 pp.

The Unclassed, *Veranilda* and *A Life's Morning* were also published by Harvester Press.

A Little of this Honey

Oscar Wilde

Richard Ellmann's Life of Joyce, generally regarded as the best literary biography of our time, was the work of his middle years. The last third of his own life was largely given to this biography of Wilde,* which was in some ways a very different sort of undertaking. There were surviving acquaintances of Joyce, but nobody who knew Wilde is available for questioning; the material, though copious, must be sought in libraries. But Ellmann was an exceptionally gifted researcher, never bragging about his finds, just folding them quietly into his narrative, as he does in this book.

For such a labour one would need not merely an admiration for the subject but a temperamental affinity, such as Ellmann obviously had with Joyce. He loved the clutter of Joyce's mind – that 'mind of a grocer's assistant' – and he also knew how to value the passion for occult patterns underlying the mess. In Wilde he chose another Irish subject: but the fantasy is different, the blarney more scented, and the achievement, in the opinion of many, of a less incontestably high order. Wilde's life, spent in a more or less continuous blaze of publicity, was far more absurd, far more spectacular, and finally far more luridly tragic, than Joyce's. His perfect biographer might be rendered incapable of writing the book by the very qualities that made him a suitable choice.

Hesketh Pearson, who wrote the best biography before this one, was advised by Shaw not to attempt it. For, as he saw it,

* Richard Ellmann, *Oscar Wilde* (London: Hamish Hamilton)

everything that could be said had already been said – by Frank Harris and others, including Shaw himself; and although Wilde was 'incomparably great as a raconteur, and as a personality . . . these points cannot be reproduced.' There is obviously some truth in this; we can hardly imagine what it must have been like to know Wilde and to hear him talk, for all the evidence suggests that there has never been anybody like him. There is nothing Ellmann or anybody else can do except report such talk as has survived – mostly epigrams and paradoxes, now for the most part too well known, too machine-made, and too often imitated, to induce hysteria. How, then, can a biographer justify going ahead? Ellmann's solution, broadly speaking, is twofold: to add to the stock of information about Wilde, and to treat him as both a great writer and a misunderstood moral genius.

The second of these is the more controversial project. This biography is at its magnificent best in its last third, for Wilde wrote very little after his disgrace, and could only with difficulty be proposed as at that stage a model of conduct, so the literary and ethical issues aren't so controversial. The section Ellmann entitles 'Disgrace' covers only the last six of Wilde's 46 years, but it occupies a quarter of the book. It could scarcely have been better done. The narrative is familiar in outline, but here the detail is everything. Even in our time, inundated as we are with accounts of even worse suffering and even worse desolation in even worse prisons, this account of Wilde at hard labour, sick, starving, cold and solitary, fills one with pity and disgust. The governor of one of his gaols is reported as saying that no middle-class person of sedentary habit (and middle age) could expect to live more than another two years after serving a sentence of two years at hard labour, and after reading this book one can believe it. Wilde, though fat, was tall and strong, and he lived on for four years: but in some respects it was only half-life.

In describing that famous fall – the three trials and their sequel – Ellmann has more to add than his own reflections. For example, it was known that the Marquess of Queensberry, the 'infamous brute' whom it was Wilde's worst bit of luck to cross, also had it in for Lord Rosebery, who at the time of the Wilde libel action was Prime Minister. Queensberry had followed Rosebery to Homburg, stalking him with a dogwhip (presumably, says Pearson, because he didn't happen to have a horse with him), and grievous bodily harm was prevented only by the personal intervention of the Prince of Wales. Queensberry's resentment was reasonably supposed to have arisen from the suicide of his son Lord Drumlanrig, private secretary to Rosebery, but its precise cause was the Marquess's suspicion that his son had been Rosebery's lover. The suicide may have been occasioned by fear of blackmail, or possibly by a desire to save Rosebery from a politically ruinous scandal. His tenure as prime minister was brief and insecure, and though it did occur to him to come to Wilde's assistance at the time of the libel action, he refrained for fear of losing the imminent general election. Later, when the jury disagreed at Wilde's first trial, there was a chance that the matter might end there, but 'the abominable rumours against Rosebery' were held to necessitate a second trial. Ellmann typically puts this little horror- or bad-luck story together from a contemporary item in the *New York Times*, a manuscript journal in the library of the University of Texas, and a published letter of T. M. Healey's.

Among other things, it shows that Wilde was not as fortunate as he may have imagined to have very grand acquaintances, the first claim on whose attention is likely to be the need to look after themselves, and the second to look after their own very grand acquaintances.

He had also to learn some hard lessons about his less noble friends. Always ready to cast himself in some mythological role, he had in his time been Narcissus, St Sebastian, Marsyas (the musician who was flayed alive for challenging Apollo); he was in the end to see himself as Timon. He fits the part pretty well. Having in happier times been prodigally generous, he was reduced in his last years to begging. When he stopped Nellie Melba in a Paris street and asked her for money, she gave him what she had in her purse. But Henry James's friend Morton Fullerton made a more typical response – he must have written this letter with Shakespeare's play open on his desk:

> I am distressed to have left your touching appeal un-
> answered for so long. But I have been on congé in the

patrie of Stendhal, and had cognizance of your *gène* only yesterday. You do me too much honour in asking me to come to the rescue of an artist such as you. And if I could have known of the situation 3 weeks ago when I had money in my pocket I should not have hesitated for a moment, especially as I had just received your play [*Earnest*] and was in the state of mind of one who says without thinking: 'it is worth its weight in gold.' But at present, after an expensive journey, I am unable, with the best goodwill in the world, to seize the event and to accept the *rôle* in this particular comedy – I use the word in its Hellenic and Gallic sense, *bien entendu*, in the sole sense in which it exists for the admirers of *Lady Windermere's Fan* and of *The Importance of Being Earnest*, etc.

Presumably there was no point in appealing to James himself, since he called Wilde an 'unclean beast' and refused to sign a clemency petition. There were closer friends who shunned him: Beardsley, for instance, who owed him so much; John Gray, an early lover, for whose *Silverpoints*, prettiest of Nineties poetry-books, Wilde had paid; Lilly Langtry, to whom he had, at one time, brought a daily lily, and who claimed to have sent him money without having actually done so. Beerbohm did not spurn him but kept his distance. Of his old friends Robbie Ross, who had introduced Wilde to homosexuality at the age of thirty-two, stood by him to the end, and he was supported by Reginald Turner and Frank Harris. They were joined by Jean Dupoirier, proprietor of the Paris hotel in which Wilde died, and perhaps of all his friends the most disinterested and serviceable.

It is easy to say that Wilde brought his distress on himself. The penury of his last years was in part due to his inability to live other than extravagantly, and in even greater part to his resuming relations with Lord Alfred Douglas – not only because the allowance from his wife was expressly conditional on his not doing so, but because, as he knew very well, Douglas was sure to bring him further disasters. It was the clearest possible proof of Wilde's self-destructiveness that knowing all he did about the treachery of this lover he should again put himself in his hands.

If one emotion prevails over all others in Ellmann's book it is loathing and contempt for Bosie, Wilde's great love and worst enemy – a callous bully, cruel in his rages and coldly exploitative, pretty and vain, autocratic and whining, jealous and promiscuous. Ellmann has no difficulty in bringing out the 'young man's close resemblance to the father he loathed, and against whom he unscrupulously used Wilde.

Ellmann conceived the whole life as tragedy, finding even in the triumphant part of it many premonitions of disaster. He attaches great importance to the fact that Wilde contracted syphilis while at Oxford, and has no doubt that the disease contributed to his early death: indeed he remarks that this conviction is central to my conception of Wilde's character and my interpretation of many things in his later life'. Wilde presumably thought himself cured, but it could no doubt be argued that he still feared the disease, and that the fear affected the writing of *Dorian Gray*, for instance.

Here as elsewhere Ellmann likes to underline the evidence that Wilde had forebodings of some future disaster, which induced him to live fully and dangerously in the present. And he certainly did take risks even before he became a practising homosexual. In an Oxford where you could be charged with the offence of 'keeping and reciting immoral poetry' it was risky to make a cult of St Sebastian, and Matthew Arnold's university was hardly the place to announce that the right way to live was to do as you like, and get what you want. Even in the larger world of London there were limits, and he achieved celebrity by continually flirting with them. When, in 1881, Gilbert satirized him in *Patience*, he was still only 26, and had published little except his first book of poems. He owed his fame to his daring in dress, talk and conduct. Such fame is inseparable from envy, and the friends made in the course of such a life could easily turn into bitter enemies, as Whistler did. No wonder Wilde had forebodings, especially when he became more or less openly and indiscreetly homosexual.

There is a sonnet in which Wilde quotes the plea of Jonathan: 'I did but taste a little honey with the end of the rod that was in my hand, and lo! I must die.' In the Bible story Jonathan has broken Saul's prohibition against eating, the announcement of which he'd missed. He doesn't die, because the people rally and save him. Wilde's poem is ostensibly about spoiling one's life by preferring pleasure to arduous study, but Ellmann thinks he is surreptitiously hoping that like Jonathan he can have his taste of honey and still be saved. It seems more likely that the poet was remembering Jonathan's earlier remark: 'how my eyes have been enlightened because I tasted a little of this honey.'

Taken together, the texts fit nicely the image of the *poète maudit*, death being the price of his gift, and sex the agent of death. This is how Wilde might wish to see himself; he can hardly, even in his most extravagant daydream, have expected to be saved by the people. The point is that he was in this instance matching himself with a fashionable stereotype rather than anticipating doom and possible redemption.

Even if Wilde himself hadn't had premonitions, there would still have been, in the ordinary way of things, events in his life to which a biographer can give the quality of tragic portents. Ellmann describes Wilde's visit to a prison in Nebraska, his consultation with a palmist called Cheiros, and several other incidents, in those terms. Once he found on a tomb the epitaph *une heure viendra qui tout paiera* – incidentally, the words are badly mistranslated in the text.[1] The motto is rather menacing, certainly, but it is, after all, a threat of very general application.

Still, there were doubtless hints and warnings of varying gravity, and it was Wilde's way to carry on being outrageous or funny rather than heed them. Whether this justifies the claim that he was 'conducting, in the most civilized way, an anatomy of his society, and a radical reconsideration of its ethics', does seem a bit doubtful. Ellmann twice brackets Wilde with Blake and Nietzsche; along with them 'he was proposing that good and evil are not what they seem, that moral tab[u]s cannot cope with the complexity of behaviour. His greatness as a writer is partly the

[1] Since the book will obviously be many times reprinted it is worth pointing out such errors. The aesthetician Baumgarten is called 'Baumgartner' in text and index (pp. 31, 85, 596). The daughter of Herodias (Salome or Hérodiade) is called 'Herodias' (p. 320). 'The cultivation of art apart from life is to build a fire that cannot burn' (p. 300) is a sentence gone astray. I have also thought fit to read 'tabus' for 'tabs' in a sentence I proceed to quote, and to emend the punctuation of the last sentence of the book.

result of the enlargement of sympathy which he demanded for society's victims.' It is true that Wilde was at his best a generous and a gentle man: he would take off his coat and give it to a naked beggar, and he was properly appalled by the meanness and cruelty with which society treated the unlucky or the criminal. But he himself would presumably have denied that these or any other virtues had any relevance to art. To call *The Picture of Dorian Gray* a critique of aestheticism that 'went far beyond Whistler and Gautier' is not necessarily false, and it may not even be false to say that 'by cunning and eloquence Wilde restored art to the power that the romantic poets had claimed for it, able once again to legislate for the world': but Wilde might have thought it odd, and so will many of his readers.

The best of Wilde, outside the theatre, is to be found in such essays as 'The Truth of Masks', 'The Critic as Artist' and 'The Decay of Lying', which are not simple in tone, but do seem to place a barrier between art and action, or legislation in any normal sense of the word. I risk the rejoinder that the implied legislative programme was meant to serve the interests not of action but of contemplation, described by Wilde as 'the proper occupation of man'. All the same, the state of the world was manifestly hostile to contemplation, and therefore required action: a requirement on which Wilde reflects at some length in 'The Soul of Man under Socialism'. One way of finding out whether one agrees with Ellmann's estimate of Wilde as an ethical force is to reread this essay, the rather camp arguments of which are here rehearsed with what seems like unqualified approval. For Ellmann was determined to prove that Wilde was a sage, a heroic figure, ahead of his time – the portent of a future ethic, as well as the agent of his own destruction.

What we are here told about Wilde's family may help us to form more mundane estimates. His parents were distinguished and somewhat bizarre. His father was a famous Dublin doctor, a man of many interests and evident vitality, who fathered three bastards in addition to his legitimate family, and managed to conceal the identity of their mother or mothers from everybody, including even Richard Ellmann. Wilde's mother was a nationalist poet, good-hearted, flamboyant, and with a bravura dottiness that

Wilde must have inherited. She called herself 'Speranza', and claimed a previous existence as an eagle, telling the youthful Yeats that she therefore needed to 'live in some high place, Primrose Hill or Highgate'. Her elder son Willie was a witty scamp famous in the Dublin pubs. Asked what he was working at, he would reply: 'At intervals.' Max Beerbohm said he was very like Oscar, with the same 'coy, carnal smile'. He was completely unreliable and irresponsible, but unlike his brother got into scrapes rather than catastrophes.

Oscar lacked Willie's malice, and his underhand ways, and also had more conscience about work. His career at Oxford left him little time for reading, but despite a failure in Divinity and a period of rustication he took a double First in Greats, aided no doubt by his famous skill as a fast reader (it is said that he could read a novel in three minutes). To have done so well at university, in the perfectly ordinary sense of the phrase, gave him much satisfaction, for at this stage, and possibly later as well, he retained some conventional values. However, as Ellmann puts it, 'he created himself at Oxford', and he did it not by writing Greek proses but by fine talk, fine clothes and a risky degree of impudence. The strain of prudence was, however, not extinct, and it showed up when he drew back at the last moment from conversion to Rome, fearing he might lose a legacy by going ahead with it. He contented himself instead with membership of a very fancy Masonic lodge.

Ellmann duly documents these and other contests between inclination and prudence, in which, as time went by, prudence had fewer and fewer successes. Yielding to Bosie's false persuasions at the time when he could have withdrawn his action against Queensberry was a crucial defeat for prudence; taking Bosie back after prison was another. But even in the days of his triumph – on the American tour, and in the days just before the disaster, when he had two successful plays in the West End – Wilde was always finding or putting himself in positions where such contests were inevitable.

Ellmann often, and rightly, reminds us of his virtues – he was only occasionally overbearing or coarse, and he was always generous; delight in his company was universal, and we see its signs wherever the biographer follows him – at his mother's salons, in Whitman's house, at Mallarmé's *mardis*, in cafés with the young Gide and Pierre Louÿs.

His power to inspire affection was extraordinary, and it depended on more than wit and fancy: he made people love him. But he also gave envy some wonderful opportunities, and knew that he was doing so. 'Of course I knew there would be a catastrophe, either that or something else,' he told Gide after his release from prison. 'To go any further was impossible, and that state of things could not last . . . there had to be some end to it.' He may not have expected that his admirers would so firmly disown him, or that the envious could be so malignant. But like his biographer, he came to see that the shape of his life was determined by its end, and was therefore tragic.

Macaulay in a famous passage spoke of the British public savaging Byron in one of its 'periodical fits of morality': 'He was excluded from circles where he had been the observed of all observers. All those creeping things that riot in the decay of nobler natures hastened to their repast; and they were right, they did after their kind. It is not every day that the savage envy of aspiring dunces is gratified by the agonies of such a spirit, and the degradation of such a name.' Ellmann catches Macaulay's mood, and it becomes our own, as we read the book – indeed it must, in some measure, whenever we think of Wilde. It is the fate of a very few writers to have led lives so remarkable that we think first of their fates and only then of their works. Merely to have written *The Importance of Being Earnest* must constitute a claim to immortality: yet when our thoughts turn to Wilde we are likely first to remember how he was tormented by a crazy nobleman, spat on at Clapham Junction, alienated from his children, and left to die in exile. After that, we may have some thoughts about epigrams, green carnations, lilies and decadence, and only then of the books and plays.

Ellmann has not sought to diminish the pity of it all, but he has tried, sometimes, perhaps, with rather too heavy a hand, to remind us of the writer, and to persuade us that decadence may be the other face of renovation. 'He belongs to our world more than to Victoria's. Now, beyond the reach of scandal, his best writings validated by time, he comes before us, still a towering figure, laughing and weeping, with parables and paradoxes, so generous, so amusing, and so right.' It is deeply satisfying that Dick Ellmann should have ended his work with that generous sentence.

London Review of Books, 29 October 1987

Georgian Eyes are Smiling

Shaw and Conrad in Their Letters

There were already good biographies of Shaw, notably those of Frank Harris and Hesketh Pearson, both of whom knew Shaw and had the benefit of his energetic interventions. Pearson in particular will not be easily supplanted. Nevertheless the archives of the world are full of Shaviana inaccessible before his death, and because there had not been a serious attempt since 1956 – the centenary year – the Shaw Estate sensibly decided that the time had come for a new biography, and invited Mr Holroyd to write it. It is not surprising that the work has preoccupied him for a great many years, nor that it will consist of three large volumes. This one* takes Shaw from his birth in 1856 to his marriage in 1898, by which time he was already celebrated or notorious, but still near the beginning of his success as a playwright.

Holroyd, needing to make a decision about how and where to record his scattered and multitudinous sources, has thought it best to leave them out altogether from the three volumes of text, and, in due time, publish them separately. His motive, which is to avoid delay in publication and avoid also 'charging general readers for an apparatus they will never use', is generous enough, but the decision is still disappointing, for some of the interest lies in spotting what is new, and even general readers – a category authors are tempted to fashion in whatever image suits their book – might like to know where it came from. Shaw produced no

* Michael Holroyd, *Bernard Shaw. Vol. I: The Search for Love, 1856–1898* (London: Chatto & Windus)

formal autobiography but wrote freely about himself – for instance, in long patiently buoyant letters to the haplessly aspiring Professor Demetrius O'Bolger of Philadelphia, and in fake interviews, as well as in some of his published writings. There is also the shorthand diary he kept for 13 years. Much of this material is now accessible in print, but Holroyd must have trawled in many other waters, and we shall have to wait, perhaps a long time, for the record of his doing so.

To be done at once with these gentle criticisms: the subtitle, perhaps also devised to please the general reader, may raise a sigh or a yawn rather than quicken interest. It pertains, but so would 'the flight from love' or the like, and neither really gives much idea of the content of the volume. Holroyd is keen to map on to Shaw's maturity his recollections of the *ménage à trois* in which he was reared. The interloper was the glamorous musician Vandeleur Lee, about whose origins Holroyd has a lot of interesting things to say. Lee had a miraculous voice-training method and is said, though not very credibly, to have been one of the models for Du Maurier's Svengali. He was a bit shady, a bit of a rogue – a type Shaw habitually fell for and habitually treated with great generosity. In conscious or unconscious emulation he liked to attach himself to married couples. These triangles recur throughout his earlier life, and crop up in *Candida* and in *The Devil's Disciple*. The wives would usually be attracted, but he seems not to have seduced them. In a well-known letter, used by Frank Harris in his biography and now given in its original form by Dan Laurence, Shaw claims to have no scruples in matters of sex, but at once goes on to admit he has two: he will take care not to get women into trouble, and he will refrain from cuckolding his friends. Here as elsewhere – in money matters, for instance, he observed his own rules very scrupulously.

Shaw wasn't always candid enough about some aspects of his youth to satisfy biographers, and although he claimed that there was nothing between the great singing teacher and his mother but friendship and professional association he may all the same – as Holroyd conjectures – have had other ideas, and even fancied himself the son of the flamboyant Lee rather than of his wretched father; Beatrice Webb, it seems, was sure he was Lee's son. What he certainly owed to Lee was his early knowledge of music, the principal positive educational attainment of his Dublin childhood. Other benefits were somewhat negative: his experience of performing badly at bad schools left him sceptical about normal education; his family, decayed aristocrats, gave him a hatred of snobbery, and Dublin a loathing of 'state superstition' and poverty.

While doing various jobs of a clerkly sort, he soaked himself in opera, and grew confident, though possibly no more than many other young men, of some sort of future greatness. At 20, having moved with the family to London, he was ghosting music criticism for Lee and writing stories, book reviews and part of a play about Jesus. The 'pale, private Shaw' he was then decided to be a writer, and doggedly worked at novels held to be so immoral, so 'disagreeable and perverse', that no one would publish them. Already a vegetarian, a teetotaller, a clothes reformer and a champion of women's rights, he was studying the realities of London life and Late Victorian society, disgusted with the falsity of conventional accounts, seeking always the hard facts, yet always, in his own way, an aesthete. His arguments for vegetarianism have ethical and hygienic components but are mainly aesthetic (one remembers how pleased he was with Almroth Wright's observation that hygiene was fundamentally a matter of aesthetics). They are also cogent: if sound argument ever prevailed over prejudice we should, under Shaw's influence, have given up meat long ago.

Along with all this he was seriously studying socialism; fired by Henry George, he was instructed mainly by Marx, whom he actually read (in French). Soon he was an indispensable Fabian. He worked like the devil – it is quite a relief to find him talking about his 'inveterate laziness', and to learn that on some days he 'did practically nothing'. But on such days he must have been working at the construction of a harder and more complex personality, a new Shaw who was always joking yet always in earnest, and always fascinating – handsome in his Jaeger suit and in the beard he grew to cover a smallpox scar.

He made interesting rather than close friends. Holroyd gives a fine account of his relationship with the amiable Ibsenite William Archer. Shaw, working as an art critic, would go with Archer to the shows. 'He didn't know much about painting then,' said Archer, 'but he thought he did, and that was the main point.' It was the same, perhaps, with women. He devoted some of his scant leisure to flirting with them, and they usually found his gallantries at once comical, infuriating and hard to resist. But he was 29 before he lost his virginity, to a friend of his mother's 15 years his senior. This affair was satisfactory to begin with, despite, Holroyd thinks, a pregnancy crisis: but Shaw was incapable of the attentiveness called for, and it ended in tears. Remembering this debacle, he later took a strong line about feminine demands on him, somewhat in the manner of Dick in *The Devil's Disciple*.

Among those he tormented were Edith Bland, whose husband Hubert was unfaithful. Failing to get Shaw into bed, she made her famous complaint: 'You had no right to write the Preface if you were not going to write the book.' Then there were Annie Besant, May Morris (especially after her marriage) and Florence Farr, for whom he had a rival in Yeats. Another whose marriage he triangulated was Janet Achurch; yet another, on whom he worked mostly by letter, was Ellen Terry. And there were more actresses, among them Mrs Patrick Campbell, some married and some not. He had a taste for actresses, and for other distinguished women. He refused to follow the way of the world and 'substitute custom for conscience', but some thought his sexual preferences, however proper by his own lights, liable to be destructive, even self-destructive. Beatrice Webb (over whose marriage he innocently hovered) spoke harshly of his brand of philandering. She had begun by disliking him, but came to know his value, and did not want him spoiled; in 1897 she complained that 'his sensuality has all drifted into sexual vanity – delight in being the candle to the moths – with a dash of intellectual curiosity to give flavour to his tickled vanity. And he is mistaken if he thinks it does not affect his artistic work. His incompleteness as a thinker, his shallow and vulgar view of many human relationships ... all these defects come largely from the flippant and worthless self-complacency brought about by the worship of rather second-rate women.' She was much relieved when (at the end of this volume) a sudden serious illness seems to have forced Shaw to stop fooling about with a first-rate woman, Charlotte Payne-Townshend – a generous benefactor of the Fabians, whose money was seed corn for the London School of Economics – and marry her ('I proposed to make her my widow'). Holroyd's account of this side of Shaw's life is admirable. His prose occasionally takes on the vitality of Shaw's, as if he were closely paraphrasing, which at times he presumably is. We shall see, in due course.

In these years Shaw's playwrighting had to be done in the spare time left by journalism and all his other exhausting activities. To give a fair notion of these activities was probably the biographer's hardest task, and he does it well, with interesting detail about Shaw's work as a vestryman in St Pancras. He campaigned against housing policy, vaccination and other evils; for honesty in local government, for independence in relation to a Parliament which forced wrong decisions on weak councils, and for the infiltration, first at local level, of socialist ideals: 'The little Socialism we have is gas and water Socialism. And it is by extension of Gas and Water Socialism that industry will be socialised.' (He might not have been surprised by the present Whitehall domination of St Pancras, though he would hardly, in his least optimistic mood, have foreseen the abolition of gas and water socialism.) In this public career he cut a certain dash, achieving only a little, but as much as he could have expected; and, as Holroyd says, he picked up a lot of information that would be useful to him as a dramatist.

This biography is unlikely to change our general idea of the younger Shaw, but it enriches and complicates the detail, making the image somewhat darker by emphasizing the insecurities that lay under the enormous affable assurance of the superman. Having found that the one reliable drug was work, he became addicted to it – reading and writing almost incessantly, studying music and economics, making himself expert in a wide variety of useful subjects, producing a mass of journalism of all sorts as well as his early plays, and writing long eloquent letters on every conceivable topic and occasion.

It might be said that the period covering the lives of Shaw (1865–1950) and Conrad (1857–1924) was not only the last age of letter-writing – the telephone was slowly taking over – but also its great age, a terminal flowering of the genre. It was still necessary to write letters and still possible to discourse fluently and informally on the matter in hand, which might be deeply personal or merely a means of setting up a meeting next day (or even on the same day). People would normally write without a thought of subsequent retrieval and collection – letters were simply the main instrument of civilized intercourse. The postal service was cheaper and more efficient than ever before or since. Paper was cheap, and no one yet thought it inconvenient or laborious to write with a pen. Typewriters, thought appropriate only to mechanical business tasks, were manipulated mostly by female labour: indeed, the word was used not only of the machine but of the typist. The first occurrence of this word recorded in *OED* – the T volume was compiled in 1917 – is dated 1885 and still enclosed in quotes, though by 1890 a Society of Typists existed to examine 'type writer operators', and the word in its full later sense was around by 1902. Its association with women workers was sometimes demonstrated in the spelling 'typiste'. Such persons were not often used for private correspondence (the later Shaw was an exception, being rich enough to have a personal secretary and having acquired a mastery of shorthand). Until quite recently, and perhaps still in some old-fashioned circles, a prejudice lingered against the use of machines for friendly or intimate letters, but at the same time personal communications from word-processors are growing more common. On the principle that the more time-saving devices there are the less time one has to spare (for a business machine converts everything into business), long, easy, digressive letters presumably don't get written except by deliberate archaists.

It doesn't of course follow that in the age of Shaw everybody, or even very good writers, wrote marvellous letters. The new Conrad volume* provides a convincing demonstration of the contrary. Conrad is by comparison with Shaw amazingly limited, almost entirely absorbed by his own admittedly awful problems, and especially by his distaste for the business of writing and his desperate shortage of cash.

Shaw had cash in quantities, though in his last years he imagined

* *Collected Letters of Joseph Conrad. Vol. III: 1903–1907*, edited by Frederick Karl and Laurence Davies (Cambridge University Press)

the Labour Government was mulcting him to the point where he paid more in tax than he earned: his allusions to this iniquity are uncharacteristically unfacetious. But these senescent grumbles form a very small part of his colossal correspondence, which, since he was, as he admitted, almost the most famous man in the world, people tended to preserve. The earliest surviving letter is dated 1872, the latest 1950.

This fourth and final volume of the Laurence edition* covers the last twenty-five years of Shaw's life, and although he grumbles a bit about an increasing tendency to forgetfulness and deafness there is only a little diminution in the vast range of his interests, the vigour of his epistolary prose, or, for that matter, his memory. Most of the 740 letters in this volume are newly published. Of course they represent only a small proportion of what is extant, and the selection is bound to be criticized by those who have frequented the archives and can claim to know almost as much about the material as Laurence himself. But everybody else is likely to feel that he has done a patient and devoted job in transcribing – even shorthand that sometimes reverted to 'antiquated grammalogues' or put dots and hooks in the wrong positions – and in elucidating carefully but without pedantry letters containing allusions to all manner of forgotten issues and interests. The list of acknowledgements to libraries, collectors and executors around the world fills three large pages and gives one a faint idea of the labour involved. Laurence mutters a bit about some carping reviews of the earlier volumes, but, having made available one of the finest collection of letters in English, he could afford to ignore them.

It is easy to see that Shaw irritated people in late as in early life. Being vain and assertive, or finding it convenient to wear a mask of assertive vanity, he writes in the same breezily authoritative tone on virtually any topic, including one or two that he was not on the face of it particularly well-qualified to undertake. Yet the collection leaves one full of admiration for the man's character as well as his casually exact prose. He claimed that although

---

* *Bernard Shaw: Collected Letters. Vol. IV: 1926–1950*, edited by Dan Laurence (London: The Bodley Head)

letter-writing had used up years of his working life, 'none of the letters was unnecessary (no time for that) . . .' Writing letters was important work. He wrote, sometimes at length, to complete strangers who sought his advice on their lives. He replied profusely – usually with sharply remembered detail, always with authority and relentless good humour – to letters from people curious about the London theatre of his youth, or anything else on which his age and fame made his opinion worth seeking. And as one reads it is hard to avoid the doubtless over-simple judgment that Shaw was not only a fantastically well-informed man, but also a good man

In a letter of 1928 he writes thus to Ada Tyrrell, whom he had known in his youth:

> My life has rushed through very quickly: I have seen very little of anyone who has not worked with me. Except with my wife I have no companionships. I spring to intimacy in a moment, and forget in half an hour. An empty life is peopled with the absent and the imagined: a full one has to be cleared out every day by the housemaid of forgetfulness or the air would become unbreathable.

But he kept up – by letter – with his old Fabian intimates, the Webbs and Wells, and had a joky intimacy with persons as diverse as Lady Astor, Virginia Woolf and the heavyweight champion Gene Tunney. He was sporadically in touch, affectionate and censorious, with Mrs Patrick Campbell, and kept a kindness for scapegraces such as Lord Alfred Douglas and Frank Harris, in whose biography of Shaw the subject had interfered so heavily and helpfully.

Being rationally opposed to the entire political, social and sexual order of the times, Shaw was professionally candid on subjects such as sex and death, which might make him seem more like Harris than he really was. His candour is without salacity or pride of conquest. In the letter mentioned above he lectures Harris (who set up as an expert on the subject) about copulation: it is not 'a personal relation', and if he were to recount every affair in his life Harris would still be no wiser about his personal, or even his sexual, history. 'You would only know what you already

know: that I am a human being.' Except, perhaps, in having no
notion of sex as a guilty thing, yet in having remained 'a continent
virgin' till the age of 29.

Rather unusually, he understood that 'chastity can be a passion,
just as intellect is a passion,' and this, I think, tells one a good
deal about him. Despite his brilliance as a debater, and despite
what Beatrice Webb called his vulgarity, he often had an intuitive
understanding of attitudes he could not share or even repudiated.
He was irreligious in the most obvious sense, unless worshipping
the Life Force is a form of religion; he disliked almost everything
about Christianity. Yet he was on friendly terms with famous
parsons like Dick Sheppard and W. R. Inge, and had a rather
remarkable correspondence with a nun called Sister Lawrentia.
Her disapproval of his *Little Black Girl in Search of God* upset him,
and when he asked her to pray for him he obviously meant it. A
report of her death proving false, he remarked that he felt 'a soul
had been dragged back from felicity. Which is queer, as of course
I don't believe anything of the sort.'

Not believing anything of the sort, he had his own way (and a
very good way it was) of offering condolence to the bereaved. He
told the newly-widowed Mrs Frank Harris to begin another life
at once 'with the wisdom garnered from your first experiment',
and enclosed a cheque for immediate expenses, since 'death does
not always select a convenient moment when there is plenty of
ready money in the house.' There is characteristic sense and
generosity in this, as there is in his letter to Esmé Percy, who had
asked for a loan on a post-dated cheque. Percy got, along with
some good advice about the dangers of such cheques, a flat refusal
– 'I shall not lend you a farthing': but he also got a present of
£100.

Shaw refused to be intimidated by death, remarking that this
was a family trait. 'Why does a funeral always sharpen one's sense
of humour and rouse one's spirits?' he asks, returning from his
mother's. 'This one was a complete success.' He enjoyed his
sister's cremation, admired the lovely garnet flames provided by
his mother, and went behind the scene to watch the crematorium
workers sorting her ashes. In the present volume he has also to
record the death of his wife: 'People who cry and grieve never

remember. I never grieve and never forget.' So he remembers being inconsiderate towards his unsatisfactory father ('unlucky, untrained and unsuccessful') and says he understands why Dr Johnson stood bareheaded in the rain at Lichfield to atone for a similar fault.

His urge to give advice was irrepressible. He lectured typographers on typography, publishers on publishing, lawyers on the law, copyright experts on copyright, Sir James Pitman on shorthand, Winston Churchill on political history, Edward Elgar on music, Gabriel Pascal on film direction, John Reith on the BBC, and especially actors on acting (he was fond of them much in the way one is fond of children: they needed discipline as well as praise). His tone is often what might have been found offensive had people not come to expect it as part of the Shavian act; and many must have come to see that he was often generous and sage as well as pretending to be both, and also denying it.

During these years he naturally had quite a lot to say about Fascism and Nazism, and although doctors, physiologists, soldiers and many other venerated professions had good cause to deplore him, it is probably for his views on Mussolini and Hitler that he is always likely to get the worst press. His attitude to National Socialism was roughly that as a socialist he himself had decided against world revolution in favour of national revolution, so that he, and all who made that choice, were in fact National Socialists themselves. He was distinctly soft on the dictators ('Fascism, or the organization of the State as a hierarchy of industrial and professional corporations, is right as far as it goes,' he tells a German acquaintance in 1933, 'but these organizations must own industry and the land'). His continuing failure to understand what was happening in the world is shown by a letter about Munich, where he argues that once it seemed clear that the British were really going to fight, 'Musso' pulled Hitler up pretty sharp and made him accept Chamberlain's terms. *Geneva* must be his biggest theatrical *faux pas*. Somebody should study the revisions he made to it in 1938 and 1939, without making it any better. Yet at the time it seemed quite good fun – more of the old fellow's paradoxes, nothing serious.

He repeatedly criticized the Nazis for wasting their energies on a silly persecution of socialists and Jews, regarding anti-Semitism as a foolish and temporary aberration, essentially unrelated to Fascism, and very bad for Germany's international reputation. In 1938 he remarked that 'Musso' had let him down by turning anti-Semite, but he also told Beatrice Webb that states have the right to make eugenic experiments 'by weeding out any strains that they think undesirable, though in such a manner as not to shock civilization by such misdemeanours as the expulsion and robbery of Einstein'. A year later we find him telling Ashley Dukes and the League of Dramatists that he wouldn't subscribe a percentage of one day's royalties to a fund for Jewish refugees (set up by Baldwin). Finally, 'Belsen was obviously produced by the incompetence and breakdown of the military command.'

On Stalin he seems merely gullible. 'With his Georgian eyes and frank smile . . . the lady killer as far as looks go, he is said to be a model of domesticity . . . Instead of making himself President he remains a nondescript nobody.' He was impressed when Stalin told Lady Astor of his indignation that the English beat their children, and charmed by the courtesy with which he himself was received.

What is one to make of all this? First, that Shaw's politics, though in his youth directly related to practical issues, grew more and more abstract. Moreover he lacked what Henry James called the imagination of disaster: he could reduce the camps, and perhaps Stalin's purges, to abstract politics or eugenics. Possibly the strain of anti-Semitism woven into the social fabric of his youth had blunted his sense of Jewish suffering. Shaw repeatedly and credibly denied that he was an anti-semite, but was incapable of being very upset about the activities of those who were. Their practical eugenics seemed a bit rough, their concentration camps badly run because they were left to the dregs of the officers' mess. A certain refusal to care is part of the Shavian style, incident to a calculated disregard for ordinary opinion. On most matters we'd still say he was ruthless on the right side, but hardly on this one.

It is sometimes said that World War One was the critical moment of his life – a purge which had no possible eugenic justification and hardened all the feeling. He could not suffer the effect of the second with quite the same force. He was old, and somewhat preoccupied with his own celebrity, which was of an intensity unmatched by any author since, except perhaps Solzhenitsyn. When he travelled, as he often did, he saw rather little and met only the nobs. Though he knew so much about everything, in one sense he knew very little about these new terrors. It is easier for us to see the horrors of Fascism and eugenics than it was for many people in the Thirties. But however strongly one would wish to do it, his case is not easy to defend. As he himself had written almost half a century before that Belsen letter, 'the worse sin towards our fellow creatures is not to hate them, but to be indifferent to them; that's the essence of inhumanity.'

Shaw's letters can be hilarious, but few other writers produce epistolary hilarity, and Conrad certainly doesn't. He was far less copious than Shaw – the present edition includes all his known letters – and was less interested in arguing and instructing than in his toothache, gout, malaria, eczema, neuralgia, depression, shortage of cash, and 'the atrocious misery of writing'. Added to his personal problems were his wife's ailing knees and heart, and his son Borys's almost continuous illnesses. He wrote repeatedly to his agent Pinker, demanding various kinds of service and urgent supplies of money in a rather peremptory way, almost as of nobleman to tradesman, except that he also says things like 'I daren't even wish myself dead.' To Wells he complains of 'creeping imbecility', and, hearing that Ford Madox Ford is in trouble, he is quick to point out that his state is 'just as bad in its way'. His correspondence with Roger Casement brings out the best in him; he was most at ease with men of action like Casement or Cunninghame Graham. His letters to the press – for example, a protest against the pre-censorship of plays – can't compare with Shaw's on similar issues.

If necessary, we can remind ourselves that he was in most respects a greater artist than Shaw, and that what he was writing, with all manner of slow torment, at the time of these miserable letters, was *Nostromo*. On 3 September 1904 he tells Garnet: 'I write you these lines just to say that Nostromo is finished; a fact upon which my friends may congratulate me as upon a recovery from a dangerous illness.' Though eloquent on their cost, he rarely says much about his books as such, and it is interesting to find him thanking W. H. Chesson for a review of *The Secret Agent* which told him something about his talent that he says he had not himself been aware of – his taste for 'the bizarre – or that which is idiotic with force and egotism'. It isn't easy to conceive of Shaw supposing that his work had senses or qualities he wasn't aware of. But one can see why the critical labour of expounding and illuminating Conrad, which calls for more delicacy and penetration than the exposition of Shaw, continues to attract so many students.

London Review of Books, 15 September 1988

V

———•——

Wells's Ladder

Wells seems to grow more and more interesting, not only because of additional information on his marriage, girls and quarrels, but because a certain conformity to deep and interesting patterns in English life is being made more evident. This new biography* is quite as satisfactory on the second point as on the first. The Mackenzies have had unlimited access to the Wells archive at the University of Illinois, which one had thought to be reserved for a huge biography by Gordon Ray, and they have put it to good use.

Wells was genial and depressive, aggressive and generous, blessed with enormous energy yet prone, at crucial moments, to debilitating illness. He knew everybody, and was, by some criteria, the most successful writer of his time. He sounds, like some of his own stories, a unique blend of the fantastic and the commonplace. He had the kind of mother necessary to English working-class genius: she was 43 when he was born, an anxious, evangelical and snobbish upper servant who married beneath her. 'What a novel my life has been,' she noted on the tenth anniversary of her wedding, 'to one who had to picture everything beautiful, and what a marriage . . . The sombre dress of black cast off for one hour.' Her husband was an easy-going vagabond who took her from luxury below stairs in a great house and installed her in his unsuccessful shop while he wandered about playing cricket. After 25 years she left him to it and went back to her old place at Up House. So Wells's youth accustomed him to what the Mackenzies

* Norman and Jeanne Mackenzie, *The Time Traveller* (London: Weidenfeld & Nicolson)

call 'a dialectic of martyrdom and self-indulgence'. He was a 'mother's boy', selfish and bellicose, and such, for all his charm, he remained. The general resemblance of his situation to Lawrence's is obvious: they are variations on the same family romance. Wells solved his problems a little less painfully; he was much more successful, but he saw no incompatibility between high living and high thinking; and he usually got his own way, especially in matters of sex.

The only way to escape the unacceptable life of a petty clerk or shopman was education. Wells's ladder was more rickety than Lawrence's, but he got up it and eventually became a teacher, first at a prep school in North Wales ('I wish I was dead') and then at a crammer. But on the way he passed through the Normal School of Science at South Kensington: his academic record was none too consistent, but he was taught by T. H. Huxley, and that experience the Mackenzies rightly call decisive.

Wells has lately had some intelligent commentary, notably from Bernard Bergonzi, and we now have a better understanding of his relation to the *fin-de-siècle* mood. It was just before the turn of the century that he made his rapid transition from hack to famous author with an astonishing series of books that included *The Time Machine*, *The Island of Dr Moreau* and *The War of the Worlds*. Probably *fin-de-siècle* suggests quite different writers, but Wells was close to the deeper fears and hopes of the epoch. In so far as they were apocalyptic in character, depending on a sense of historical crisis, they are best understood in Wells, and not only in the Science Fiction. His finest novel, *Tono-Bungay*, also commemorates a deeply imagined crisis of English life: 'It is like an early day in a fine October. The hand of change rests on it all, unfelt, unseen; resting for a while, as it were half reluctantly, before it grips and ends the thing for ever. One frost and the whole face of things will be bare, links snap, patience end, our fine foliage of pretence lie glowing in the mire.'

Wells's messianism, another aspect of this feeling for crisis, is a secularized version of an older millenarianism, of which it occasionally retains visible traces, as in *The War of the Worlds*. Even in the Thirties he was talking, in *The Shape of Things to Come*, of an Elect which, after a great catastrophe, would take over the world and establish the New Jerusalem. He may even have thought of the Fabian Society as a sketch of his Elect: but his mind was of a catastrophic rather than a gradualist cast, which is why Shaw and Beatrice Webb had so little trouble in beating him on platforms and committees. He was typically a man for apocalypse, living at the moment of a major historical crisis of which only he was fully aware, and claiming here and now, in the manner of older prophets of the same kind, some of the privileges, especially the amorous privileges, which would be part of the future his sagacity had enabled him to discover.

Huxley's importance was that he taught Wells to see the crisis on a historical scale, a scale greater than the social or national: it became nothing less than a crisis in evolution. This helps to explain a deep pessimism in Wells's thought. The Mackenzies cite Huxley's Romanes Lecture 'Evolution and Ethics' as a clue to Wells's private blend of evangelical apocalyptism and modern science: somehow the evolutionary process, itself indifferent, has produced an ethical animal, and if there is any progress for men the motive force must be ethics, not evolution. Evolution can only produce the end of man, which was for Wells an obsession. His Utopias, whether in fiction or tract, are ethical. No more than Huxley could he be sure that ethics might prevail, but he thought we must behave as if it were so. It used to be thought that there was a radical change, to be explained by the miseries of war and old age, in the thought of Wells's last books. Yet ethics didn't, in the Forties, seem to be working, and in his own way he was consistent enough. Lawrence, another evangelical apocalyptist, tried, in his wartime novels, to hold together Utopia and despair in a not altogether different way: he could believe in the smash as a prelude to regeneration, and to the rule of a non-proletarian Samurai. Lawrence's supermen were, of course, not scientists, but the patterns and contradictions are similar and belong to the times.

It was not only in the matter of historical epochs that Wells found himself betwixt and between. He was habitually so. He lived handsomely and met the best people, but according to Odette Keun, who lived with him long enough to know, he never lost his hatred of the upper classes. Even the means by which he had escaped the oppression of the class system – his writing – took him into a profession where he was neither one thing nor the other, neither journalist nor artist. He would probably never have got started had there not been a vast new low-level literary public. The Mackenzies remark that the man of letters was in those days in a seller's market: almost anything would sell, and Wells could write almost anything.

Yet the older sanctions and ideals were still powerful. In the eyes of Conrad and James, Wells was always likely to betray his talent, to move away from art into publicity, for which he indeed had a developed gift. For a time he flourished in this situation of betwixt and between, arguing that the high notions of the novelist's art associated with James and Conrad were actually harmful. The novel was spoilt by their 'fierce pedantries of technique': it should be lax and spacious, an open medium for dealing with social problems, a container for anything. 'Before we are done,' he said, anticipating one of Lawrence's exultant claims, 'we will have all life within the scope of the novel.' That was said in 1911, after which date Wells wrote no novel that wasn't more of an argument than a work of art. He was set on a collision course with James, whom he provoked, with characteristic brashness, in *Boon*. The old man beautifully put him down. At one time Wells might have grasped what James meant when he said that only art '*makes*' life, makes interest, makes importance', but he could do so no longer.

That quarrel, of course, shows Wells at his worst – brash, inconsiderate, selfish, uncomprehending. It is more significant than the Fabian rows, or even the marital rows, because it explains why he was to write so much, yet make so little importance, in the years that followed. James admired him enormously in the early days, when, however fluent, he was true to his imagination, to his nightmares, to his remarkable sense of the uniqueness of his moment. Afterwards he took impossible liberties, and outlived his art by many years. He was still interesting, as a revolutionary encyclopaedist. But by 1938 he could say: 'My epitaph will be: "He was clever but not clever enough." I write books because I have a habit of writing.'

The Listener, 14 June 1973

Forster and Maurice

Forster died very old, 67 years after the publication of his first story, 46 years after the appearance of his last novel. He was older than Lawrence, who indeed treated him with some impatience as belonging to a dying world. When Henry James pronounced on the state of the novel in 1914 he admitted to his list of considerable novelists Lawrence ('lagging in the dusty rear' of Cannan, Walpole etc.) but not Forster; perhaps he thought him too old at 35 to be promising, or perhaps his failure to identify him socially (he mixed him up with G. E. Moore) was symptomatic of a deeper lack of recognition.

Beginning work in the first decade of the century, amid the rising tumult of modernism, Forster was already, it seemed, a man of the past. He was a scion of sects forgotten by all save the chroniclers of Victorian philanthropy and curious inquirers into the antecedents of Bloomsbury. Unlike most of the 'bloomsberries' in all kinds of ways, he nevertheless did share their meditations on election and salvation – that dream, as it has been called, 'of a coterie of lapsed Protestants'. Most of what is now conventionally recognized as seminal in the thought of the early years of the century failed to engage him deeply. Cambridge in some of its greatest years was his chosen world, but Dickinson and Wedd meant more to him than even G. E. Moore, and he looked back with McTaggart to Hegelianism rather than forward with Russell to Wittgenstein. His moderns were Wagner, Ibsen and Samuel Butler, rather than Gertrude Stein, whose *Three Lives*, in the year of *The Longest Journey*, offered a new style to fiction, and also admitted the poor on new terms. Two years later they were pronounced, in *Howards End*, unthinkable.

Forster thought about the instruments of fiction for himself, but seemed to show no special interest in the apparently intense contemporary researches of James, Conrad and Ford: the great 'contriver' was still Meredith. *Ulysses*, virtually the contemporary of his own greatest achievement, he could never bring himself to like ('an attempt to make crossness and dirt succeed where sweetness and light failed'). Like all the great Edwardian novelists he saw that the real task was to register the crisis or the decline of the culture, but he did not see in this a duty to make radical formal innovations; and although he thought Lawrence the greatest imaginative novelist of his generation, he neither explained why he held this view nor showed, in his last novel, the slightest sign of having read *Women in Love*. It is characteristic that his *Aspects of the Novel*, which, patiently read, contains more deep insights into the theory of fiction than any other book, is swaddled in whimsy, as if to preserve the speaker's amateur status.

The *sprezzatura* was, no doubt, something he took over from his social milieu, and there is certainly, in the early novels, a similar coloration. This is not, of course, to say that they do not reflect the developing conscience of the rich as money began visibly to ruin even their England, the plight of the poor grew more visible and scandalous, and there was heavy recruitment, from all social classes, to 'the vast armies of the benighted'. Forster eventually tried his hand at the benighted poor, and though most people think Leonard Bast a failure, Lawrence was right to call him a brave try. But what Forster really knew about were the ways in which members of the bourgeoisie go into the dark – when, for example, 'they have sinned against passion and truth' like Lucy Honeychurch.

Sometimes these novels make one think of field reports from anthropologists on some tribe that is strangling itself in the complexities of its own social structures, where manhood is established by adroitness with a railway footwarmer, and it may be thought improper for a young woman to sleep in a room newly vacated by a young man. The gentle poor (Italian peasants, natural sons like Stephen Wonham) are exempt from such concerns; the Bast poor would like not to be, and they are thus as in all other ways 'inferior to most rich people'. The rules exist because the rich feel they have to keep so much out of their lives – not only the wicked poor but wicked passion; and their homes and schools are dedicated to the initiation of the young into their weirdly restrictive rites.

In such a world it seems impossible that people should make love; and in Forster's novels, which are so often about the impact of passion on such a tribe, they do so only unconvincingly. Love erupts from some thicket as a disguised deity, momentarily transforming the maimed and benighted, causing even kisses. It is in these scenes that the prose, like conduct, goes wrong: compare the love scenes in *A Room with a View* with the extraordinary moment in the same book when murder is committed. All is justified later, when the nameless beast runs out onto the Marabar road and Ronnie and Adela experience their first sexual impulse, an evil one because of the absence of the god – a wonderfully delicate passage in the building of a unique structure. But the earlier books, though of very complex design, cannot aspire to such subtle order: they are restricted by the society whose restrictiveness they represent, and they break through those restrictions with machinery as clumsy as Ansell's 'operatic' speech at Sawston school, in *The Longest Journey*.

More generally, love in Forster is what binds together the true élite, those who would and may be saved from the armies of the benighted. It is 'the Beloved Republic', free, honest, sensitive, not indifferent to money (the chief preservative of the Wilcox tribe) but caring about what money can destroy, the expressiveness of a person, the beauty of a countryside. Yet like money it is conservationist; and like money it develops, necessarily, its own fictive universe. It was by prolonged meditation on the dimensions of this universe that Forster arrived at his masterpiece, which is one of the greatest novels, and so of a quite different order from his earlier books, distinguished as they are.

Love, translated into the realm of art, is once more a way of achieving a unity and completeness abnormal in life, for art, unlike life, never shows 'the sadness of the incomplete'. That is an early view: in *Passage to India* the wholeness of the book is intended to include incompleteness. But always, for Forster, the work of art is 'a self-contained entity with a life of its own', and he could hardly conceive of one that was not 'complicated and passionate'. Making it so is a work of love, of that heightened conscious-ness in the author which conveys itself to the whole design as well as to the detail. The book is like Professor Godbole's universe, always testifying to the presence (or the absence) of a god.

So the dealings of people with other people, with what they perceive, with the ground they walk on, are of a piece with their dealings with the whole, 'beyond and beyond'; and the few who know the truth know it altogether, as a knowledge of presence or of absence. The motto of *Howards End*, 'Only connect,' is, for all the book's complexity, only the beginning of a programme for *A Passage to India*.

After a lapse of fourteen years Forster was no longer so involved in the literary difficulties imposed by convention. The new book has some of the same qualities of social comedy, the kind of inventiveness represented by the story of Aziz's lost collar-stud and his game of polo with the subaltern; and it is still animated by a hatred of Sawston and the hegemony of the benighted. But it is more boldly about the possibilities and limits of love in a whole world, no longer about tribal quirks. As an account of the social conditions of British India it was powerful enough to have influenced events, and to be condemned, as it still is even today, for its inaccuracies and omissions (no Congress Party, no Gandhi, no reforming civil servants, no really sensible Hindus). Forster's own denial that it was a political novel was not taken quite seriously, and it isn't surprising that he greeted Peter Burra's essay of 1934 (reprinted in the Everyman edition) with relief and gratitude, though Burra left nearly everything to be said.

For a work so complicated, so passionate, so obsessed with the world tragedy of negatives and exclusions and yet so committed to its own wholeness, must not be confined to such narrow contexts, or even to the geology and topography of a continent. Forster alters these too: the ornamented Buddhist caves of Barabar become the un-ornamented un-Buddhist caves of Marabar, and the fists and fingers of these hills are moved hundreds of miles, so that the mud of the Ganges can slowly cover them. Forster, when I asked him once about the shape of his opening sentence, confirmed that he had constructed it so as to make the first word of the book 'except', and to end the first sentence with 'extraordinary', which thereafter has its special meaning at every appearance. This is a hint about the complicatedness of the whole work. I would find it difficult to suggest parallels, in the whole history of the novel, for this first chapter, or for the astonishing boldness and beauty of the opening of the second part, which establishes the book's mystical geology: the mud creating, as it covers the sun's flesh, possibilities of life and spirit – monkey, ghost, god and throw-backs to Marabar, like the 'sun-dried bureaucrat' who, however much he calls, can no more persuade his servant to come than Marabar can make Krishna come (Heaslop's servant is called Krishna). But Krishna does come, and Godbole smears himself with mud at the moment when division and time end for a moment. So love's epiphany at last happens, in the midst of muddle. Then the rock thrusts up again, divides friends and lovers: the world falls back under the rule of time.

Forster, who cared a great deal about the need to 'hand on' experiences of value in art, said that they were like religion, in that anybody who had them *needed* to hand them on, whether by teaching or criticism, however imperfect. One book of his at least seems necessary and fit for the process, not dulled by trafficking with a dead social grammar, fully human in that it is a fiction of a whole but inexplicable human world. It is essential to a recognition of the true nature of human poverty and riches, and so it will be handed on. No foreseeable revolution in our culture can invalidate its complicated passion; and with it Forster ceased to be a man of the past and, more than some more obvious 'modernists', is now everybody's contemporary.

In 1913, E. M. Forster returned from a visit to India and began work on his fifth novel. He wrote, it appears, seven chapters and some bits, and in one of the bits arranged for a young Englishwoman to be assaulted by an Indian in a cave. Then he got stuck, and put this book aside. Meanwhile, since he was staying in Yorkshire, he visited Edward Carpenter, the yogi-Christian socialist-homosexual reformer-poet – 'a rebel appropriate to his age', Forster remarks. 'He was sentimental and a little sacramental . . . He was a socialist who ignored industrialism and a simple-lifer with an independent income and a Whitmannic poet whose nobility exceeded his strength and, finally, he was a believer in the Love of Comrades, whom he sometimes called Uranians.' As Forster says, the prestige of Carpenter is now hard to understand, and it has been his fate to become a footnote in books on Lawrence, and now on Forster, whose reticent note on the centennial of Carpenter's birth in 1944 mentioned *Love's Coming of Age* and *The Intermediate Sex* only in passing, for it was still necessary to conceal the fact that in Forster's own homosexual loneliness he saw Carpenter as a possible saviour.

The only thing that happened worth mentioning on Forster's visit was that George Merrill, Carpenter's Uranian comrade, touched the novelist's buttocks. The effect of this was striking; Forster went straight back to Harrogate and began a new novel about homosexual love. It proved easier to write than any of his other books, he says, and he finished it in 1914, strengthened it a bit, and put it away, certain that since it had a happy ending it stood no chance of unmolested publication. He was still sure of this in 1960, when he wrote the Terminal Note from which I have quoted, though as it happens he was wrong. The recommendation of the Wolfenden Committee of 1957 was eventually accepted by Parliament, and homosexual behaviour between consenting adult males became legal, a reform which Forster, who thought it could never happen because – as a doctor says in his book – 'England has always been disinclined to accept human nature,' lived long enough to see. At the same time, the law on obscene publications relaxed a little, and Forster's Uranian story could have been published without the least danger of its undergoing the sort of ordeal suffered by Radclyffe Hall's lesbian novel *The Well of Loneliness* in 1928.

Meanwhile, to get back to 1914, the war came, and it was not until it was well over that Forster could make the second and indispensable visit to India. On his return he had an arduous time finishing and revising the book he had put aside in 1913. The hard one was *A Passage to India*, published in 1924, and the easy one was *Maurice*, only now before us.*

'It's a queer business,' says one of Forster's men to another as they discuss the history of their coming together. And so is the novel. Forster himself says that there are necessarily a lot of 'anachronisms' – half-sovereign tips, pianola records, and the like – but not to the extent where the reader would conjecture that the whole conduct of homosexual affairs has changed radically since 1914, and that sex itself, the mere biological basis, is no longer quite what it was. The only alternative is to attribute the oddness or queerness of the book to Forster's own imaginative needs and perhaps his social limitations. In a measure greater than any other of his novels, this one is a fairly simple wish-fulfilling fantasy; it has symbolic patterns in the usual Forster way, and these will no doubt be made much of, but they seem to be relatively inert and self-indulgent – almost shamefully so if you think of *A Passage to India*.

Of course, *Maurice* belongs with the four prewar novels and not the later one; and theirs is a world we may find increasingly hard to inhabit. It is worth remembering that while Forster was writing *Maurice*, Lawrence was at work on *Sons and Lovers*, a work which seems to belong to a different genre and to deal with a different society. In fact it *was* a different society. What Forster knew about was the way in which members of the upper classes sin against passion and truth, how they 'go into the dark'. Rickie, in *The Longest Journey*, does it by marrying; Lucy, in *A Room with a View*, by not. The crisis such characters face is one which the poor are spared. Through no fault of their own they are 'inferior to most rich people', unless they are Italians or children of nature like Stephen Wonham. Forster, who admitted that he hated but respected money, also hated and respected class; Leonard Bast in *Howards End* is killed on its electrified fence, though inside the fence there are mostly Wilcoxes and Pembrokes and people who send their children to Sawston school. There is of course a small elite in there too – 'the sensitive, the considerate and the plucky' will do to describe them. They are usually men who have been

* E. M. Forster, *Maurice* (New York: Norton)

awakened at Cambridge from the barbarous sleep of Sawston. Leonard Bast was not eligible. Such people are in the habit of saying, modestly and firmly, exactly what they mean, and acting in accordance with their beliefs; but these may include the belief that people who do not resemble them do not exist, a view held by Ansell in *The Longest Journey*. Women rarely belong, unless old and fey.

This unfair (but not inaccurate) characterization of Forster's prewar world may help us with *Maurice*, and *Maurice* may help us with the earlier books. To begin with, it is well known that in those books effective lovers are scarce and usually ungentlemanly – handsome Italians, or desirable peasants like the one at the funeral in *Howards End*. Nothing passes between Gerald and Agnes in *The Longest Journey* that could not be predicated of a prefect and a handsome boy. When there is real fun and comradeship, the arrival of ladies puts an end to it, as in the bathing scene of *A Room with a View*. At least in *Maurice* we are dealing with the real thing, with sexual good and evil; and if it helped the author to handle the sex in *Passage to India*, it justified its writing on that ground alone.

However, the sex is still very odd. The opening chapter is set in a school. Maurice is fourteen and three quarters, and about to leave, 'healthy but backward, to receive upon undefended flesh the first blows of the world'; that *backward* is rich in itself. A master takes him for a walk on the beach and undertakes an explanation of the facts of life, which he illustrates with diagrams scratched in the sand. The boy takes a polite interest, but is bored. In one of the heavily sententious intrusions of the author (Forster always did them, but never, I think, so irritatingly) we are told that 'puberty was there, but not intelligence, and manhood was stealing on him, as it always must, in a trance'; Maurice cannot be got at 'before his hour'. As they walk off, ladies appear, and the teacher panics because he has forgotten to erase those diagrams. Fortunately the tide, as in a Petrarchan sonnet, has come in and washed the love emblems away, just in time. For an instant the boy despises the man: 'Liar, coward, he's told me nothing'; then he sinks back into his protracted latency.

This is neat and interesting, but the boy, after all, is fourteen *and three quarters*. Off he goes to his suburban home, to astonish himself and his mother by weeping because the gardener's boy has been fired. 'Who was George? Nobody – just a common servant.' And he wins the servile approbation of the gardener and his wife by bullying them. The importance of this lies in the fact that the book concerns itself with the relation between homosexual freedom and the breaking down of the class barriers. In the end Maurice acknowledges his love for a successor to George and goes off to live with him. Where? Not in society, of course, but in the 'greenwood'. Forster says in his note that the biggest anachronism of all is this greenwood, which ceased to exist after 1914; you could no longer drop out into it. All that was left, until the law changed, were antisocial substitutes – secret affairs, guardsmen, Italian boys.

Maurice's protracted adolescence, here portentously allegorized as a descent 'into the Valley of the Shadow', yields two prophetic dreams which, since Forster was a master of the contrivance he admired in Meredith, have high structural importance. One is of George running naked toward him, but he wakes up on contact. The other is of a face, later compared to that of God at the end of the *Paradiso*, and a voice saying, 'That is your friend.' The coming of the friend, recurrent in *Maurice*, is a theme Forster realized finally in the coming of Krishna, after many failed invocations, in *A Passage to India*. Here the friend is a Cambridge product. Maurice has already experienced, among the dreary banalities of his school, a revulsion from women, but he knows nothing whatever about sex except that it is obscene, and when he meets his comrade he sees no significance in the romping and stroking they go in for. When the other boy primes him with the *Symposium* and then tells him he loves him, Maurice is outraged.

This is just about credible. But then Maurice gets the point, and goes to his friend's room at night (from the outside; there is a lot of symbolism about this kind of love coming in from the dark outside), and they call each other by their first names and sleep together. Nothing else; for Clive, the other boy, has long recognized in himself 'the impulse that destroyed the City of the Plain', and determined that 'it should not ever become carnal'. He is an intellectual, a Hellenist. The relationship goes on for three years ('precarious, idealistic and peculiarly English', Forster remarks in his Terminal Note: 'what Italian boy would have put up with it?'), outfacing Mother Nature, who enters the text saying, 'with even voice, "Very well, you are thus; I blame none of my children. But you must go the way of all sterility."' This sentence of genetic death, for all its obtrusiveness, has weight; a weight that is lacking at the big moment of *Room with a View* when Lucy is accused of sinning 'against Eros and Pallas Athene, and not by any heavenly intervention, but by the ordinary course of nature, those allied deities will be avenged.' At least we are now talking about something real. When Clive gets sick he feels a spurt of desire for a nurse, and then goes to Greece to commune with Pallas Athene, 'motherless and a virgin'; but Hellas has the surprising effect of normalizing Clive. He seems to have been confusing love with death; or he had homosexuality in the head.

That he continues the relationship with Maurice on a best-friend footing, though now disliking him physically, shows class. 'Blessed are the uneducated, who forget [love] entirely,' says the novelist. Maurice goes through a bad time, for Clive now has a 'horror of masculinity' and even takes an interest in Maurice's sister. Clive marries and at once becomes one of those characters for whom Forster can find nothing but nasty things to say, as he admits in his Note. Maurice goes into a sexual slump but emerges when he finds himself lusting for an inaccessible young gentleman, and finally falls in love with Clive's under-gamekeeper. Forster claims that this bisexual peasant is 'senior in date to the prickly gamekeepers of D. H. Lawrence,' which is not true, since Annable appeared in *The White Peacock* in 1911; but it probably is true that he owes 'nothing to their disquisitions'. Forster's young man is simply an animated greenwood, a dream of the situation where comrades of different classes can get together outside.

The novel foresees this criticism, and strives for a verisimilitude which will defeat it, and a symbolic patterning which will transcend it. This is attempted by means of what Forster calls 'rhythms'; a particularly laborious one uses a recurring figure of evening primroses, and there is repeated calling and coming. In the end Maurice is 'saved' (Forster's word, borrowed directly from the secularized evangelism of Bloomsbury). What is he saved from? Lucy Honeychurch was saved, but her lover was only a bit like a peasant, only a little of the outer darkness; it is more complicated with women. Maurice is diagrammatically saved from the joyless but compulsorily heterosexual lives going on all round him, from the conventional chivalry and intellectual falsity of Clive, from the rotting society and its ruined boys.

Lytton Strachey told Forster that Maurice's relation with his gamekeeper was based on curiosity and lust, and would not last six weeks. Forster himself could not write the ending he wanted, a Carpenterian vision of Uranian woodcutters. What he knew for sure was that the only kind of love worth having was this kind, so difficult to get. He displays a society in which women are all bores, nuisances, substitutes, interrupters, and powerful rivals; they have Nature on their side and are more powerful than the motherless Greek virgin. Because this display is so unqualified, so revealing, *Maurice* is valuable as an explanation of what restricted Forster in the earlier books. It makes the liberated sexual vision of *A Passage to India* the more remarkable; but even in that book the only sexual contact – between Heaslop and Adela on the Marabar road – is evil, and indicates the absence of Krishna; a woman's sexual fantasy produces the catastrophe; and Fielding finds no sexual satisfaction in his new wife. Aziz, straightforwardly heterosexual, has no profound feelings for women, and is, in any case, not English.

Maurice is, however, 'peculiarly English'. English society created the conditions under which Uranian love could best flourish, and at the same time held that kind of love in horror. Consequently there grew up within that society a secret society – that aristocracy of the sensitive, the considerate, and the proud – which cultivated the love that dared not speak its name, and gave it a cultural frame of reference (Plato, Whitman, Swinburne, etc.). Under such conditions it was possible to regard ordinary non-Uranian love – pandemic, Venerean – as *déclassé*, base, and finally unintelligible. *Maurice* is a monument to this very queer business.

The Listener, 18 June 1970 & *The Atlantic Monthly*, November 1971

Yes, Santa, There is a Virginia

There has of late been a transformation in the fortunes of Virginia Woolf. It is not that she has belatedly grown famous; her name has been a household word since the mid-Twenties, and even at the start of that decade she was able, as this new diary* shows us, to predict with sardonic accuracy the reactions of reviewers ('Mrs Woolf . . . must beware of virtuosity. She must beware of obscurity . . . her great natural gift &c . . . She is at her best in the simple lyric . . .'). She lived to see a good deal written about her; and even in the years when her reputation went into its posthumous slump there was a steady stream of books and articles. But what is happening at the moment transcends mere fashion. She is being received into the canon.

There appear to be two main reasons for the alteration in the kind of attention her novels are getting – apart, that is, from a developing recognition of their own merits. The first is a renewed interest in her feminism, now seen as constituting precisely that serious and intelligent commitment to the affairs of her society and the world that was formerly supposed, by arrogant males, to be impossible in a woman of her temperament and talents. This aspect of her work is now, and quite justly, thought to be far more important than her clever men friends could understand. There are even attempts to develop, from some of her remarks, a theory of androgyny, founded in her reading of Coleridge; Roger Poole, sympathetic to feminism, nevertheless makes some sturdy qualifications

---

* *The Diary of Virginia Woolf, Volume Two: 1920–24*, edited by Anne Olivier Bell, assisted by Andrew McNeillie (New York: Harcourt Brace Jovanovich)

here,* and one is glad of them, for a bass voice strengthens the chorus.

The second intrinsic reason for the change I speak of is the renascence of Aubreyan candour in literary gossip, especially about Bloomsbury. When Michael Holroyd wrote his *Strachey* few of the survivors seemed to care what was said about them, and in a sense it is *their* candour that has now grown popular. Virginia Woolf shared it; sometimes it seems that for her the word 'bugger' was virtually a synonym for 'male', and her autobiographical writings (published a couple of years ago under the title *Moments of Being*) reflect the passion of the Bloomsbury buggers for intimate and even embarrassing truth.

Leonard Woolf, who long ago published an excellent selection from her diary, spoke with loving candour of Virginia in his multi-volume autobiography, and so did her nephew Quentin Bell in the standard biography. The world knows pretty well by now that her half-brothers interfered with her sexually, that her father oppressed her, that from time to time she was insane, and that these and other sufferings were not unrelated to disadvantages shared by others of her sex. Six volumes of letters and five of the diary will make her intimate life as well known to the public as that of any author in history.

A second wave of biography, interpretative and revisionist, is inevitable. And so people turn again, with curiosity or veneration, to the novels, and may find that at any rate two of them, *To the Lighthouse* and *Between the Acts*, are among the greatest of the century. They may then reflect upon the prejudices that delayed this recognition.

The new volume of the diary covers a period during which *Jacob's Room* was published and *Mrs Dalloway* written. One purpose of keeping it was simply to satisfy her endless desire to be writing; another, as she discovered, was that she liked to '*practise* writing; do my scales, yes & work at certain effects'. Work was necessary to happiness; she and her husband both thought so. Running the Hogarth Press was work therapy; filling every chink of the day

* Roger Poole, *The Unknown Virginia Woolf* (Cambridge University Press)

with usefulness was a way of avoiding or delaying the long blank months of illness. In these years she wrote two books and a hundred articles and reviews. She doesn't say a lot about the novels; the diary is not in the least like James's notebooks. She does mention the moment when the story of Mrs Dalloway 'branched into a book ... The world seen by the sane & the insane side by side – something like that. Septimus Smith? – is that a good name?' Friends died – Kitty Maxse, thought to be the original of Mrs Dalloway; Katherine Mansfield, for whom she felt a mixture of affection, respect, and envy. She is not profoundly disturbed. She moves house, and leaving Richmond reflects upon her times of sickness there: 'I've had some very curious visions in this room ... lying in bed, mad, & seeing the sunlight quivering like gold water, on the wall. I've heard the voices of the dead here. And felt, through it all, exquisitely happy.'

She liked to think that it was this visionary power that compensated for her lack of the tough, honourable reasonableness she associated with Leonard; she felt screened from the world in which he was effective, and tended to exaggerate her lack of practical intelligence, but claimed instead a susceptibility to 'the poetry of existence', often, she says, associated 'with the sea and St Ives'. Sometimes she speaks of reality as if it were something everybody except her had a right to be easy with. *Mrs Dalloway* helped her to overcome her fear of this exclusion, and *To the Lighthouse* was the masterpiece that resulted from her giving the sea and St Ives their full due.

In 1922 she reached forty. The Group was still flourishing, though 'we all grow old; grow stocky; lose our pliancy and impressionability'. The triadic sentence is characteristic; in one sense *Between the Acts* is an extraordinary set of variations upon it. These triads are imposed upon her world. There they all are, Keynes and Strachey and Fry, Bell and Forster and Grant; on the fringes Ottoline Morrell, Mansfield, Eliot. Affection and admiration never make her uncritical. Forster was for a time her adviser; but, he said, 'one waited for her to snap'. Strachey she deeply admired, but envied the sales of his books. Keynes's intellect she thought wholly out of her reach, but saw him 'by lamplight – like a gorged seal, double chin, ledge of red lip, little eyes sensual, brutal, unimaginative'. Clive Bell made the mistake of growing fat and bald. Acquaintances untouched by the glamour of Cambridge have an even worse time; Eliot flits in and out, suavely double-tongued, pitiable, evasive, admired.

The record of Woolf's reading often shows the same capacity to admire and snap simultaneously. In *The Wings of the Dove* there is much 'juggling & arranging of silk pocket handkerchiefs' and Milly disappears behind them. 'He overreaches himself . . . The mental grasp and stretch are magnificent. Not a flabby or slack sentence, but much emasculated by this timidity or consciousness or whatever it is. Very highly American, I conjecture, in the determination to be highly bred, & the slight obtuseness as to what high breeding is.' Resisting Eliot's propaganda for *Ulysses*, she calls it 'an illiterate, underbred book . . . The book of a self-taught working man'. Proust is another matter, unquestionably upper class: 'his command of every resource is so extravagant'.

Occasionally, and understandably, she would say she wished she knew some 'normal people', but when she met them they tended to be either underbred or boring. Class mattered enormously, and the English upper-middle-class horror of being mistaken for the English lower middle class. She criticized her friends for dressing badly; they should not smell of the bargain counter and the suburb. Forster and his friends tried to escape the class trap by taking working-class men as their lovers; she had a weakness for great ladies, freely confessed in the essay 'Am I a Snob?' There, for instance, is Mrs Asquith, 'stone white: with the brown veiled eyes of an aged falcon . . . She rides life, if you like.' (She herself wanted to ride work 'as a man rides a great horse'.) She was a little afraid of these great persons: 'The thing about aristocrats is that they veil all pretence very humbly; & let one ride on their backs; & then suddenly turn seigneurial.' Victoria Sackville-West, on first acquaintance 'florid, moustached, parakeet coloured, with all the supple ease of the aristocracy', was to become her lover.

For servants she had a contempt that is sometimes simply odious. She seems never to have looked critically at the class attitudes of her set, perhaps because she was herself socially insecure. It was when she was ill that her disgust with the lives and bodies of the poor grew most violent. Of the oppression of women as a class she was of course acutely aware, but at this stage she wanted the great ladies to handle it: 'The lady R[hondda]s ought to be feminists . . . if the rich women will do it, we neednt; & its the feminists who will drain off this black blood of bitterness which is poisoning us all.' The two main feminist works, *A Room of One's Own* and *Three Guineas*, came out in 1929 and 1938.

Anybody reading this volume without some awareness of the whole story might well suppose its author to have been a rarely gifted, rarely industrious (filling up gaps by refreshing her Greek or learning Russian), and for the most part rarely happy person. The editing, it must be said, reinforces this impression of calm, even of gaiety; Anne Olivier Bell's touch is light and amusing, and even the excellent index is rather jolly. But few will read it with so innocent an eye. The breakdowns and the suicide are so well documented, and the sexual assaults, and the recurring sense of exclusion and aridity, and her doubts about her intelligence, sanity, and achievement. All this needs explaining, and two more explainers are at hand.

Roger Poole is polemical as well as apologetic, and the main objects of his assault are Quentin Bell and, especially, Leonard Woolf, both of whom said repeatedly that in what Poole calls her 'very distressed periods' Virginia Woolf was mad. This is the expression they – and Virginia Woolf, and many other people, for the usage, though blunt, is normal – use of persons who claim to hear the birds talking Greek and the king uttering obscenities among the azaleas. Poole prefers to say 'her nerves gave out'.

That he can claim to show plausibly why this occurred doesn't alter the fact that the sufferer was quite properly described as mad, and it is a pity that Poole, a combative writer, should want to fight over this semantic eggshell. He needed all his powder for the assault on Leonard Woolf, who, so far from being a model of patience and devotion, is held to have subjected his wife to a peculiar tyranny, here characterized at length, and no less disastrous to her nerves than the tyranny of her father and the outrages of her half-brothers. On these earlier traumata Poole has persuasive things to say; for example, he makes a brilliant guess why the birds spoke Greek to Virginia. He uses a variety of psychoanalytic ideas, some less plausible than others (the famous episode of the six-year-old Virginia's frightening experience with a looking glass is related to the 'mirror stage', but six is surely rather aged for that?). It is, however, in his treatment of Leonard that he fails to persuade.

It is doubtless true that Woolf ('a penniless Jew', as Virginia liked to call him, of lower-middle-class origin) remained, despite Cambridge and the Apostles, uneasily aware of his social ambiguity, unduly vain of his intellect; and possibly, over the twenty-nine years of their marriage, he sometimes mishandled his sick wife. But Poole thinks he was always wrong. He consulted doctors about her health even before they were engaged, took her collapse after the honeymoon as a recurrence of the old troubles (instead of seeing that it had its cause in the honeymoon itself), went to some trouble to find doctors who would say his wife should not have children, and indeed entered into a lifelong conspiracy with the medical profession against her. Her refusal to eat he countered stupidly, unflaggingly persistent with his spoonfeeding; he reinforced her fear of being stared at in public. All this Poole connects, very skilfully, with the account of the madness of Septimus Smith in *Mrs Dalloway*.

Yet it is surely wrong to represent Woolf as so malignant. Perhaps his choice of medical advisers was, if not premature, unfortunate, and Septimus admittedly did jump out of the window. *Anorexia nervosa* (Rose's diagnosis) was and remains a difficult disease to treat. He made other mistakes, and it may be true that his masculine passion for reason made it especially hard for him to understand madness. Yet he struggled for such understanding, and a less partisan view of the record would surely suggest that he had some success.

Virginia Woolf was almost thirty and without much achievement when she married; in spite of two lost years she was at forty intensely productive, working on her fourth novel *Mrs Dalloway*, conscious for the first time of the genuineness of her gift, and even quite famous. It would be difficult to argue that Leonard had no part in making all this possible, that he and his wife were totally incompatible, that the marriage, though like other marriages *sui generis*, was not in many ways a happy one. Poole would so argue; and he is, in the end, bound to confront the suicide note, in which Virginia wrote 'I don't think two people could have been happier than we have been.' This he describes as an honourable lie, 'the only fraud of her career', intended to spare Leonard some of the guilt of the survivor. There is small reason to believe this, or to disbelieve the reasons for suicide given in the note to Vanessa, which was perhaps not available to Poole: 'I am certain now that I am going mad again. It is just as it was the first time, I am always hearing voices, and I know I shan't get over it now.'

Phyllis Rose does quote the note to Vanessa.* Though she certainly does not neglect the pathogenic elements in her subject's early history, or their relation to the novelist's gifts, Rose's book is distinguished less by its new discoveries and new theories than by its extremely sympathetic and balanced view of Woolf as a woman of letters, with the emphasis on 'woman'. Poole stresses the dichotomy between male rationality and female imagination, and this is also part of Rose's theme. She is very good on the difficulties that stood in the way of some kinds of achievement in a man's world, and on the men in question, from the moaning father to the absurd, sick half-brothers and the brilliant boring buggers. In *Three Guineas* Woolf argued a relation between normal male antics and fascism. She thought the conventional assumptions about registering reality in fiction were also essentially masculine; but in this respect she was less sure of herself, of the value of her quite different methods.

Rose is particularly good here – she identifies Woolf's characteristic successes with her victories over male precept, with her refusal of the poetry-fact dichotomy. There were lapses, even as late as *The Years*; but feminism won, and the poetic and 'experimental' survived, so that certain good aspects of modernism are to be seen as a triumph for the sex. This success was achieved, as Rose is careful to show, without loss of serious engagement with great public issues, though that engagement was also different in style from the male version.

* Phyllis Rose, *Woman of Letters: A Life of Virginia Woolf* (Oxford University Press)

Yes, Santa, There is a Virginia

Rose naturally speculates about the *mariage* (practically) *blanc*, and the strain it must have entailed; but decides, sensibly, that a woman who at twenty-nine describes herself as a failure, childless and insane, and at forty claims to have found her own voice and to be happy, has not suffered a disastrous decade. In fact she had done much to discredit the 'pre-existing (masculine) model of the novelist'. It is not quite dead even now, as much fiction reviewing testifies; but it is very shabby. Rose has written an admirable book; she is perceptive about Woolf's madness, in particular about its tendency to recur as a novel was being finished; and she understands some of its usefulness, to which Woolf herself testified. In Rose's view the whole story of Virginia Woolf illustrates the problems still facing women of achievement. Sometimes I think that she is wrong, for example that she misunderstands *Between the Acts* and especially Mrs Manresa; but the portrait as a whole seems right, and does something to explain the somewhat belated revision of the canon to which I alluded at the outset.

New York Review of Books, 21 December 1978

The Feast of St Thomas

'The idea that Eliot's poetry was rooted in private aspects of his life has now been accepted,' says Lyndall Gordon in the Foreword to her second volume of biographical rooting among these aspects.* This acceptance, which she evidently approves, has undoubtedly occurred, as a root through the enormous heap of books about the poet, now augmented by the centenary of his birth, will quickly demonstrate.

By the time of his death in 1965 people had long been curious about this very famous man. Collections such as the one made by Richard Marsh and Tambimuttu for his sixtieth birthday in 1948 contained much pleasant anecdote, and there were respectful reminiscences in Allen Tate's memorial volume of 1966. Meanwhile, off the page, there was some gossip about such matters as a putatively vast pornographic poem, and about Eliot's first marriage. I once heard J. B. Priestley explaining that the Eumenides in *The Family Reunion* were a direct representation of Vivien(ne), which I couldn't understand since in the play only Harry sees them ('*You* don't see them, but I see them,' he claims), whereas Priestley's point was that Vivien would storm unexpectedly and embarrassingly into parties where everybody could see her. As for the poem, it seems to have been a fitful series of mildly obscene verses included in letters to such friends as Conrad Aiken. Gossips are not on oath.

While these oral versions of biography paid tribute to the celebrity of the poet, the poetry was usually treated as quite impersonal. It had come, in the post-war years, under heavy

* Lyndall Gordon, *Eliot's New Life* (Oxford University Press)

academic protection: this was a time when potent professors wanted to exclude biography from the institutional study of literature. Eliot's own doctrine of poetic impersonality had contributed to the formation of this austere doctrine, and though quite often subjected to more severe scrutiny than literary journalism normally attracts, the early essay 'Tradition and the Individual Talent' remained influential, and suited the New Criticism well.

As Gordon suggests, we have moved on from there, not just because we like gossip better than professorial personality purges, but because many people have come to think that the impersonality business was nonsense anyway. This is roughly the position of Maud Ellmann's brisk first book.* Eliot called Pound's *Cantos* 'a reticent biography', and she thinks we should apply the same description to Eliot's work. According to her, early Modernism, despite the contrary pretence, was always individualistic, and steeped in Bergson. Now Eliot certainly went to Bergson's lectures, and was for a time much affected by his very fashionable philosophy: but he soon changed his mind, as is clear from the satirical assault on Middleton Murry, a Bergsonian surrogate, in 'The Function of Criticism' (1923). And of course he was well aware that impersonal poetry was produced by persons: but this doesn't make the impersonality argument bogus, as Ellmann supposes, or entitle us to think that it has sinister ideological implications – that Eliot 'inveighs against personality for much the same reasons that he ostracizes the Jews from his Anglo-Catholic utopia'.

Eliot notoriously remarked that 'only those who have personality and emotions know what it means to want to escape from these things', which implies a claim to poetic or spiritual election, and this is no doubt what gives rise to the notion that poetic impersonality has, in the long run, some nasty political implications. But one ought to reflect that among the poet's preferred models are Aristotle and Dante, Pascal and Baudelaire; impersonality and intelligence, as he understood them, are the achievement of heroic personalities, and it is hard to see that they *necessarily*

* Maud Ellmann, *The Poetics of Impersonality* (Hemel Hempstead: Harvester Press)

imply political wickedness. What Eliot himself says about the topic in 'The Perfect Critic' still seems innocuous: 'In an artist . . . suggestions made by a work of art, which are purely personal, become fused with a multitude of other suggestions from multitudinous experience, and result in the production of a new object, which is no longer purely personal.' Many artists – Milton and Picasso, to name two at random – might have subscribed to some form of this statement, without suspecting that to do so might, on such evidence alone, get them called fascists, or even Anglo-Catholic utopians.

Even in the years when the impersonality approach generally prevailed there were many books about the more polite and discussable aspects of Eliot as a person who had, for example, thought a bit and read a bit. Some writers tried, as Eliot himself never did, to work his critical observations up into a coherent theory; others, like Grover Smith, read what he had read, so far as this could be ascertained, and examined his sources with what looked like, but cannot quite have been, exhaustive care: for recently there has been a boom in such research. A procession of students combs the archives in New York, Cambridge and elsewhere. The poet's early philosophical studies and his work on F. H. Bradley have been very carefully examined; and those early slogans, Impersonality, Tradition, Dissociation of Sensibility, Objective Correlative, have been dissected again and again. One might even say that no other English critic except possibly Coleridge has had his ideas and his reading more intensely studied. The reason for all this activity isn't merely that there are so many more aspirants looking for something interesting to investigate, though that is not wholly irrelevant. It may be true that too much has been written and published about him, but it is also true that there is a lot to write about.

At the same time, however, the poet's life, and especially the first half of it, has been examined with a persistence that is beginning to seem prurient: it certainly goes well beyond what Eliot, or any other private and reserved person, would have thought tolerable. The Letters offer several instances of his rage at intrusions into his privacy, and one remembers him forcing the withdrawal of John Peter's article from *Essays in Criticism* because it suggested a homosexual element in his relationship with Jean Verdenal. Lyndall Gordon reports a conversation with Mary Trevelyan which makes him seem mildly amused about this imputation, but his first reaction was quick and indignant. After his death the sanction of his disapproval no longer worked, and almost anything goes.[1]

Now that so much has been said it seems impossible not to say more, and even Valerie Eliot is obliged to take part. The sufferings of both partners in the poet's first marriage have been amply described, sometimes, as by Peter Ackroyd, with reasonable delicacy, but research continues to discover more painful details. What will not be fully uncovered until 2019 (Gordon's date; Mrs Eliot says 2020) are the letters Eliot wrote to Emily Hale. He had known her since 1912, but most of the letters were written between 1927 (Gordon's date; 1932 according to Valerie Eliot) and 1947. We learn from Mrs Eliot that in the Sixties the poet, 'in a private paper' whose privacy has now gone the way of all privacy, said he had discovered, a year after his marriage to Vivien, that he was still in love with Miss Hale, though 'it may merely have been my reaction against my misery with Vivienne' – we are told that he gave her name the two extra letters when exasperated – 'and desire to revert to an earlier situation.' He attributes the muddle to his timidity and immaturity, and to his worries about a choice of profession – for academic philosophy was still a possibility.

When she heard about Eliot's second marriage, Emily Hale presented his letters (numbering about a thousand, says Gordon) to Princeton University Library. He had wanted these letters preserved, but Mrs Eliot says he was irritated by Hale's act, calling it 'the *Aspern Papers* in reverse'; and when the Princeton Librarian informed him that they were to be sealed until fifty years after the death of the survivor he got somebody to burn all Hale's letters to him. There would appear to be an understandable difference in the attitudes of Mrs Eliot and Gordon to the Princeton letters. Gordon is far from wanting to minimise the import-

[1] Frederick Tomlin, in his memoir of a long, respectful and predominantly churchy acquaintance with the poet, describes his reaction to Peter (*T. S. Eliot: A Friendship*, London: Routledge).

ance of the triangular relation between the poet, his first wife and Emily Hale: indeed she makes it central to her account of Eliot's wife. It was on Vivien's death in 1947 that he broke with Hale. It is true that at various times he abandoned other friends with equal abruptness (as, when he remarried, he dropped Mary Trevelyan, who had twice proposed to him), but it seems clear that Hale was not just another friend, and any doubt on the subject is likely to be dispelled by Gordon's researches. She is able to quote in full a letter of Hale's, written in 1947, which says she had understood that Eliot had intended to marry her if Vivien should die; during one of his visits to the United States, when they had actually discussed the prospect, he had spoken of a *mariage blanc*. And Gordon has seen, in another restricted Princeton archive, a copy of her sad last letter to Eliot, written as late as 1963.

Indefatigable and resourceful, Gordon has interviewed many witnesses, and had the co-operation of Maurice Haigh-Wood, Vivien's brother; she draws on Vivien's diaries in the Bodleian, the copyright of which, as we learn from the *Letters*, belongs to Eliot's widow. And, familiar with virtually all the archives, she has read a great many of the letters. Her acknowledgements make interesting reading. Mrs Eliot, who helped with the earlier book, is absent from the list.

Emily Hale is Gordon's heroine. Her book has the pattern of a morality: Hale was 'the higher dream' and Vivien 'the sense of sin'. Out of the conflict between these forces come 'the great works of Eliot's maturity, as he converts life into meaning'. Vivien, we gather, 'was Eliot's muse only so long as he shared her hell', and Hale as heavenly muse took over the role in *Ash Wednesday*, 'a dream of sexual purity to set against Vivien'. The *vita nuova* referred to in Gordon's title was announced in a vision inspired by Hale, and it involved a vow of celibacy.

It has long been known that it was with Emily Hale that Eliot visited Burnt Norton, probably in 1934. But Gordon adds much detail about their relationship, and about many other aspects of the long years between the poet's marriages. Even if we may doubt that Hale was his Urania or his Beatrice it seems clear that they were rather close. But I'm bound to say that there is something disturbing about Gordon's handling of all this. Her religiose attitude to the facts, a sort of muckraking sublimity, affects her prose as well as her argument, and the whole pseudo-allegorical and hagiographical enterprise is vaguely disgusting, though I ought to add that it might seem just right to readers of different disposition.

Volume One of Mrs Eliot's edition of the letters* takes us up to 1922, when the poet was 34 and had suffered seven years of marriage. It is not, on the whole, an enlivening collection. Quite a lot of it is familiar in one form or another from earlier books, and the depressing events, as well as the successes, of Eliot's first London decade are fairly well-known to all who have any interest in the subject, so there is sometimes a sense of *déjà lu*.

Mrs Eliot's brief and slightly odd Introduction, already mentioned in connection with Emily Hale, explains that she had persuaded Eliot to sanction such a publication. In the nature of the case, a lot of correspondence had been destroyed or lost, especially from the poet's schooldays; these lacunae are, as it were, filled by the inclusion of letters by other people, including Eliot's mother and Vivien, whose letters are very nervous and lively: she seems to have been a more vigorous and disconcerting correspondent than her husband. There is also a letter from Alain-Fournier, and a number from Jean Verdenal, the dedicatee of *Prufrock and Other Observations*, '*mort aux Dardanelles*'. Their relationship wasn't of the kind improperly suggested, but it was close and involved some elegant youthful posing. *Ce n'est pas facile de se faire comprendre, et puis d'ailleurs ce n'est pas mon métier* is the kind of remark that would appeal to Eliot, who was fond of Byron's lines about not understanding his own meaning when he would be *very* fine: he quotes them in a letter, and again, a decade later, in *The Use of Poetry and the Use of Criticism*. Verdenal also complains about the way small artists form gangs for mutual support and start short-lived movements – a remark that might, at the time, have been less welcome. The mother's letters are eloquently maternal, calm but worried. Some are to schoolmasters; the boy

* *The Letters of T. S. Eliot*, edited by Valerie Eliot (London: Faber & Faber)

wasn't robust and as the editor reminds us had to wear a truss, which can't have made things easier at school.

Some of the jollier letters are to a Boston cousin, Eleanor Hinkley, through whom he had met Hale. She had an interest in the theatre, and with her Eliot can go in for the sort of joshing he kept up in one way or another throughout his life. More important, though in essence well-known, are the letters to Conrad Aiken, later dismissed by Eliot as stupid, but a principal confidant of the earlier years. The jesting is intermingled with worry about intellectual constipation, 'nervous sexual attacks', and fantasies about Saint Sebastian, including a version of the poem already known from Mrs Eliot's edition of the manuscripts the poet gave to his American patron John Quinn: though rejected, these verses bear his true voiceprint. It was to Aiken that he could speak of fantasies of flagellation and the murder of women. He also speculates, in what at least by hindsight we can call a characteristic manner, on the necessity of pain: 'what is necessary is a *certain kind* (could one but catch it) of *tranquillity* and *sometimes* pain does bring it.'

Aiken was also the recipient of this meditation: 'The idea of a submarine world of clear green light – one would be attached to a rock and swayed in two directions – would one be happiest or most wretched at the turn of the tide?' This fancy probably owes something to some strenuous lines in *Antony and Cleopatra*:

> This common body
> Like to a vagabond flag upon the stream,
> Goes to and back, lackeying the varying tide
> To rot itself with motion.

This is a good illustration of one of that 'multitude of other suggestions . . . which result in the production of a new object' without eliminating the personal: if you had to guess which distinguished poet wrote that little reverie you might well think first of Eliot. He also had a way of assimilating some particular line or passage that has provided him with what he calls 'a bewildering minute'. In *The Revenger's Tragedy* that expression refers with excitement and disgust to the sexual act: its transfer to the impact of poetry is presumably not insignificant. In the same way, the Shakespeare passage is the comment of chilly Octavius on the fickleness of a populace which switches support from him to the burnt-out lecher Antony. Lyndall Gordon rightly remarks on the psychological importance of these letters to Aiken, but they have interest, too, for students of poetry.

Mrs Eliot includes a series of letters from the young man to his Harvard professor J. H. Woods, which seem to have eluded Gordon. These have a certain dry interest. Eliot, at 26, was at Oxford, and engaged in the serious professional study of philosophy. He kept in touch with Woods, who had taught him some Indian philosophy at Harvard. At Oxford he was working through Aristotle's *Posterior Analytics* with Harold Joachim, reading the *Metaphysics* in Greek, and at the same time struggling with Husserl, whom he found 'terribly hard'. He offered to send Woods his notes on the *Posterior Analytics*, the *Ethics* and the *De Anima*. Although his 'fatal disposition to scepticism' interfered, he said, with his appreciation of Joachim, he was clearly working very seriously at philosophy. And it might be conjectured that the commentaries written since his thesis on Bradley turned up have not taken enough notice of his Aristotelian studies. They ought at least to be remembered when his famous dictum 'there is no method except to be very intelligent' is trotted out, for it occurs in a context extolling Aristotle, and specifically the *Posterior Analytics*, as a great example of what he means by intelligence.

Much has been written of late concerning Eliot's views on, and indebtedness, to F. H. Bradley. Richard Wollheim, an authority on Bradley, has argued that the famous quotation from *Appearance and Reality* in the note on l.412 of *The Waste Land* is misleading because out of context. Either Eliot is using it because its decontextualized sense fits his purpose, or because he had simply forgotten the context – in later years he professed not to understand his own book on Bradley. Wollheim detects a progressive loss of interest in philosophy. Eliot more than once spoke of his incapacity for abstruse thought (though this may not be wholly serious – the diligent young birdwatcher, possessor of Chapman's *Handbook of Birds of Eastern North America*, and closely acquainted with the water-dripping song of the hermit-thrush, tells Eleanor

Hinkley that he is not sure whether some birds he sees are sparrows, for he knows nothing about ornithology).

He certainly had to decide between a steady job as an academic philosopher, probably at Harvard, and a rougher career in London, where he would have to support his poetry by lecturing, reviewing, and to the dismay of his mother, school-teaching, which she thought beneath him; in the end, it came to banking and publishing. But the philosophical years must surely have left some traces. It has been suggested that Josiah Royce, another Harvard philosopher, was more important than is usually realized, having a congenial theory of tradition and community; some think Russell, who was very close to Eliot in the early London years, cured him of Bradleyan idealism, so that Bradley's continuing influence depended finally on Eliot's admiration for his prose style. Not everybody agrees, and it can still be maintained, as by Lewis Freed in his book *The Critic as Philosopher* (1979), that Eliot's critical theories are Bradleyan almost through and through. Now, however, we have Richard Shusterman with a new view of the whole matter.* He believes that Eliot is much more interesting as a philosopher than even his supporters think, and that the easy dismissals on the part of such detractors as Terry Eagleton and Christopher Norris are founded on political prejudice and uninformed assumptions. Shusterman emphasizes the Aristotelian studies, and the attack on Descartes in the unpublished Clark Lectures of 1926, which deplores that philosopher's upsetting of Aristotelianism. As to Bradley, he was thoroughly anti-empiricist, whereas Eliot was from the outset expressly not so: indeed he adopted, around 1916, the analytic empiricist realism of Russell, and did not abandon it till his conversion in 1927, when he moved to 'a non-realist hermeneutical perspective'.

Shusterman's efforts to map Eliot's thought onto twentieth-century philosophy may be too systematic, or too opportunist – he makes little allowance for accidental resemblances, claiming, for instance, that Eliot anticipated the thought of Gadamer. What Eliot calls 'the historical sense' is much the same as Gadamer's

* Richard Shusterman, *T.S.Eliot and the Philosophy of Criticism* (London: Duckworth)

'effective historical consciousness', and he is also said to share some of the later thinker's idea of aesthetic activity as a form of play. Moreover their ideas about tradition and community look rather alike. More interesting is the idea that his study of Aristotle's *phronesis* led the poet back towards a native American pragmatism, recalling William James at Harvard but also providing critical anticipations of Richard Rorty.

The truth is no doubt messier than these formulations suggest – say, that Eliot after a time was content to assimilate rather than extend his philosophical learning, but that the philosophical layer of his mind continued to influence an application to matters not manifestly philosophical. Shusterman's is an interesting book, but he seems to forget that even very intelligent people may have cluttered minds, and may be incapable of sustaining the kinds of prescient synthesis he discovers in Eliot's.

The decision to stop doing serious philosophy and take his chance in London was much influenced by Vivien and by Ezra Pound, who almost single-handed launched his protégé into the literary scene. Russell – despite his over-zealous and finally damaging interventions in Eliot's marriage – was probably the main influence on the social side, so important to Eliot. But the tale of Eliot's settling down here is long and tortuous. Arriving from Germany at the outbreak of war, he tells Hinkley (September 1914): 'I feel I don't understand the English very well … It's ever so much easier to know what a Frenchman or an American is thinking about, than an Englishman.' A neutral in an embattled country, he felt partisanship for neither of the conflicting parties. By October he is saying he doesn't think he can ever feel at home in England 'as I do for instance in France', though he admires the English more 'in certain ways'. By 1917 he has come to loathe the snobbish English middle class ('its family life is hideous') and informs his Harvard professor that the English lack of respect for education is amazing.

However, as the war nears its end he can say that he gets on better with Englishmen than with Americans, who 'now impress me, almost invariably, as very immature'. Occasionally regretting his loss of contact with 'Americans and their ways', and also the 'spiritual decadence of England', he nevertheless urges his brother to come here and escape the appalling gregariousness of American life. 'You are unfortunate in having a consciousness – though not a clear one – of how barbarous life in America is. If you had, like all other Americans, no consciousness at all, you would be happier.' In London, he tells Henry, he would have to 'fight very hard, in order to survive', but that would surely be better than having friends notable only for their '*immaturity of feeling*'. Mrs Eliot rather wickedly prints a letter to the poet from a distinguished and aged kinsman who says he finds it unintelligible that Eliot 'or any other young American can forego the privilege of living in the genuine American atmosphere – a bright atmosphere of freedom and hope'. It's a remark the poet might have found somewhat wanting in consciousness.

His dwelling on the rarity of this possession reminds one of the cold put-down in *The Family Reunion* when Harry fails to be moved by the news that his brother has been concussed in an accident:

> A minor trouble like concussion
> Cannot make much difference to John.
> A brief vacation from the kind of consciousness
> That John enjoys, can't make very much difference
> To him or anybody else.

To Eliot most people, and by this time all Americans except his brother, resembled John. He would presumably have excepted members of the social circle he had entered, but they did make life difficult.

> It is damned hard work to live with a foreign nation and cope with them – one is always coming up against differences of feeling that make one feel humiliated and lonely. One always remains a foreigner – only the lower classes can assimilate. It is like being always on dress parade – one can never relax. It is a great strain. And society is in a way much *harder, not* gentler. People are more aware of you, more critical, and they have no pity for one's mistakes or stupidities. They are always intriguing or caballing, one

must be very alert. They are sensitive, and easily become
enemies. But it is never dull.

So much for Bloomsbury and Garsington, and it must really have
been hard going. Clive Bell found Eliot's 'studied primness'
deliciously comic, and Virginia Woolf was a great tease. But this
was his chosen milieu, and although Eliot could call himself
'Metoikos' (meaning 'exile') as late as 1945, he had obviously
acquired the censorious Bloomsbury habit. Russell, he discovered,
'has a sensitive, but hardly a cultivated mind . . . in some ways
an immature mind'. Lowes Dickinson is 'very common'. But
Americans are of course far worse, witness Aiken and Max Boden-
heim, an American Jew who made the mistake of supposing he
could pick up a living in London as easily as he had done in
America. 'He received his first blow,' Eliot contentedly tells his
mother, 'when he found that no one had heard of him. I told him
my history here, and left him to consider whether an American
Jew, of only common school education and no university degree,
with no money, no connections, and no social polish or experience,
could make a living in London.'

His pride in his own achievement is understandable. It called
for extraordinary industry as well as talent, and at the age of 31
it was with much satisfaction that he told his mother he had been
asked to write for the *Times Literary Supplement* – 'the highest
honour possible in the field of critical literature'. Yet despite such
signal distinctions he continued to be poor: Vivien had to darn
his worn-out underclothes, and although the family was generous
with hand-outs, he never had enough money to stop worrying
about it. At one rather amusing moment, near the end of the war,
he says he would be willing to go into the (US) Army 'if I could
have a rank high enough to support me financially' – an élite
stipulation if ever there was one.

These embarrassments did not prevent the metoikos from quite
quickly becoming an insider in the London literary world. He
was offered the editorship of the *Athenaeum* but after careful
financial consideration, declined. He belonged to the party which
scorned Squire's *London Mercury*: 'you must understand that
writers here are divided into at least two groups, those who appear

regularly in the London Mercury and those who do not. The Mercury has no standing among intelligent people ... It is socially looked down upon.' It gives one some notion of what he meant by 'society' that literary and social scorn should be so commingled. He was at home in that small world, to the extent of having not only confederates but enemies. Gosse, for example, hated him. Yeats, he fancied, disliked him. Katherine Mansfield was a thick-skinned toady. Of Middleton Murry, toward whom he had once felt quite warmly, he says: 'I think something conclusive must be done about Murry.' A month later he is thanking Murry for an exceptionally pleasant weekend, but, as we have seen, he was quite soon to do something fairly conclusive by making him the representative of the Inner Voice in 'The Function of Criticism'. Above all, he was *papabile*. Herbert Read remarked that 'by the time he was given the *Criterion* Eliot was our undisputed leader.'

There is a good account of his complex early relationships with London writers in Erik Svarny's *The Men of 1914*.* One can hardly miss a certain ruthlessness, even some opportunism, in the Eliot of these years. For all his personal unhappiness he was remarkably successful; he knew how to make alliances and deal with misalliances, and how, amid all the bustle, to sustain his really important literary relationships, which were with Pound (sometimes sharply criticized) and Wyndham Lewis, for whom his admiration seems never to have flagged. He had other friendships – for example, with Brigid Patmore, Mary Hutchinson and Sydney Schiff, people less involved in the literary struggle, and perhaps for that reason recipients of some of his most interesting letters. All in all, he seems to have made himself as much as home as it was in his nature to be.

Yet the letters testify, if we needed reminding, that these were also wretched years, plagued by overwork, illness and marital misery. Eliot himself suffered with his teeth, his chest, with repeated attacks of influenza and the sense of breakdown. Vivien was more or less permanently sick, sometimes quite horribly – 'lying in the

---

* Erik Svarny, *'The Men of 1914': T. S. Eliot and Early Modernism* (Milton Keynes: Open University Press)

most dreadful agony, with *neuritis* in every nerve, increasingly – arms, legs, feet, back', and in such pain that she feared for her sanity. Everything conspired to augment their unhappiness – cold weather, hot weather, his mother's failure to visit and then her visit, moving house or staying where they were, the ill-fated Bel Esprit plan to help him by the subscriptions of well-wishers, an insult in the *Liverpool Daily Post*'s report of the matter.

Apart from nursing Vivien, Eliot had to prepare lecture courses and to read, very quickly, writers he had no interest in, such as George Eliot. He knew he was writing too much for literary journals, but needed the money. In September 1922, the nervous collapse associated with *The Waste Land* only recently past, he told John Quinn that he found himself 'under the continuous strain of trying to suppress a vague but acutely intense horror and apprehension'. Vivien at least understood what an achievement it was to edit the *Criterion* when 'tired out by eight hours in the City', meanwhile filling hot water bottles and making invalid food for her. He also had a sense of his own guilt to contend with, telling Pound, in 1922, that his mistakes were 'largely the cause' of Vivien's 'present catastrophic state of health'. And while there was all this to deal with there were also poems needing somehow to be written.

Such a man, in such a plight, could plausibly suppose himself different not only from the *Massenmenschen* but even from his gently bohemian, quite well-off writer friends: and so, after all, still metoikos, always an exile – not merely in the sense of being physically *dépaysé*, like Turgenev and James Joyce, but in the more general sense *dépaysé* anywhere, suffering an exile of the spirit right here in the London that so fascinated him, as the exile of one of his spiritual heroes, Baudelaire, was undergone in his native Paris. How much suffering, and how much guilt, is enough?

For all his social uncertainties and worries about money, Eliot seems to have been remarkably secure in his sense of class and calling. Yet it was still necessary to be separate. There was an apparently instinctive withdrawal from others, shown not only in the abrupt way he sometimes ended relationships, whether male friendships or *amitiés amoureuses*, but in a coldness which could affect even an obituary notice. He needed isolation, not as a *prince d'Aquitaine* pose, but because it was entailed both by his idea of poetry and his idea of intelligence. Some social success was obviously necessary, but so was a deep reserve and a deep self-esteem. He found Joyce to be 'a quiet but rather dogmatic man' who had '(as I am convinced most superior persons have) a sense of his own importance'. And Eliot was certainly a superior person.

It happens that the letters have little to say about Eliot's early life in St Louis, a city which, if only because of its river, grew increasingly important to the poet in the second half of his life. The scholars have looked into his early background, and although Herbert Howarth wrote well about it in *Some Figures behind T. S. Eliot*, Robert Crawford has made a substantial addition. His patient Oxford D.Phil. thesis* is intended more generally to illustrate Eliot's preoccupation with the primitive and the city, but its opening chapters are about St Louis and the Mississippi. He illustrates them with gems from the *St Louis Globe-Democrat*, such as the daily advertisement of a Dr F. L. Sweaney, which promised relief to fatigued brains and bodies. The youthful poet carefully copied the drawing of the bearded doctor's face, together with the exhortation: 'When other fail consult . . .' Did the doctor form one of the multitude of suggestions incorporated in Sweeney? Does the young poet's interest indicate a consciousness or a fear of debility? We must make up our own minds. And there may be an additional clue in an early story, printed in the school magazine, in which a man is almost eaten whole by vultures. Eliot, we may conjecture, was closing in on his subject.

Crawford also has a lot to say about Gloucester, Mass., another place of obvious importance to the poet. And as he goes he finds much to say about Eliot's reading in ethnology, even documenting his loss of interest in it, dated by an admission that he did not bother to read Malinowski. The book is a little dogged in manner, as the genre of dissertation requires, but it provides some hard information as well as many conjectures, which might be useful and can certainly do no harm. Stanley Sultan's book† can be said to do likewise for the period of *Ulysses* and *The Waste Land*.

* Robert Crawford, *The Savage and the City in the Work of T. S. Eliot* (Oxford University Press)
† Stanley Sultan, *Eliot, Joyce and Company* (Oxford University Press)

The Feast of St Thomas

Scofield's* is for the most part a modest exercise in reading the poems. All such books, and there are lots of them, with the centenary likely to produce more, are bound to repeat much that is available already, but beginners will not suffer from using them.

Finally, it is curious that we seem to be keener than ever on centenaries. They are part of the *Aberglaube* of a secularized tradition, taking the place of religious feasts. Of course they are commercialized, but still fairly innocently so, and they serve to affirm, or on rarer occasions to disconfirm, canonical values: which of course makes it all the more apposite that we should celebrate Eliot on 26 September, continuing, if we choose, for the ensuing octave, in the manner prescribed by the best ecclesiastical authorities.

London Review of Books, 29 September 1988

* Martin Scofield, *T. S. Eliot: The Poems* (Cambridge University Press)

Poetry à la Mode

The original *Oxford Book of English Verse* came out in 1900, was revised by its editor, Sir Arthur Quiller-Couch, in 1939, and has kept going to this day. The tradition might be represented as even longer than the three-quarters of a century claimed above; in the preface to his first edition Quiller-Couch acknowledged his debt to an earlier anthology: 'Few of my contemporaries can erase – or would wish to erase – the dye their minds took from the late Mr Palgrave's *Golden Treasury*.' Since Palgrave made his selections on the advice of Tennyson, we can identify the dye as laureate crimson; *The Oxford Book of English Verse* was already, in a sense, archaic when it came out. Q was certainly not the kind of professor who revises his views to accommodate the new, and the 1939 edition makes only a few concessions to changing fashion. He added a hundred pages and updated the collection to 1918, but his heart wasn't in it, and there is real bitterness in his comments on the poetry of his own later years. 'It were profane to misdoubt the Nine as having forsaken these so long favoured islands,' he remarks, adding that in 1939 he is 'at a loss what to do with a fashion of morose disparagement; of sneering at things long by catholic consent accounted beautiful; of scorning at "man's unconquerable mind" and hanging up (without benefit of laundry) our common humanity as a rag on a clothes-line.'

Perhaps 1939 was the last possible date such prose could have been written, and by very old literary gentlemen still stunned by the wickedness of 'The Waste Land'. It was the year of Yeats's death, but 'The Lake Isle of Innisfree' was as far as Q cared to go. As Dame Helen Gardner hints in her preface to the new edition,* the 1939 revision of *O.B.V.* was a disaster, though it's much easier to be confident about this in 1972 than it was in 1939.

The character of the difficulties Q faced in 1939 will help us to understand the magnitude, and I fear the hopelessness, of what Dame Helen has tried to do in 1972. What the old man undertook to revise was, in some perfectly real sense of the word, a classic; he had assembled in 1900 a body of verse which won cultural acceptance as in some way canonical. The well-read could argue about its balance, but the normal reader, who might accord to poetry a measure of respect or even love, but associated it primarily with all that was fine in bourgeois sentiment and piety, went on buying it for his children and his pupils. On both sides of the Atlantic the book appeared in so many different guises – morocco bindings, India paper, and many other such variations – that it clearly had acquired some of the status of the Bible, issued (by the same publisher) in just such a range of editions. It may therefore be said to have become a social symbol: it could lie around or stand on a shelf as an index of the owner's participation in the culture. In due course it ousted Palgrave (though I was given *The Golden Treasury*, in leather, as a school prize in 1934) as the single volume associated in the public mind with English poetry – beautiful and true, all you know and all you need to know.

What made Q so doleful in 1939 was the sense that this state of affairs was coming to an end; as indeed it was, and precisely because the phase of culture which made it possible was nearly over. Almost anything written in the present century that he could bear to include in the new edition was bound to be very old-fashioned; as the rude young poet Auden might have put it, he had, in the age of the Bristol bomber, tastes appropriate to the age of the penny-farthing bicycle. The entire constitution of the poetry-reading public was changing fast, and the lower-middle-class public, which once assumed that virtue lay in the imitation of a better-educated and more polite class above it, was acquiring different habits. A smattering of poetry was no longer socially

* *The New Oxford Book of English Verse*, edited by Helen Gardner (Oxford University Press)

301

necessary. Meanwhile, a new public was adjusting itself to a new poetry, and the universities, using different methods in the United States and Great Britain, began to turn out readers who found in poetry strict but pleasing challenges, moral or intellectual, and had sophisticated ways of talking about it. Q's book appeared before anybody taught English literature at Oxford or Cambridge: its public was unlearned, unsystematic. Nevertheless, simply by accepting that the poetry it needed was contained in those eight hundred or so pages, the book's audience constituted a kind of unified literary culture which all the efforts of the universities have not replaced.

It was, no doubt, a culture of a humble, even tiresome kind. Some notion of its lower reaches – occupied by the newly literate, the products of compulsory education, trained largely by special newspapers such as *Titbits* to pick up the scraps that fell from the inaccessible table of literature – may be had from the 'Nausicaa' episode of Joyce's *Ulysses*. The date, only four years after the publication of *O.B.V.*, is June 16, 1904: 'The summer evening had begun to fold the world in its mysterious embrace. Far in the west the sun was setting and the last glow of all too fleeting day lingered lovingly on sea and strand . . .' The sickening stew of poesy, facetiousness, clerks' witticisms, novelettes, and girls' weeklies, concocted by the abstemious Joyce, reminds us that he once claimed to have the mind of a grocer's assistant. Into it he drops not only St Bernard's Litany of the Virgin but lines of poetry that had somehow peeled off the parent poems and sunk into the popular mind: 'with all his faults she loved him still' or 'golden opinions' or 'more sinned against than sinning', all worn smooth in Gertie's dialect, like the Latin of the *Tantum ergo*: *Tantumer gosa cramen tum.*

Yet however extreme this debasement of literary culture, Gertie nevertheless belongs to such a culture; the tags from *Macbeth* or *Lear* drift down to her almost without meaning, yet her culture is continuous with that of the future King Edward VII Professor at Cambridge, Quiller-Couch; and no one would dream of saying any such thing about the relationship of any comparable modern girl with Professor L. C. Knights, the present incumbent, who, as it happens, has written a good deal about such sad dissociations.

Gertie's literary tags have no meaning except as signs of a deplorable but large cultural class, and as the unconscious tribute of that class to notions of literary excellence imposed from above.

Q acknowledges, in his original preface, the advice of a large number of literary men: they include Bridges, Binyon, Kipling, Swinburne, Francis Thompson, and Yeats, and contrast sharply with the donnish consultants of Dame Helen. The poet and man of letters has retreated into the university, like his audience. We may not feel altogether badly about this if we consider some of Q's other advisers, such as Frederick Locker-Lampson, whose own poem 'At Her Window' Q gratefully included in his selection. Gertie would have loved it:

> Beating Heart! we come again
> Where my love reposes:
> This is Mabel's window-pane;
> These are Mabel's roses . . .

> Sing thy song, thou tranced thrush,
> Pipe thy best, thy clearest; –
> Hush, her lattice moves, O hush –
> Dearest Mabel! – dearest . . .

Even Q dropped this one from his revised edition, together with others, notably a truly incredible outburst by the Irish poet John Todhunter, another cinch for Gertie, though Yeats must have had his doubts; not that leaving Todhunter out made room for Yeats, but the times were changing.

To come at last to the new version; one may say with absolute confidence that Gertie has nothing at all in common with Dame Helen Gardner; and that you will look in vain in the new O.B.V. for farcically corrupted fragments of Eliot, comparable with the decayed Tennysonianisms of the old collection. Of course, chips from Eliot's poems have never been used to stuff lower-middle-class conversation either. Palgrave said he hoped his anthology would prove 'a storehouse of delight to Labour and Poverty'. That function of poetry is now obsolete; the work is done instead by television advertising. If you take a London child to the

Christmas pantomime nowadays you will find that he understands the jokes and you don't, simply because he watches commercial television more than you; the dialogue is a continuous allusion to advertising gimmicks and slogans. So is normal supermarket conversation. Whether you prefer this is a matter of taste; but it's worth remembering that the culture of the newly literate in the late nineteenth century might be represented not only by Gertie and Wells's Mr Polly (whose neologisms are a tribute to culture) but by D. H. Lawrence. Poetry was still something you might read without embarrassment, and without taking a course in it; it still had some place in the conversation of all the literate. Whether the admen in any sense supply its place I don't know. What seems quite sure is that there is no longer an easily recognizable public for *The Oxford Book of English Verse*, and no generally acknowledged corpus of English poetry.

In spite of all this, Dame Helen has remade the book for a new public. In her preface she has a few words to say about changed taste, but this really means the taste inculcated in the universities. Dame Helen is a don, a scholar, as Q was not; she has edited Donne (a poet in whom Q was a little too old and a little too old-fashioned to be very interested) and Eliot, whose existence Q ignored. She offers the public a qualified version of the view of English poetry which on the whole prevails in the universities – qualified because the book is not intended for use there; because some poetry carries on into the new edition as if by inertia; and because she has quite rightly not thought that this is a proper occasion to stimulate controversy.

Some of her inclusions are due, I feel, rather to the constraints of the academic conscience than to any persuasion that there is a public which will respond: these are mostly seventeenth- and twentieth-century poems. The editor's dilemma is illustrated by her inclusion of 'The Waste Land' entire, except for the notes. It has to be there, but how odd it looks in this context! Who will read it here, even first time? It simply doesn't belong; it will never be canonical in the old sense; it is too self-conscious about tradition ever to find a place in the messy continuum of taste I've tried to describe; it is the work of a poet who actually announced that tradition was not something you could acquire passively –

you must work for it. So with Yeats; it is necessary for Dame Helen, as it was impossible for Q, to include such poems as 'Sailing to Byzantium' and 'The Circus Animals' Desertion', which can never be the poetry of people who read it only in the *Oxford Book*.

Sometimes the changes introduced in conformity with standard modern taste have their own interest. For Q there was no sharp distinction between English and American poetry – he had Whitman (in a wretched selection) because Whitman was early domesticated in England, but he also had Whittier and Longfellow. Apart from Auden (an exception needing no excuse), Gardner includes only one American, Ezra Pound, though having made this endearing decision, she spoils it by including only three pieces: 'The River-Merchant's Wife', a bit of 'Hugh Selwyn Mauberley', and 'What thou lovest well remains', from the *Pisan Cantos* (she ignores Q's ban on extracts). Her stated reason for leaving out the Americans is that she needs the space for the great English moderns, Hopkins, Hardy, Yeats, and Eliot; but of course it is also true that since Whitman (who might have been left in on the same grounds as Scottish poetry – 'part of the cultural heritage of England'), American poetry isn't susceptible to the kind of levelling that has to go on in such a book as this, and is for the most part unknown in England. Some American poets – say, Stevens, Williams, Lowell, Plath, Berryman, and Ginsberg – are extremely important to people who read poetry; but neither their names nor their poems have become household words.

The revaluation of styles and periods is also subject to conventional restraints. Gardner greatly increases Skelton's share, and Fulke Greville's. She puts in eighteen pages of Donne, against Q's meagre five poems, one of which, lifted from Palgrave, isn't by Donne anyway. Although she rather surprisingly contents herself with the same single lyric of Chapman selected by Q and the same two poems by Quarles, she adds a whole batch of minor seventeenth-century poets ignored by Q – Samuel Butler, John Cleveland, and Aurelian Townshend, for example. She adds a beautiful poem to Davenant's portion, doubles Herbert's share, slightly enlarges Marvell's, and allows bits of *Paradise Lost*, rather forlornly one feels, in the Milton section. Pope and Dryden benefit largely from the lifting of Arnold's ban on them; and Romantic poetry is much better represented. So principle is upheld; but whether representation is the object of such a book is a question.

The major changes naturally occur late in the anthology. Q, as we have seen, was at his worst here; even his Browning selection is disgraceful. Gardner ruthlessly cuts down his favourites: Sydney Dobell, Beeching, William Watson, T. E. Brown, Henry Newbolt, W. D. Howells. James Thomson, who is the author of lyrical trifles in Q, is the author of 'The City of Dreadful Night' in Gardner. John Davidson, who appears in Q as a nothing poet, a trifler, is now the author of the splendid 'Thirty Bob a Week'. Q left out of his first edition certain contemporaries with evident claims on his space – Dowson, Lionel Johnson, Wilde, not to mention John Gray and Arthur Symons. Perhaps they were all too wicked; certainly they were very much advanced for Gertie.

Gardner is very brisk about all this. Just as she imports Edward Lear and Lewis Carroll into the Victorian pages, she also includes Chesterton and Belloc, as well as Housman, Johnson, and Wilde. Willing enough to be conventional (as when she includes anthology pieces by W. H. Davies, Ralph Hodgson, Walter de la Mare, and John Masefield), she can also surprise us, as when she adds to the obvious Binyon choice, 'For the Fallen' (which, incidentally, did, between the wars, acquire a wide cultural spread as an Armistice poem), a beautiful and little-known work written during World War II and called 'The Burning of the Leaves'. This, together with Edmund Blunden's 'Report on Experience' and the Davenant dialogue, strikes me as the best Gardner does toward matching Q's great coup, the discovery of a sonnet by Mark Alexander Boyd which Ezra Pound later called the most beautiful in the language.

Dame Helen's stars are Hardy, Yeats, and Eliot. She is a bit skimpy on Lawrence, and it might be said that Graves deserves more, perhaps at the expense of Edith Sitwell. She stops at 1950, doing well by Edwin Muir, William Empson, Louis MacNeice, Auden, Roy Fuller, and Dylan Thomas. American readers may be pleased and surprised by Stevie Smith's poem:

Poetry à la Mode

Nobody heard him, the dead man,
But still he lay moaning;
I was much farther out than you thought
And not waving but drowning –

But Miss Smith's work is now quite widely known in Britain. She may travel as well as John Betjeman or the two poems of Henry Reed which 'everybody' knows, and which are properly reprinted here.

It would be silly to argue long about choices, or even to dwell on a suspicion that the book is somehow a shade pious, a little light on erotic poetry. Dame Helen has done her work well. She knows a lot more than Q and has strong preferences, but she has seen the need, if the thing was to work at all, for sticking quite close to the only norm available, 'the critical consensus', as she herself calls it. She has not tried to avoid a family resemblance to Q's collection, or even to Palgrave's.

The question remains: who is going to read this book? Not students, not schoolboys, though I suppose they may still have it thrust into their hands. There is the huge army of poetry in paperback, for the truly interested; and there is no longer any need for those who aren't to pretend. Will it console lonely ladies in London apartments, or provincial reading groups? They no longer exist, at any rate in the form such words conjure up. And modern Gerties feed their fantasies at the telly. I wouldn't for a moment argue against the proposition that this is in most ascertainable ways a better job than Q's; but that it can have a comparable place in our lives is surely quite impossible.

The Atlantic Monthly, January 1973

On William Gerhardie

Gerhardie is one of those writers who are periodically rescued from near-oblivion. In 1947, a temporary revival of interest was brought about by the publication of a 'uniform Edition' of his novels, and there was another in 1970, when the same edition was republished with prefaces by Michael Holroyd. Gerhardie himself prefixed to the reissue of his first book, *Futility*, an important essay called 'My Literary Credo', which is unfortunately omitted from the new Penguin Modern Classics reprint.* (*Futility* is the only novel in paperback, another omission that Penguin ought to rectify.) The most recent upsurge of interest has been caused by the posthumous publication of *God's Fifth Column*, in the preparation of which Mr Holroyd, sticking to his noble task, has sensibly enlisted the help of a historian expert in the period reviewed by the book.[1]

Gerhardie died in 1977 in his eighty-second year – fifty-five years after the publication of *Futility* and nearly forty years after his last novel. As the editors point out, he early acquired a reputation for failure, and there was little in the second half of his life to suggest that this judgment was seriously wrong. He was a shadowy survivor, living round the corner from Broadcasting House but known to few. The press noticed that he added a final 'e' to Gerhardi, and that the Arts Council gave him a writer's

---

[1] William Gerhardie, *God's Fifth Column: A Biography of the Age, 1890–1940*, edited and with an introduction by Michael Holroyd and Robert Skidelsky (London: Hodder & Stoughton)

* William Gerhardie, *Futility* (London: Penguin)

grant, tacitly waiving the rule that such grants are made in the expectation of a return in the form of new publication, and not in recognition of services rendered or for considerations of need. Of course there were said to be works in progress: but few supposed that they would come to much. Gerhardi(e) belonged to the Twenties and Thirties.

He himself has a good deal to say, in the 'Credo', about the fickleness of reviewers and the transience of praise. If one book does well, the second is disparaged; or, if it is not, the first is forgotten. He compares novel-reviews to strings of sausages, churned out by writers impatient to get on with their own work. This doesn't prevent him from quoting the best reviews given him by illustrious critics: but in the end, he says, 'something incomplete and alien wafts upon us even from the friendliest notice'. Nobody ever seemed to have time to achieve an understanding of what he was really up to.

In some ways he resembles Ford Madox Ford, though Ford was much more prolific, indeed embarrassingly so. Both were dedicated to the art of fiction; and Ford also died a failure and three parts forgotten. Repeated attempts to establish at least *The Good Soldier* and *Parade's End* as canonical masterpieces have never quite succeeded, despite very distinguished sponsorship. But *The Good Soldier* doesn't disappear completely, and perhaps an increasing number of people take it for granted as one of the great novels of the century: so it hovers on the margin of the canon. No book of Gerhardie's has acquired even that status. Neither books nor theses (as far as I know) are written about him. In an age when large numbers of people are maintained by the public to read English literature, and to train even larger numbers of readers to be a proper audience for good writing, Gerhardie finds no place in syllabuses which find room for, say, Vonnegut or Doris Lessing.

Since Henry Green, arguably the best English novelist of his time, is little better off, we need not waste our time being surprised at this neglect. It would be agreeable to believe that the present stir of interest might alter the situation: but the rather freakish *God's Fifth Column*, even supported by *Futility*, does not seem a strong enough base on which to rebuild a reputation. It may even reinforce the old view that Gerhardie was no more than a quite interesting and rather peculiar kind of failure. In fact, everybody interested in good novels should read him. I speak as a new convert, for although I read *Futility* forty years ago I knew nothing else until this posthumous book induced me to look out some of the other novels. I bought *The Polyglots* and *Of Mortal Love* for four dollars in a New York second-hand bookshop, and was quickly persuaded that Gerhardie is a novelist of high order. To explain how such a writer may come to be overlooked would call for a whole book about the way we live now as a literary community. At one level we behave like Time in *Troilus and Cressida* – that is,

> like a fashionable host
> That slightly shakes his parting guest by the hand,
> And with his arms outstretched as he would fly,
> Grasps in the comer. The welcome ever smiles,
> And farewell goes out sighing.

In other words, there are fashions in reputations. At another level, where there is a responsibility to provide good writers with appropriate readers, we are enslaved to habit or inertia. Under such conditions it is all too easy for valuable work to disappear.

Gerhardie's 'Credo' takes account of these facts and their consequences. He had developed a rather Proustian theory of time and habit (the signs are that he knew Beckett's *Proust* rather well). His defence of poetry is Romantic, expressly Wordsworthian, for it remembers the definition of poetry as 'the pleasure which there is in life itself'. Here, and again in *God's Fifth Column*, he remembers, without quoting them, Wordsworth's lines about those 'higher minds' which

> from their native selves can send abroad
> Kindred mutations; for themselves create
> A like existence; and, whene'er it dawns
> Created for them, catch it, or are caught
> By its inevitable mastery.
> Like angels stopped upon the wing by sound
> Of harmony from Heaven's remotest spheres –

where the 'mutations' and 'existence' are kindred to those of
nature. The link between this primary Romantic idea and Proust
is provided by Blake: 'eternity is in love with the productions of
time' – having, as Gerhardie adds, nothing else to be in love with
outside itself. Poetry is the means by which we sense that love,
and so experience 'the pleasure that there is in life itself'. But by
poetry he meant the novel, now our principal means of achieving
glimpses of intemporal realities, the 'unknown laws of the kingdom of heaven'. It follows that good novels must be serious, which
entails a distinction between seriousness and earnestness, and a
claim that the serious is also humorous. The genre of his own
novels he defines as 'humorous tragedy', adding that they have
their origins in emotion recollected in tranquillity, '*Wahrheit*
made fragrant by *Dichtung*'.

Not surprisingly, the man who holds such views believes also
that good novels are neither obvious nor transparent: to read
them is a task calling for slow research, and few will undertake
such work. Reviewers prefer what is familiar and easily dealt with,
and may therefore destroy a book whose whole object is to remove
what Wordsworth and Coleridge called 'the film of familiarity
and selfish solicitude' which prevents our seeing and understanding. So Gerhardie's aesthetic merges into his complaint about his
reception. Not that he hopes for many 'ideal readers': given an
audience of genius, he whimsically remarks, the writer of genius
would lose his distinction. But there should be some, capable of
reading 'stereoscopically', serious but not earnest, participators in
the work of 'humorous tragedy'.

The 'Credo' is an odd document, mingling grand claims with
a muted disappointment and in the end leaving the whole matter
to posterity – a weak conclusion, since posterity is only more bad
readers, with perhaps a few good ones who could easily miss him.
But it does convey his sense of the justice of his claims without
sounding merely vain. Not that he was without a saving vanity.
He was always surprised by the slowness with which he made his
way. *Futility* was turned down by thirteen publishers before he
sent it to the dying Katherine Mansfield, who got it published at
once; it was a success, but not the wild one he seemed to expect.
His choice of reader was shrewd: for all that he has to say about

the English Romantics and Goethe and Proust, his true Penelope was Chekhov, a humorous tragedian whose 'insight . . . penetrates to a level immeasurably deeper than the superficial differences of men and race, to a bed-rock of common humanity where *all* human beings, as human beings, are frail, irresponsible, weak. Against this, their success or failure is shown to be irrelevant.'

Futility is a Russian novel, Chekhov naturalized. It is even about three Russian sisters. It is set in the period of the Revolution and immediately after, a period on which Gerhardie's imagination would continue to dwell, but it is mostly concerned with Chekhovian irresponsibility and charming weakness. One sees why Shaw said to him: 'If you're English you're a genius, but if you're Russian . . .' What would he have said had he been allowed to finish? Epigone, or thief? Gerhardie's people are always saying such things as 'how tiring this is, Andrei Andreiech . . . to be always waiting to begin our lives.' Or: 'The three sisters always sat in some extraordinary positions, on the backs of sofas and easychairs, and Fanny Ivanovna and Kniaz sat in very ordinary positions . . .' The manner is playfully high-handed, the narrator running the show to suit himself, introducing whenever he feels like it observations on life and on the relation between life and his novel. The book ends with a tiny *Liebestod*. Back in London, the 'I' of the book again thinks he loves Nina (*staying* in love is always a major problem in Gerhardie) and slogs back to Vladivostock, via Port Said, Colombo, Hong Kong, Shanghai and Peking, to find that Nina has christened her parrot Andrei Andreiech. She no longer loves him, nor, he finds, does he love her. She leaves for Europe; her boat is subjected to a 'heart-rending delay', and Andrei ends the book in an alternation of relief and overwhelming sadness, a mood which has no visible excuse except perhaps 'common humanity'.

The futility lies in being unable to make purposeful moves, even in courtship, even when the girl is so charming that her lack of real substance merely enhances her charm. The lover, like his elders, is incapable of acting except foolishly, except when the occasion doesn't require it, because he is self-bewilderingly odd. There is a character who claims to have no father, only a grandfather, and when that is called an odd omission, cannot see why:

he is a type of all Gerhardie's sympathetic characters, and nearly all of them *are* sympathetic. *The Polyglots*, published three years after *Futility*, has much the same ambience, including the setting in time and place, but is a more definite and more powerful book. Now the girl is Sylvia; the narrator's marriage to her is continually postponed and they grow tired of each other. Eventually she marries a bore, but her farcical mother, having arranged the match, prevents its consummation, and the hero, the young writer, sleeps with her on the wedding night. Then they go off to Europe, leaving the husband behind. The love-relationship is serious and silly, passionate and tedious. The writer remembers from Chekhov's notebook the saying that love is 'either a remnant of something degenerating, something which once has been immense, or ... a particle of what will in the future develop into something immense; but in the present it is unsatisfying, it gives much less than one expects ...' *The Polyglots* is a study of love in the light of that remark, but also in the light of other facts of life, such as war and death. The events of the Great War and what followed it left Gerhardie with a hatred and contempt for war, and the people who made war, sentiments which grew stronger with time; and on this subject there are notable pages in *The Polyglots*. The Chekhovian eccentrics are still there. One uncle claims that he can construct an electrical machine in such a way that the hero can press the keys in his attic while the typewriter types in the basement. But he agrees that the arrangement offers no discernible advantage, and goes away 'swinging his hammer, and wondering if there was anything by way of a nail anywhere that wanted driving in'. Now, however, these pleasant idlers are marked for death. Throughout the book one is charmed by the accurate rendering of the funniness of children's talk, Chekhovians in miniature as they all are; later one understands that these pleasures have softened one up for the tragic climax, which is beautifully and very painfully written.

In *Of Mortal Love*, which gets Gerhardie's main preoccupation into its title, the manner changes a little; it appeared, though its writing may have begun very much earlier, in 1936. It is again a story of an irresponsible and delightful girl, of an off-and-on love affair, which ends not in parting but in death. The final section, written with great delicacy and candour, takes all the risks and succeeds. Why it is not sentimental is a good question. There is a sort of epiphany near the end, the dead young woman seen as a being perpetually alive, as a defeat of time, as a truth from which the 'film of familiarity' has been wiped away. Then time and habit resume their rule.

If books such as these can remain out of circulation for decades, it is not easy to believe that *God's Fifth Column* will do well with posterity, though it is an interesting experiment, a biography of the age that is as much from the hand that wrote *The Romanovs*, a study of the Russian dynasty, as from the imagination of the novelist. It is divided into five books, one for each decade, and the story is told by means of casually apposed and anecdotal biographies, with the author's reflections on politics, metaphysics and anything else he chooses thrown in. The editors explain that the work engaged Gerhardie for a great many years; 'finished' early in the second war, it was retrieved from the publisher for improvements and additions.

It seems obvious that on the method employed a book becomes indefinitely expansible: you need never run out of lives, or even out of Plutarchan parallel lives, which, as in the case of Hitler and D. H. Lawrence, Gerhardie rather enjoys. There are interwoven chapters on Margot Tennant, the Kaiser ('the greatest ass of the last half-century to wear a crown'), Lenin and Chekhov, Bismarck, Curzon, Balfour, Tolstoy, Wilde, Proust, a couple of Czars, and so on. All are written with care and informed by strong opinions. Lenin, who 'gave no more thought to the unbearable burdens of the Russian peasant' than the Czar Alexander, is, like most statesmen, treated with contempt, unlike Chekhov, who remarked that if the upper classes could depute their bowel movements to the working classes they would do so, explaining that the best people should not waste on these merely eliminatory functions the time indispensable to the task of ensuring cultural progress.

Gerhardie had a profound hatred of class, especially in England, and in general he thought his own country mediocre, dirty and hypocritical, with its grotesque educational system, its affairs placed in the hands of 'feeble-minded wives and their not much wiser husbands'. The Boer War is treated as a turning-point in our moral history and a useful example for Hitler. The system of international finance is responsible for twentieth-century wars in which the people kill one another ruthlessly, having been encouraged to treat the opposition as the embodiment of evil until the rulers make up the quarrel, reassign the frontiers, and carry on.

The tone varies from the mildly Swiftian to the ecstatic. On Hitler:

> He had no culture; so he invented his own brand. He had no mind, no intellect; he was practically illiterate; so with his secretary's assistance he wrote a book to say that he despised education, and forced everybody to buy and read it . . . He had no sense of accuracy or of history; so he decreed that his own accession to power was henceforward to be the chief study of the school curriculum. He had no well-founded right even to his name . . . so he decreed that his name should be on every lip as a greeting.

On Proust:

> He had re-lived an isolated moment in its crystal purity, free from the strain of anxiety and the blight of habit which had dulled the actual moment and made it nebulously unreal. He had re-lived it, this time, with insouciance because his being recognized it as real and ideal. Utterly real, with nothing in it to abstract from simultaneous realization, the moment was also the ideal of contemplation. Man no longer stood in his own shadow. The duality had been bridged.

As these quotations suggest, the artists come off better than the politicians: in fact, the characters are divided into those who, like kings and politicians, are the slaves of time and chance, and on the other hand artists, who deal in eternal reality. There is a further distinction between poets and prophets: the poets include Wilde, Chekhov and Proust, the prophets Tolstoy, Shaw and Gorky. Artists, who introduce eternity to the productions of time, do not preach or teach. They may not be virtuous: Proust remarked that 'great artists often, while being thoroughly wicked, make use of their vices in order to arrive at a conception of the moral law that is binding upon us all.' Gerhardie's Twenties section ends strongly with a comparison between Proust and Lenin, the analyst of vanity and the 'man of narrowly premeditated action' who declared that he was prepared to exterminate three-quarters of the human race if only the remaining quarter survived to be communists. The Thirties were perhaps too close, and the writing loses force, though God's fifth column – the power which, working for God, sabotages human complacency and human ambitions – was certainly hard at work in those years.

The book is full of deft juxtapositions and fine, self-indulgent moralizing, but it is a failure all the same and somehow seems to know it. It has a sort of loneliness, as of a work that knows it has no real audience. Nor is it impeccably served by its editors. Gerhardie regarded printers as the enemy of authors, especially authors who quote foreign languages; and perhaps, as he complains, they ignore or garble proof corrections also. The text of this last book has a good many errors including some in foreign languages. The editors sometimes translate (or mistranslate – see the first Proust quotation on page 98) passages of French and German, and sometimes don't. There are obvious mistranscriptions, as on page 165, where 'stillness' should be 'silliness', and Gerhardie is permitted to attribute a remark about 'bloody instructions which but return to plague the inventor' (*sic*) to Kipling. There is a scatter of simple misprints, which Gerhardie would have hated. Perhaps Mr Holroyd, when he supervises the next Uniform Edition at the next Gerhardie revival a dozen years hence, will put them right.

London Review of Books, 2 April 1981

The Essential Orwell

Professor Crick's subject is important and his research has evidently been diligent. We now know a lot more about Orwell than we did, and the increment of knowledge is not always trivial. Why, then, is it impossible to commend this book* with warmth? For two main reasons: first, in a work of such length the prevalence of carelessly written pages is a strong disincentive to continuing (and of course they are shown up all the more by their proximity to quotations from Orwell); and secondly, Orwell was a literary figure as well as a political thinker, and Crick's literary touch is far from certain.

Take, for instance, the conclusion. It is sententious, but we may feel that two hundred thousand laborious words have earned the author the right to pontificate on the final page. '"Our prerogatives as men," wrote the young Auden, "Will be cancelled who knows when . . . ?", if we cannot radically alter our relationships with public power; but neither a transformed nor a reformed public realm will be worth having if individual creative values do not flourish, indeed fructify in abundance for the majority of people, not just for the chosen or even the self-chosen few . . .' Crick often praises Orwell's style, and even observes its progressive refinement. He must have been conscious throughout of a formidable reader over his shoulder: but he evidently did not ask himself how many faults. Orwell would have found in that sentence. And there are many passages worse than that one, sentences that flop randomly onto the page, or make sense only by an act of charity on the part of the reader. I've chosen this one because

---

* Bernard Crick, *George Orwell: A Life* (London: Secker & Warburg)

it also contains a factual inaccuracy. The verses quoted were written not by the young Auden but by the young MacNeice, who went on to say that he was writing these lines 'before/The gun butt raps upon the door' – an encounter less abstract than 'relationships with public power'. The poet is to that extent more Orwellian than Crick. As it happens, MacNeice's poem is a poor one, but we remember it because he often wrote well, and because he, sometimes more accurately than Auden, caught the mood and posture of that moment, expressed a foreboding necessarily a bit spurious in the face of fears not yet capable of being fully imagined.

Other writers also suffer from Crick's difficulty in reporting literature. Spotting a source for a famous line in *Animal Farm*, he misquotes Milton ('And render me more equal, and perhaps,/A thing not undesirable, sometime [not *something*]/Superior . . .'. Moreover it is untrue to say that 'Orwell was to put this thought more pithily in *Animal Farm*.' Eve is talking about the possible advantages of withholding her forbidden knowledge from Adam, not about totalitarian perversions of democracy. It is even more reprehensible for a professor of politics to misquote Hobbes's most famous remark, about the horrors of living at a time when there is no state power to keep men in awe. The catalogue ends with the words: 'And the life of man, solitary, poore, nasty, brutish, and short'. There are five partners in this ghastly firm, and to leave out 'poore' is to destroy the rhythm that made it memorable in the first place.

So it is not surprising that Crick has little of interest to say about Orwell's achievement as a critic of literature. The essay on 'Lear, Tolstoy and the Fool' is described as 'a profound comparison of the didacticism of Tolstoy with the tolerant humanism of Shakespeare', and indeed it is profound: but if you are doing Orwell in some depth you surely need to add that it is also, in some respects, profoundly silly ('One wicked daughter would have been quite enough, and Edgar is a superfluous character; indeed it would probably be a better play if Gloucester and both his sons were eliminated'). This kind of thing is interesting because it shows that Orwell, in his literary criticism as in his other writing, sometimes yielded to the temptation of saying too much. Crick quite often catches him doing so. In one of the wartime London

Letters to *Partisan Review* Orwell reported that when the authorities tore down railings for scrap they ravaged working-class parks and squares but left upper-class ones alone. When his wife pointed out that this allegation was demonstrably false, he answered that it was '*essentially* true', rather as he accused pacifists of being 'objectively Fascist'. Sometimes from ignorance, sometimes from a pamphleteer's sense of the need for emphatic illustration, Orwell quite often said the thing that is not, quite. Getting some things wrong (or only *essentially* right) was probably the price he paid for getting some hugely important things right – the nature of totalitarianism, for instance. The struggle to get that vision of evil across, to give it very sharp definition, may be what led him to dogmatic excess or distortion in lesser matters.

The need to be extremely unequivocal, to present arguments without conventional rhetorical shading or contemplative half-tones, helped to form the mature prose style. It was a product of the same extremism that sent Orwell out on the road as a tramp, preferring the dosshouse to the comfort of more prosperous working-class homes (though they were his image of paradise). He 'went native in his own country', said V. S. Pritchett. He also went native in his own language. But to do either of these things called for extreme self-discipline, for an almost military upper-class rigour. Orwell's style is of course not the style of tramps. Nor is it the style of cosy tripe shops. In fact, it is the enemy of the *lumpen* and the *gemütlich* just as certainly as of bourgeois evasion and euphemism. The achievement of such a manner is unmistakably an achievement of high culture – almost an inverted mandarinism. The humble style has a grand history: to match it with great subjects calls for virtuosity, which is why it cost Orwell such time and effort to learn how it was done, and also why he was keen to distinguish it from pulp prose, which he regarded as an instrument for the oppression of the poor.

His hatred of cliché, and all kinds of carelessness in expression, is quite properly said to derive from his conviction that clarity of language was necessary to clear thinking, and that clear thinking was essential to social health. This explains his choice of Harold Laski as a principal target in the essay on 'Politics and the English Language'. But his extreme fastidiousness goes beyond that intelligible concern for straight as against crooked or muddled thinking. Good prose must have a force, a dignity, that inevitably make it sound aristocratic in a context of shoddy writing and unachieved thinking. There is a ruthlessness in Orwell's prescriptions for good prose, a characteristic excess – for example, in his proscription of *not un-*: 'a not unblack dog chasing a not unsmall rabbit across a not ungreen field'.

The last of his rules for good writing states that none of the others should apply if barbarism resulted: but there was in him a strain that was, if not barbarous, then barbarian. It emerged in his life. We read of him lashing out at tiresome Burmese students with a heavy cane; attacking Rayner Heppenstall; killing an adder with sadistic deliberation. He once wrote of a wasp that was eating the jam on his plate. He cut it in half with his knife, and watched it continuing to eat jam, which squirted out of the back end: flying off, it had a sudden understanding of disaster. Orwell was not interested in his own part in these proceedings; he presents the story of the wasp as an allegory of the condition of England. He liked military service and rather enjoyed the war. In Scotland he carried a service revolver. Most of his eccentricities have a barbarian flavour. Working men never mistook him for a working man; his friend Jack Common notes that 'breeding' was what you first noticed about him. He did not conquer a dislike for proletarian over-familiarity; he always kept some upper-class ideas of order. His ideal society had a ritual basis, and pieties he might have been expected to think obsolete. He would not use broken tombstones to mend a wall. While *Down and Out in Paris and London* was in the press he was taking an active part in Anglican services and reading the *Church Times*. He asked to be buried in consecrated ground and in accordance with the rites of the Church of England. Such a man would not have agreed with Auden's statement that a poem was a fascist organization (a whole population of words locked in cellars) or with more modern assertions that well-formed sentences are fascist. What distinguishes his prose is not merely the plainness of its language but also the authority of its ordering, which at times may exhibit a certain brutality.

As the prose was shaped, so was the life. A biographer who

can't do justice to the prose will, in that measure, fail with the life. Still, Crick's book has the virtue of getting better as it goes on. The childhood and youth of the hero make heavy reading, partly because Crick is obsessed with the question whether 'Such, such were the joys' is a fair account of the prep school Orwell attended with Cyril Connolly. No doubt Orwell would have said it was *essentially* true. He once praised *Martin Chuzzlewit*, with its mixture of travel book and fiction, as 'a good example of Dickens's habit of telling small lies in order to emphasize what he regards as a big truth'. The power of prep schools to corrupt children was, to Orwell, a big truth, though it may be noted that he gave quite usual bourgeois reasons for not sending his own adopted son to the local primary school: 'Any child that has a chance should be rescued from them.'

Similar difficulties arise from the essay called 'A Hanging', for it cannot be certainly stated that Orwell ever attended one. (Hanging interested him as a possible consequence of murder: in 'The Decline of English Murder' he is nostalgic for 'the old domestic poisoning dramas, product of a stable society where the all-prevailing hypocrisy did at least ensure that crimes as serious as murder should have strong emotions behind them'.) Then again there is the problem as to whether, leaving Wigan by train, he actually saw a woman 'poking a stick up a foul drainpipe'. Probably not – he was on foot, and saw the woman in 'a horrible squalid side-alley'. Such are the issues that arise when writers work in the no-man's-land between fiction and reporting, slipping over the border into the former in search of essential truths. Orwell often made such raids, not least, perhaps, in 'Such, such were the joys'.

His years at Eton are relatively well documented. He was not particularly miserable, but had no social or academic success. Always low in the class list, he was also physically unattractive: 'large, rather fat face, with big jowls, a bit like a hamster'. 'He was not impressed by Eton,' says Crick, 'and most of his contemporaries were not much impressed by anything else about him' (*else*?). Orwell himself says that at seventeen he was 'both a snob and a reactionary', and we might say he retained both of these characteristics, though in wonderfully transformed versions. From Eton he went to Burma, and Crick has collected a lot of information about the Burmese days, and the slow onset of anti-imperialism. Back in England he was determined – very implausibly, as it must have seemed – to turn himself into a writer. 'He wrote so badly,' said Ruth Pitter, who knew him in those days. 'He had to teach himself writing. He was like a cow with a musket.' Though Eton left its mark, this was the time when he did all his learning, as a writer, as 'amateur pauper'. Learning seemed often to require the conquest of an aversion, usually an aversion to dirt and human smells, but perhaps also an aversion to the humble style. He knew very well that education, not identification, was his purpose. In *Down and Out in Paris and London* he did what any good writer must, rearranged the facts and told 'small lies'. But 'he never claimed to have been a tramp, only to have been among tramps': it would have been a real, perhaps a fatal lie, to pretend otherwise.

His education thus far complete, he changed his name from Eric Blair to George Orwell, or rather adopted Orwell as his writing name. Crick, who makes little of this, thinks others have made too much. But although he never gave up his original name, it seems obvious that the change was of more than trivial import: it marked his emergence from the long period of preparation into a life that was very different, not only because he was a writer, but because he was making his name as a writer. An earlier biographer, who thought the change had an enlarging and liberating effect on Orwell, is teased by Crick for adding that the effect is not 'easily defined': 'what cannot be "easily defined" had best be ignored,' says Crick, but that does seem a rather limiting attitude for a biographer to take.

Nevertheless, it is at about this point in the subject's life that the biographer hits his stride. Orwell was making his way towards his peculiar kind of sanctity, full of crotchets and rather irritable, as is the case with other saints, but clearly marked by the continuity and intensity of his concern with suffering, amounting sometimes to a secular form of victimage. There is, thanks to the detail assembled by Crick, a fair representation of this aspect of Orwell. But of course the animating vision was a vision of evil, and had to be expressed in terms of politics. Here Crick is strongest. He gives a very sane account of *The Lion and The Unicorn*, and is extremely helpful about the tortuous history of the English Left in the Thirties. Who now knows about internal dissensions in the ILP? For that matter, who is absolutely clear about the relations between POUM and the Communist Party in Spain? These matters, and especially POUM, were intensely important to Orwell. The ILP was to be our defence against fascism 'when this appears in its British form', and his experiences in Barcelona helped to constitute his image of comradely socialist society. He could be wrong or wrongheaded on detail, but he clearly identified the great evil, totalitarianism. Stalinism and Hitlerism were virtually the same thing: fascism was not 'advanced capitalism' but a grim perversion of socialism. 'Every line of serious work that I have written since 1936 has been written, directly or indirectly, against totalitarianism and for democratic Socialism, as I understand it.' Crick spells all this out with care and skill, though he also quotes Stevie Smith's portrait of Orwell in her novel *The Holiday*, which catches well the occasional absurdity introduced into Orwell's conversation by his obsession with the big truth. He

> said that very soon the population would be only forty million. He said that the cruelty of the Germans was nothing to what the cruelty of the English would be if the English were really up against it in the matter of losing their property . . . He said that America would be the ruin of the moral order, he said that the more gadgets women had and the more they thought about their faces and their figures, the less they wanted to have children, he said that he happened to see an article in an American women's magazine about scanty panties, he said women who thought about scanty panties never had a comfortable fire burning in the fireplace, or a baby in the house, or a dog or cat or a parrot . . .
>
> Or a canary, I said.
>
> Or a canary, went on Basil, and he said that this was the end of the moral order.

As Orwell grows famous, the anecdotes accumulate. In Spain, he had at once established himself as a natural leader (a bit careless, though – his wound could probably have been avoided), and at home during the war he took charge of his section in the Home Guard, drilling the awkward squad, which included Fred Warburg, with great seriousness, and teaching them to make bombs out of milk bottles. He saw in the Home Guard the makings of a revolutionary militia, his view no doubt affected by a persistent after-image of Spanish POUM comrades. He really knew what it would mean to be free, and defended the right of opponents to say what they wanted: but the steadiness of his vision of the good life didn't prevent him being at times grouchy or paranoid. When the publication of *Animal Farm* was delayed by Warburg's shortage of paper, he maintained that Nye Bevan had held it up, fearing its effect on the outcome of the 1945 election. Later, in the days of *Nineteen Eighty-Four*, he kept a notebook listing the names of people he thought might be Communists.

He had a conscience fit for a Jesuit confessor. After the death of his first wife he several times proposed marriage to women he had just met. 'What I am really asking you,' he wrote to Anne Popham, 'is whether you would like to be the widow of a literary man. If things remain more or less as they are there is a certain amount of fun in this, as you would probably get royalties coming in and you might find it interesting to edit unpublished stuff, etc . . . if you think of yourself as essentially a widow, then you might do worse . . .' Crick thinks this letter self-pitying, but Orwell was saying no more than the truth when he called himself 'a bad life', and it would have been unfair not to say so, not to make it quite clear what he could offer. He had fully earned this measure of unconventionality, though it is interesting that in other respects he had more trouble shaking off the manners of his class, as when he had trouble deciding how to address the young woman who acted as nurse to his child. Common sense often co-existed with a tendency to fuss over matters of this sort, and with an occasional foolish wildness, as when, by his own fault, he endangered his own life, and the lives of his guests, among the whirlpools of the Hebrides.

Crick is no mythmaker, and easily disposes of some received ideas concerning the last years of Orwell's life. The documents prove that *Nineteen Eighty-Four* was not the product of a race against death: it was conceived before *Animal Farm*, and though he wrote it under great difficulties, he did not think of it as his last book – indeed he was planning another in his last months. His early death was a quite unmeasurable loss. 'He hated the power-hungry, exercised intelligence and independence, and taught us again to use our language with beauty and clarity,' says Crick at the end. Unfortunately the last part of this remark is untrue, as Crick, like the rest of us, demonstrates. Still, he does achieve something unusual. Biographies as thoroughly researched as this one often cut down the subject to human size, but Orwell here seems rather to have gained in spiritual force: an achievement for which the biographer, after all, deserves our thanks.

'Since about 1930,' wrote Orwell in 1945, 'the world has given no reason for optimism whatever.' But the Thirties are interesting again, even glamorous, and authors unborn in that low dishonest decade now pour out books and essays seeking to explain and defend it. The two listed are collections of essays. The first* contains two especially interesting pieces: one by John Coombes on Orwell's despised Popular Front, and one by Valentine Cunningham on the famous pamphlet 'Authors take sides in the Spanish War'. The second collection† is much more interesting because it contains material by survivors: in fact, it is dedicated to a vindication of the 'radical culture' of the Thirties, a period when intellectuals first allied themselves with workers, opposed that 'high culture' which could no longer sharply distinguish itself from fascism, and 'saw the force of the Marxist analysis'.

The late James Klugmann, in an introductory essay, proclaims the achievements of the period: 'it is a great compliment that people who are reactionary fear it so much.' Margot Heinemann writes with exceptional authority on MacNeice, John Cornford and Clive Branson; there are studies of left-wing theatre, and of the *Left Review* and the Left Book Club; and, only a little to the side, a very judicious article, by Iain Wright, on Leavis. The purpose of the book is said to be to help us understand our time

* *Class, Culture and Social Change: A New View of the 1930s*, edited by Frank Gloversmith (Brighton: Harvester Press)
† *Culture and Crisis in Britain in the Thirties*, edited by Jon Clark, Margot Heinemann, David Margolies and Carole Snee (London: Lawrence & Wishart)

by grasping the role of a simpler and more practical Marxism fifty years ago. It is not very surprising that Orwell is coolly treated, or that little mention is made of Stalin, except that his influence 'bedevilled our work'. So this isn't a dispassionate book, and one can't help entertaining the useless thought that the right man to review it was Orwell.

London Review of Books, 22 January 1981

Half-way Up the Hill

The Young John Betjeman

John Betjeman was nicely eccentric, and droll in a way mysteriously suited to English taste. His being so droll allowed him to display an out-of-the-way learning that might otherwise have seemed remote and ineffectual, but on which it was his gift to confer a certain centrality. He liked to seem lazy, which is why, having repeatedly failed the easy examination in Divinity then compulsory at Oxford, he went down without a degree. He enjoyed best, and studied energetically, what others neglected to know – not only forgotten Victorian architecture, but the verse of Philip Bourke Marston or that of Ebenezer Jones (whom Mr Hillier, by an un-Betjemanian slip, confounds with Ebenezer Elliott, the Corn Law Rhymer).

In such matters it was good and original pedagogy to be droll. To be so on the subject of the extremely upper classes may seem less useful. They evidently caused him to suffer, to fear that they might think him common, or, nastiest of all their put-downs, middle-class. Betjeman was undeniably middle-class, and this unhappy accident of birth occasionally induced in him bouts of self-contempt.

That this portrait* of him should be so enormously detailed testifies to the author's confidence that a reasonably large readership will be fascinated by the whims, fantasies and extravagances which spread like Alpine plants over the rock-like social assurance of its betters. At the end of this first volume the hero is still under

* Bevis Hillier, *Young Betjeman* (London: John Murray)

thirty, with a long and droll career, presumably at least as well documented, still before him. Long biographies are in fashion, and the serious case for this one must be that Betjeman's influence on insular taste really has been quite profound. He persuaded the nation that some things were interesting, or even frightfully interesting, which the constraints of fashion, and a general readiness to be tasteful within existing bounds, had not formerly permitted to be either.

Betjeman was the son of a man called Betjemann, an able man with a solid up-market cabinet-making business. John dropped the final 'n' because during the first war it was more comfortable to look Dutch than German; at school he was persecuted as a German spy. Except when signing the marriage register he stuck thenceforth to the shorter spelling, though his father chid him for it. As late as 1976 the son said he felt that as one held to be German he hadn't 'any right to be in this country'. T. S. Eliot, who taught him for a while at school, would sign himself 'Metoikos', and it seems that in this, though in few other respects, Eliot and Betjeman shared a feeling. As a matter of fact, the Betjemann family seems to have been settled in London from 1797 on. It was not without talent – its various branches produced musicians as well as drunkards and wastrels. The poet's great-grandfather invented the locked tantalus, to keep the servants from the drink, but unwisely carried a key, and died at 34 of 'the things he was locking up'. This somehow sounds more English than German, but in some matters reassurance is not to be had.

When his very grand mother-in-law described him as a middle-class Dutchman, he must have thought himself out of the frying-pan into the fire: still a despised European. It made things worse that he detested abroad; Osbert Lancaster said that Betjeman abroad had to be surrounded by friends, like a rugby player who has lost his shorts. He also disliked Betjemann, who, though a man of parts, was at times quarrelsome and censorious.

Mr Hillier's book is stuffed with detail about family and school. Born at Gospel Oak, Betjeman moved up with his parents to better-off West Hill; fans will remember his touching invocation of the house there ('Deeply I loved thee, 31 West Hill!'), as well as some very subtle verses ('Lissenden Mansions! And my memory sifts/Lilies from lily-like electric lights'). A bit more information on this period is welcome, though at times one cannot help asking fretfully whether we really need to know this much about Betjeman. Hillier acknowledges what, if Martin Gilbert had been a shade less thorough, might be a record number of helpers and informants. Flagging only in the last stretch of the alphabet, they range from Sir Harold Acton to Douglas Woodruff, and like his subject the author has evidently 'made it his business to know people whom he thought worth knowing'. He dissociates himself from what he calls 'the vacuum-cleaner school' of biographers, but remains defiant about the length of this volume, advising us to look elsewhere if we seek not 'a fully-fleshed portrait' but 'a deckchair book on Betjeman'.

At West Hill the poet, an only child, consoled himself as best he could with his teddy-bear, and, quite in the tradition, owed to a sombre nursemaid his terror of hell and the devil. Occasionally he went farther up the hill and the social scale to The Grove, Highgate, where once, at the end of a children's party, he heard the hostess describe him as 'that strange, rather common little boy', just the kind of thing he would make a poem about, and strongly confirming his opinion that by birth his place was, sadly, only about half-way up the hill.

As a schoolboy he was already a poet, and confidently predicted for himself a poet's career. Some of his earliest pieces sound quite like his later work, though teacher Eliot did not admire them. He was not an industrious pupil, and claimed only that Highgate Junior taught him how to get round people, how to lie, how 'to show off just enough to attract attention but not so much as to attract unwelcome attention', and also to mistrust human beings. He went on to the Dragon School, where his fellows included Hugh Gaitskell and J. P. Mallalieu, who once challenged him to a fight but honourably accepted Betjeman's mendacious excuse that his mater was very ill. He now began his acting career as the maid Ruth in *The Pirates of Penzance*, with Mallalieu as Edith and Gaitskell as Chorus of Police. He was already exploring churches; the set of his interest seems not to have changed much after his schooldays.

His parents moved to Chelsea, and 'the budding bard', as his father satirically called him, to Marlborough, a school remembered by more than one witness as, at that time, 'the most awful barbarous place . . . it was extraordinary that people were willing to pay large sums to subject their children to it.' The bard was duly tormented. Some comfort could have been derived from the reflection that the rigours of school were a good preparation for those of the social life to come, but more immediate relief was available from schoolfellows such as Louis MacNeice, T. C. Worsley, Ellis Waterhouse and Anthony Blunt. The school magazine printed his poems, he played Puck, and Maria in *Twelfth Night*; he had love affairs, and was recognized as an aesthete. The best evidence of aestheticism was his refusal, when the postage was reduced from 2½*d* to 2*d* in 1924, to use the new and cheaper orange stamp, which clashed with his envelopes: he continued to use the expensive, matching blue.

One of his elegantly-enveloped letters was addressed to Lord Alfred Douglas, whose verses Betjeman admired. Betjemann discovered this fact, and felt obliged to explain to his odd and difficult son that his correspondent was a bugger – that is, one of those men who 'work themselves up into such a state of mutual admiration that one puts his piss-pipe up the other one's arse'. Betjeman claims to have been shattered by this revelation, as well he might have been.

After school, Oxford was, as usual, a great relief. 'First college rooms, a kingdom of my own.' Influence got him into Magdalen, and droll charm into a famously smart set. He spent Betjemann's money, loathed his tutor, C. S. Lewis: 'What's wrong with you, Betjeman, is that you've no *starl*. No sense of *starl*.' He was taken up by Maurice Bowra, and through him grew friendly with Kenneth Clark, John Sparrow, Henry Yorke, Alan Pryce-Jones, Osbert Lancaster, Robert Byron, Anthony Powell, Peter Quennell, Tom Driberg, Harold Acton, Christopher Sykes, Randolph Churchill, W. H. Auden, and lots of others, including Gaitskell once more ('Hugh, may I stroke your bottom?' 'Oh, I suppose so, if you must'). With Auden he went to bed; also, according to Hillier (citing Peter Quennell), he collaborated with him and MacNeice in the composition of what Driberg described as 'the shortest erotic poem in the language', which Hillier gives as follows:

> I sometimes think that I should like
> To be the saddle of a bike.

But this story cannot be quite true. Auden quotes the poem in *Letters from Iceland* in this form,

> I think that I would rather like
> To be the saddle of a bike,

and calls it 'a touching little cri du coeur made by a friend', so evidently he claimed no part in its writing; also he attributes it to a single author. Auden mentions an Icelandic variant, 'in terms of horses'.

All these Oxford friends were very clever, and above all rejoiced in their new freedom. Betjeman was as famous as any of them, writing for *Isis* and *Cherwell*, becoming known as the naughty boy of OUDS, and as an expert on architecture and high society. He caught the mood of elegant libertinism and sheer privilege. To be sent down wasn't a serious problem; you could get work on the *London Mercury* (Alan Pryce-Jones), or, in Betjeman's own case, Bowra would help you to get fixed up at the *Architectural Review*. If all else failed, there was the safety-net of the educational agency referred to by Auden as 'Rabbitarse and String'. It was, in fact, through them that Betjeman was enabled to spend some time as an eccentric prep-school teacher (£30 a term plus board). During the week he suffered the little children, occasionally engaging in venomous feuds with them; at weekends he would be off to various grand houses, which grew even more accessible after his appointment to the *Architectural Review*.

One such house, which happened to be near Oxford, was rented by Maurice Hastings, a man described by James Lees-Milne as 'a capricious alcoholic . . . rich, clever and slightly mad'. Hastings would lash his landlord's family portraits, which were by Kneller, with a hunting crop, and fire his rifle at the private parts of the garden statues. Lees-Milne was so shocked at this behaviour that he vowed there and then to devote his life to the preservation of English country houses – one of the more permanent conversions in an age when briefer ones were not uncommon. However, it was by no means compulsory to disapprove of Hastings, and Bowra would bring undergraduates to the house, where they might observe its monocled and drunken master 'put his hunter to the dining-room table, when it was fully charged with silver and crystal, and jump it'. So Alan Pryce-Jones, who adds that their host would attack his guests in the corridors, while his wife hid, sobbing, under a bed. Betjeman often visited, with Bowra and Pryce-Jones; Hastings responded to his charm, and since his father owned, and his brother edited, the *Architectural Review*, these visits were as decisive for Betjeman as they had been for Lees-Milne. Leaving the schoolroom behind, he went to the *Review* at the fairly handsome salary of £300, and in his very individual way made a great success of the job, though presenting himself to the world as an idle joker. One practical joke is here described at length, and in two separate versions.

Out of office hours he lived in the gossip-column world. He fell in love with several high-born Angela-Brazil-like girls. There are some religious undertones, but as far as possible life was a continuation of the 'endless party' of Oxford. Astutely making friends with J. C. Squire, he got into the *London Mercury* and the *New Statesman*. His first book of poems, *Mount Zion*, was published in 1931, gorgeously; it was paid for by a friend. Betjeman carefully arranged a claque of reviewers. He did not care for criticism: when Geoffrey Grigson at *New Verse* turned down his poem about the arrest of Oscar Wilde he stood on the backside of the White Horse at Uffington and cursed him.

In these years he must, despite all the appearances, have been working extremely hard. His output included newspaper gossip, profiles, film criticism, articles about houses, trains and timetables. His pursuit of girls culminated in his courtship of Penelope Chetwode, daughter of a Field Marshal, and his marriage to her forms the final chapter and grand climax of this volume. It does make an interesting story. They were an oddly assorted couple, yet truly compatible. She was a learned archaeologist, but also enormously patrician. Her parents thought the very idea of marrying the middle-class Dutchman absurd ('we ask people like that to our houses, but we don't marry them'), but the children were clearly in love, though tending to communicate by mutual insult, in mock-Irish with the nastier words in Greek script; he was, with this degree of concealment, named Dung or Filth or Poofy. Lady Penelope commented affectionately on her lover's green teeth and his smell. He irritated her parents by ostentatiously wearing a made-up white tie, which he snapped back and forth on its elastic.

After many vicissitudes there was a secret marriage, and after many more peace was established with the Field Marshal and his lady. Betjeman had put himself into a position where he was bound to be snubbed – as Hillier notes, he had from childhood put himself into such positions, almost treasuring his rebuffs – and yet, as was his wont, proved that 'this shabby, shambling figure was tougher' than the snubbers.

Hillier was manifestly well qualified to write this book, having a mastery of architectural detail and much affection for his weirdly attractive subject, so much the product of a particular time and place, yet so unlike anybody else. Betjeman's influence is not to be doubted, though there could be argument about the degree to which it was beneficial. It must mean something that for all his oddness and erudition he became a sort of national pet, a TV personality, a poet who ignored not only the Modernist canon but the un-Modernist one as well, and an expert who could make people look closely at familiar or forgotten buildings and objects. Here was a personality neither Dutch or German – the *echt-English* exponent of an upper-class bohemianism impossible elsewhere.

London Review of Books, 7 July 1988

Connolly's World

Long before he died in 1974, Cyril Connolly had grown accustomed to the idea that he would never produce a masterpiece, though he professed to believe that nothing else was worth writing. He must have expected to be admired and remembered for his other accomplishments: as the exponent of a certain upper-class *vie de bohème*, the representative of an obsolescent variety of literary polish and conversational wit; as a man with exceptionally interesting friends, wives, and mistresses; and as the founding and also the terminating editor of the magazine *Horizon*.

Michael Shelden's chief concern is with the decade of that journal's existence, of which he provides an authoritative history.* But since *Horizon* was inseparable from the fabric of Connolly's life, and was the focus of his celebrity – it was, with all its faults, Connolly's central achievement – Shelden couldn't, even if he'd wanted to, withhold some account of the charms and the absurdities of the editor's private life. His book, therefore, can hardly help being amusing (the work keeps some of its old London, Noël Cowardish flavour), though it is less amusing than Barbara Skelton's extraordinary autobiography *Tears Before Bedtime*, in which the candid bedside mug shots of her 'slothful whale of a husband' achieve a sort of outrageous and loving hilarity.

Shelden can afford to be a little less intimate than Skelton, but the figure under analysis is recognisably the same. In matters of business, as in private life, Connolly was charmingly selfish and incredibly unreliable, literally out to lunch most of the time,

---

* Michael Shelden, *Friends of Promise: Cyril Connolly and the World of Horizon* (New York: Harper & Row)

usually in expensive restaurants with somebody else paying. He rarely rose before noon, and was out or entertaining most evenings; he was constantly enjoying the sweet melancholy of competing and time-consuming amorous claims; he travelled in Europe, and later in America, whenever he could find somebody to pay for the trips. So it seems he had little enough time to spare for the *Horizon* office and the dull duties of an editor.

Such wanton behaviour on the part of people who choose to edit little magazines is by no means unheard of (the stock example being Ford Madox Ford, who is supposed to have edited the *English Review*, an exceptionally important little magazine, in his music-hall box). It wouldn't work with a weekly, or perhaps even with a fortnightly, but a monthly publication might allow you to get away with a certain editorial *désinvolture*, as long as there were enough devoted women to do the office work. What the editor needed most was a wide and amiable acquaintance among writers and artists, plus something not so easily specified, and usually called, rather weakly, editorial flair.

Connolly had both. When the review became famous, and he along with it, a surprisingly large number of people felt unable to do without either of them. Meanwhile Connolly, who was easily bored, was often bored with the paper, as he was often bored with a woman, at least until he'd been separated from her for a while. The wonder is he didn't abandon *Horizon* long before he did in 1949, and then write it sad, petulant, and beautiful letters of longing and regret.

Of course, it was not enough to have a gifted editor; there also had to be somebody patient to pick up the tab. In the case of *Horizon*, this paragon was Peter Watson, a very rich, rather sad, and moderately exploitable patron. A long-suffering friend, he was after the war robbed of his fine collection of paintings, and eventually forced to give up his Paris apartment, by his drug-addicted homosexual lover. He died in 1956, a perfectly healthy man mysteriously drowned in his bath. Suspicion fell on another lover, but no case was made against him. That lover inherited most of Watson's large estate, but quite soon he died in his turn, drowned in his bath.

Watson was one of those people like James Pope-Hennessy

who, whether willingly or not, inhabit more than one *bohème*, Connolly's kind and another one closer to Joe Orton's. His strange, introspective, and mostly melancholy life has not been well known, except to such friends as Sonia Brownell (who later married the dying Orwell) and Stephen Spender. No doubt the main reason for this neglect is that Watson was a modest and retiring man (he refused to have his name on the masthead of the paper, though he did much more for it than provide cash). But another reason for his obscurity may be that Connolly could be relied on to take any bows that were going. Shelden has illuminated Watson's life, which was not deficient in other good works. He helped found the Institute of Contemporary Arts, and to some extent internationalize British assumptions about the visual arts and music. He was in his way a notable patron, even, it has been said, 'the last true patron of the arts'.

But Shelden's title is justified by the inevitable dominance, centre stage, of the editor himself. It was generally thought that December 1939 was a crazy moment to start a new magazine of the arts. There was a growing list of restrictions on all publications, writers were being drafted, and the eerily calm bewilderment of the phoney war was confidently and rightly expected to give way to real terrors and privations. But somehow it turned out to be the right time. The insouciance of the paper and its editor, their dedication to an idea of civilized pleasure in art, even their general air of irresponsibility, made a strong appeal to far more people than Watson or even Connolly had expected.

Among the items of mail that I, and many others, irritably awaited in all the parts of the world into which our unwelcome duties impelled us, *Horizon* was almost the most desired. That was partly because it took so little direct notice of the war. Perhaps we made too much of it – there were certainly some dull issues; but it seemed to fill a need that nobody, and especially the bureaucrats, had foreseen. For most of its life *Horizon* could have had a far larger circulation if the government had allowed it enough paper. (The German occupation of Norway in April 1940 cut off 80 per cent of Britain's supply of pulp.)

As Shelden remarks, one of Connolly's best ideas was to enlist his old schoolfriend George Orwell, who contributed essays that might at the time have struck other editors as bizarrely out of place – his essays on 'Boys' Weeklies', 'The Art of Donald McGill', and 'Raffles and Miss Blandish'. These pioneer investigations of popular culture appeared alongside poems by Auden and reproductions of work by Graham Sutherland and Lucien Freud, in a general atmosphere of highbrow art and criticism. Connolly himself, until he got bored, contributed a monthly editorial comment, often provocative, always written with that inlay of unexpected, slightly fantastic jokes and surprising locutions that give his style its undoubted though sometimes maddening distinction.

It wasn't what might be called an avant-garde journal. Connolly had no programme, except to publish what pleased him. On a celebrated occasion he told an indignant contributor who had read a proof and wanted to know why his article wasn't published that the piece was good enough to set in type but not good enough to print. He more or less discovered Mary McCarthy, he recruited the young Clement Greenberg, and he published the memoirs of Augustus John: so there was no discernible pattern in *Horizon*. Still, it had the impress of the editor's personality and taste, and it had no successor. It was meant to satisfy Connolly, and it contrived to provide much more general satisfaction.

It would be only proper to credit Connolly with some courage; it was no joke living and working in London during the Blitz. Still, it is probably fair to add that it was his indifference to anything that interfered with the satisfaction of his own desires that kept the paper going. He also had some valuable friends in high places, Harold Nicolson, for instance, who could be persuaded, as so many could in other phases of his life, to give him what he wanted. At Eton, though lacking the good looks supposed to be an essential prerequisite for election to the elite group called Pop, Connolly got in by being famously witty and amusing. Later the charm continued to work in much the same way. It took a measure of social genius to be simultaneously friendly with Auden, Spender, and MacNeice on the one hand and with Evelyn Waugh on the other. Waugh, who was later very satirical about all these writers, allowed Connolly to devote a whole number of the magazine to *The Loved One*, and eagerly dined at Connolly's apartment, because he enjoyed the cooking of the current mistress.

One understands why Anthony Powell says of Connolly that 'there was undoubtedly something hypnotic about him'.

The editing of *Horizon*, with all the subplots of friendships and love affairs that were based on the office, makes a fascinating story. One aspect of it that may strike modern writers as belonging to an entirely different period is the availability of rather splendid and incredibly cheap accommodation in a London that was nightly losing a proportion of its housing, splendid or not. These people lived their charmed lives in a city that no longer exists, on incomes that would nowadays hardly allow them to eat more grandly than in fast-food joints; but we find them in all but the very best restaurants, accompanied by their infinitely obliging women. The story and its milieu are competently reconstructed by Shelden from an ample collection of letters and papers, and from the stories of nostalgic informants. It is a genuine piece of cultural history.

Some of the names that recur are of people still living and more or less famous. Some that at the time seemed likely to become important – Anna Kavan, for example – have more or less disappeared from view. Connolly himself achieved great celebrity with the publication of *The Unquiet Grave*, much admired by Hemingway and also by Edmund Wilson, and certainly one of the strangest war books ever written. Published in 1,000 copies in 1944, it purported to be by 'Palinurus', though the identity of the author was hardly a secret. Palinurus was Aeneas's pilot. One night he fell asleep, and disappeared overboard; reaching the shore, he was murdered by savages. Aeneas met him on his visit to the underworld, when Palinurus asked to be properly buried, worried that he had only an unquiet grave. This ancient hero, a skilful failure, fascinated Connolly, who published under the name of Palinurus an account of opportunities refused, of women pursued, caught, and lost – a series of poignant, silvery, self-pitying meditations on his life and culture, on his beautiful failures that made success seem vulgar.

Wilson's approval was understandable. Connolly once described Wilson as 'a passionate, sensual Johnsonian polymath', and Shelden remarks, quite wrongly I think, that the expression could equally well be applied to Connolly. There are vast differences between the men, not only in their approaches to polymathy, but in the character of their sensuality, as readers of Wilson's notebooks and journals, and Barbara Skelton's book, or indeed *The Unquiet Grave* itself, should see at a glance.

Connolly's book, once it was republished in an unlimited edition, succeeded in the United States as well as in England. When the war was over he visited the States, edited a remarkably percipient 'American' issue, and was feted to the point of delighted exhaustion in New York. Americans appeared not to resent his famous appeal for relief from postwar life in Britain, that infamous American Begging Bowl, introduced with the slogan 'too long a sacrifice can make a stone of the heart', and demanding all manner of food, especially peach-fed hams. Americans had been sending the British food parcels for years, but now, victims of that celebrated charm, they came through with more.

Connolly was one of those writers whose bright ideas for a book – an exquisite study of Flaubert, a travel book about southwest France – fade once the advance is spent and the region is luxuriously visited. The books he actually published were largely collections of reviews. They are intelligent, flighty, and charming, but he knew that it was not for them that he would be valued. One of his books is called *Enemies of Promise*, and his was a promise that was all too vulnerable to hedonism, and to a kind of sweet, half-amorous melancholy. It was almost by accident that Connolly became the most influential figure in English writing in the 1940s. He gave it a colouring derived from a former time, from the world of Waugh's early novels, and Anthony Powell's, with a dash of Elizabeth Bowen – upper-class refinement, a rather weary vice, a snobbishness at once appealing and appalling. It was remarkable that such a colouring could survive that awful decade, but it did. It has still not quite faded, though doubtless it will soon be gone for good, like Connolly's own taste for the refinements of Latin poetry, for the high pleasures of Paris, for women who are both intelligent and submissive.

It is so long since most writers had the necessary education, or could afford the pleasures and find the women, that if they were made available we should hardly know what to do with them. But looking at my own battered, surviving copies of *Horizon*, I remember that among the myths that animated me in those years was that perhaps someday I should possess and know how to value that *douceur de vie*, even if it meant being rather deliciously sad for quite a lot of the time. If anybody enjoys it now, he or she doesn't edit a literary journal, and almost certainly has very little interest in what used to be called, in all innocence, literature.

The New Republic, 18 September 1989

Oldham to Blackheath

Roy Fuller

Forty years ago, Roy Fuller was taking a close look at himself and finding the image unsatisfying, already a little disappointed.

> This one is remembered for a lyric,
> His place and period – nothing could be duller.

In his new book of poems* there is one called 'On Birkett Marshall's *Rare Poems of the 17th Century*':

> Coppinger, Pordage, Collop. Fayne,
> Fettiplace, Farley, Chamberlain –
> They could be the darling poets of my youth:
> I almost search among the names for mine . . .
>
> Three hundred years ago they were consoled
> For lack of genius and fame by some
>
> Astonishing trope or stanza's tailoring.
> Strange that the consolation still should work
>
> – Prujean, 'Ephelia', Cutts, Cockayne,
> Cameron, Allott, Fuller, Raine.

And in the very considerable body of verse he has produced in

* Roy Fuller, *The Reign of Sparrows* (London: London Magazine Editions)

between there are a good many poems tinctured by the same kind of self-justifying self-deprecation. He very soon ceased to make tremendous statements, preferring on the whole to notice whatever seems to deserve that favourite epithet 'odd', and to meditate on the *trouvaille*. *The Middle of the War* carries on its rough, browning wartime pages lines that almost anybody might have written at the time – on the first page, 'the enormous finger of the gun'. But there are others that suggest a more characteristic insight: 'ruins are implicit in every structure.' It is an insight proper to its date, but wittier than it first appears. The implicit is Fuller's special interest, and it goes with a sense that poetry, working on it, will not quite destroy it; it makes the visible a little hard to see, as Wallace Stevens, early admired by Fuller, once remarked. Or, in another favourite Fuller locution, it ought to be not unimplicit, which doesn't mean it shouldn't be clear.

I particularly like a poem in *Buff*, the volume of 1965, about a little girl:

> there's a suggestion of the primitive
> In her physical anthropology – the span
> Of the stance and the residual stagger; too
> Stubby the velvet legs, and the lovely head
> Over-large . . .

It goes on to celebrate the child's marvellous moving out of infantile jargoning into language ('Odd, all the same, that we find her genius/In doing badly what all do pretty well'). But the jargon, the milky vocables, was not only that in which language was implicit: it is also what remains, like something that remains behind explicit poems.

> The best part of my life is bringing out
> Jargon with words – but how minute a part,
> Since ordered language is most loath to admit
> The excited dream-soaked gibberish of its start.
> Therefore must be preserved, if possible,
> A struggler with the uncommunicable,
> A chanter of enchantment, underneath

The honoured inventor of a unified
Field theory or detector of gravitons
Or prince's perfectly proportioned bride.

In another poem he put the antithesis clearly as between 'the neat completed work' and what it might be better to leave to posterity:

The words on book-marks, enigmatic notes,
Thoughts before sleep . . .

It is almost as if the need to be explicit reduced the poetry and made it 'minor' in relation to poems more obscure and tremendous. But respect for the implicit and a desire to be decently communicative are, for good or ill, the poles on which the world of this poet turns.

Sometimes it helps one's inquiries into the implicit to move a little away from being simply oneself. Or, as Fuller once remarked, it 'probably happens to most poets as they grow older that their personal experiences are less immediate and varied, and therefore they are inclined to assume *personae* which don't properly belong to them.' However, as he added with customary scruple, 'one wouldn't assume [a particular mask] unless one personally felt that this was an appropriate mask to put on.' Of late years, conscientiously minor in relation to Yeats's brassy major, he assumes the persona not of a Wild Old Man but of a Sad Though Sharp-Witted Old Buffer. This person speaks many of the poems in *The Reign of Sparrows*. He was indeed implicit in that young fellow who looked disappointedly at himself in the middle of the war, expecting only a modicum of fame, perhaps the Pordage of his day. The old chap collects his pension, tends his garden, and, quite rightly, finds intimations of mortality in almost everything. But he remains very sharp. Long ago the first novelist to note the peculiar smell of a newly-turned-on electric fire, he now becomes, I dare say, the first poet to notice a funny thing about shrimps:

Shrimps and their shadows on the contoured sand
Of the shallows: oddly, the shadows more apparent . . .

343

'Oddly' because it suggests something *other*; the poem will not quite say what that is, though it establishes an otherness.

The old man, in one of his manifestations, reports a letter from his teacher which says that when we grow old we lose the sense of here and now:

> 'one's as it were transposed
> Into infinity, more or less alone,
> No longer with hopes or fears, only observing.'
> That's how I feel, though much less stoical!

Even that last line is not spoken in the poet's proper person, but it was presumably an appropriate mask to put on. A niggling alarm about the approach of death, a sense of minor terminal disappointment, belong both to mask and wearer. A shoe salesman unconsciously puns in German: 'I'm afraid it's your welt that's gone.' Kids kiss on the bus; the poet sneers and returns to his obituary column. One poem is called 'In His 65th Year', another, modelled on 'Rugby Chapel', is 'On His 65th Birthday' and starts out at the Mini-Town Hall where with others he queues for the 'baksheesh of the State'. It is quite without the pensive uplift of Arnold, being less interested in moving on to the City of God than in remaining as long as possible in the 'Philistine world'.

This deliberate, carefully qualified bathos is not without its own un-Arnoldian charm, and will be especially attractive to readers who are themselves on the point of trying out for the part of Old Buffer. They will also enjoy *Souvenirs*.* The title alludes to an ancient pop song – 'You've left a broken heart among my souvenirs' – as old buffers will recognize. I do not say that *Souvenirs* will not exercise its antiquarian charms on the younger generation, but the best readers will be those who can unhesitatingly answer questions of the following kind: Who was Horatio Nicholls? Lya de Putti? Wilkie Bard? Muriel George and Ernest Butcher? Can you at once sing the opening bars of 'Shepherd of the Hills' and 'The Sheik of Araby'? Or 'Horsie, keep your tail up' and 'Does the Spearmint lose its flavour on the bedstead over

* Roy Fuller, *Souvenirs* (London: London Magazine Editions)

night'? Did you play the book-list game (*The Tiger's Revenge* by Claude R. Sole, *The Passionate Lover* by E. Tudor Tittiov)? Did you have a relation who said, 'Never trouble trouble till trouble troubles you,' or, more idiosyncratically, something like 'Dearie me the day!'? Were your tonsils extracted on a scrubbed kitchen table? Are you pre-orthodontic?

If, like the present reviewer, you find these questions easy and could do the exam at a higher level, you will enjoy this book not as an account of the inexplicably odd childhood of a famous poet, but as a reminder of a culture which spawned a good proportion of contemporary intellectual bufferdom. Fuller distances it by introducing little bursts of Powellish syntactical virtuosity – as in the model, they don't always quite work – and a number of wrily posh words like 'rugeous', 'edentulousness' and 'obstipated', all looking odd against a background of plain sad prose: but his pleasure in the souvenirs is unmistakable and also communicable.

The book is not a chronological account of the poet's youth but a 'set of variations' on themes proposed by a memory often self-deprecatingly described as cold and faulty, guilty of 'blanks and blunders', 'morbidly defective' – and not only in respect of what one would prefer not to remember, though adolescent randiness is not exactly foregrounded. A keener memory, we are given to understand, would have been used to improve the registration of 'the material reality of life' in the poet's novels, rather than profounder Proustian evocations. Yet we are given a view of the poet's youth in Oldham and particularly in Blackpool, where everybody knew who Horatio Nicholls and Wilkie Bard were; of a mother able to support herself, though a widow, on money left her by her husband; of the self-education of a poet, especially in music, and of the joky idleness of youths in a solicitor's office. Fuller comes from the upper levels of that large lower middle class which at any rate in his and my youth tolerated or even encouraged so much fertile eccentricity in kinsman and friend. Perhaps a general sense of oppression made our response to the concert-party comic so spontaneous, and gave us the giggles when somebody oddly or elegantly varied the social norms – Fuller's grandfather, who would occasionally say, not '' ow do?', but 'How now, Tubal! What news from Genoa?' I once worked in an office where the tedium of the nine-hour day was relieved by exactly the kinds of catchphrase that are still on the poet's lips, and where, at intervals, the senior clerk would raise his bald head and huge parrot nose above the partition and croak such memorabilia as 'Take it out or I'll snap it off!' He drank two cases of fizzy lemonade a day and died of throat cancer. So muttering over his cards, the poet's grandfather would remind the company that 'there's many a man walking the streets of London with his shirt hanging out of his britches through not drawing trumps.'

'One must be struck,' writes Fuller, 'setting down such brief lives, by their suitability for the fiction of, say, Arnold Bennett's best period – their illustration of the petty bourgeoisie's social mobility coupled with its immersion in the more or less sordid details of human existence, yet with a readiness to cope with life's material side and in many ways – some the ways of art – to rise above it.' This catches very well the ambience. A young artist might well thrive in that scene. Fuller may be right to discover in himself, all those years ago, something of the *tristesse* of his present; and perhaps blame that early milieu for a reluctance to take chances, whether in business or in literature, which has 'prevented great achievements'. About combining business and poetry he is half-apologetic, half-defiant, remembering that Stevens also led 'rather a routine life'. But what his memory recalls without failure is the England that made him a poet.

So the memoir will strike old buffers as being true and funny as well as sad. There are acute recollections of school, the extraordinary individuality of certain boys; of landladies and family. Always there is evidence of what Fuller calls the lawyer's knack of hearing 'faint bells ringing'. *Souvenirs* is a collection of *trouvailles*, like his poems – excogitations of the implicit. Once again one thinks of the poems that begin with such a *trouvaille*:

> Looking up 'love' in Roget's useful charts
> (Itself a curious activity),
> I find the astounding entry 'nothing'. Why
> Should the mind's assent lag behind the heart's?

To make many such finds is to work in defiance of the tremendous, to practise, however reluctantly, a minor art.

Some of life's sense, I think, if sense at all
Resides in the minor artist's artifact:
The variations on a small perception
Heroically destined for neglect . . .

Fuller is on record as regarding his era as a period of good minor poetry: 'it may be that our poetry will survive as a sort of great anthology of the first part of the twentieth century' – somewhat anonymously, that is, rather than as the work of particular poets; the work, almost, of 'one collective poet'. I doubt this: there are the quirks of vision and language that distinguish him, and others, from the rest; there is a substance that prevails, as Stevens said, and a private contribution to the study Fuller once described as the proper study of poets – 'the anomalous and not altogether unmysterious place of organic life in a universe largely of quite different stuff'.

This* is the third and last volume of Roy Fuller's memoirs, and it takes him up to the end of the war. It may sound ungracious, but I can't help wondering why I find all three books so appealing that the strong implication of finality seems quite unacceptable. Though literate and pleasantly, even amusingly morose, these are not what are commonly called compulsive reads. Not everybody will experience an irresistible need to go on turning their pages. But I do, and would like three or four more, all about the Woolwich, the Arts Council, the BBC and Oxford, with incidental observations on the conduct of the young, the remembered follies of youth, the tiresome defects of age, and so forth.

One reason may be that Fuller, to an even greater degree than most of us, delights in coincidence, in those random and often tenuous connections between people which for a moment give one the pleasant delusion that the world has some order and is

* Roy Fuller, *Home and Dry: Memoirs III* (London: London Magazine Editions)

even a bit comic. In the second volume, *Vamp till ready*, he mentions a connection with me so slight as to be almost imperceptible to anybody caring less about such things; it is actually slighter than our real-life relations, though I wish they were stronger. In the first volume, *Souvenirs*, he spoke of his childhood trips to the Isle of Man. I reviewed the book, and the coincidence that I was born in the Isle of Man *and* reviewed his book was pleasant to him. I'm delighted to say that I can strengthen the link. The poet's mother used, on medical advice, to travel back and forth between Fleetwood and Douglas on the Isle of Man boats. Now in those days I was a purser on those very boats, and, so, familiar with the phenomenon of contract passengers. It's a reasonable bet that I sometimes examined Mrs Fuller's contract, or even – since these stoical voyagers were not very numerous – came to recognize her and dispense with the formality. Did we chat? I wish I could say she often talked about her son the solicitor, but the thing has gone far enough.

Another characteristic I find myself looking for with a measure of longing is the sentence of deliberately awkward elegance, very much Fuller's own but owing something, I believe, to certain not dissimilar contortions in the work of his friend Anthony Powell. Here he is telling us the circumstances under which he allowed to go forward an absurd requisition for flying-helmets–30,000 for a Fleet Air Arm that probably needed about a quarter of that number. 'It is no defence,' he writes, 'to recall that some of the more commonplace aspects of the appointment still held mystery – a proper form of minutes ("I propose the following minute" was the opening for an underling), meaning of initials and acronyms, whereabouts of liaison officers, departmental sections, other Government and service departments – for having worked in a large organization the pennies quickly dropped.' The infolded parentheses, the confusing catalogue, the wonder as to what organization the pennies worked in before being called up, the suppression of the first person 'I' except in citation – all combine to convey a powerful sense of what it is to be a small cog in a huge and inefficient war machine.

A similar artful indirection may be observed in the Fullerian periphrasis, such as 'the prescribed baksheesh' for 'tip'. The most quirky of these is the author's almost invariable practice of calling anything that has to do with Scotland 'Hibernian'. A piper enters, playing a Hibernian instrument; the Navy sends young Fuller to Aberdeen, where he enjoys a 'Hibernian idyll'. Since on other evidence the poet is a football fan, it may be that he was long ago misled by the name of a Scottish team: but can it be that his publisher, Alan Ross, suffers the same inveterate delusion? Perhaps this is one of those tiny harmless in-jokes of which the author is so fond, and which contribute so much to one's entertainment.

This last volume is mostly concerned with the Navy, a service in which Fuller spent five years. He has retained, or perhaps developed by subsequent contemplation, a certain tenderness for what he likes, using Naval slang, to call 'The Andrew'. I myself spent an even longer portion of my life in the Navy and, perhaps because I felt no affection for it, have few memories of it, which makes the ease and quality of Fuller's recall the more impressive to me. He was a radar mechanic, was sent to Ceylon but stopped in East Africa, and eventually came back and ended the war in a cushy Admiralty job with the amazing income of £700 p.a. Though never at sea except in troopships, he saw and heard and remembers enough to bring back all manner of old unhappy far-off things and happily forgotten words: figgy duff, tiddly, tiddy oggies, ammicks, and the best thing of all about The Andrew – namely, *leaf*. Clearly he really got fell in. On being commissioned, he was put out that the gold braid on his cuffs was but semicircular, and explains this as wartime shortage: but I think the real reason was that full circles tended to fray the doeskin jacket, so that the motive was thrift, a virtue of which the poet often expresses his approval.

I dare say many of these memories arose spontaneously as he wrote, which is why they are more affecting than a more systematic history might be. Sometimes he recalls half-forgotten songs or recitations, like the story of poor blind Nell, who prospers but neglects her loving parents:

Did she send them goods and parcels?
Did she? Did she f— —g a— —s.

Reading these lines, moving as they are, I could not doubt the superiority of the variant version they brought to my own memory:

> They sent her books and parcels.
> But did she send them anyfink in return?
> Did she f— —g a— —s.

It is for the reader to choose, though I am quietly confident.

Of course many memories are more distressing, and what is really impressive is the quiet fidelity with which they are recounted. There is a half-page about the 'leisurely pace of catastrophe' at sea, as when in a large convoy two ships are hit, so far away and somehow so unreal that one watches them blaze or explode almost with disinterest, though not without entertaining the possibility of being next on the list. Another truth recalled is of the slight derangement of sense and of dreams attending watchkeeping, four hours on and eight off, at any rate if one had a night watch; a brief experience of the more rigorous routine of four on and four off showed one that the derangement ceases when the whole point of living is to sleep.

Another sensation here recollected in tranquillity is that of deep quiet panic at leaving on an overseas draft, hardest of all no doubt if, like Fuller, you had a wife and a child. For in 1942 or thereabouts there seemed to be no obvious reason to think the war would end in an imaginable future, or that anybody would be concerning himself with getting you back from India or Kenya or wherever, for no discernible cause, you might be going. I myself careered around the world like a pinball, but by chance was never away for much more than a year; Fuller had a longer absence but got back for good and finished the war in domestic content at Blackheath, eating lunch at Schmidt's or even the White Tower with the likes of Joe Ackerley, John Lehmann and once, E. M. Forster. Though a virtual civilian, he remembers getting demobbed at Olympia, choosing from the millions of pinstriped suits and raincoats, one of which proved, in his thrifty hands and posh language, 'longevous'. And I should like here to mention that about the same time I too was kitting myself out for post-war life, but not at Olympia. I had to go to Oldham, where the Fuller story began.

Though he complains a bit about having accomplished so little in these years, Fuller's ruling passion was writing. Considering how nearly impossible it was to find the place and the will to write, he did what seems to me an enormous amount. He published his second volume of poetry, *The Middle of a War*, in 1942, one of the best books of the time, and immediately recognized as such. The author complains of its 'scruffy paper', but looking at my copy (second impression, 1942) I see that it has yellowed and crumbled less than some much younger books. Much of the pleasure of these memoirs comes from remembering *The Middle of a War* and *A Lost Season*, which followed two years later. Fuller was also writing prose, and here reprints a narrative called 'The People Round About' which I read I suppose nearly forty years ago, yet recalled well enough to anticipate the surprise of its concluding line.

Though written in a determinedly relaxed manner ('I dare say I could write a bit about evenings in the POs' mess, though monotonous'), these books give the poet an outline unassertively his own. He admits a youthful tendency to get up to tricks and even to go in for a bit of dodging; once he even lost his temper, though the occurrence was evidently unusual and is remembered as such. And it is a certain purity of response that best defines him. Most survivors of his generation will share his sense that one should let determined things to destiny hold unbewailed their way, and look with some kind of happiness at the unpredicted shapes their lives have taken. Fuller sometimes represents this happiness as a sort of disillusion, looking with pity on the socialist dreams of his nonage and with contempt on the actual ruin of post-war youth. 'Perhaps my whole life could be depicted in terms of the destruction or modification of public and private illusions,' he wrote in *Vamp till ready*; and now: 'I have always considered generalities about one's spiritual state from time to time of little validity, most epochs of one's life requiring one simply to soldier on, anything less landing one in a state utterly foreign to one's being.'

Fortunately, soldiering on may be held to include the business of validating experience by writing about it, and doing so in this idiosyncratic way, very literary yet always marked by the ancient Lancastrian mistrust of affectation and by a straightfaced sense of fun – of the 'comic nature of minute-to-minute existence', letting the longer view descry what it may. That is why these books are both credible and memorable, and why they need sequels.

London Review of Books, 22 May 1980 & 5 April 1984

Remembering the Movement

It seemed to be happening only yesterday, but Blake Morrison was born in 1950, and for him the Movement is something you have to work on in a library. So it suddenly comes to seem rather remote, as deep in the past as those files of the *Spectator* where he found the famous pieces by J. D. Scott and Anthony Hartley, or the scripts of John Wain's Third Programme magazine *First Reading*, or copies of the Reading limited editions of Wain and Amis. Mr Morrison claims to have eschewed gossip and attended instead to such questions as: 'Did the writers know each other? Is there any evidence of mutual admiration, mutual influence, or collaboration?' It is almost as if he were seeking information about Spenser, Gabriel Harvey and the Areopagus. Yet most of the poets he is writing about are ascertainably hale and not yet eligible for the Old Age Pension; even the few living elders they respected are still around, and capable of spry conversation – Empson, Fuller, Graves. Mr Morrison, of course, knew this, and addressed some inquiries to relevant survivors. Some responded – not Amis, I notice, and not Larkin, for reasons no doubt easily guessed at; but Conquest, doyen of the group, co-operated, and so did Davie, who is quoted more than anybody, though in my view (and in that of certain members of the group) he was never really in the middle of it, partly because he was an interloper from Cambridge, and partly because of all the talents assembled his was the least identifiable with the Movement's mood and programme.

Still, researchers have to use what material there is, and although there is a certain air of unreality in this study,* a Martian

* Blake Morrison, *The Movement: English Poetry and Fiction of the 1950s* (Oxford University Press)

postcard quality, it's well enough and conscientiously done. Morrison decides, unsurprisingly, that there really was such a thing as the Movement, that it wasn't a 'gigantic confidence trick' to get the *Spectator* over a circulation crisis; less unsurprisingly, he goes on to describe it as 'a literary group of considerable importance ... probably the most influential in England since the Imagists'. He believes that a lot of good poems ('key texts') in the post-war period originated in the play of influence between members of the group, and by extending the term to include writers who weren't among the *New Lines* poets, but nevertheless felt some sympathy for them, he makes a fair case. Whether he's right to maintain that the Movement was as central to the Fifties as the 'Auden Group' to the Thirties depends a bit on whether you believe, as he does, that there was a 'Movement ideology' existing in some significant relation to the social and political mood of the time.

Robert Conquest's anthology came out in 1956, the year of Suez, so the 'ideology' must have been formed during the administrations of Churchill and Eden. The first Attlee Government carried out the programme enthusiastically endorsed by the troops in 1945, but the second, hampered by the exhaustion of its leaders and the smallness of its majority, did little, and it was easy to feel that six years after the end of the war many of its more depressing aspects, such as ruins and rationing, were here to stay. But in 1951 the thirteen continuous years of Conservative rule began, and so, in a way, did the post-war period. Labour in opposition devoted itself to a masochistic doctrinal argument which ended only with Gaitskell's defeat of the Left in 1961. But often people no longer found ideology very interesting, and indeed its end was announced.

These facts have a bearing on the mood of the Movement. When John Holloway, in an article here quoted, spoke in 1956 of 'the recent social revolution, gentle though real', he was of course talking about something that happened between 1945 and 1950. Part of the cost of the revolution was the measure of privation I've already mentioned: the queuing for your weekly egg and shilling's worth of meat, the bread, petrol and clothes coupons, the terrible shortage of beer. All that soon ended, and so did the revolution. But some effects of the war and its immediate aftermath persisted. It seemed possible to opt out of the old class system; as Holloway observed, it was no longer inevitable that lower-class talent should be 'decanted' into the upper class. New writers could stay where they were, in the provincial universities perhaps; enjoying, or reconciled to, a mildly proletarian life-style, free of the affectations of the metropolitan literary world.

There is no doubt that thoughts of this kind occurred to the writers in question, and even to their enemies; the classic document on the fears of the latter is Somerset Maugham's attack on *Lucky Jim*. But Maugham and Amis became quite good friends after a while, and of course there never was anything very proletarian about the Movement. Most of its members were formed under the old system, scholarship boys from lower-middle-class backgrounds; they retained some expectation of being 'decanted' and in due course they were – into All Souls, Professorships of Poetry, positions of power in London. After 1951, such expectations were no longer muted – if they ever were – by a confidence that their suppression might contribute to a just society, and in the new world then dawning these exceptionally able men found themselves rather well placed to make it. It's worth remembering that the only university owing its origins to the period of Labour idealism was Keele; the other new universities, established in cathedral towns and other pleasant places, and for a time at least extremely fashionable, belong to the Macmillan era. Lucky Jim's having to start life in a redbrick was, as it turned out, merely a consequence of being born a bit too early.

In short, there was nothing much in the education of this essentially Oxford group of poets that made it hard for them to flourish under the new Toryism. By 1951, they were already fed up with their little suburban houses and rotten pay. I remember my surprise when John Wain told me he intended to vote Conservative in the 1951 election; it shows how naive I was, but it also explains why the Movement's later 'drift to the Right' did not surprise me. Indeed, it is a bit of a puzzle why Amis drifted so late; and Conquest cannot have had very far to drift in any case. He alone, I think, had a strong sense of politics, but it was never true of the others that they weren't in some sense political; it is never true of anybody. They were, I suppose, typical Butskellites, with a preference for the But end of the term. At the time, it was noticed that the novels of both Amis and Wain exhibited a tendency to hypergamy – marrying upwards – and one might, without being too fanciful, represent that as a rapprochement with the upper classes parallel to the attitude of the Labour revisionists who came to terms with what, despite the 'revolution', remained a society of rich and poor.

Morrison dutifully records the careers of the members of his group at Oxford; Larkin's introduction to the 1976 edition of *Jill* is good testimony, though a rather different sense of the place may be had from Wain's *Sprightly Running*, with its magnificent memoir of E. H. W. Meyerstein. The young man from the Potteries was greatly taken with this weird upper-class eccentric, and for a long time afterwards plugged his un-Movementish poetry. Wain was also close to C. S. Lewis, who had very little in common with these young men except a liking for beer and (important in Wain's case) a love of scholarship. But it is a fact rarely mentioned that even in wartime, Oxford was a highly competitive place, and these men thrived on competition. They were not unambitious. They wanted things – their own journal, *Mandrake*, access to the BBC and the highbrow weeklies. They required to be noticed, and were.

Here the importance of Amis is obvious. He had a formidable talent for sending up whatever seemed phoney or affected (see Larkin's introduction), and pretty well all the preferences of London literati might be so classed. The positive programme of the Movement was formed in reaction to the assumptions of these powerful phoneys: an Orwellian emphasis on lucidity, accompanied by a dislike of snobbish preferences in the arts; a preference for tight verse forms (with Empson as an ambiguous progenitor, and some historical support from Davie's *Purity of Diction*); in prose, common sense, plain dealing and blunt speaking, in contrast with the mandarinism of the capital, whose fashions they affected to deplore in the manner of Leavis. It was possible to claim that such a programme restored a broken contact with a genuinely English tradition, long obscured by foreign modernism and London xenophilia.

I suppose the main charge against the group has been philistinism or little-Englandism, expressed in general terms as a dislike of Abroad and some kinds of Beauty – these being what people you loathe tend to go in for. And certainly the writers in the group encouraged a belief that they read no language but English and hated music (except jazz) and pictures and theatres. This was largely nonsense, but it had its importance, especially for Larkin and Amis. To get the balance right, one needs to ask naively whether Amis would be the fine novelist he is if he truly shared the *Weltanschauung* of Jim Dixon. Actually much of his best writing is about privation and the intolerable terms on which life has to be accepted (this is as true of 'A Dream of Fair Women' as it is of *The Anti-Death League* and *Jake's Thing*). The hilarious rejections are a comic aspect of this almost metaphysical sense of loss and division, and if it were not so the joke would have long ago worn thin. The same is true, with variations, of Larkin.

Morrison looks at these and other matters very carefully, considering the relation of his subjects to their audience, their attitudes to society and literary tradition, and so forth. He is scrupulous and balanced. But he does not succeed in supporting his judgment that these writers are of importance by writing well of their work. The chief failure here is with Larkin, who crops up over and over again, and understandably, since *The Less Deceived* is by common consent the best volume the Movement produced. There seems to be some quality in Larkin's verse that repels Morrison's analytical instruments. For example, he treats at some length the beautiful early poem 'At Grass', which he describes as 'post-imperial'. The horses have only their memories of 'faded, classic Junes'; they are, however, enjoying their superannuated peace. So they stand for England; and elements in the language of the poem – 'Squadrons of empty cars', for instance – are equally reminiscent of imperial pomp. Morrison backs away from his own reading by saying that the allegory is unconscious, though it has to be supplied because 'the emotion of the poem is in excess of the facts as they appear.' But this comment is open to the same criticism as Eliot's remark about *Hamlet*, which it echoes: where but from the poem did he find the evidence of what was needed to make it work? A more profitable approach might have been rhetorical. For example, the last two lines –

Only the groom, and the groom's boy,
With bridles in the evening come –

get their power from a ghostly and very inferior unwritten version, which puts the groom and the groom's boy in reverse order and supplies the half-rhyme that is promised by the inversion in the second line. The Marvellian assurance and purity of this is a 'fact' no emotion in the poem is in excess of.

Indeed, I don't believe the poem has anything to do with imperial splendour and the Welfare State, any more than I think 'Church Going' provides evidence of the Movement's muted concern with Christianity; Morrison's comment simply bounces off that wonderfully paced and original concluding stanza. What he says about 'The Less Deceived' is again characteristic of a certain failure to *read* Larkin, because 'fulfilment's desolate attic' surely shouldn't be treated as a general proposition about 'post-coital disillusion'. The difficulty arises from the method of the book, which is to use the works of these poets as evidence of Movement attitudes to this, that and the other (the Empire, Christianity, Sex) rather than to consider them as poems. In just this way, the author, despite strong guidance from Donald Davie on the point, simply misunderstands a poem by Amis (pages 79–80). It's coming to something when these apostles of the new lucidity, proponents of the view that the poet must do his share and not leave the reader to work out his obscure half-written verses, find their poems subjected to the kind of rival interpretations that used to be reserved for 'A Cooking Egg'.

This isn't to say Morrison is dull or imperceptive. He is good, for example, on Larkin's characteristic silent transitions from 'I' to 'we', and on the verbal tricks ('seems', 'of course', 'surely') that are trademarks of the Movement. But his chief interest is in placing the group historically, and in doing that he is often shrewd: for example, when he asks what sort of audience the Movement thought it needed and deserved, he catches its members out in all kinds of contradictions. And he works hard at the question as to why this batch of highly educated, very literary people should have put together a programme which, however vague on some things, quite certainly rejected 'Modernism'. 'The modern movement began with a brilliant blaze,' said Enright. 'Unfortunately the flames got out of control, and ever since we have been warming ourselves at the embers.' Davie, in his youth, argued for consolidation, for a healthy 'loss of nerve'. Neither he nor Wain found it simple to reject Pound, but they both had a strong interest in English eighteenth-century poetry, and a wish to return to a more English tradition.

It would be wrong to suppose that the anti-modernism of the Movement was anti-academic. Nobody taught Pound or Joyce in the universities of those days, and Davie's books on diction and syntax were respectfully received. At the end of the decade an academic, Graham Hough, spelt out in his *Image and Experience* the view that modernism was an interruption of the native tradition, cogently questioning the method by which Eliot and Pound claimed to have built structures dependent upon a 'logic of imagination' different from other logics, and intelligible only to selected readers. He gave organized expression to something the Movement poets already believed. They particularly resented the snubbing of 'ordinary readers', whom they wanted for their own work; of course they knew that even their more accessible verses weren't going to find a large readership. As Amis remarked, they really wrote for dons, and a slightly shamefaced sense of election comes through in an early poem of Wain's:

And so my speech must be confined
To those who taste our epoch's plight –

nothing, it seemed, could be done for 'the limping, the half man'. It was probably this difficulty about the audience for poetry that induced Wain and Amis to try their hand at fiction. The novel also provided better opportunities for bashing the phoney cultured, who were still, before the academics took over, the protectors of modernist art.

I've suggested that the best work of the group was a poetry, and a fiction, of disappointment: work that was aware of what it had given up to be as it was. The worst work is that in which the need to seem philistine has made the poet be philistine; the need arose, as Lindsay Anderson remarked, from a fear of being thought to be something even worse than a philistine – namely, an intellectual.

Donald Davie, looking back at his ex-colleagues, thinks they had to pretend to be cultural teddy-boys in order to 'put the house of English poetry in order', but condemns them nevertheless because in place of the old pretentiousness and cultural window-dressing they provided something 'painfully modest . . . deliberately provincial . . . inevitably marginal in importance'. Morrison, surveying the activities of the members of the group after it broke up, is more generous, and insistent on their continuing influence. I think he's right: a form of their anti-modernist position is still strongly held, the resistance to innovation in the novel and poetry may even have increased, and a native tradition is not so much something one argues for as what is taken for granted, like a fact of nature.

D. J. Enright's anthology is,* among other things, an example of this quiet acceptance. It comes a quarter of a century after his *Poets of the 1950s*, which was more combative, a blow in the struggle to establish the new, right kind of poetry. He looks back at the Movement, is glad that its members, 'after a brief cohesiveness', went their separate ways, and that he is making this new collection in times which, as he reads them, do not call for schools and manifestos. All is calm. Alvarez upset things for a while with his accusations of Gentility, but what really counts, and what in fair measure we have, is Civility. Of the eight poets in his first collection five survive: Conquest, Enright, Amis, Davie and Larkin. Three drop out: Holloway, Jennings, Wain. The temporal qualification for inclusion is to be a poet 'whose staying power is attested' by work published between 1945 and 1980, but writers who flourished in the Thirties are excluded. The oldest poet present is Stevie Smith, who, like Earle Birney, was older

* *The Oxford Book of Contemporary Verse 1945–1980*, chosen by D. J. Enright (Oxford University Press)

than Auden; A. D. Hope was born in the same year as Auden, and is older than Spender. The poets who do get in are all pretty well known and mostly unexceptionable. Certain Americans pass the Civility test: Lowell, Berryman, Nemerov, Wilbur, Simpson, Hecht. When the two first named are uncivil, as sometimes happens, they are below their best, and Berryman is represented by work 'which may well though not indisputably be judged unrepresentative'. We are offered poetry which aspires to 'civility, passion and order', but which above all makes sense. The editor shuns surprises, which might be bad surprises, and bad surprises are not better than being boring. There are, I needn't say, a great many good poems in this book. Anybody who turns on to less civil American, or indeed British, stimuli will of course avoid it. It's an Oxford Book that shows how wrong it would be to think the Movement, an Oxford phenomenon, fell apart around the time of Suez; or that the period of consolidation, of the preferred neutral tone, might be short.

London Review of Books, 5 June 1980

Obsessed with Obsession

Julian Barnes

Julian Barnes is an English writer still in his thirties. His first
novel, *Metroland*, appeared in 1981, his second, *Before She Met
Me*, in 1982. With his third, *Flaubert's Parrot*,* he is beginning to
attract the kind of attention reserved for serious novelists. Yet he
is still, I should say, better known in Britain as a television critic.
Television criticism is on the face of it a peculiar and unpromising
genre, and that it should have been brought to such a high degree
of polish in the English Sunday papers may suggest that something
important though obscure is going on in British culture. Reviews
of books and exhibitions and plays are about what you might
conceivably read or visit; television reviews are about shows you
either have already seen or never will. More often than not
they never needed discussing anyway. The TV critic has to
contemplate a wholly forgettable recent past as material for a
piece that will have to be loved for itself alone. Wit, charm,
fantasy are his instruments (TV criticism is apparently a male
preserve). The genre was invented by Clive James, who actually
collects his reviews in volume form, so that you can savour all
over again two years later the giggly charm of a lost Sunday
morning you spent reading about nothing.

The hour brings forth the man, or the men, and the London
Sunday papers have nourished a generation of writers capable of
wit on many subjects, among them Barnes and the slightly

* Julian Barnes, *Flaubert's Parrot* (London: Jonathan Cape & New York:
Knopf)

younger, very much more hectic, Martin Amis. Sooner or later – rather later in the case of Barnes – these sharpened wits will be applied to larger enterprises, and most obviously to fiction. As a novelist Barnes is less *'épatant'*, to use a word he associates with adolescent cultural enthusiasms, than Amis; but they share a world. To belong fully to that world you need to have been born in England after 1945. Your parents belong to the generation of Philip Larkin and Kingsley Amis, writers regarded as funny, subtle, mildly chauvinistic, slightly disgusted with the state of England but suspicious of 'Abroad'. You understand these attitudes but think them in need of refinement. You have a different past, which includes them and their obsolete sexual hang-ups, their fits of social conscience, and the imprint on them of that lost long-running TV spectacular, the War. Of course you sometimes feel the awfulness of things too, but it is mitigated by the undoubted coziness of literary London, and a witty sadness is the appropriate response.

In *Flaubert's Parrot* Barnes's narrator is a physician in his sixties, a veteran of the Normandy landings. A passion for Flaubert may seem a little out of character, but two strategically placed and only half submerged quotations from Philip Larkin in the first three pages reassure us. They come from 'Church Going', a poem that might be called the anthem of a literary generation that accepted Larkin as its laureate; to 'place' a contemporary of Barnes by the same method one would plant a line or two by the poet Craig Raine. And indeed even the elderly doctor in *Flaubert's Parrot* can't help seeing the world through Raine's 'Martian' eyes: looking at the remains of Mulberry Harbour off the Normandy coast, he sees it as 'curving morse', a code sending out some sadly pointless message about the past.

The heroes of Barnes's two previous novels were men of his own age. *Metroland* (1981) is a *Bildungsroman* without the solidity or the desperation the term may seem to imply. It records the private jokes and amusements of a bright London schoolboy with his bright friend, and it does so with such accuracy that other ex-clever school-kids who hated sports, built a secret repertory of jests and allusions, and baffled adults by their choice of reading matter, will have the pleasure of self-recognition. Forced to spend an afternoon with a comic old twister of an uncle, the hero brings along Flaubert's *Dictionary of Received Ideas*, but is as usual conned into digging the garden.

In 1968 we find him in Paris, supposed to be studying, and certainly keeping a journal about his first love affair. So preoccupied, he missed the *événements* of that spring: 'Absolutely typical,' said his pal. 'Only time you've been in the right place at the right time in your whole life, I'd say, and where are you? Holed up in an attic stuffing some chippy.' But he had gone to Paris not for the barricades and the *chie-en-lit* but, replete with a knowledge of the 'classics of passion – Racine, Marivaux, Laclos', to lose his virginity. He also loses the girl because when circumstances required him to say *je t'aime*, he couldn't stop himself from adding *bien*. His dad would never have allowed himself to get into such a position; but he wouldn't, either, have missed the *événements*.

Another index of current Englishness is the treatment of women. Barnes's women resemble those of the previous generation of wits in that they are easily superior to men, more mature, more moral, more candid. The chief difference is that they are also less inhibited and usually unfaithful to their devious, dishonest, but faithful men. Some of the problems that arise from this state of affairs are treated in Barnes's second novel, *Before She Met Me*, a remarkably original and subtle book not yet published in the US. The novel takes as its premise that sexual jealousy ought not to exist in the permissive present, but it isn't dead, and can turn up, absurdly, in the past. Here is a man who leaves his awful wife for a woman in whom he finds a sober certainty of happiness. She is a candid woman who has in the past been a minor movie actress. He is not interested in movies, but is tricked by his ex-wife into seeing one, in which his present wife commits adultery. Soon he is devoting his time to tracking down every terrible film she appeared in, and every terrible film her screen lovers appeared in without her. He meets them in dreams, reconstructs affairs off-screen. Perfectly secure in her present love for him, he questions her about the past (he is by profession a historian). She answers patiently and honestly, except once. It is that one lapse from complete candour that turns sad farce into bloody tragedy.

What seems clear from this excellent novel is that Barnes is obsessed with obsession, and since he finds no obvious occasion for it at the moment it is always placed in some past that can be speculatively reconstructed only by minute attention to trivial and treacherous records. So the hero, a calm, amusing, peace-loving, unrandy historian, fanatically constructs, on the basis of the film archive, his own disease. Its cure of course must be in the present. He accepts the advice of a treacherous friend and treats himself with booze and masturbation. All this is horribly funny, and idiosyncratic without seriously departing from the tradition of the modern English farcical novel. If we want evidence that Barnes is an original artist we can find it in the inexplicit links and echoes that declare themselves only on a second reading, or in small acts of observation that turn out not to be marginal but of the real substance of the book.

At one such moment the wife is standing in line at the butcher's. The butcher wears a blue-striped apron and a straw hat, as butchers will. Suddenly she sees him with a Martian eye; and now there seems to be a strange contrast between apron and hat.

> The boater implied the idle splash of an oar in a listless, weed-choked river; the blood-stained apron announced a life of crime, of psychopathic killing. Why had she never noticed that before? Looking at this man was like looking at a schizophrenic: civility and brutishness hustled together into a pretence of normality. And people *did* think it was normal; they weren't astonished that this man, just by standing there, could be announcing two incompatible things.

Later, waiting for her husband to come in, she imagines herself waiting for two interrogators, 'the gentle one who only wanted to help you, and the anarchically brutal one who could freeze you by merely flicking your shoulder blade'. These two are the doubleness in her husband, which is also the doubleness of past and present.

Flaubert's Parrot opens with a similar moment: six North Africans are playing boules beneath the statue of Flaubert in Rouen.

Clean cracks sounded over the grumble of jammed traffic. With a final, ironic caress from the fingertips, a brown hand dispatched a silver globe. It landed, hopped heavily, and curved in a slow scatter of hard dust. The thrower remained a stylish, temporary statue: knees not quite unbent, and the right hand ecstatically spread. I noticed a furled white shirt, a bare forearm and a blob on the back of the wrist. Not a watch, as I first thought, or a tattoo, but a coloured transfer: the face of a political sage much admired in the desert.

These modern French North Africans wear Mao on their wrists as Flaubert's Carthaginian soldiers in *Salammbô* bore the sign of the parrot. The living statue ridicules the dead one. The Germans destroyed Flaubert's statue in 1941, but the original cast survived and a new statue was made, mostly of copper, and now weeping cupreous tears. In the stone version of Trouville there is damage to the thigh, and part of the moustache has fallen off. Barnes's physician is in search of the crumbled, junky past, of the truth about Gustave Flaubert, which, like the truth about his own life, is on some views both unimportant and inaccessible.

Among the decaying rubbish that testifies to the existence of Flaubert is the parrot he borrowed when writing *Un coeur simple*, in which Félicité comes to see a parrot as the Holy Ghost. However, there are two rival claimants, stuffed parrots that are both certified as authentic, though the evidence presented at the end of the doctor's quest suggests that neither can be. Quietly obsessed, randy for relics, as he puts it, the doctor finds that Flaubert's house at Croisset was pulled down to make way for a factory extracting alcohol from wheat, itself later replaced by a paper mill. He encounters an American scholar who has acquired Flaubert's letters to the English governess Juliet Herbert. This man claims that the letters showed Miss Herbert to have been Flaubert's mistress, but adds that, obedient to the author's stated wishes, he has burned the correspondence. Our hero goes ahead all the same, quietly searching for every deliquescent and delusive trace.

The parrot is at the centre. The dossier for *Bouvard et Pécuchet* tells of a man who thought he had turned into a parrot. In *L'Education sentimentale* there is an empty parrot perch, now an emblem of the author himself. Information of all sorts is assembled under various arbitrary headings, rather as in the *Dictionnaire des idées reçues*. Maxime du Camp places the business card of one 'Humbert, Frotteur' on top of a pyramid for Flaubert to find. Flaubert acquires a freak sheep. On his first appearance in print he was named 'Faubert'. (Did Joyce remember this when Bloom appeared in the list of Paddy Dignam's mourners as 'Boom'?) A book published by the Reverend G. M. Musgrave in 1855 describes the cabs of Rouen as 'the most dumpy vehicles . . . of their kind, in Europe' – they ' "cut" about the streets like Tom Thumb's coach'. This throws a new light on the lovemaking of Léon and Emma in a scene so famous that within a year of the publication of *Madame Bovary* cabs hired in Hamburg for sexual purposes were known as Bovarys.

The doctor sharply distinguishes his kind of search for truth from the academic kind. Academics may be too puritanical about truth, or they may be too careless. The most violent pages in the book consist of an assault on the late Enid Starkie, famous in her day for her flamboyant Oxford rooms and her intimate knowledge of Flaubert. Apart from speaking French badly, she dared to accuse Flaubert of getting into a muddle about the colour of Emma's eyes. The doctor is able to refute the charge with contempt.

Flaubert's Parrot can be read as a very interesting Flaubert miscellany, interspersed with disquisitions on the modern novel and much else. It offers information about the books Flaubert thought he might one day write, including one about Thermopylae, another about a sarcophagus he might have seen in the British Museum in 1852. It is also instructive about his sexual habits and diseases. Louise Colet appears, first as the second-rate poet and nuisance that she has, on Flaubert's evidence, been called, but then, in the most surprising moment of the book, as her own apologist – a candid, unillusioned woman who has forgiven Flaubert's profound sexual vulgarity. 'He feared me as many men fear women: because their mistresses (or their wives) understand them. They are scarcely adult, some men: they wish women to understand them, and to that end they tell them all their secrets; and then, when they are properly understood, they hate their women for understanding them.' Gustave thought of himself as a wild beast, a polar bear, a buffalo, excusing his egotism as a proper pride and distinguishing it from vanity, the chattering parrot; but 'perhaps he was really just a parrot.'

The doctor obviously likes Louise; perhaps she resembles his dead wife, who was both candid and unfaithful. Remembering his happiness and unhappiness, he is never capable of keeping it separate from his Flaubertiana; his account of his marriage is lavishly illustrated by quotations from Flaubert. This is quite brilliantly written and deeply obsessive; the work of mourning is done by sifting through these surrogate and fading archives. His wife's secret life was inaccessible, too; her one fault that she was unable to look steadily, as Gustave Flaubert did, at despair.

Our last view of the doctor is in a limbo of stuffed birds, sprinkled with pesticide; not two but three parrots gaze at him 'like three quizzical, sharp-eyed, dandruff-ridden, dishonourable old men'. The lost past is the ground of nightmare and mourning, seen, as far as may be, with the calm and wit proper to the comfortable present. *Flaubert's Parrot* is a very unusual novel; people who think they know exactly what a novel is tend to say this isn't one, just an eccentric essay on Flaubert. That's nonsense; the book does feel disorderly at times, but it is true to the laws of its own being. It lacks something of the fine tuning of *Before She Met Me*, but perhaps doesn't need it for its purposes. And it has the voice, witty and sad, of the peculiar civility of modern London – liberated from the constraints of the past, yet obsessed with its pain and with its missing dates, the *événements* never to be experienced except in fantasy.

New York Review of Books, 25 April 1985

Losers

Anita Brookner

So far as the evidence of five novels goes, Anita Brookner has one basic theme, which she varies with considerable and increasing technical resource. All five books are quite short, and all have some of the qualities of what James called the beautiful and blest nouvelle, since they are intensive in plot and on the whole refuse the temptation to broaden into novels. This limitation, if that is the right word, is not at all the consequence of any diffidence or lack of skill in the registration of milieu or of character: Brookner is good at both, so we had best say we are dealing with works that exist in a no man's land between two genres. We should be glad of this, for we escape on one side the danger of an obsessed narrowness of treatment, and on the other some possibility of failure consequent on the too obvious stretching of the great central topic, which is, after all, the central topic of long romantic novels already in existence, and usually lacking the humour as well as the fineness of the pathetic moments in this writer.

The heroines have hitherto been mostly writers of one sort or another. *A Start in Life* tells us how Ruth Weiss, a scholarly woman, elegant and capable, has had little success with men. She is writing a thesis on Balzac's women, and of any handsome man is likely to say, with Eugénie Grandet, *Je suis trop laide, il ne fera pas attention à moi.* How such an attractive woman got into this state is explained by her family, a crazy actress mother and a useless father, a car salesman manqué – all rather like early Angus Wilson. It is a family call that aborts her affair with a handsome Sorbonne professor, dragging her back to London; her other men are a do-gooder, and an unsuitable husband whose early death leaves her to look after her decrepit father.

Ruth has the luck of most of Brookner's women. Modest, intelligent, dutiful, they are surrounded by irresponsible raffish family and friends, observing them, envying them, but condemned to disappoint and to the full understanding that nice women finish second, or worse. Their special fate is the theme of all the books. *Providence* is about Kitty Maule (a name bearing a curse). Her beautiful clothes contrast strongly with the standard garb of her academic colleagues, inhabitants of a provincial Senior Common Room 'where low armchairs house many spreading bottoms and stomachs clad in grey flannel or beige tweed, where legs may be seen protruding in maroon socks and ginger suede shoes, where shirts and blouses give off the dingy glare of nylon.' Kitty develops a passion for a devious Christian history professor with a tragic romantic past. We watch her teaching, taking a class through *Adolphe*, a work important to her own book on *The Romantic Dilemma*, and one which enables her to reflect sombrely on such painful sentences as the one beginning: *Mais quand on voit l'angoisse qui résulte de ces liens brisés . . .* Again the frieze characters, students and teachers and others, have a Wilsonian weirdness. The big moment, well-prepared, well-written, but not altogether unexpected, is Kitty's discovery at a party that the history professor, after all his messing about with her, has chosen another. Of course she behaves very well, being expert in the dissimulation of 'separation anxiety'.

Look at me, probably the best of the books before this new one,* has an 'I' narrator, Frances Hinton, who works in a medical history library and writes; writing is her panacea, her cure for separation and anxiety. She is, as usual, a very superior young woman, and very acute on the grotesque citizens who use the library; but she falls victim to handsome Nick, whom they all adore, and so to his spoilt and even rather gross wife Alix. For a while she seems to be bridging the gap between these people, the fortunate and wicked, and herself. There is her kind of person, and there are 'the others, the free ones'. She tries to learn from

* Anita Brookner, *Family and Friends* (London: Jonathan Cape)

them: 'I needed to know that not everyone carries a wound and that this wound bleeds intermittently through life.' An oddly ambiguous sentence but it comes off. Then: 'I needed to learn, from experts, that pure egotism that had always escaped me, for the little I had managed to build up, and which had so far gone into my writing, was quickly vanquished by the sight of that tremulousness, that lost look in the eye, that *disappointment* that seemed to haunt me.' And her addiction to the perfectly awful free ones leads her to an ultimate disappointment and deception: a lover she couldn't dispose of in her book, who offers tenderness but not desire, and leaves her, 'foolish with desire', for another free one.

The famous *Hotel du Lac* has another writer and self-acknowledged loser, this time Edith: as a tortoise, she knows that hares win. The setting is an expensive hotel, with more grotesque and more or less free ones. Edith is there because she disgraced herself by leaving an unsuitable fiancé at the registry office. She writes novelettish letters to her unsatisfactory married lover, to whom she will return, resuming her unfree though refined existence. As in other instances, the man who irrupts into the young woman's life at the hotel is not without a perhaps deliberately novelettish quality. Such men are handsome and tend to be immaculately dressed (an expression Brookner is a bit too fond of – she doesn't appear to mean simply that they manage not to get food stains on their lapels or ties).

The central myth of *Family and Friends* is the same one, though interestingly varied. The men now matter a bit more, though much less than the women – especially, of course, the loser woman; and in all sorts of ways the texture of this book is richer (it is less an extended nouvelle than a shrunk saga) and a great advance, I think, on *Hotel du Lac*. It starts with a wedding photograph and ends with one, these frozen frames being interrogated and explained by an inquisitive knowing narrator, who uses only the present tense except when demonstrating that she really knows all the outcomes: 'When he is a little older, this imperviousness will drive women to unwise acts and statements, which they will later regret,' or 'Alfred possesses both types of love, sacred and profane. He will grieve for such plenitude for ever after.' Thus, although the surprises are fewer and the ethical positions less idiosyncratic, this book has a slight flavour of Muriel Spark.

The family of the title is rich London-Jewish, established, we are told, from the debris of its European predecessor: living in pre-war London and enjoying what it offered, but without altogether sacrificing traditional Middle-European manners and style. It is presided over by the widow Sofka – herself European but possessing four English children, two boys and two girls: Frederick, an amiable playboy adored by his mother; Alfred, who knows he is destined to prefer duty to inclination, whose dreams are foiled because he must go into the family business instead of Frederick; Betty is selfish, beautiful, ruthless; and Mimi, who has to carry on the Brookner tradition in this new setting, is modest, considerate, and not good at flirting, which ought to be her principal occupation. The book gives the story of their lives, recounting in a newly hectic mode and with notable modifications the triumph of the hare over the tortoise, of the free ones over the disappointed. This time the triumph is hollow and the disappointment far from unmitigated.

The book has a central episode very characteristic of this author, though more richly developed than before. Betty has escaped to Paris, where she means to be a dancer and do a double act with Frank. Mimi and Alfred go to fetch her back. Mimi takes over the negotiations; she knows Betty won't come back, and hopes to have Frank herself. Even before she sets out we know she is hoping that the union of Frank and Betty has not been consummated. 'She begins, in the way of all those who are born to lose, to imagine her way past this terrible damage.' In Paris she is convinced that Frank will prefer her as more honest than her sister. 'Mimi thinks this is how hearts are won,' observes the narrator, 'not believing for a moment that Betty's is the surer way. Behind this certainty lies an unbearable vision of the world's duplicity that must not come to full realization.' It has, of course, done so in the mind of the narrator.

But Frank gives Mimi some cause to think she is right. A finely written page, which has its congener in every one of Brookner's novels, describes Mimi as she waits for Frank in her Paris hotel room, dressed first for dinner, then, as the time goes on, for bed.

Finally she lies on her bed alone, wearing, as we are quite ready to believe, a smile 'tinged with intimations of absolute horror'. This horror, and a sense of deep disgrace, stays with Mimi over the years, and her appearance reflects her 'total dereliction of spirit'. 'Somehow she knows, correctly, that without this false start, this disgrace, this defeat, she could have taken her chance like any other woman.' The plight of Mimi, and of others like her in these books, is an image of some aboriginal catastrophe, not merely the betrayal of a modest passionate woman by a good-looking man who turns as if by some law of nature from the unfree to the free. Mimi's disaster proceeds both from her unfreedom and from her willingness to shed it if she can, as she appears to be doing while she waits confidently for Frank as the hours pass; meanwhile Frank is with her sister. Had she been more like her mother none of this could have happened, for Sofka has always avoided passion and 'knows nothing of that voluptuous flight from the contingencies of normal living, that surrender of will, that rich harvest of inner thought and memory' which is said to accrue from letting go.

Betty, free, ruthless but finally less passionate, marries a film director whose 'films are interesting because they concentrate on emptiness, on the time before things happen, the time when the outlaw might just get away with it'. Failing to get into the movies, she grows fat beside her Beverly Hills pool. Frederick marries a vulgar but satisfactorily carnal heiress, and is given a hotel to manage at Bordighera, where he is able to get on well with enemy officers during the war and maintain into late middle age his role as *homo ludens*: a happy life, though hardly what was promised, and a shade *mauvais genre*, as Sofka would say. Virtuous Alfred enriches the business and pursues his fantasies of country living, meanwhile developing affairs with the wives of friends. Mimi eventually marries a devoted servant of the firm, indispensable but subordinate, and much too old for her. Alfred is disgusted: but she achieves pregnancy and her husband is more deeply attached to the family than most of its true members. However, she still suspects that the good live unhappily ever after.

Sofka dies, knowing she misses Betty and Frederick most. But there is a final wedding photograph, and in this Mimi is the matriarch, while Alfred slyly indicates his relation to a child born late and unexpectedly to an old friend, whose husband stands off to the side. If Mimi replaces Sofka, Alfred replaces her discreetly libertine husband, and the dancers appear to be in place for the next set.

The book moves from such static poses to the intricacies of lifelike movement and plot; it is about rich and not very interesting people, but is itself rich and interesting. There is great assurance – in the contrasts between the manners of the generations, in the registration of types and variants in families, in the ways a house can be ruled and servants included as members of the clan, in the varying degrees of intimacy achieved by friends. One ends it with some surprise that Mimi and Alfred have come out of it so well, their siblings languishing in vacuous California and dull Bordighera while the unfree become the family in their place. The surprise reminds us that Brookner continues to prefer the shorter forms, even when the richness of the material available must tempt her to the longer.

London Review of Books, 5 September 1985

The Horse of the Baskervilles

Umberto Eco

Semiotics is a fashionable subject, but semioticians do not normally become international best-sellers, which is the fate that, in apparent violation of this familiar cultural assumption, has befallen the Professor of Semiotics at Bologna, Umberto Eco. Academic novelists aren't rare, of course, but it's hard to think of one who regards fiction as not only entertainment but material for the practice of a professional discipline. Eco's novel* is a very complicated instance of what he would call semiosis, of the production of signs and their vicissitudes in a network of codes. It also contains many disquisitions on semiotics and related subjects. If that were all, it might be expected to give keen pleasure to a rather small audience: but it seems to go down well with a very large one. That is because it is also, for the most part, as lively and interesting as it is weird and extravagant.

Eco's best-known book before this one was his *Theory of Semiotics* (1976), a vigorous but difficult treatise. One point it makes is that signs are not meaningful in themselves but only in relation to the codes in which they are seen to function: a sign, that is, means nothing save in terms of a network of changing relationships. It has no fixed referent beyond the codes, whose relationship to the world is determined by cultural predispositions, and is thus fundamentally arbitrary. It is accordingly possible to understand a set of facts or clues in very different ways, for the reading

* Umberto Eco, *The Name of the Rose*, translated by William Weaver (London: Secker & Warburg)

depends on the code chosen. This state of affairs is well known, whether by intuition or ratiocination, to writers of detective stories. That a cultural assumption may lead to false interpretation of clues is a donnée of all those crime stories in which a nursery rhyme seems to provide a key to a sequence of murders – *Ten Little Indians*, for instance. And of course the work of the detective often consists in distinguishing between the apparent relations of the clues, which might well be a creation of the murderer (intuitively or otherwise aware of our weakness for pre-established or coded consonance), and a relation more occult, arbitrary and novel, which happens to be the right one. Eco makes some mention of this literary convention in his *Theory*, where he contrasts clues with symptoms. Red spots on the face mean 'this child has measles': but clues can be falsified and are seldom coded. Their interpretation 'is a matter of complex inference . . . which makes criminal novels more interesting than the detection of pneumonia'.

It is not difficult, then, to see why Eco might want to try his hand at some kind of detective novel, like many a don before him, though with a special semiotician's twist. But this book has so much in it that differs from any known kind of detective story that we must look to Eco's pre-semiotic career for help. He began as a Medievalist, and his first book was about scholastic philosophy. Evidently he takes extraordinary pleasure in the art and architecture, the learning and the politics, of the thirteenth and fourteenth centuries: a world 'so organized' – to quote again from *Theory of Semiotics* – 'that a cultural unit corresponding to say "transubstantiation" could find a place within it, i.e. could be a precisely segmented portion of the content of a given cultural background'. The background included fantastically elaborate symbolic systems for herbs, gems, devils and vast agglomerative allegorical codes. Eco likes to describe these as they might have appeared to a forward-looking monk who had been a disciple of Roger Bacon, and therefore believed in machines and science, and a friend of William of Ockham, and was therefore opposed to the multiplication of beings (and signs), sceptical of universals, a sort of proto-semiotician but also a common-sense Englishman, suspicious of Continental flimflam. He is called William of Baskerville, and takes drugs to assist intuition, though he appears not to play a musical instrument.

In case all this sounds a bit tricky to lovers of the historical novel, it should be added that Eco gives his story a solid foundation in the politics and theology of the early fourteenth century. John XXII is Pope in Avignon. A decision of his predecessors had opened a division among the Franciscans by relaxing the original Rule in respect of poverty. The Spiritual Franciscans, who adhered to the letter of the Rule, were condemned by John, and became allied to his mighty opposite, the Emperor Louis of Bavaria. So the Pope, anyway much disliked in Italy and England because he was French and preferred French cardinals, had more than one grudge against the Spiritual Franciscans, who were his enemies in politics as well as in doctrine.

The Emperor had his own theological supporters, notably Marsilio of Padua, an intellectual imperialist in the tradition of Dante; and William of Ockham was to support the Spirituals on the issue of poverty. But they were disobedient and in certain respects heretical at a time when it was very dangerous to be so. In the previous century the successes of the Cathars and other heretics had led to the development of the Inquisition, which retained the equipment necessary to deal with the extremists among the Fraticelli, as they came to be called. Among them there were those who had a special animus against John XXII because of their Joachimite opinions.

These men accepted the teaching of Joachim of Fiore and his followers: a new age should have started about 1250, organized by doctrinally pure Franciscans; and one of the signs of this new age would be the advent of the Angelic Pope. John XXII in Avignon was clearly not this personage. The logic of the situation as the Spirituals understood it is neatly expressed by Marjorie Reeves: 'the true Pope could not err, the Rule of St Francis could not be modified, therefore a pontiff who did so and manifestly erred must be the pseudo-Pope of prophecy.' John XXII, then, was the pseudo-Pope, or Antichrist. To get all this straight, Eco introduces into his novel the historical figure of Ubertino of Casale, who had been an influence on Dante, and who believed that the Papal assault on the Spirituals was the final conflict with

Antichrist. There was an imperialist element in this kind of apocalyptic speculation, for there was also expected an emperor, probably a Hohenstaufen, who would preside with the Angelic Pope over a renewed world in a Third Age. The desire for such an emperor led to all sorts of extraordinary charismatic outbursts, familiar from the work of Norman Cohn. Fra Dolcino, one of the chiliasts Cohn mentions, figures prominently in Eco's book.

The story is supposed to be told by an old Benedictine monk, Adso of Melk, writing near the end of the fourteenth century. As a very young man he had become the scribe of William of Baskerville, who, equipped with his newfangled spectacles, compass and hallucinogens, undertook a mission on behalf of the emperor. The Pope, professing a desire to mend his relations with the Order, has summoned the General of the Franciscans to Avignon. They fear a trick; John will perhaps arrest the General and have him tried for heresy. It is arranged that a delegation from Avignon will meet representatives of the other side for preliminary discussions at a Benedictine abbey in Tuscany; and William, with his scribe, makes his way there to attend the discussions. However, he discovers on arrival that a monk has just been murdered, and the abbot asks him to investigate.

This narrative is doubly framed. There is a joky introduction describing how the author discovered Adso's manuscript, and a prologue in which Adso provides information about the general political scene. This is also whimsical ('heaven grant,' he says of John XXII, 'that no pontiff take again a name now so distasteful to the righteous'). And there are bits of fun like this in the story itself. This taste for pleasantry doesn't prevent Eco from going all out in his creation or reproduction of period detail. The abbey is very minutely described, and its plan appears on the end-papers – though we are denied the help given to Italian readers, who also have a plan of the labyrinth. The heart of the abbey is its library, which preserves, under the protection of various secret signs and architectural complexities, all the learning of the past, licit and illicit. It seems that in the most secret recesses there is a book thought by somebody to be so dangerous that it ought to be kept from readers even if to do so necessitates the killing of monk after monk. Of course that is only one possibility.

The Horse of the Baskervilles

William of Baskerville interpolates into his inquiries many lectures on logic, poison, love, metaphor, poverty, laughter, heresy, the millennium, and so forth; he is by no means our only informant, for Adso picks up elsewhere all sorts of information about the Cohn-like vagrants, about necromancy and witchcraft; but, as the abbot seems to notice, William, who also has long periods of simply lying down and doing nothing, exhibits a strange lack of urgency, especially considering that monks are being put down at the rate of one a day. He is interested in everything as an instance of meaning-production; and right at the outset we get a simple introduction to his semiotic detective methods. As he rides up to the abbey with Adso they meet a band of monks and servants led by one who announces himself as the cellarer, and greets them courteously. William thanks him, the more appreciative of his courtesy in that the cellarer is engaged in an urgent search.

> 'But don't worry. The horse came this way and took the path to the right. He will not get far, because he will have to stop when he reaches the dungheap. He is too intelligent to plunge down that precipitous slope . . .'
>
> 'When did you see him?' the cellarer asked.
>
> 'We haven't seen him at all, have we, Adso?' William said, turning toward me with an amused look. 'But if you are hunting for Brunellus, the horse can only be where I have said.'
>
> '. . . Brunellus? How did you know?'
>
> 'Come come . . . it is obvious you are hunting for Brunellus, the abbot's favourite horse, fifteen hands, the fastest in your stables, with a dark coat, a full tail, small round hoofs, but a very steady gait; small head, sharp ears, big eyes. He went to the right, as I said . . .'

A few minutes later the servants come back rejoicing, leading Brunellus. Adso, of course, asks how it was done. The world, William explains, is an endless array of symbols, some obscurely related 'to the ultimate things', some speaking clearly of what is at hand. William had observed a horse's footprints in the snow, headed to their left. From the spacing and the shape he could tell that the hoofs were small and round, and that the animal was galloping regularly, not in a panic. Above, some twigs were broken off at a height of about five feet, and some long black hairs had caught in a bramble. What about the small head, sharp ears and big eyes? Well, whether the horse had these features or not, the people of the abbey would think it did: Isidore of Seville affirms that beauty in a horse requires them. The missing horse must be the finest in the stable, for otherwise the cellarer wouldn't turn out himself to conduct the search, he would send stableboys; being a monk, the cellarer would be able to see an excellent horse only in the light of what the *auctoritates* say such a horse ought to be. Why Brunellus, though? Well, in logical examples, horses are always given that name.

The method, then, is Holmesian, with a touch of upmarket Father Brown, and a dash of semiotics. Using it in conjunction with his vast learning, William solves the problem of the library, understands the repeated discussion of comedy and laughter, and evaluates the relevance of the apocalyptic symbolism which heavily punctuates the narrative – whether correctly or not perhaps depends on one's own reading of the final scenes.

Here one is compelled to treat the book as a detective story, and prevented from saying what really needs to be said about the coding operations, whether of the type that diagnoses pneumonia or the type that interprets novel constellations of clues. Perhaps one can enigmatically say that carnival and metaphor, inversions of normal cultural style, may, as Aristotle possibly hinted, be enemies of the normal and the literal, without being enemies of the truth. And since in our own time we have seen a major change in the understanding of signs, and also a serious reappraisal of the meaning of carnival, it may appear that Eco is alluding to this more recent *renovatio* when he sets against the stored and controlled learning of the Benedictine library the anti-traditionalist scepticism of the modernist William.

But that certainly makes the book sound too heavy. I am told by Italian friends that Eco is not considered to be a writer of very distinguished prose, but his translator William Weaver contrives to give him, in English, an extraordinary richness and energy. This is true, for example, of the breathless descriptions of heretical vagrants and frauds, of the abbot on the abbey's possessions, of Adso's one-night affair with a village girl, after which William discourses on the relation between physical and spiritual love. There is a dream of Adso's, a dream of carnivalesque reversals which is a remarkable feat of invention (if, as I ignorantly assume, the book *Caena Cypriani*, which is said to be its source, is also Eco's invention). Another achievement is the coming together of the diplomatic and the murder plots; when the Papal delegation arrives the inquisitor takes a hand, ensuring the failure of the peace move, and handing out a tremendous grilling (probably based on the plentiful records of the Inquisition) to a monk suspected of both heresy and murder.

In one of his lectures to Adso, William observes that 'books are not made to be believed, but to be subjected to inquiry. When we consider a book, we mustn't ask ourselves what it says but what it means . . .' So perhaps one ought to treat this book as a complicated footprint from which to infer horses and the names of horses. Certainly it has itself something of the carnival spirit, and something of Borges and perhaps the Nabokov of *Pale Fire*. People not particularly interested in receiving detailed instruction on fourteenth-century imagery, theology and philosophy may find some of the supply of information redundant, and although I have observed the conventions about giving too much away, single-minded lovers of detective fiction may find their progress a bit painful. But take it all together and *The Name of the Rose*, though it complies with no genre (logically it couldn't, it must be a-generic), is a wonderfully interesting book – a very odd thing to be born of a passion for the Middle Ages and for semiotics, and a very modern pleasure.

London Review of Books, 6 October 1983

VI

——•◆•——

The Faces of Man

One good thing about going back to the Isle of Man: it's the only place in the world where my name doesn't look or sound odd. It settles in comfortably with the Cannells and the Cubbons, Kennaughs and Kerruishes, Mylchreests and Qualtroughs, Quines and Quayles. There's a long list of such names, more, one might think, than are needed for a population of 60,000, many of whom are English anyway, 'comeovers' with foreign names. But the Manx are many tribes within a tribe, and very strong on kinship; they distinguish themselves not only from all who live outside their island, but from one another. Not that their differences from the non-Manx are gross and obvious; the names are often variants of more familiar mainland names, as Kermode is of McDermot. This slight but positive deviation seems very characteristic. To the Manx, England is not quite a foreign country, but it certainly isn't home. They call it 'away' or 'across'; they are proud of having what they call, not altogether absurdly, home rule; but only a few of them want to be lumbered with passports and customs, and practically all of them freely express allegiance to the Crown.

I spent my first eighteen years in Man; higher education and the war took me to England, and for forty years I've been 'away'. My accent, which used to return as soon as I boarded the steamer at Liverpool, has gone, practically, for good. And I hadn't been back for years. The immediate cause of my flying over the other day was a desire to see whether, in the year chosen for the celebration of the millennium of Tynwald, the old place had changed as much as I had.

Tynwald is the peculiar Manx parliament: nobody knows

whether it really started in 979, though it is quite possibly even older. The celebrations of 5 July will have a characteristic mixture of styles and motives: the Manx will recall, with traditional ceremony, the genuine antiquity of their institutions, but will do so in full consciousness of the cash value of such displays to a community that needs to attract tourists, 'visitors' as we used to call them. The chief visitor this time will be the Queen. The Manx are understandably proud of their mountains, glens and beaches, but have long known the value of spectacular supplementary attractions; the great though lethal motorcycle races serve to give the season an early start and a delayed end; the Tynwald ceremony marks, as it always did, the midsummer peak.

As children we didn't bother much about the visitors, though the whole place felt different in the summer, an interlude of hard work for the natives and, as we supposed, licentious living for the tourists, before everybody relaxed and the chaste, cosy winter closed in. To our elders the tide of visitors that poured in every weekend in crowded steamers – six hours from Ardrossan, four from Liverpool, three from Fleetwood or Heysham – had another, grimmer meaning; for in the three months during which these transients took the place over, nearly all the work of the year had to be done. Few working people were employed the year round; my father was, on the unspoken condition that he should never join a union, and this set him a little apart from those who could hope, during the forty weeks between seasons, for no more than a spell of roadmending at forty-five shillings a week.

All that is changed; the Isle of Man is, relatively, rich. An unemployment rate of 3 per cent is something to boast about, and, combined with the low income tax, is beginning to attract British *Gastarbeiter* in slightly embarrassing numbers. Moreover, the contribution of tourism to the GNP is now only 8 per cent, little more than a third of the product of banking and finance; for the Island is now, though the description is resisted by many, a tax haven.

All the same, it didn't look very different to my anglicized eye. It remains beautiful, rather grimly so in winter or in a cold late spring; there is something forbidding in the abruptly rocky seacoast of the south, and a large part of the island is more or less barren upland: gorse, heather, sheep. Yet here the palm tree flourishes, and hedges are thick with fuchsia – more gentle indications of a warp in the ecological system, hints of slight but positive deviations from the mainland norm.

To return to such a place, with only a memory of one's own native difference, is to invite unease, a mild dismay perhaps, such as must accompany a clear view, voluntarily undergone, of the road not taken. Placenames, long forgotten, return to the mind with no real sense of strangeness, yet with an absence of immediate association; a rise in the road yields a view, again familiar enough, but signifying not affinity but loss. In my hired car I could drive from one end of the Island to the other in an hour, over roads sometimes much as they were, mere ancient tracks, and sometimes straightened and superbly metalled for the two-hundred-mile-an-hour motorbikes; roads unlike any others in the world, perhaps, yet not extravagantly different, for the Island never is. I, on the other hand, was extravagantly different. For one thing, I was in a car, as I hardly ever was in my youth, when the notion that I should ever *drive* one would have seemed a wild speculation. For another, to know the place as I did, on foot or bicycle, takes years, and the place is different anyway. Should I have rented a bike instead? Would the loss have seemed less? I doubt it; nothing can restore a fully Manx eye for Manx places.

I found myself obsessed by the idea of the modest peculiarity of the Island. But of course nobody who truly is Manx would talk so, however proud of his independence, or of the antiquity and difference of his institutions. If you live your life in a certain culture, vote for and accept a particular form of government, you do not concern yourself with speculation about their interesting oddities. What you do feel about them is something I can no longer know, except by means of memories too vague to be of service. So it was another mark of my alienation that I should have this obsession, and that I should explore the question – of 'modest peculiarity', of 'slight but positive deviation' – by conversing with people whose business it is to understand Man and the Manx from positions of authority: the Lieutenant Governor, the First Deemster, the Speaker of the House of Keys, a rich English immigrant.

Since the millennium approaches, we talked a lot about Tynwald, and we talked also about the relations, now on such a different footing, between Manx natives and British immigrants – two principal aspects of slight but positive deviation. The Manx have a democratically elected lower house, called the Keys, with twenty-four members (the number has never changed). A Speaker presides – a bit like the House of Commons. There is an Upper House, a bit like the House of Lords; but it is presided over by the Governor, a Crown appointee and never a Manxman. What makes the Court of Tynwald modestly peculiar is that the two Houses meet together, the Governor presiding; and the Speaker on such occasions takes part in the debates as a simple member of the lower house. So when the Court meets in its specially designed chamber it combines three layers of government – the two houses and the Governor – into a fourth.

I went to a session of Tynwald: national government on a local scale. One thing the Court had to approve was the sale, to an Englishman, of Bishop's Court, the palace for some 800 years of the Bishop of Sodor and Man. Both Houses had agreed in principle already, and the proceedings should have been merely formal; but members of both Houses, including, very eloquently, the Speaker, asked the Court to think again – to make this a victory for national pride against fecklessness or avarice. They won some votes, but not enough; the Keys contains some very unsentimental members. But the debate was impressive, formal without being overpoweringly so; and the Speaker's freedom to express himself thus marks a difference from Westminster. So does the absence of an official Opposition. There are no Whips. People say what they like, and accept the Speaker as Leader of the House; another deviation.

The Manx, of course, would claim that the deviance is at Westminster. Tynwald is older than the Mother of Parliaments, a heritage of the long Norse occupation. The ceremony on 5 July remembers this fact. Tynwald then assembles on an artificial mound of great antiquity, at St John's, smack in the middle of the Island. The top layer of the mound is occupied by the Governor and the Bishop, another Englishman; they sit, undoubtedly, in seats formerly occupied by a Norse king and a priest of Odin, who did not associate Midsummer's day with St John the Baptist.

On the level below them, the Legislative Council or Upper House; then the Keys and the law-giving Deemsters. They hear the laws of the past year read aloud in Manx and English.

The functions of the great officers of state are as peculiar as Tynwald Hill, or tailless cats and four-horned sheep. The Governor is an instance. The present incumbent, Sir John Paul, came to the Island from the Bahamas. Offhand, he said, he couldn't think of any respect whatever in which the job of being Governor-General there resembled his present one. In the Isle of Man he has, in principle, very great authority, too much in the opinion of some; he himself prefers to devolve it, and it is being reduced, though at a very slow rate; it will be a long time before the job is merely ceremonial. Since he could, if he chose, advise Westminster to withhold the Royal Assent to any bill he disliked, he has something close to a power of veto. In certain circumstances he might act more positively. In my youth a Governor sent for British troops to break a general strike (fortunately the strike ended before they arrived). Sir John seemed a bit surprised when I told him of that incident; but there is no doubt he could do likewise, if he thought public order was threatened, and if there were any troops available.

However gentle the incumbent, the Governorship can be represented as symbolising a millennium of foreign interest in the Island. Why, since the country is not rich, has it persisted? The answers are various. The Vikings wanted a raiding base, the English nobles were after land and customs revenue. In the early nineteenth century the place was a haven for English debtors; the Manx obligingly passed laws to protect them. They needed English money, as they still do. Now they have laws to protect the English who want to protect their wealth by living their last years, and dying, in the Isle of Man. Income tax is a flat 21 per cent and there are no estate duties or capital transfer tax. For various reasons, too complicated to go into, Whitehall does quite well out of the arrangement, and doesn't interfere; it might if the Manx decided they would like to run their own Customs.

The Governor, who doesn't think the income tax rate is all that low, told me he thought the present arrangements beneficial to the Manx; and anyway there was no chance of a major change, since the probability of huge reductions in UK tax is so small as to be ignored. But tax exile isn't for everybody. I talked to Sir Roy Matthews, former director of a dozen City companies, now, in his seventies, amusing himself with a couple of miniature Manx ones. Scope for investment, he said, was very limited; your money may be forced back to the UK and the taxation you hoped to avoid. But more important, he said, was the fact that people should make sure they really like it in the Island; merely saving money and being bored literally to death at the same time isn't worth it. He and his wife loved it.

What about the dangers of a two-level society, with a sort of leisured class of Anglo-Manx on top? Sir Roy dismissed them. There might be some risk in the existence of a small group of ex-colonials, 'when-I-wazzers' he called them, with their clubs and ingrown ways, and disregard for the natives. But for the most part the important thing was to be accepted by the Manx, who accept all who deserve acceptance.

Still, there are, in a sense, two cultures. The price of prosperity is to share one's home with strangers; in the end, I think, the best to be had is an affable coexistence. Talk to the Manx and you see why. I'd been away for 40 years; yet forgotten girlfriends were forced back into my memory, they and their sisters, the husbands they later married, the deaths of their parents and uncles and aunts, the careers of their children. Conversation often consists of an intricate piecing together of the family history of such persons, mere acquaintances perhaps, yet studied in depth, over several generations and in collateral lines. No disaster, no peccadillo even, is ever wholly forgotten. In its way it's rather aristocratic. And since the comeovers can't, for the natives, have a comparable depth of history, they lack reality.

The First Deemster is, I suppose, with or just after the Speaker, the most important Manxman. I knew him almost fifty years ago, when he was an organist and I a choirboy. He is now seventy, very small, amazingly friendly and energetic, very Manx. I tried to get him to feed my interest in slight but positive deviations, this time in respect of Manx law; he is one of the few who are members of the English Bar as well. He swept the topic aside, and spoke of his years in London, reading for the English Bar, as a sojourn in a strange land. We talked about a locally famous tenor who, over 40 years ago, committed suicide on the eve of his wedding; and of a long-dead Deemster who taught me enough Manx to sing Matins in that language. We recited the Lord's Prayer in Manx, though I soon dropped out. Here was a man of considerable power, expert in the new kind of Manx lawsuit, which might involve deals running into millions (the Isle of Man Companies Act of 1976 is much admired, far better, they say, than its UK equivalent). But the First Deemster, who on 5 July will read the laws in Manx before the Queen at Tynwald, is, in his accent as in his interests, positively not English; though some of his best friends are.

It was to the Manx who can never quite be English that I went back. They all accept their difference, and often, with a little irony, represent it as inferiority. The Manx, as no less a man than the Speaker told me, lack 'go'. The Clerk of Tynwald illustrated the point with an old story of a fisherman who had a catch of crabs in his sack. Somebody passing by warned him that one crab was about to escape. 'Don't worry,' he said. 'These are Manx crabs – the others will pull him down.' But some crabs have to get out, for instance, to go to university. It isn't always easy for them to return; so they live among strangers and forget their part in the great Manx conversation, which still goes on, however much times change.

The Manx, said the Speaker sadly, are always 20 years behind; but even so, times do change. You can eat better than you could, at English prices, but not the wonderful cheap fish of my youth; the rich waters round the coast are now trawled by the vacuums of the big EEC boats, and local fish, though still good, is dear. Complaints about food or comfort or prices may get you not so much dislike as tolerant suspicion – you must be English. People stay 20 years behind only when there is some advantage to be had from doing so. In the Isle of Man the advantage may simply be the satisfaction of an instinct for staying slightly different, holding on to one's peculiarity.

The same instinct requires, on occasion, a show of fight. Some young people now learn Manx, study the folksongs, seek greater autonomy. Mostly people are content unless affronted by a show of unjust power, as when the British Government issued an Order in Council for the suppression of Radio Caroline, then anchored in Manx water, without consulting the Manx Government. The Manx have always had some sympathy with smugglers or 'pirates', a reflection of their quizzical attitude to English power. Governors are carefully observed and set down, as in a child's history book the Good, the Lazy, the Arrogant. The very good ones, like Sir Montagu Butler, stay in the conversation; so will the present one, who has made a great success after coming at short notice.

I remember what it felt like to be Manx. There are faces, now aged, that I know; I can join falteringly in the conversation, as in the Lord's Prayer. Much that is alien to others – the Norse placenames, certain peculiarly shaped hills and rocks, the curve of a bay – I shall have in mind as long as I live, though seeing them from a rented car added very little to their effect. And everything reminds me that I got out of the sack. The trouble is that I retain, awkwardly and uselessly, a little of that slight, positive deviance; going back reminded me forcefully of something I can never forget anyway, that I always feel slightly other than English; and no amount of anglicization, either of me or of the Island itself, will ever change that.

The Observer Magazine, 1 July 1979

The Men from Man

Last summer my passport expired and I applied for a new one; since I'd had a British passport for forty years it didn't occur to me that Her Britannic Majesty's Principal Secretary of State for Foreign Affairs might cease to afford me his protection. But one of his assistants noticed that I was born in the Isle of Man, and I was asked to furnish proof that one of my grandparents, at least, was born in the UK. The penalties for fraudulent declarations being what I suppose they must be, severe, I was unable to comply, and for a while it appeared that I should never be able to leave the UK again except to visit my native land. A declaration that I'd worked here for over forty years, if you count war service, wrung from the Passport Office the indulgence I sought, and they undertook to send me a new one when they had collected enough paper to print it on.

All this came about at a time when the British had a tighter grip on the Manx than ever, though the Manx still have what is called Home Rule and are not part of the UK. Analogously, they aren't full members of the European Community, though they share most of the disadvantages of membership, plus a special one of their own – they aren't free to take work in Europe. Since the low rates of direct taxation enjoyed in the Island are chiefly a benefit to English tax-avoiders, and the birching of children a benefit to nobody, it would not be easy to represent the Manx as a privileged people.

It is certainly not Christopher Killip's intention to do so, either in his photographs or in his text; he wants rather to suggest that the Manx are underprivileged to the point of extinction, and John Berger's somewhat hectic preface makes the same point with more rhetorical force and less concern for the facts.* Mr Berger admires the photographs, as well he might; he finds their modest skill entirely appropriate to the task of depicting the lives of the 'under-privileged indigenous inhabitants' of a rocky, inhospitable island. He has never been there, though the pictures admittedly tell him a lot. He acutely notes that a photograph of a father and his son states a resemblance which goes beyond heredity, being improved by a common occupation, and by exposure to the same weather; and when he mentions the 'cunning innocence' of a teenage boy one can applaud, for cunning innocence is certainly a Manx trait. But Mr Berger's notions of the Island are otherwise inaccurate. He supposes it to be occupied by two nations, one consisting of Manx fishermen and small farmers, and the other of the tax-avoiding English who have arrived since the war, and are wiping out the peasants. This formula ignores the existence in the towns, where a very large majority of the Manx live, of a large population that is neither one nor the other, and which has always been in various ways dependent on the English.

Mr Killip's subjects helped to deceive Mr Berger, for they are mostly of the peasant remnant and their landscapes. The portraits are very interesting. All have a certain dignity – the poetry of sheep and mountains has prepared us, and the photographer, for that. But they have other qualities in common – the mouths tight or turned down, the gaze defensive, suspicious even; weathered, and somehow moral. Interspersed among the portraits are the landscapes of rock and mountain and cloud with which, allowing for some excess in Berger's prose, one can agree that the faces have an affinity. The mood is of unadorned, Wordsworthian pastoral, the mood, say of *Michael.*

Yet it should be said, I think, that the Manx, perhaps even the rural Manx, will have difficulty in recognizing themselves in the fantasy of isolated poverty and brutalized survival offered by the text of this book. I don't suggest that the tax-avoiders are good for the Island. Mr Killip is right to ask how a young Manx farmer can ever hope to buy land when land is 'a good investment, at any

* Christopher Killip, *Isle of Man: A Book about the Manx,* introduced by John Berger (London: Arts Council of Great Britain)

price'; the farms, like the fishing industry (now entirely supplanted by the trawlers of the EEC) may well fall into ruin; the well-off Manx will take their profits and join the Anglo-Manx who have come only to save their fortunes and have no real interest in the country. Mr Killip found an apt quotation in *Moby Dick*: Ahab points to the old Manx sailor and says: 'Here's a man from Man, a man born in once independent Man, and now unmanned of Man.' It is true that Man has been unmanned, but not just recently; there has been much emigration not only of workers but of all who seek higher education. And some unmanning of those who stayed at home has been accomplished by the exploitation of Scots and English for 700 years. But the Manx are used to it, and used to living off the English, whether by sheltering their debtors, by smuggling, by tourism, or by serving in their navy (a Manxman steered *Victory* at Trafalgar; press-gangs were paid extra for Manxmen). And most of them would deny that they are worse off at present than before the arrival of the 20,000–plus English *colons*; the unemployment rate is 3 per cent as against the mass seasonal unemployment of the prewar years when tourism was the main source of income.

There has been no open rebellion for over 300 years and there will be no arson now. Even in my youth the great herring fleets had shrunk and the smallholders were hard pressed. I am able to feel with Mr Killip that one could love the Island more, and feel less guilty in voluntary exile, if it were self-subsistent, if those country faces looked less oppressed, more capable of merriment. But I don't think it's true to speak of the Manx as at the end of their history. They are close-knit, very un-English, cut off by a rather expensive stretch of water; the need to emigrate has gone, and few will do so of their own free will. The tax-avoiders may continue to arrive; they will be greeted politely but with that same defensive, weathered stare, and left to get on with their rootless existence while the Manx, whose names like their faces really belong to the Island, carry on living.

The Listener, 1 May 1980

My Formation

Formation – *les années de formation* – sounds perfectly natural in French, but the English equivalent is somehow rather grand. Oddly enough, the word, in the sense that is now exercising us, is absent from the *OED* and from the Supplement. I suppose this must be an oversight, since one hears the word used from time to time; but there is some feeling that the usage is strained, a bit posh or a bit foreign. Formation implies some pretty rigorous process of shaping, some deliberate attempt to put a person together for a particular purpose, on a particular pattern, something that happens elsewhere all right, but not very conspicuously here.

Certainly nothing of the sort happened to me, though it must of course be true that teachers have some vague notion of what it is they wish to make of the material entrusted to them, and equally true that somehow one's mind assumed a serviceable shape. It seems likely, however, that the real shaping was done before the official teachers got their chance. If we push formation back that far we shall have to admit that it is the proper study not of the literary critic brooding on his past but of the psychoanalyst. Still, it must be fairly clear that the circumstances and influences of one's extreme youth allow certain predispositions to develop at the expense of others. I was perfectly well aware that something of the sort was happening when, as a child, I recognized that there were things I couldn't hope to do because my family was relatively poor.

From 1919 to 1939, the first twenty years of my life, my father earned £3 a week, a sum he augmented by what he called 'doing foreigners', or, in modern parlance, 'moonlighting'; but his annual income cannot ever have exceeded £200. That was enough to pay the rent, eat decently and dress warmly. It was not enough for trips abroad, books, or a piano. The last of these lacks was the one I was most tedious about, for I was very early certain of a musical vocation. How genuine it was I can't say; I took up the clarinet, and was told I was the only performer who invariably made the instrument sound like a trumpet, so perhaps not much has been lost. Still, not being able to be a musician was part of my formation. Soon I found ways of acquiring books cheaply and founded the large nondescript library that has become, in these my latter days, such a domestic nuisance.

The first poet I knew anything about was T. E. Brown, formerly much respected in the Isle of Man, where the dialect poems still made sense. Fragments of these poems have been in my head since early childhood, for my mother would read or recite them, and allude to them in passing. I doubt whether many people read them now, but I remember the large crowds at the centenary celebrations of 1930. The principal speaker was Sir Arthur Quiller-Couch, King Edward VII Professor of English Literature at Cambridge. His address was, I fear, coldly received; the Manx don't like the English (even the Cornish) to come over and tell them about their own affairs; and I doubt if the most ambitious boy in the audience envied Q his job.

Brown's school was the only public school on the Island, and the question of my going there never arose, for it was as much beyond our means as Clifton, the school where Brown taught. The local grammar school (almost the first to go comprehensive in later years) was a good one; that is, it got good results in examinations. We were beaten a good deal; there was with some masters a desire to terrorize one into knowledge, perhaps as a substitute for the more difficult method, which is to inculcate love for the subject taught. Still, it was possible to get excited about Browning and moony about Lamartine; Latin was laboriously taught throughout the school, and Greek and German were available, so that anybody determined to get himself formed as a scholar might just about do it. He would then have to win one of the three scholarships annually available to Manx children (few of whom had any money) and go to university on the mainland.

The best scholarship was tied to Liverpool University, and there I went in 1937.

It may seem that I did so for the same reason that I took up the clarinet, and in a way that is true. There simply wasn't the money for anything else. But it would be quite wrong to allow the inference that I felt deprived. We knew nothing about universities anyway; it seemed an amazing bit of luck to be going to Liverpool. And so, I think, it proved. It was quite splendid enough for me, and the teaching was good, to a reasonably adventurous syllabus. I had to learn some Anglo-Saxon, willingly learnt some Italian, and continued Latin under no less a teacher than Mountford. It might be thought that one defect of a provincial university would be that Oxbridge could cream off the brightest students; but if that is the case now, which may in part be doubted, it was not the case in the 1930s, when, as the Franks Report informed us, the number of applicants to Oxbridge tallied pretty exactly with the number of places available to them. All the rest went somewhere else, or stayed at home and attended the local university. Later on I shall mention three people who, academically speaking, did most to form me; one of them was an undergraduate at Liverpool.

There was little use thinking of careers or even futures if you were twenty in 1939. I graduated in 1940, and embarked upon five and a half years in the Navy, properly, in the present context, to be thought of as a protracted period of deformation. It is a large claim, but I doubt if many people spent the war years in a condition of inutility more absurd than mine. All that survived of previous habits was a lust for print, often hard to come by. A friend agreed to be a sort of private book-of-the-month club, and I still have some battered relics of his taste: *Between the Acts*, *New Year Letter*, *Plant and Phantom*, D. W. Harding's *The Impulse to Dominate*. But he was a pacifist, and went to prison. For a couple of years I could go, for two days every two months, to Reykjavik, where there was little comfort except a bookshop well stocked with Everyman editions; I am reminded of it when I see my copy of *The Brothers Karamazov*, volume 2, still swollen from its ducking in an Icelandic hurricane. (I probably know more about hurricanes than all the Conrad scholars together, but they did not interest me much.) I wrote many verses, the poetry, I now see, of a

398

corrupted mind. When Yeats complained that 'conduct and work grow coarse and coarse the soul', he was not talking about our war, but I think of the words as appropriate to my deformation and to an aspect of the war years that everybody seems to have forgotten: they were base, dirty and ugly. London was so disgusting that one was astonished by the brilliant streets and buildings of New York and Sydney. It was in Sydney, as a matter of fact, that I had my sole literary experience of the war years, for I fell among poets at a time when better poetry was being written in Australia than in London.

Like many others, I found the immediate aftermath of the war, which included the ghastly heatless winter of 1946–47, depressing, especially as it was not easy to live on £4 a week even in 1946. Though I was in no shape to do so, I started work on a thesis. I dare say I should never have been formed at all if at this time three people had not intervened rather decisively and tried to do the delayed or spoilt work for me. All are prematurely dead. The first of them was Peter Ure, before the war the undergraduate I spoke of. He died in 1969, just before his fiftieth birthday, and is remembered outside his circle of friends for a handful of books and articles on Yeats and Shakespeare and the Jacobean drama; his first book on Yeats, published in 1946 though written much earlier, really inaugurated modern Yeats scholarship. I have written a memoir of some length, and will not repeat it here. Ure made a prolonged attempt to prove a poetic vocation, and then tackled scholarship with the same seriousness (not that he thought poets could manage without being scholars).

He was a classic by training, but before he came up to 'read' English he had pretty well read it. He knew the English poets with an intimacy I have not seen rivalled, and assumed that all freshmen reading English had read them all, and also Racine and Dante and Joyce and Kafka and Rilke and Dostoevsky. He read incessantly, without haste and without rest, and as he read he made notes. After his sudden death James Maxwell and I could say, from the notes we found in his perfectly tidy study, what he had been reading and why; and why he had stopped. He annotated his own pain.

A solitary man and given to melancholy, Ure spent the last

twenty-two years of his life in Newcastle, and was not much celebrated in the important south. But I think no one who did know him would deny that he was probably more fully 'formed' than anyone else in the business, a scholar of exemplary serious-ness whose achievement fell rather short of his great powers. It was the most marvellous luck to have him as colleague, friend, and occasionally, rival for so long. To me, at eighteen, extravagantly provincial and (as I now saw) desperately ill-read, he was an image of the possibilities of living seriously with books, of undertaking to study them.

When he got out of prison Ure went to the Middle East and finished the war an important figure in UNRRA, ordering people about in his newly-acquired modern Greek, and drinking gin, he said, with generals who cannot have known he was a conscientious objector. This experience of power did not make postwar Liver-pool, when he got back, any less depressing; but his return was a blessing to me. I was, since I had to embark on something, embarking on an edition of Abraham Cowley, under the eye of L. C. Martin, whose long-term plan was an O.E.T. edition like his own Vaughan and Crashaw. However, I found that the only poem of Cowley's in which I could maintain anything like the degree of interest necessary to the project of living with him for several years was the *Davideis*; and of the *Davideis* the only parts that really held my attention were Cowley's notes. At this point Martin very properly decided to shed me. He transferred me to Donald Gordon, then about thirty and, I think, an assistant lecturer.

Anybody who knew Gordon in his prime will at once under-stand why I shall not be able, in the space of this article, to give the reader any idea of what he, the second of my belated formers, was like. He was at the time of our meeting working on that series of articles on the Stuart masques which are now admired as virtuoso examples of a kind of scholarship previously unknown in the subject, though I don't think they initially won much attention. The first task I performed for this strange new supervisor was to read the final typescript and check the quotations of the monumental essay on Jonson's *Hymenaei*; his virtue both then and later, when he had his own department, was to insist on the young taking an active part in his work, as he did in theirs. For the first time I saw how this kind of research was done, and conceived a desire to do some of it myself.

There were, however, a number of reasons why this ambition seemed less than wise. That I quickly lost my scholarly innocence under Gordon's instruction was clear from the inroads I was making into Cowley's notes; but I still had a very long way to go before I could do his kind of thing at all, let alone do it with his magisterial confidence. Working with Gordon meant using the Warburg Institute, then as now entirely hospitable to all scholars, but at the same time generating a daunting atmosphere of high scholarship. I once asked the director, Fritz Saxl – I think in 1946, certainly in the old Imperial Institute days – about some research I was contemplating and he asked me in the most natural way whether I thought my Arabic was equal to it.

In the course of the conversation he gathered, with what must, I think, have been a polite affectation of astonishment, that I didn't even have Hebrew. Fortunately these shameful revelations went no further; but it seemed clear – and the presence of such figures as Frances Yates and Ernst Gombrich silently enforced the conclusion – that at 26 or 27 I was simply too old to switch decisively from being the sort of literary critic and historian (with a huge gap in my 'career') I was, to being even a very minor scholar of the kind Saxl and the others would really want to have around.

So seeing how it was done and actually doing it were not the same thing. What looked like a conjuror's skill – for Gordon, Ficino, Cartari, Comes, Brisonius' *De Ritu Nuptiarum*, Xylander's *Plutarch*, always seemed to open themselves at the right page – could be acquired only with long drudgery. I was ready enough for that, and proved it to myself with a minute reading of Kircher's *Musurgia Universalis*, which took many hours a day for many weeks. But more than hard work was needed, and I doubted whether I really had that sixth sense which made the spectacle of Gordon at work a bit like that of Alex Higgins playing snooker, all dash and accuracy. He got stuck so rarely that when he did the strongest measures seemed justified; everybody within reach was conscripted to work on the problem, letters and telephone calls recruited the world of learning.

Quite apart from my other deficiencies I was temperamentally incapable of this kind of thing. Gordon was a showman, a *régisseur*; his public performances, whether you liked them or not, were extraordinary – very dramatic, always turning on some moment of revelation or recognition. He dressed and talked the part. His dandyish figure was very exotic amid the dirt and ruins of Liverpool. He wore his hair long for those days, and had the kind of laugh that I can only think unsociable, though it made everybody in a room turn towards him; a loud laugh, always scornful even if he was amused. His voice and way of speaking also alienated the orthodox. He had a habit I've known in no one else, of uttering, or innering, words on the intake of the breath; somewhere, still faintly audible beneath the hooting and gasping, there remained a trace of refined Lowland Scottish, like that of the Edinburgh ladies whom Muriel Spark remembers from her youth as for ever beginning their remarks with the word *niverthelace*. He spoke Italian with the greatest fluency and assurance, though with a sometimes embarrassing archaism of vocabulary. With his long hair and swarthy good looks he was, as an Italian colleague remarked, *scozzese italianato*, a dangerous breed. He liked to remind one that James VI and I, a monarch with whom he was on excellent terms, favoured a scholar named Gordon (John, unluckily) who wrote a French panegyric on the King's accession, and was at once made Dean of Salisbury.

I had no share in his fantasies about the great world, its honours and its rewards. There was a disparity, too, of sexual inclination. Nothing bound us except literature and scholarship, and, as I have explained, there were difficulties even in those affinities. That a fruitful friendship might exist between two such persons seems unlikely, but it developed; we were made, as he would say, 'as notes in music are, for one another though dissimilar', the last word spoken ironically on an indrawn breath. The same formula could be applied to his little department at Reading in the early 1950s, the most productive, if not the most harmonious, I have ever worked in before it (and he) broke up. He was not a popular man for he was conceited and scornful and ambitious. The work he did so brilliantly struck few as important; he was envied because, in the days when there were relatively few chairs in the subject, he had one at 33 and let everybody know and feel it. After 40 he was sick and apparently unproductive; his first book appeared not long before his death, and it was put together by another hand. He, who loved acclaim more than most men, was not honoured by the British Academy. But at Vicenza, where his studies of the Teatro Olimpico had made him a familiar figure and a member of the local academy, the local newspaper carried an elegant obituary, which it might not want to do for any other British scholar. He deserved that; he knew how to leave his mark on a topic, on a group of *eruditi*, on a library (witness the Liverpool collection of emblem books, and the Renaissance and modern collections at Reading) and on a pupil.

I was too late, and of the wrong stuff, but he generously gave me what form he could, and later acquired some from me. He was a great gossip and also subject at times to bouts of foolish envy, and because of that we eventually quarrelled; we were reconciled, but the days of shaping were then long past. My close connection with him stretched from 1946 into the 1960s, but it was interrupted by my two years at Newcastle, where I worked (with Ure) under the rule of John Butt, the third of my formers. It isn't easy to imagine two men of the same profession who differed more than Gordon and Butt, though I suppose that they were equally learned and Butt knew as much about music as Gordon did about painting. He was shy and rather severe in manner (one needs to remember that in those days subordinates were quite unaffectedly treated as such) though he too was capable of stunning public performances; his Warton Lecture is remembered as the only one in which the audience was moved to applause in the middle of a lecture by the force of a particular conclusive demonstration.

By modern standards we were cruelly overworked – six lectures a week throughout the year, and extra ones as called for, quite apart from classes. The students were ex-service men, hungry for degrees; they might mention to Butt that they wanted to be straightened out on the subject of, say, I. A. Richards, and he would casually ask me to put on a couple of lectures next week.

But he himself did far more teaching than we did, as well as attending those of his juniors and explaining what was amiss in them. Thursdays he spent editing *R.E.S.*; I have a memory of him bent over proofs, wholly concentrated, in the weak light of a candle during some power cut. He launched Ure and myself on our careers as reviewers – which causes me to reflect that in thirty-odd years I have written several hundred reviews, an example I would strongly urge the young not to follow. It is, once one begins, all too easy. Somebody mentioned me to J. R. Ackerley at *The Listener*, and so was born the journalist who has wasted so much of my time.

I think of those Newcastle years as formative, certainly; but when Gordon succeeded to the Reading chair in 1949 he took the first opportunity to summon me, and I went without much hesitation. I was 30 by this time, and any more remaking I should obviously have to do myself, though chance or grace might take a hand. I went on working on Shakespeare and the Renaissance, but in the summer of 1955 something decisive happened: I had written a lecture, *In Memory of Major Robert Gregory* (a lecture rather Gordonian in method), and it turned almost spontaneously into a book called *Romantic Image*. It was not a book either Ure or Gordon or Butt would have written, though it owed something to all three, and especially to Ure and Gordon. Soon after it came out Gordon moved into the same area and began to do the work in his own way, with the usual blend of thorough preparation, intuitive discernment of sources, and, at the climax, splendour of public display. I have not much time for that book now, though it does not trouble me that people still read it. What was good about it was that, however belatedly, I was, in my thirties, my own man, with a future doubtless full of follies and errors, but my own to choose. In so far as I was capable of formation, I was, at last, formed.

Times Higher Education Supplement, 30 January 1981

A Stroll Around the Block

Anybody oppressed by the thought of the torrent of prose that pours out upon us daily might well be tempted to give quiet thanks for the existence of the psychological condition known as *writer's block*. To suffer from it is another matter. Most people experience a mild form of it at some time or another, perhaps merely as an inability to write a letter; but it can be much more disagreeable, and is often a really serious affliction.

Freud, who knew about it rather as a doctor than as a writer (if we are to judge by the bulk of his published work) classified it with other inhibitions, including the one familiar to us, though not to him, as *anorexia nervosa*, a pathological reluctance to eat that is now not uncommon among adolescents.

Freud, however, talked only in a general way about 'inhibition in work'. He did make some specific remarks about writing, inhibition of which, he thought, might have a sexual origin, though it might equally result from a transfer of psychic energy to more important work, such as mourning. But for him the condition was simply a special case of a more general theory of depression.

Nor does he, though writing in 1925, use the expression 'writer's block'. The term appears to be of more recent origin. The Oxford Dictionary (Supplement) assigns the first use of the word 'block' in neurology to 1882: 'an obstruction to the passage of a nervous or muscular impulse'. As late as 1931, the term was transferred to psychology: 'the term block refers to those periods, experienced by mental workers when they seem unable to respond and cannot, even by an effort, continue until a short time has elapsed.' It took even longer to get into common speech; the

Dictionary quotes the *Times* as remarking, in 1969, that at a certain period Henry James could have been observed 'freeing himself from emotional and work blocks', but the term 'writer's block' still finds no place in this most august and complete of lexicons.

What is writer's block? Of course it may be an indication that one's energies are needed for something else; but more often, I suspect, it is a panic attendant on the mysteriousness of actually writing down what it is one has, or hopes one has, to say. I refer not to the well-known sexual implications of putting pen to paper, nor even to the remotely numinous quality of writing in itself (a message from elsewhere, the tablets on Sinai, the veneration accorded the Torah or the Scriptures) but rather to the fact that a writer, unless he is almost literally writing 'off the top of his head', is obliged, in some degree, to make that descent into himself of which Conrad spoke with such feeling. The fear that attends this descent may be transferred to the unwelcoming aspect of the paper set out before him: *le vide papier*, as Mallarmé called it, '*que sa blancheur défend*'.

That inviolable whiteness also suggests the specific difficulty of *beginning*. It's the first step that counts; the marks that sully the paper provide the beginning of a context for subsequent sentences. Monologues as well as conversations are easier to manage once there is a context. Healthy people can create one easily enough, simply by saying what it is they propose to say: 'In what follows I shall discuss the question of writer's block.' Technically such remarks are said to belong to what is called a metalanguage, and they are used to say what the impending message is about, which helps the writer as well as the reader.

I gather that in the speech disorder called aphasia there are broadly two varieties. One (a 'similarity disorder') prevents the patient from saying things except in a context already provided; the other (a 'contiguity disorder') deprives him, among other things, of the use of a metalanguage. Perhaps similar distinctions might be found in writer's block, which we could call 'agraphia' if the doctors hadn't appropriated the term for something else, a pathological inability to write correctly.

I know a good many people who suffer from the block; it is

especially prevalent among research students. Writing a doctoral dissertation is a quite formidable professional test; you may spend two years collecting material, and must then devote a year to writing it up. The position of such students is in any case depressive, for they are likely to be lonely and to suffer many crises of self-confidence. I always tell them, though they pay no attention, not to get themselves into a situation in which to write connected prose is an unfamiliar activity – to write every day, and to remember that paper burns easily.

Not everyone, however, can reconcile himself to producing pages of 'wildtrack' writing just to keep his hand in. I myself write very wild drafts which have little relation to what is done in the end; but I remember Muriel Spark showing me, in 1963, the exercise book in which she was writing 'The Mandelbaum Gate', and noticing that apart from a few verbal alterations everything was carefully written to stay exactly as it was. I find the clatter and buzz of an electric typewriter helpful; others need, as well as dread, the intimate contact of the hand on the paper.

In short, there is no prophylaxis against writer's block that will suit everybody. Mme Guyon was an automatic writer, and worked so fast, she tells us, that a scribe 'could not, however great his diligence, copy in five days what I wrote in a single night.' Flaubert and Joyce could labour a whole morning on one sentence.

Most people, even if not afflicted with the block, find it hard work to take on a language, as in some measure one always must. The worst moment is the beginning, the empty white paper. The best thing to do is to start, knowing that what you are doing is probably hopeless, but knowing also that you can throw it away. In that way you will provide yourself with a context to speak to, and then your conversation with yourself can begin. If this fails, telephone the doctor. Don't try to write to him.

Daily Telegraph, 12 April 1975

On Being an Enemy of Humanity

Earlier this year Dame Helen Gardner, Fellow of the British Academy, Emeritus Merton Professor of English Literature at Oxford, editor of Donne, and (to be brief) the doyenne of English academic criticism, published a book entitled *In Defence of the Imagination*. It consisted for the most part of her Charles Eliot Norton Lectures, given at Harvard in 1979–80. I was aware that in the course of her lectures Dame Helen had made some adverse comments on my book *The Genesis of Secrecy*, which happened to have had its origin in the Norton Lectures for 1977–8, for Dame Helen had been kind enough to write a letter saying that she had done so, and expressing the hope that I would not think her attitude hostile.

For reasons that will emerge I have come to feel that I need to make some reply to her polite accusations, and I ought therefore to begin by stating with equal candour my hope that what follows has no offence in it. Dame Helen thinks modern literary criticism is in a bad way and, however sadly, attributes a surprisingly large part of the blame to me. I too think literary criticism is ailing but suppose that a more accurate diagnosis might be had from an examination of her Norton Lectures than of mine.

No copy of Dame Helen's book reached me at the time of its publication, but the English literary press left me in no doubt about its drift. *The Times* (London) praised its wit and wisdom and affirmed that it reduced me 'to a heap of cardboard ruins', but the standard of literary comment in *The Times* is now about the same as its standard of typography, which is a national disgrace. A review in the *Times Literary Supplement* by Denis Donoghue, which made it equally clear that Dame Helen, though doubtless without hostility, had not exactly been flattering me, asked whether her use of the Norton Lectures as a medium for reviewing a predecessor in the series was in perfect taste. There is, after all, some tacit understanding that these lectures should make or attempt a constructive contribution to knowledge; what can the people at Harvard have thought when this particular mouse was proudly deposited on their hearthrug? According to Dame Helen herself (in a private communication) they mostly wondered why she had been so much nicer to me than to Stanley Fish. But Donoghue's notice did not make it appear that she had been very nice at all. He was soon to pay for this impudent suggestion. The Dame did not lack a champion. In the very next issue of *T.L.S.* there was printed a strong challenge from Howard Erskine-Hill. 'When such fundamental issues are at stake,' wrote this heroic and unillusioned scholar, 'many will be glad that her frank defence of her discipline overrode the fear of indecorum.' He spoke on behalf of 'the human world', in whose service all means are presumably justifiable.

No one, I suppose, will fail to be impressed by the moderation with which Erskine-Hill deploys an argument earlier used by, among others, Stalin against the kulaks. Perhaps he may, like Bentley, an even more distinguished Cambridge scholar, acquire a reputation for 'singular humanity', but in the course of his letter he attributes to Gardner the expression *une liberté pour rien*, which she borrowed from my book, where it was duly credited to Jean Starobinski. But even if Erskine-Hill laboured under the disadvantage of not having read the book under attack, he knew by instinct, or perhaps by virtue of his singular humanity, that it needed purging.

Another reviewer, Peter Conrad, as celebrated for his modesty and charity as Erskine-Hill for his wit and charm, wrote ecstatically of Dame Helen's 'lethal courtesy' and hailed my demise with understandable *schadenfreude*. Other literary figures of almost equal eminence and authority, such as the poet Thwaite, have, I am told, joined in the exultation, rejoicing that Imagination, Humanity, Principle, and perhaps other valuable qualities, have been saved from my assault by the vigilance, learning, and courtesy of Dame Helen. She, of course, is not responsible for the exuberance of this volunteer claque; but I was rather pleased that David Lodge, whom no doubt she would rather have had as a supporter than those she actually got, made it clear in his review that he was not delighted by Gardner's attempt, in the lectures, to enlist him, and indeed went so far as to remark on the Dame's tendency to substitute rhetoric (or sarcasm) for argument.

Anyway, I confess to doubting that a book capable of eliciting the unstinted admiration of Peter Conrad can be worth reading, and Erskine-Hill's communication only made me wonder at Shakespeare's genius in coining, so far in advance of its imperative occasion, the epithet 'forcible-feeble'. So I still did not read the *Defence*. But soon afterwards the editor of a London journal telephoned me. He asked how I was. 'Oh, fine,' I said. 'Really? From here you look to be covered in blood.' He wondered if I wanted to defend myself. Might it not appear, if I omitted to do so, that I had no defence to offer? Although I was prepared to believe my book vulnerable to informed criticism, I did not think it could be totally destroyed, reduced to ruins, or whatever. Perhaps I should defend what could be defended. So at last I acquired and read the *Defence*.

Dame Helen's title echoes, I suppose, Sidney's as well as Shelley's, though *The School of Abuse* would have been more apposite. My first surprise came when I discovered that my sins against the imagination were not confined to *The Genesis of Secrecy* but had long antedated that work, in other books which my critic had obviously been skimming, pencil at the ready to mark offences against humanity, etc. Since she holds it proper for good humanists to accept correction with grace, Dame Helen will not mind if I mention that she twice misrepresents the title of one of those books – a small matter, admittedly, but one must start somewhere. For the *Defence* is so heavily committed to the business of exposing, and then decrying in appropriate tones of lamentation or ridicule, my faults and those of other sinners, that its author has, I dare say uncharacteristically, failed to take proper humanist precautions against errors of her own.

Her motives in writing this book can only be surmised. In the course of one of her lectures she recounts a conversation with me which took place between the two series of lectures. There is no inaccuracy in her account of that occasion, so far as it goes, but, using the same liberty, I will supplement it by recording that she professed herself very worried because, as the time of the lectures approached, she had nothing new to say. I tried to cheer her up by remarking that very few people had, and that the old, suitably recycled, is often called into emergency service on such occasions; but it is clear that the worry persisted, for Dame Helen says much the same thing in her first lecture. She adds that, having for many years been attending to other business, she was, so far as modern literary criticism went, 'a kind of literary Rip Van Winkle'; she had awakened into an entirely unfamiliar world. These are about the least contestable statements in her book, though their purpose is tactical; the point is that being so strongly endowed with humanity and common sense, she can see through all this nonsense without wasting much time on reading it. Her positive purpose is to provide 'a restatement of the humanist belief in the value of a study of literature as the core of a liberal education'. 'Humanist' is here used, of course, in a single eulogistic sense; like 'imagination' it has been commandeered by people who want their cause to seem nobler than a mere disinclination to be disturbed. Indeed Dame Helen suggests that humanism is the enemy of 'spite, meanness and cruelty', though she must know that these disqualities are in fact strongly connoted by some varieties of humanism.

Let us however agree that all humanists, of whatever moral stripe, acknowledge an obligation to get things right. Yet Dame Helen's restatement of her humanist faith opens with a series of remarks which betoken a lack of acquaintance with the topics under discussion so total as to give a new sense to the expression 'learned ignorance'.

Consider her spanking condemnation of 'Deconstruction'. It is a doctrine I certainly do not regard as immune to criticism; nor, for that matter, do its principal exponents. But Gardner speaks of the 'Deconstructionist image of the reader as importing meanings into texts instead of attending to what he is reading'. Dame Helen condemns other critics for being playful, but she herself too often abandons an argument with an attempt at dismissive humour, and possibly this remark is meant to be funny. It is, of course, quite absurdly inaccurate, and could hardly have

been made by anybody who had read even a few pages of Derrida
or of Paul de Man, whose attention to what they are reading is
of an intensity beyond (on the evidence of this book) Dame
Helen's conception.

There is, next, the tiresome matter of hermeneutics to be
disposed of. It is hardly too much to say that every remark in this
section of Dame Helen's book is false. She simply hasn't bothered
to find out what she is talking about. Interpretation, she asserts,
was now – after her Rip Van Winkle period – 'being given the
more impressive name of "hermeneutics", a term adopted from
Biblical criticism via Heidegger.' All that remains of this sentence
when its two errors of fact are discounted is the sneer. 'Hermeneutics' is not a synonym for 'interpretation', and it was applied to
secular literature long before Heidegger. It stands to 'interpretation' roughly as 'philosophy of science' stands to 'science'; only
roughly, because it originally dealt with the rules governing
interpretation, and more recently has acquired wider philosophical connotation. (To give a simple instance: E. D. Hirsch's well-
known *Validity in Interpretation* is not, in fact, a work of
interpretation but of hermeneutics.) Dame Helen, researching
the matter, looked up the word in the Supplement to the *OED*
and decided that an example from 1965 was the earliest the
dictionary gave, though like a good humanist she says she can
push it back a few years from that date. The Supplement claims
in a rubric to be supplying 'earlier and later examples'; a really
thorough humanist might have looked up the word in the big
dictionary itself and found that it defined 'hermeneutics' as 'the
art or science of interpretation, esp. of Scripture', citing instances
from 1843 and 1871. But what is really surprising is that one
ready to intervene in these matters does not know that by the
mid-eighteenth century it was already held, strongly though not
universally, that there was no essential difference of method
between secular and sacred hermeneutics. It is a point often still
made, as for example by R. Bultmann, a theologian much involved
in hermeneutics and one with whom, as we shall see, Dame Helen
claims some acquaintance.

The difficulties into which one may run in the course of
condemning methods and ideas of which one has not the slightest

conception are further illustrated by Dame Helen's oddest claim, which is that hermeneutics is somehow related to Gnosticism, which, on the authority of Henry Chadwick (which few will challenge), she describes as a 'sombre and repellent theosophy'. The expert in hermeneutics, she claims, does what Gnostics do; he distinguishes between the fleshly majority and the few 'spiritual' men or *illuminati*. So Professor Chadwick's censure of Gnosticism is transferred to hermeneutics, but only by an argument which, if employed by a less austere humanist, would surely be described as transparently disingenuous.

It will not now seem surprising that Dame Helen appears to think what she calls 'the *nouvelle critique*' and 'hermeneutics' to be alternative names for the same thing – a very sombre and repellent thing. She ventures some historical explanation of how and why this wickedness took hold. There was the New Criticism, and there was the literature of what she calls (surely incorrectly; but French is very alien) 'the years of *entre deux guerres*'. At that time, she informs her audience, there occurred a Great Depression and much political instability, producing literature that called for *interpretation*; and so the rot set in from which we continue to suffer.

These large historical gestures are sketched with all the authority Dame Helen habitually confers upon the commonplace, upon her own mistakes, and upon her condemnation of the mistakes, real or supposed, of others. She enjoys severity for its own sake, as when those who pervert the teachings of Freud and Marx are strongly censured, though the perversions are not characterized, and their perpetrators not named. The point is, one supposes, to issue a general ban on any kind of critical discourse that departs from the manner of her own, tacitly proposed as the only one adequate to the continuance of the 'humanist's quest, which is to understand the nature of man as it manifests itself in time and history'. Or anyway, in Anglo-American time and history; for these preliminary salvos end with the announcement that 'the literary situation in France is very different from that in England and America', so that 'French new criticism' has 'little relevance' in our countries; indeed its importation signifies 'a real loss of belief in the value of literature and literary study'.

And here we might expect a humanist to offer some sort of demonstration that the French, though in some sense human, are nevertheless alien, at any rate in their critical practice. But what we get is something quite different, an assault on me for using the word 'unfollowable', which she says she cannot even pronounce.

This, to be sure, is only one of her little jokes, and no speech therapy seems to be called for. But of course I did not make this word up. It was given currency by an undeniably British philosopher, W. B. Gallie, in a famous book published in 1964. Perhaps this was during the Rip Van Winkle period, though, like a conscientious humanist, I gave a reference in my book.

Dame Helen politely notes that she doubts the 'genuineness' of 'some' writers – meaning, I think, me – largely, it seems, because she has herself no difficulty in making sense of the world. But one isn't, with the best will in the world, persuaded of the genuineness of this criticism, made as it is by a commentator who has real difficulty in attending to any train of thought she has not already entertained herself. A good instance of this incapacity occurs when her eye lights upon a passage in my book *The Sense of an Ending* which she thinks deserving of more serious reprobation. In that passage I wrote about Christopher Burney, elaborating a saying of his (in his book *Solitary Confinement*) to the effect that in the stratagems he devised for the defeat of time and solitariness we might find an image of 'certain characteristic fictions in a pure state'. Looking at the passage (as I needed to since it was written seventeen years ago) I note that I develop the idea at some length, and also carefully qualify it. I do not know whether Dame Helen read Burney's book (she quotes a sentence of his as if it were mine, which suggests that she hasn't) but there was in any case no need to garble my argument. 'It seems a kind of outrage,' she says (doubtless without hostility), 'an insensibility to real and terrible suffering to relate the extremity in which [Burney] found himself to the epistemological anxieties which afflict some modern writers and intellectuals.' It seems a kind of outrage that a famous humanist should read so perversely. She could, of course, count on the audience not having read Burney or me. If anybody wants to pursue the matter they need only look at pages 156–64 of my book. When I conclude by saying that 'we

414

can, if we like, think of Burney's book as a model of a more general solitary confinement,' I am summarizing what is quite explicitly a discussion, initiated by Burney himself, of the fictions he invented during his confinement. To read the passage, as Gardner does, in order to justify a display of humanist indignation is basely to misrepresent it.

Misrepresentation, however, is one of the principal instruments employed in this defence of the imagination. Speaking of another book of mine, *The Classic*, she remarks: 'He takes as seriously intended the test of a century, which Horace cited only to mock at, and arrives at the notion that the status of a classic is not given through the centuries by the judgment of the common reader, but by the possibility of its providing sufficient material for a *Casebook*.' Of the two statements here one is a misrepresentation and the other an untruth, compounded by the suggestion that there is a causal relation between them; or perhaps this is another of her jokes. It is true that Horace ridicules the argument that exactly one hundred years must elapse before an author can be accepted as *vetus atque probus* (why not ninety-nine, etc.?). But as good humanists are aware, he placed a high value on past literature which enjoyed continuing esteem, and the point is that in imitating Horace, Pope used the word *classic* to represent *vetus atque probus*, as Horace of course could not. The rest of the sentence is a travesty of an argument which in no way depends upon the validity of the hundred-year test, and has nothing whatever to do with casebooks. It is followed by what appears to be an adverse comment on the chapter of my book that discusses Hawthorne, but since it never engages the argument but merely rambles on about Lionel Trilling, Wordsworth, and Dickens, one may take it that its main object, since she admittedly has nothing to say, is to fill in some time.

But her most obvious piece of time-filling is the fifth lecture, more or less entirely given over to a courteous assault on *The Genesis of Secrecy*. It is the work of a scholar never for a moment uncertain of her own authority. Modestly disclaiming specialist knowledge of the field, she nevertheless issues a stream of corrections and rebukes. And I must indeed admit that although I took pains to avoid error, and consulted biblical specialists, I did not expect to escape criticism. The experts, incidentally, seem inclined to regard my biblical scholarship as sound enough but unoriginal (see, for example, the detailed critical comments in *Religious Studies*, viii (1) [January, 1982], pages 1–9), and of the eminent scholars with whom I have discussed the book either because they wrote to me or because we met at conferences, none has suggested that it was full of ludicrous mistakes. Perhaps they were too polite; perhaps they did not feel a desire to administer correction that may testify less to a passion for humanist accuracy than to velleities more obscure and reprehensible.

Some thirty years ago, she tells us, Dame Helen found herself able to introduce Oxford philosophers and literary critics to the theology of Rudolf Bultmann, and no doubt she did so with proper modesty. She mentions this historical fact as a preface to remarking, correctly, that Bultmann is not mentioned in my book. But she very charitably excuses the omission, since 'Existentialism is no longer very fashionable' – the implication apparently being that if it were I should certainly have put Bultmann in. But I am not to be excused for saying so little about Form Criticism.

Now I have already noticed Dame Helen's curious tactic of admitting that she knows very little about a subject before making authoritative pronouncements about it. She says that thirty years ago she was 'a little hazy' about Bultmann; what she knew was that he had something to do with Existentialism, and something to do with 'demythologising'. But as her severance of the topics shows, she did not, and still does not associate him with Form Criticism, and that is very odd, since Bultmann, as everybody with any qualification to speak on these matters must know, was a principal exponent of the method. His *History of the Synoptic Tradition* is, if I may so put it, a classic of that genre. It dates from 1921, and it had been around for a generation before 'demythologisation', which Bultmann thought up during the war, became a fashionable topic. Ignoring this fact, Dame Helen is further disadvantaged by not knowing that during her long remission of attention to such matters Form Criticism suffered severe criticism and modification. The subject is too large to enter upon here, but the alteration of emphasis can be described in a few words. Bultmann, like Dibelius, was applying to the New

Testament a method of studying the evidence for the existence, in the biblical text, of traditional oral units. He classified this hypothetical oral material and considered how it had taken the literary form it now has – how the original material was adapted to the needs of the community for which the literary version was written, its *Sitz im Leben*.

Dame Helen professes annoyance at my speaking of a certain 'circularity' in form-critical method; yet the point is obvious. The judgment as to whether a 'unit' is traditional, or as to what its traditional content may have been, depends on what you suppose the community to have done to it, and most of what you say of the community is inferred from that. Without some prior decision or fore-understanding (Bultmann, as Dame Helen doubtless knows, called this *Vorverständnis*) about the community and the tradition there is nothing to be said. Moreover, the practice of using the text simply as material for disintegrative enquiries inescapably gave rise to the criticism that the texts were after all *written*, composed. The gospels, even when they exhibit common material, are remarkably various. Each *Sitz im Leben* no doubt called for its own handling of that material, but no *Sitz im Leben* ever took up a pen and wrote. In their enthusiasm for the oral tradition the form-critics tended to neglect the fact of composition, and attempts to correct this false emphasis led to the development of a new method, labelled *Redaktiongeschichte*, a term first employed in 1959 and therefore not exactly newfangled. Indeed, people who know anything about these matters have long since abandoned Form Criticism in its original style, now sixty years old if we count from Bultmann's book, and even older if we start from Gunkel, who first applied the method to the Old Testament. It is, in fact, far more dead than the New Criticism, in which, since it is so often said to be dead, Dame Helen now finds some virtue.

A new interest in the gospels as the work of writers has, not surprisingly, led to their being considered as composed narratives. I confess I do not understand why such considerations strike Dame Helen as offensive. When I remark that in developing this new interest some biblical critics have shown themselves a little naive, she hurries, quite unnecessarily, to their defence. The evidence I gave for this contention – that biblical scholarship has been imperceptive of certain narrative devices and qualities in the gospels – is ignored by Gardner, though biblical scholars have found it persuasive. Incidentally, while we are on the subject of naiveté, Dame Helen announces, ex cathedra as it were, that Mark's gospel is a 'naive text', an instance of *Vorverständnis* that disqualifies her from following much of the argument of my book.

Given the chance, she always does turn aside from the real issue with a jest or an ex cathedra pronouncement. For example, I mentioned in passing Defoe's 'True Relation of the Apparition of One Mrs Veal' as a 'rhetorical success'. I hesitated before doing so, for the example is none of the freshest, so I was surprised to be instructed that 'we know now' that this 'was part of the recorded account of Mrs Bargrave herself'. I suppose 'we' are the true and accurate humanists. However, what 'we' know is actually rather different. Defoe collected four different accounts of the apparition and altered them, using, as Professor James T. Boulton observes, 'a literary method which emphasises circumstantial detail', and so 'achieves vividness of narration'. I dare say the undergraduates in the audience enjoyed the neatness of the put-down without suspecting that it was false. In rather the same way she derides my remarks on the historicity of Fulke Greville's account of the death of Sidney; but instead of attempting a refutation she rambles on about Oscar Wilde and in the end seems unable positively to disagree.

Since she is so concerned about 'historical accuracy' I will mention my surprise at finding Dame Helen (*In Defence of the Imagination*, chapter 6) saying that she will 'never forget [her] first reading of ["East Coker"] on that dreary day in late March 1940', at a time when the war news was depressing and she was suffering from 'the bungled débâcle of Norway'. The Germans did not, in fact, invade Norway until April 9, and the 'débâcle', 'bungled' or otherwise, was not evident until the evacuation of British forces in late May. The historical cause of her sadness must have been something quite different.

If she dislikes what I have to say about written history, Dame Helen is even less pleased by my remarks on institutions and the control of interpretation. This is partly because she has a rather restricted notion of institutions, saying that to belong to a church does not feel like belonging to an institution, a term she apparently reserves for lunatic asylums, workhouses, and banks. As to the relation of institutions to interpretations, she simply operates on the assumption that she already knows what it is that preserves the reputation, and the texts and the interpretation, of books she admires, and regards all enquiry into the means by which these things are maintained as superfluous. Yet she complains plangently that we live in a time when 'values' aren't being satisfactorily transmitted, at least in part because of what happened in the universities in the sixties. Does it not make sense, then, to stop simply repeating that 'the common reader' is the sole preserver of our classics, and ask what is? Or is the common reader responsible for the sad state of affairs she laments elsewhere?

All this is very odd if you consider that Dame Helen has possessed, and continues to possess and enjoy, institutional authority. It seems a kind of outrage, if one may say so, that having enjoyed this power and had such authority over a couple of generations of readers, she should set up as, or defer to the sovereign notion of, the common reader. In providing some account of her differences from me on this issue, she misunderstands what is perfectly simple, and argues that to recognize the possibility of multiple interpretation is to take away 'the possibility of agreement'. But the assertion is ridiculous; the possibility of agreement, as I have often pointed out, is a fact of experience. The nature of such agreements, and the testing of dissent from them, are matters which ought to be of interest to all teachers of literature, and it seems reasonable that they should be discussed rather than waved away.

On more specifically biblical issues, there is a strong suggestion that Dame Helen's accomplishment in biblical scholarship, though admittedly very defective, is quite good enough to put *me* down. Hence some amusing but inaccurate sniping at detail. For example, almost any reading in the subject over the past thirty years or more would have enabled her to discover that what I say about collections of *testimonia* is not original; far from exemplifying my intoxication with the *nouvelle critique*, it derives in large part from the work of C. H. Roberts, a distinguished member of two of her own institutions, Oxford University and the British Academy. When she finds fault with me for saying 'There are good reasons for thinking that the first Christian book was a book of Testimonies' and that another such book was a 'collection of proof texts about the Messiah found in a cave at Qumran' she is, perhaps inadvertently (though I made due acknowledgment), criticizing Roberts, a task for which she might well disavow her competence. Indeed I sometimes suspect that apart from a general intention to give me and some other wretches a bad time she is not altogether clear what she *is* trying to do. I felt this particularly when she announced, as if in opposition to me, that 'The interpreter can cast light here or there . . . but he can never become the text's master.' Of course! Yet it is for expounding this view and trying to explore its implications that my book so offends her.

But I must now come to the one matter of substance she discusses in any detail; for here we may suppose her to be even surer than usual of her ground. She maintains that I ignore the insistence of commentators from Augustine on that there is a main or literal sense which may be figuratively expressed but which remains basic to the other senses. And well may she maintain it, for it is what all the world knows, including even me. She refers me to Augustine. There is a well-known passage in *The City of God* (XVI.1) in which Augustine directly confronts the relation between the historical and the prefigurative. He says of the narrative of Noah and his sons that the 'former obscurity' of its meaning has been cleared by its 'true event', which means that its significance is established only by its typological reference to Christ. And he goes on to ask what may be the point of the 'historical relations' which have no such typological fruition. They are there, he says, only for the sake of those that are 'mystical' (i.e. typological). As in ploughing, only the ploughshare turns the earth, though you need a whole plough; or as in making harmony the organist touches only the keys, though there is a lot more to an organ; so in the scriptural narrative 'some things are merely relations, yet are they adherent unto those that are significant, and in a manner linked to them.' That is: there are historical details which are not susceptible of typological interpretation, but

420

they are present for the sake of those which are. It should not be difficult to understand Augustine's priorities. Dame Helen has simply taken 'literal' too literally, as her reading, ancient and modern, could have shown her.

It is characteristically generous of Dame Helen to refer me to books by Beryl Smalley and Auerbach, a kindness I might reciprocate by advising her to read Bradley before she next ventures to speak of *Othello*. To be blunt, everything she says about my treatment of types and testimonies is either superfluous or false. No one listening to her could suppose that the points she makes are considered, though from a less dogmatic and indeed un-Christian angle, in my fifth chapter. The relations between the two Testaments as I describe them are in accord with most informed thinking on the subject; Dame Helen should read, for example, Hans von Campenhausen's *The Formation of the Christian Bible*. Since she finds it incredible that many people expected the New Testament, which provided antitypes for the Old, to offer in its turn types to be fulfilled in a third gospel, I could recommend a good many books for her list, including those of another of her institutional colleagues, Marjorie Reeves. That one terminus of such thinking is the Nazi Third Reich is another topic upon which ample instruction is available.

Well, the whole parade of superior learning and wisdom is comically shabby, and in the end I thought I should wash off the stage blood and say so. But the true import of Dame Helen's book is different. It doesn't much matter that she unwisely used me as an expedient to supply her want of something to say. What does matter is the claim in her book's title. It is a large part of the purpose of *In Defence of the Imagination* to suggest that I and others are the enemies of imagination, and of the young who might imitate us. Her book is offered, and has been welcomed, as an example to these young persons of the real right thing. It may therefore be well to end by looking at the imaginative fare offered them by Dame Helen. Here is a sample:

These [Dickens, Trollope, and James] are three of the novelists I find myself most often re-reading, if I confine myself to novelists writing in English. Yet for all the pleasure and reward I find in reading novels, it is in the experience of reading poetry that I find the deepest pleasure and the greatest rewards. In poetry language reaches its highest expressiveness. Meaning is carried into the heart and the mind by the pulse of its rhythms, by repetition and echo, by the sweetness or force of rhyme and assonance, and by the sense we have of difficulty surmounted with ease and of limitation made a source of fullness. These things combine to give it another precious quality, memorability, so that we come to possess it, and, with it, capabilities beyond our natural powers. Something of Milton's mastery of language communicates itself to me as I move with him through a long, winding, periodic sentence, which continually defeats the expectation of a close, until at last with a sense of triumph I arrive at the true close. I too have soared, with no middle flight, and guided down have come safely to rest.

Here – to borrow one of Dame Helen's most inspired quotations – is God's plenty. 'Who prop, thou ask'st, in these bad days, my mind?' is another such quotation, and she does not shrink from being the fiftieth person to call it 'a strong contender for the worst opening line of a sonnet in English'. But she asks the question seriously, and her young auditors might well ask it, too.

They have a choice of props. We are all concerned with the future; we all acknowledge (whether or not we profess to leave such matters to the common reader) that a new generation can be taught, somehow, to read well. But we differ about the means. Dame Helen, in passages such as the one I have quoted, tacitly proposes herself as the representative of what she calls a humanist approach. In this response I have necessarily been busy to defend myself against her charges, and only incidentally to suggest that she lacks understanding of those different approaches to literature which, in view of the example she offers of the humanist approach – its arrogance, its condescension, its *prose* – many critics besides myself will be content to have described as anti-humanist. Yet if to be a humanist means taking pains to get things right, making some effort to understand unfamiliar ideas, and engaging in discussions intended to promote mutual understanding and avoid rancour (as I dare say she would maintain), then Dame Helen is also an anti-humanist.

The labels are unimportant; what matters is the choice of the young. It would be absurd to pretend that the anti-humanist side doesn't offer examples quite as bad in their way as the self-congratulatory crooning of the passage I quoted. But even they are likely to have more appeal to lively minds. And perhaps the moral of all this is simply that, if humanism is what Gardner's book represents it as being, the future will, in that respect, look after itself. It is therefore important that the anti-humanists accept their responsibilities, for the inheritance of literary intelligence, critical accuracy, speculative boldness, and genuine civility has devolved upon them. They will be fiercely opposed; but they can take heart from Gardner's book, for nobody could have written it who didn't feel seriously threatened. If this is humanism, the humanists are running scared.

Raritan, Fall 1982

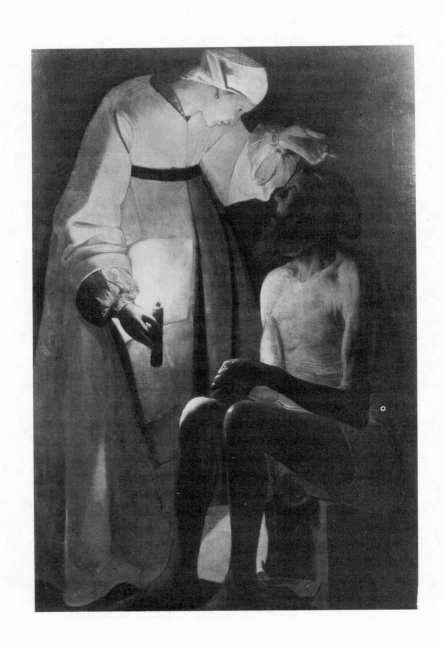

The Uses of Error

Sermon Before The University
King's College Chapel
11 May 1986

And the Lord said unto Satan, Behold he is in thine hand;
but save his life.

So went Satan forth from the presence of the Lord, and
smote Job with sore boils from the sole of his boot unto
his crown.

And he took a potsherd to scrape himself withal; and he
sat down among the ashes. Then said his wife unto him,
Dost thou still retain thine integrity? curse God and die.

But he said unto her, Thou speakest as one of the foolish
women speaketh. What? shall we receive good at the hands
of God, and shall we not receive evil? In all this Job did
not sin with his lips.

Job II: 6–10

That one remark, 'Dost thou still retain thine integrity? Curse
God and die,' is the whole record of the sayings of Job's wife. It
has ensured her a pretty bad press for two thousand years. This
woman had shared Job's prosperity and borne him seven sons and
three daughters, but when these distresses come upon him all she
can do is scold and taunt. She has been regarded as one of Satan's
chief instruments. 'The blessed Job,' says one early commentator,
'was whipped in two different fashions: Satan flogged him with
scourges, his wife with words (*cum verberibus . . . cum verbis*).' Job,

of course, is patient. He only says that in urging him to take a
quick way out of his misery – for if he cursed God he would surely
be struck down – his wife is talking foolishly, as some women do.
He doesn't say she is wicked. Perhaps he thought that after all
she meant well. But that, as I say, has not been the common view
since his time.

It may seem odd that in the Hebrew text of the Book of Job
what the wife says is '*bless* God and die'. But it has long been
understood that this 'bless' is a euphemism. It would have been
improper for the author or a scribe to write the words 'curse
God', and so here, as in the first chapter of the book, the difficulty
is avoided by using the exactly opposite word, 'bless'. Saint Jerome,
who sixteen hundred years ago translated the Hebrew into Latin,
was well aware of this euphemism, as we know from one of his
letters. He was a good Hebraist and an ardent seeker after the
truth, *hebraica veritas*. Yet when he translated this passage he
wrote *benedic Deo*, bless God. And his translation, the Vulgate, is
the Bible of the Latin church, which has read *benedic Deo* ever
since.

Why did Jerome say 'bless'? Perhaps he thought that the
Hebrew truth required it. And perhaps he felt certain that all who
could read would be aware of the euphemism. At any rate he left
the matter there, with the word possibly meaning one thing to
some people and another thing to others. The translators who
produced our English Bible were afflicted by no indecision and
tolerant of no ambiguity. They knew the Hebrew really meant
'curse', so 'curse' was what they wrote. And there has been very
little ambiguity in our subsequent thinking about Job's wife.
Indeed there has never been much in anybody's. In popular
literature and in the pictorial tradition she is nearly always represented as straightforwardly shrewish and cruel, taunting her
husband and impatient with his patience.

I know of only one possible exception to this generalisation.
The populace didn't read the Bible, and the popular tradition
could continue under its own momentum to show the wife as
unsympathetic. But after the Council of Trent affirmed the sole
authority of the Latin Bible it seems just possible that Jerome's
'bless' might have been taken at its face value by some of the

literate and pious. And it is indeed at this point that there is some confusion in the pictorial record. Here, perhaps, the wife's gesture is pitying or protective; there she is pouring a bucket of water over Job, not, it may be, to insult him, but to give him some ease.

The most interesting picture known to me is the 'Job Visited by his Wife' of Georges De La Tour, painted probably about 1640. It is the work of an artist firmly rooted in the Counter-Reformation tradition. As you will see from the reproduction, he owed much to Caravaggio. On the left side is a female figure carrying a candle in her right hand, while the left is held in a distinctive gesture above the head of a practically naked male figure on the right. He sits with his hands clenched above his knees. The man and the woman stare into each other's face. The light comes from the candle. There is nothing in the picture apart from these figures, except for a broken pot and a piece of it.

For a very long time the subject of this painting was not correctly identified. Some thought it represented the angel liberating St Peter from prison. Others said it was an allegory, 'The Clothing of the Naked'. Only in 1935 did an art historian, taking account of the pot and the potsherd, propose 'Job Visited by his Wife'. This prolonged failure to identify the subject can have only one explanation: De La Tour's painting was markedly different from others of this not unfamiliar subject. And it is interesting to note that once people knew what the picture represented they began to see it differently. Hitherto the female figure had been an angel, or Compassion personified. No one suggested that she was scowling or scolding. But after 1935 there was a change. The standard French study of De La Tour describes the woman's face as angry, her gesture as cruel; and the interaction of the glances is said to be one of conflict. The author is willing to allow that the treatment is a bit softer than usual, but he has no doubt about what Job's wife is saying, nor of what she means by it.

Yet one cannot but observe that this woman, once taken to be an angel, bears more than a slight resemblance to the angel in another of De La Tour's works, the 'Angel Appearing to St Joseph'; and there are other commentators who say they do not see her as taunting her husband; rather she is a simple soul

427

confronted by misery both physical and mental; scandalised by it, she urges her husband to rebel. Because of her pity she cannot bear his torment or the calm with which he accepts it. And it does occur to me that the painter and his patron may really have read the words *benedic Deo* quite literally, and seen Job's wife as tender, however foolish she might be; she may be saying that death is the only way out of such misery and that he should seek it, and make a good end. So far as I can make out her gesture could mean either 'depart' or 'bless' – the code of gestures is not well understood, but either of these seems more likely than 'curse'.

Here, at any rate, is an ambiguity we are very unlikely ever to resolve; and it has existed, potentially, ever since the author of Job wrote 'bless' when he meant 'curse'. If only because it was possible for him to write one and not the other, both form part of our experience of the story. We may see in his 'bless/curse' fidelity to our own experience, indeed to human experience in general. It was of interest to Freud that in Latin the word for 'holy' also means 'accursed', and what he called 'the antithetical sense of primal words' could be far more elaborately documented. Maimonides includes some remarks on the phenomenon in his *Guide for the Perplexed*; the observation is not very new, and it interested Freud mostly because he thought that dreams also had antithetical senses. But it is in any case a matter of common experience that words bear apparently impossible double senses, especially words having to do with love.

It would doubtless be convenient if words could only be used to mean one thing at a time; there would be fewer misunderstandings. But there would be much less poetry; and the whole field of human experience that exists only because language exists, with all its treacheries and ambiguities and those magical powers we honour when we use euphemisms, would dwindle to almost nothing. It is tempting to be decisive and say that only one reading of the verse in Job can be right: choose bless or curse and don't try to have it both ways. But matters are not so simple. Those looks exchanged between husband and wife are an image of mystery. Is the female figure angelic, or does the very shape of her lips signify anger and disgust, as some think? We have our private experience of such mysterious exchanges, such indissoluble ambiguities, and need not deny them to picture or text; they are part of language and part of life.

A few years ago Muriel Spark wrote a novel called *The Only Problem*. It is about a man who is writing a book about Job. He is a great admirer of De La Tour's painting. What is called in the title 'the only problem' is, for this man and many other people, the problem of why God allows unmerited suffering. It seems that Mrs Spark's hero finds De La Tour's painting of some use in his research on this problem. It may be that such minor puzzles reflect greater ones, and in particular one that is so great as to deserve to be called the only problem.

We do well to remember that in the Bible the great problems are repeatedly studied by means of stories and poems. In both the Jewish and the Christian traditions these stories and poems are frequently rewritten, expanded, adapted. It is only necessary to think of the two Nativity stories, or the apocryphal stories about the childhood of Jesus, or the remarkable later additions to the history of Pontius Pilate, as martyr and saint. Poems can be changed, too, as when St Luke's Magnificat borrows and adapts the song of Hannah in the Old Testament. It is part of our experience of the past that we change it as it passes through our hands; and in changing it we may make it more puzzling in making it more our own.

Let me give an example of the way in which one Christian poet can transform the work of another, reversing its symbolism and giving it, on the basis of what might be called a misinterpretation, a new sense, antithetical but acceptable. The first poet is St John. In the third chapter of his gospel there occurs the story of Nicodemus, a 'ruler of the Jews' who 'came to Jesus by night', saying that he recognized Jesus as a teacher come from God. Jesus, as so often, replies obliquely: to see the kingdom of God a man must be born again (or, born from above). Nicodemus, misunderstanding the answer, points out the impossibility of re-entering one's mother's womb. Although Jesus reproves him, a 'master of Israel', for not knowing these things, he favours Nicodemus with an important discourse. We do not learn that he went away instructed. It seems that he shares the ignorance of the world and is condemned with it. 'Light is come into the world,

429

ar.d men loved the darkness rather than the light.' For this they are condemned.

John has further uses for Nicodemus, but at this point he is of the darkness, unable to know the truth though interested enough to ask about it. He goes out into the dark, as Judas will do later. We have known from the very beginning of the gospel that the world is the dark and Jesus the light and that they are opposites. Nicodemus still belongs to the dark.

The second poet is Henry Vaughan, writing in Wales around 1650. Here are the opening lines of his poem, 'The Night':

> Through that pure virgin shrine,
> That sacred veil drawn o'er thy glorious noon
> That men might look and live, as glow-worms shine
>   And face the moon,
> Wise Nicodemus saw such light
> As made him know his God by night.
> Most blest believer he!

Nicodemus is now wise and blessed and a believer. He has chosen the right time to visit Jesus, since night made him accessible to mortals who could not look on the face of God and live. Moreover, Vaughan says in the sequel, Nicodemus probably met Jesus in the open air, among plants that grow at night under stellar influences. The night, so strongly associated with ignorance and evil in the gospel, is now represented as preferable to the day – indeed it is called 'the day of spirits'. And Vaughan goes on, in a passage of quite extraordinary beauty, to call the night:

> God's silent, searching flight;
> When my lord's head is filled with dew, and all
> His locks are wet with the clear drops of night . . .
>   His still, soft call,
> His knocking time, the soul's dumb watch,
> Where spirits their fair kindred catch.

Here he is remembering another biblical poem, the Song of Songs: 'I sleep, but my heart waketh: it is the voice of my beloved that knocketh, saying, Open to me, my sister, my love, my dove, my undefiled: for my head is filled with dew, and my locks with the drops of the night.' Now night has become the time when the lord is at the door like a lover, the time when the heart or the soul wakes, and when the sky, full of stars, is God's hair filled with dew. The Song of Songs was an allegory to everybody, but I do not know that anybody else had thought of the lover's wet hair as a figure for the night sky. And Vaughan converts the Song to his own purposes, as he converts St John. Under the influence of these two poets he transforms the darkness of Nicodemus into something antithetical – into that 'deep but dazzling darkness' some mystics associate with God. And Nicodemus, originally too dull to understand the idea of a second birth, now becomes the revered model of the later poet, who also wants to join his God in the dark:

> Oh for that night, where I in him
> Might live invisible and dim!

It is easy to see that Vaughan distorts the original, yet few would deny that this is a great poem. When the Song of Songs, a work of high importance in the mystical tradition, is unexpectedly introduced into the story of Nicodemus, we have no conflict, no perversion or distortion, but something antithetical and enriching.

The history of interpretation, the skills by which we keep alive in our minds the light and the dark of past literature and past humanity, is to an incalculable extent a history of error. Or perhaps it would be better to say, of ambiguity, of antithetical senses. The history of biblical interpretation will provide many instances of fruitful misunderstanding. It arises because we want to have more of the story than was originally offered, or we want to see into the depths of that story. We have always been pretty sure that the literal sense is not enough, and when we try to go beyond it we may err, but sometimes splendidly. Job will serve the argument as a book which always was and always will be enigmatic, which will always attract interpretation. A mysteriousness pervaded the whole book, and if felt also in isolated verses like the one I have discussed. The more deeply we consider what time and the world have made of Job's wife the more obvious it becomes that the mysteries of such stories, and perhaps of language itself, are familiar to us from our interpretations of our own lives. The reasons why Nicodemus comes to be called wise are very curious reasons: because an earlier poet wrote about the night in a different way from St John's, and because a later poet could imagine that a lover waiting, his hair wet with dew, outside his girl's room, could be a figure for the starry heavens; and that the Song and the gospel story belonged wholly, though mysteriously, together. It was, if you like, an act of genius; but it is what, in our more humdrum way, we all habitually do – make new combinations of disparate experience, settle for ambiguity, confront the antithetical senses. So I think that there is a peculiar truth in Job's wife when we cannot decide whether she is tender or cruel, blessing or cursing; and a peculiar truth also in a poem which, on the face of it, falsifies the gospel itself. We bring ourselves and our conflicts to words, to poems and pictures, as we bring them to the world; and thus we change the poems and the pictures, or perhaps it is ourselves we change.